THEY STOLE A CITY

ALSO BY LAUREN COLLINS

When in French:
Love in a Second Language

THEY STOLE A CITY

Wilmington's White Supremacist Coup and the Families Who Live with Its Legacy

LAUREN COLLINS

PENGUIN PRESS NEW YORK 2026

PENGUIN PRESS
An imprint of Penguin Random House LLC
1745 Broadway, New York, NY 10019
penguinrandomhouse.com

Book design by Daniel Lagin
Family trees by Alexis Sulaimani

LIBRARY OF CONGRESS CATALOGING-IN-PUBLICATION DATA
Names: Collins, Lauren (Journalist) author
Title: They stole a city : Wilmington's white supremacist coup
and the families who live with its legacy / Lauren Collins.
Description: New York : Penguin Press, 2026. | Includes bibliographical references and index.
Identifiers: LCCN 2025049525 (print) | LCCN 2025049526 (ebook) |
ISBN 9781984878816 hardcover | ISBN 9781984878823 ebook
Subjects: LCSH: Wilmington Massacre, Wilmington, N.C., 1898 |
African Americans—Civil rights—North Carolina—Wilmington—History—19th century |
Coups d'état—North Carolina—Wilmington—History—19th century |
White supremacy movements—North Carolina—Wilmington—History—19th century |
Collective memory—United States | Wilmington (N.C.)—Race relations |
Wilmington (N.C.)—Biography | LCGFT: Biographies
Classification: LCC F264.W7 C38 2026 (print) | LCC F264.W7 (ebook)
LC record available at https://lccn.loc.gov/2025049525
LC ebook record available at https://lccn.loc.gov/2025049526

Printed in the United States of America
1st Printing

For Claudia and Louis

In loving memory of Cynthia Jevette Brown (1955–2023)

The Lord said, "What have you done? Listen! Your brother's blood cries out to me from the ground."

—GENESIS 4:10

The blood of Joshua Halsey still cries, and the question is, can we hear it?

—REVEREND WILLIAM BARBER,
PINE FOREST CEMETERY,
WILMINGTON, NORTH CAROLINA,
NOVEMBER 2021

Contents

PART 2
HELL JOLTED LOOSE
1898

PART 3
SUBSTANTIAL DENIALS
1899–1979

PART 4
THE TRUTH IS COMING ON THE SCENE
1990–2026

Moore Family Tree

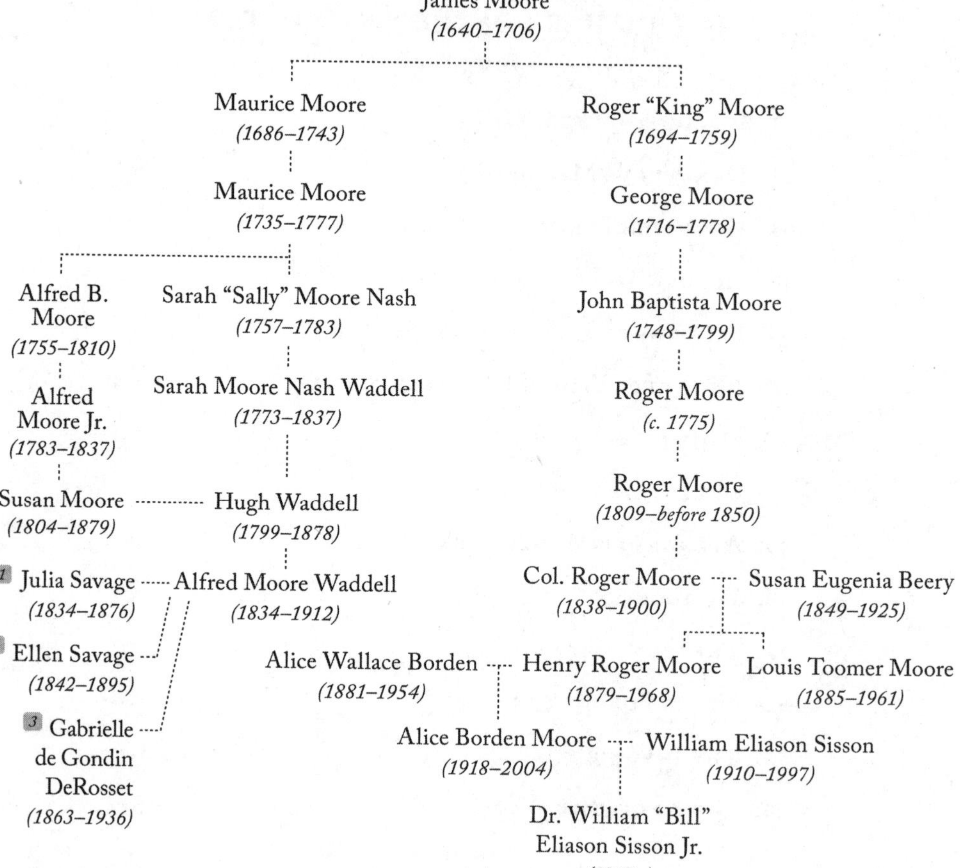

MacRae Family Tree

Caroline Price (1806–1875) — Alexander MacRae (1796–1868)

Julia Norton (1834–1867) — Donald MacRae (1825–1892)

Hugh MacRae (1865–1951) — Rena Nelson (1869–1963)

Nelson MacRae (1893–1942) — Marguerite Grist Bellamy (1899–1988)

[1] Rachel Cameron (1929–) — Hugh MacRae II (1924–2018) — Eunice "Bambi" Taylor [2] (1934–)

Hugh MacRae III (1957–)

Marguerite "Meg" Bellamy MacRae (1970–)

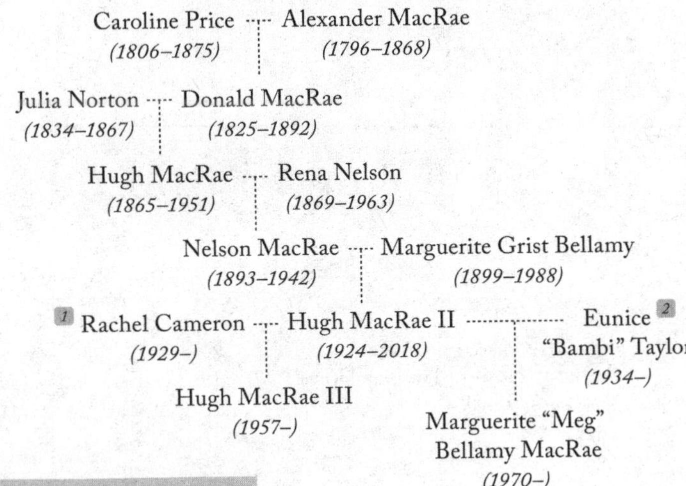

Bellamy Family Tree

John Bellamie (1650–1710)

John Bellamy (1675–1760)

John Bellamy (1720–1792)

John Bellamy (1750–1826)

Dr. John Dillard Bellamy (1817–1896) — Eliza McIlhenny Harriss (1821–1907)

Mary Elizabeth "Belle" Bellamy (1840–1900)

Marsden Bellamy (1843–1909)

Dr. William James Harriss Bellamy (1844–1911)

Eliza Bellamy (1847–1929)

Ellen Douglas Bellamy (1852–1946)

Emma May Hargrove (1857–1944) — John Dillard Bellamy Jr. (1854–1942)

George Harriss Bellamy (1856–1924)

Kate Bellamy (1858–1858)

Chesley Calhoun Bellamy (1859–1881)

Robert Rankin Bellamy (1861–1926)

Marguerite Grist Bellamy (1899–1988) — Nelson MacRae (1893–1942)

[1] Rachel Cameron (1929–) — Hugh MacRae II (1924–2018) — Eunice "Bambi" Taylor [2] (1934–)

Hugh MacRae III (1957–)

Marguerite "Meg" Bellamy MacRae (1970–)

Howe Family Tree

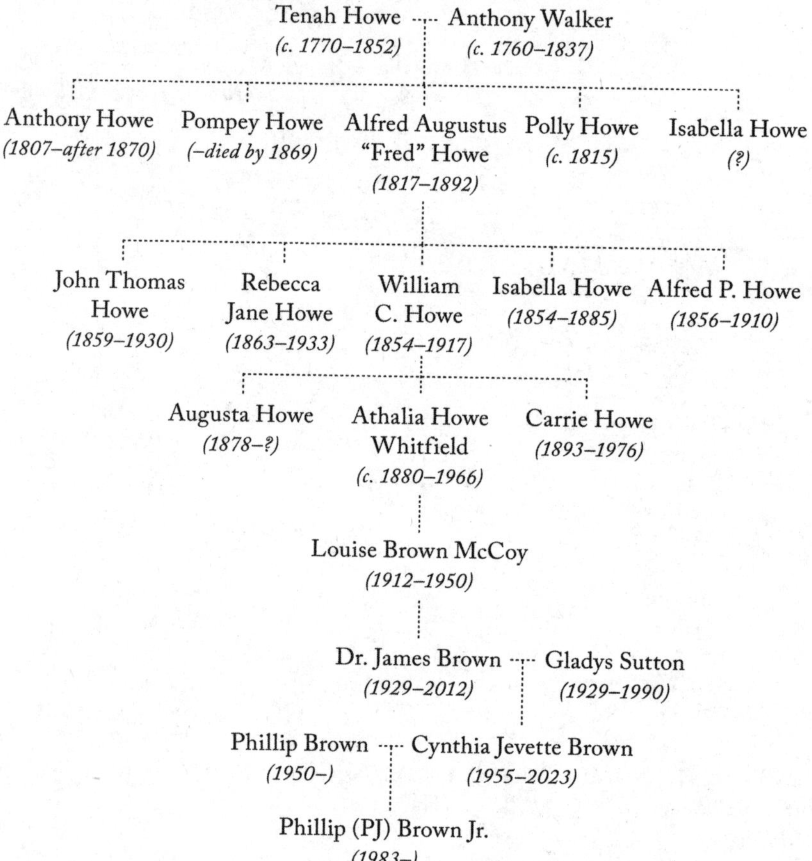

Halsey Family Tree

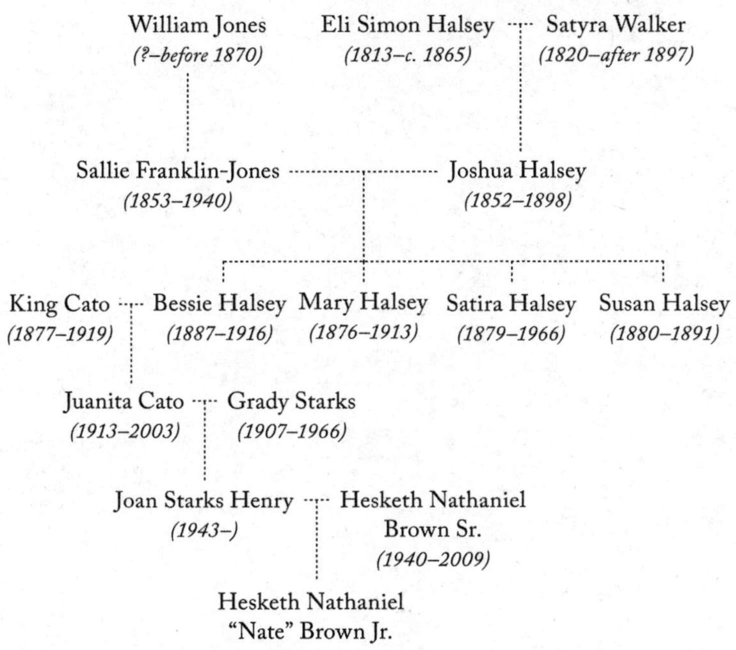

Introduction

Our understanding of history depends on where we place the parameters of an event, on when we believe it begins and ends. I started this book thinking I was writing about a massacre and coup d'état that white supremacists committed in Wilmington, North Carolina, on a Thursday near the end of the nineteenth century. I finished it understanding that November 10, 1898, is a centuries-long day that isn't over yet.

I was born in Wilmington and lived there until I was eighteen. I return frequently, but I didn't know much about 1898 until 2016, when I watched a documentary called *Wilmington on Fire*, directed by Christopher Everett. The film showed how white Democrats murdered Black men in the streets, banished Black leaders and their white Republican allies, and overthrew the city's biracial government, establishing a precedent of impunity for racial terrorism and paving the way for Jim Crow. It demonstrated that the incident had been overlooked and even actively suppressed ("Before Rosewood. Before Tulsa. A massacre that was kept a secret for a hundred years."). I agreed that the story needed to be known by as many people as possible and, in hopes of drawing attention to the film, decided to write a short article about it for *The New Yorker*.

Everett and I arranged to meet in Wilmington, where I was visiting family. He was raised by his grandparents in Laurinburg, about an hour and a half west on Interstate 74. After getting laid off from a graphic design job in Atlanta in 2010, he moved back home and used his unemployment money to make *Wilmington on Fire*. He suggested that we meet in front of the former headquarters of the Wilmington Light Infantry (WLI), a socially elite volunteer military organization that operated from before the Civil War until after World War II. Its members were all white men, and they were all Democrats. (Before the political parties essentially switched ideologies in the mid-twentieth century, the Democrats stood for states' rights and social conservatism.) It was there at the WLI Armory, on the morning of November 10, 1898, that a crowd of heavily armed white men gathered to impose their will by force.

Everett and I sat on a pair of pedestals that flank the entrance to the elegant marble-clad Greek Revival building. It stands at 409 Market Street, a few blocks from the Cape Fear River, amid the moss-draped oaks and proud spires of the downtown historic district—*The New York Times* once deemed the city a "poor man's Charleston," while *Southern Living* recently named it one of the ten "dreamiest places to live" in the coastal South. Everett confessed that Wilmington had given him a weird feeling since he was a kid. "It just always felt like something was off here," he said. The pedestals we sat on were topped with cannonballs, like finials. They had been captured in Cuba and installed just after 1898 to commemorate the WLI's mobilization in the Spanish-American War. Nothing acknowledged that in the same year, the city's white people prosecuted a local war of conquest, setting out from this very site to slaughter and subjugate their fellow Americans.

THE WILMINGTON AREA HAS BECOME ONE OF THE FASTEST-GROWING places in the United States, but when I was a kid it was a snug town of around sixty thousand people, tucked between the Cape Fear River and the Atlantic Ocean. During my childhood, Wilmington was aggressively segregated. Even now, the average white inhabitant lives in a neighborhood that is 75 percent white. The county is 11 percent Black, but Black people account for less than 5 percent of residents in twenty-three of forty-eight census tracts. In recent decades, wages have increased for white workers but declined by an equal margin for Black workers, and roughly a third of Black residents live below the poverty line.

As I began my research, I learned that Wilmington had once been a very different place, on a very different trajectory. In 1898, Black people and white people lived side by side in all five wards of what one visitor recalled as "a pretty little city" of "oxcarts, fried bananas, red bandanas, hot biscuits, honking geese, and wandering shoats." Black people constituted a slim majority of the population. A thriving middle class—dyers, pharmacists, architects, lawyers, doctors, wheelwrights, oystermen, restaurateurs—gave the city a nationwide reputation as "a Mecca for Negroes."

After the Civil War, Reconstruction ushered in an era of political equality and economic opportunity for Black people, and it lasted longer in Wilmington than almost anywhere else. This was due to a unique experiment called Fusion, which in the 1890s brought white Populists and Black Republicans in North Carolina together under the banner of common class interest. In 1898, the Fusionists controlled Wilmington's municipal government. Three of the city's ten aldermen were Black, as was the justice of the peace, the coroner, the supervisor of streets, and a member of the influential board of finance. The collector of customs, a Black man named John Dancy, made more money than the governor. According to one historian, Wilmington represented "the heart of Black political power in the state."

North Carolina Democrats were desperate to lure white voters back to the party. In 1898, they explicitly chose to center the year's election campaign on "the all-absorbing and paramount question of WHITE SUPREMACY." Party leaders barnstormed the state's hundred counties, bankrolled by business barons, whose taxes they promised to cut. Newspapers fulminated against "Negro domination" and printed sensational articles: "Negro on Train with Big Feet Behind White," "Stole Cheese: Negro Man Boldly Purloins a Cheese." For the illiterate, there were racist cartoons. A typical production depicted a winged, taloned Black man as the "vampire that hovers over North Carolina," snatching up white women and kids.

As the elections approached, Democrats were especially intent on "redeeming" Wilmington from Fusion control. In August 1898, the *Wilmington Morning Star* printed a grotesque speech in which a prominent white woman characterized Black men as habitual rapists, urging her male peers to "lynch a thousand times a week if necessary." The editor of the Wilmington *Daily Record*, the state's only Black-owned newspaper, published an unblinking rebuttal, in which he argued that white women's sexual encounters with Black men were often consensual. He furthermore confronted the ultra-taboo subject of white men's sexual violence against Black women during slavery and since.

The Democrats pounced, calling the piece "a horrid slander" that white men were duty-bound to avenge. Members of white government clubs hassled their white neighbors into political lockstep and advertised physical and financial retribution for any Black person who dared to vote. The patriarchs of elite white families banded together, organizing secret paramilitaries that could be activated on a moment's notice. One aristocrat took the stage at City Hall and thundered, "Shall we surrender [our heritage] to a ragged rabble of Negroes?" He continued, "No! A thousand times no!" White men had a "right to rule" and they would exercise it, he vowed, "if we have to choke the current of the Cape Fear with carcasses."

The white supremacy campaign worked: Democrats swept the elections on November 8, taking the state legislature and the governorship by outlandish margins. The Fusion-dominated city government, however, wasn't up for reelection for another year. Success at the polls had only made the Democrats greedier for power. Unwilling to wait, or to take their chances with the democratic process, they initiated the takeover that they'd been covertly plotting for months. On November 9, nearly five hundred white men signed a new city charter, calling it "The White Declaration of Independence." The document proclaimed, "We, the undersigned citizens of the city of Wilmington and the county of New Hanover do hereby declare that we will no longer be ruled, and we will never again be ruled by men of African origin."

EVERETT AND I SAT FACING THE SOUTH SIDE OF THE CITY WHERE, IN 1898, *The Daily Record* occupied a two-story wood-framed building at 417 South Seventh Street. After mustering at the WLI Armory, the white men arranged themselves into military columns and marched to the newspaper's offices, class distinctions effaced by their shared sense of racial superiority. "The lawyer and his clients were side by side," one eyewitness wrote. "Men of large business interests kept step with the clerks." Everett squinted in the sun. "This was meticulously planned," he said. "But for years it was branded as something that just spontaneously happened."

When the white supremacists got to the *Record*, they doused the offices with kerosene and watched them burn. They would have lynched the paper's editor, but he had already fled town. A photograph taken that day shows dozens of white men—they're in suits and derbies, long rifles slung over their shoulders—posing with flushed satisfaction in front of the charred framework of the *Record*.

Everett and I set out on foot for Brooklyn, a working-class, historically Black neighborhood on the north side of the city. It was a sweltering day with a baby-blue sky and low, powdery clouds. Looking down Market Street, the sun nowhere and everywhere, we could make out an eight-foot-tall cast-iron statue of George Davis, the final attorney general of the Confederacy. Local legend claimed that Davis's right hand was raised in the direction of the liquor store, but he could just as easily have been pointing to the county courthouse, where his grandson and grandson-in-law composed the White Declaration of Independence—their articles of secession from democratic norms. No one ever stood trial, there or elsewhere, for the crimes of 1898 or for the immediate and long-term damages that they caused. One block

A white mob poses in front of the smoldering remains of the Wilmington *Daily Record*, November 10, 1898.

farther, yet another monument paid tribute to Confederate soldiers. In 2000, a drunk driver knocked the statue off its foundation. You'd think this would have presented a convenient opportunity to retire it, but instead it was restored and reinstalled at a cost of fifty-four thousand dollars.

We walked north on Fourth Street, passing the county jail, Victorian houses, corner stores, shotgun shacks, and a Black Pentecostal church that white investors had recently turned into a "stunning event venue." Hardly anyone was out in the heat. After Campbell Street, we crossed over the former Atlantic Coast Line Railroad tracks—a void chugging into the distance, a still river of dark green, deep summer grass. To the right, we could see the Sixth Street truss bridge, the longtime conduit between Brooklyn and the rest of the city. The longer we walked, the quieter it got. Soon, we had reached the intersection of Fourth and Harnett streets, bounded by a community health clinic, shuttered storefronts, a bar, and an empty lot.

"Right here is where they started shooting Black folk," Everett said.

In 1898, as word of the violence at the *Record* spread, Black workers around the city put down their tools and ran home to Brooklyn. The white mob flocked there, too, joined by Red Shirts—white supremacist paramilitaries connected to the Democratic Party—and a WLI unit careening around town in a horse-drawn wagon. In the lead-up to the election, white leaders had ordered a state-of-the-art machine gun that could fire four hundred rounds a minute. The WLI men mounted it on the back of their wagon and rampaged through the neighborhood, shooting and killing at least a dozen Black men. At the same time, Democratic leaders, backed by a rabble, stormed City Hall and seized control of the local government. Then they swore their own men into office, completing what is thought to be the only successful coup d'état on American soil.

Black people fled to outlying swamps and forests, where they hid for days in "bone-chilling, drizzling rain." While they shivered in the darkness, the paramilitaries rounded up their most effective advocates—Black ministers, lawyers, and politicians, along with white Republican officials and activists—and marched them to the railroad station, forcing them onto northbound trains. At least twenty-one men were run out of town and told they'd be killed if they ever set foot in Wilmington again. They and their families scattered across the country, a diaspora of diverted potential and unresolved grief. Their exile effectively eliminated political opposition in the city, sending a lasting message to anyone who might seek to challenge the white regime. That Sunday, the pastor of the First Presbyterian Church, one of the city's eminent white congregations, ascended the pulpit and boasted, "We have taken a city."

NO ONE KNOWS HOW MANY BLACK PEOPLE WILMINGTON'S WHITE SUPREMACISTS murdered on November 10. Though a 2002 report put the number at twenty-two deaths, estimates range from a dozen to several hundred. The higher figures are more convincing, as it's likely that some victims were never found and that others were buried quietly amid the terror. Black people had few forums in which to publicly memorialize the dead, particularly given that their newspaper had just been incinerated. Only eight of their names are known: Silas Brown, John L. Gregory, Joshua Halsey, William Mazon, Samuel McFarland, John Townsell, Daniel Wright, and a man whose last name was Bizzell. Even using the conservative estimates, New Hanover County ranks fifteenth nationwide on the Equal Justice Initiative's list of counties with the most lynching victims between 1877 and 1950. To this day, folklore among both Black and white Wilmingtonians holds that the Cape Fear River ran red.

Everett and I turned left on Harnett, then right on Third, bringing us to the outer limit of the city, where the street turns into a highway and whisks you out of town. From the sidewalk, we walked up a little set of stairs into the 1898 Monument and Memorial Park. Six bronze paddle-shaped pillars stood in a semicircle. A plaque noted that they symbolized the importance of water "in the spiritual belief system of people from the African continent," and that they were erected in 2008 "as a memorial to those who suffered as a result of the violence of November 1898." An inscription explained further: "Wilmington's 1898 racial violence was not accidental. It began a successful statewide Democratic campaign to regain control of the state government, disenfranchise African-Americans, and create a legal system of segregation which persisted into the second half of the twentieth century."

The monument faced a parched brownfield enclosed by a chain-link fence. A few fancy streetlamps that the city had put in only seemed to emphasize the loneliness of the site. We were the sole pedestrians around, but a trace of human presence caught my eye. Nearby, someone had nailed a piece of plywood high on a telephone pole. Against the hot blue sky, I could just make out the message, stenciled in red and black letters: "1898 WAR CRIME."

The signs spoke in eloquent juxtaposition: one a handsome, official monument tidily summarizing the events of 1898 and what they meant; the other, a homemade, guerrilla effort that challenged the neat closure of that narrative. What they told me, together, was that 1898 was still being adjudicated. The conversation posed high stakes and held deep meaning for people living today.

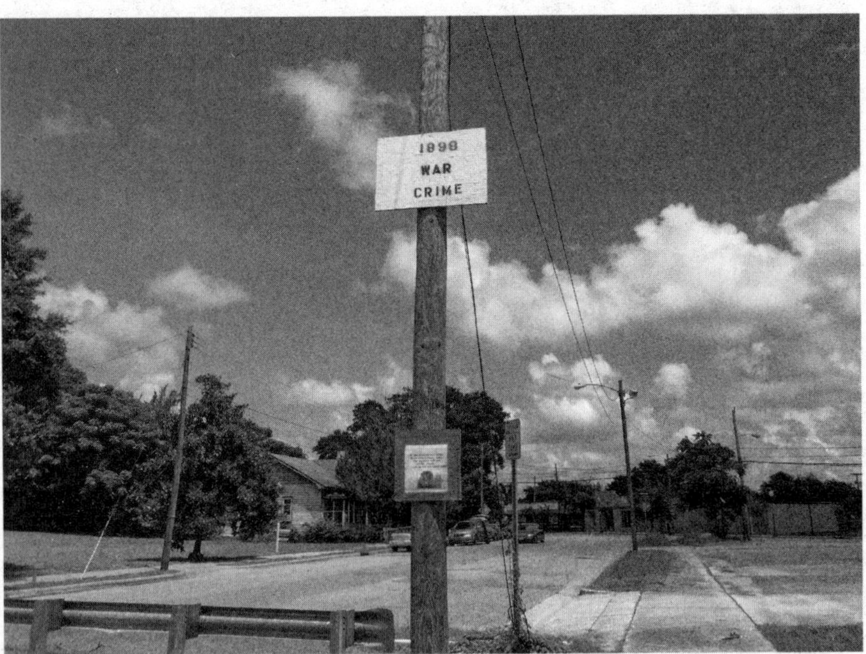

Near 1898 Memorial Park, August 10, 2016.

As I dug into the generational stories of the families involved, I became ever more convinced of the direct and urgent relevance of 1898. The article I wrote about Everett's film led to a deeper questioning of how 1898—a period of white backlash against Black success, the violent harassment of elected officials, the undermining of democratic norms, the weaponization of misinformation—relates to our current political moment. There is no more explicit example of the vulnerability of American democracy and of the magnitude of the task of repairing it once it is breached.

I came to the subject with some personal knowledge of the people and places involved, but I have no family connection to 1898. My roots in Wilmington reach back to 1973, when my parents, from New York and Pennsylvania, moved there after attending college in North Carolina. My father's legal career prospered; when my brother and I came along, we attended for some years an overwhelmingly white private school. My parents didn't know, exactly, that it had been founded as a "segregation academy," but they didn't *not* know either. (The school mascot was a rebel.) Eventually, I transferred to New Hanover, a public high school, and gave garden tours as a hoop-skirted "Azalea Belle." It wasn't until several years later, in college, that I encountered a more complicated picture of American history—and began to understand the connections between white femininity and white supremacy—and realized what a bad decision that had been.

The white elite, many of whose members descended from 1898 ringleaders, formed a cliquish society, sanctioning any deviation from their unchanging manners and codes. This was the 1990s, not the 1890s, but my family and I were sometimes dismissed as "Yankees"—still considered a stinging epithet. We benefited from passivity, from not asking questions whose answers would have made our lives difficult. As white, upper-class newcomers, we were part of the Wilmington cover story, alibis for a New South that didn't quite exist.

I consider myself an "implicated subject," per a category of political responsibility defined by UCLA scholar Michael Rothberg—enmeshed and liable even though I don't have a direct tie to the 1898 massacre and coup. As Rothberg argues, the traditional binary of victims and perpetrators (or descendants thereof) doesn't sufficiently account for the complexity of our relationships to historical violence and the contemporary inequities it creates. There is no such thing as what the German chancellor Helmut Kohl once called "the mercy of late birth," expressing relief at having missed the Nazism by simple demographic luck. If you're a German, you're part of the Nazi story. If you're a Wilmingtonian—an American, for that matter—you're part of 1898.

1898 is twenty-first-century history as much as it is nineteenth-century history. It's white history as much as it is Black history. It's incumbent upon white people to learn it, to grapple with it, and to shoulder the full truth. My forebears were designing backwater valves in Pennsylvania and digging potatoes in Ireland in 1898, but I live, as they did, entangled in what the historian Tessa Morris-Suzuki calls "structures, institutions, and webs of ideas that are the product of history, formed by acts of imagination, courage, generosity, greed, and brutality performed in previous generations." The day that we met, Everett and I walked through a city dotted with the landmarks of these earlier choices: First Presbyterian Church, where I was baptized in the light of a rose window dedicated to one of the coup's perpetrators; the empty lot where *The Daily Record* burned to ashes, when, had it survived into the twenty-first century, Everett might have found a job in Wilmington, instead of having to move to Atlanta to pursue his career in graphic design. We did not create 1898, but in various ways, 1898 created us.

MOST ACCOUNTS OF 1898 BEGIN WITH RECONSTRUCTION OR, MORE OFTEN, with 1894 and the creation of the racially diverse Fusion movement. They conclude in late 1898, with the McKinley administration's refusal to send troops to Wilmington or to extend any other form of aid, emboldening white terrorists nationwide. At the outer limit, they continue to 1900. That year, the passage of voting restrictions, accompanied by a grandfather clause exempting anyone whose forebear could vote before 1867 from disenfranchisement—that is, almost all white men—achieved the white supremacists' goal of evicting Black people from political life. It seemed to me that 1898 had been put into a historical container that couldn't hold its copious antecedents, its complex consequences spilling into the coming centuries in messy, unpredictable streaks. The event begged to be examined in its longitudinal fullness. I stuck a note card to the shelf above my desk: "American coup—and then what?"

In addition to extending the timeline of 1898 into both the past and the future, I have enlarged the human scope of inquiry, focusing on families rather than individual players. Twenty thousand people lived in Wilmington in 1898. They passed their experiences down to their children, who transmitted them to their own, and so on: hundreds of thousands of lives, interrupted, consolidated, dispersed, concentrated, thwarted, redirected, punctuated, complicated, elevated, degraded, enriched, ruined, marked, transformed. Families are both the incubators and the life-support machines of memory. The North Carolina legislature's recent efforts to disenfranchise Black voters through gerrymandering and voter identification laws are nothing if not the grandchildren of the grandfather clause. Tracing the intergenerational transmission of racial terror is critical because it allows us to see who made its instigators and survivors the people that they were, and to assess how their legacies shape the choices that their descendants make today.

Wilmington's Black population declined moderately in the immediate wake of 1898, as did the number of Black-owned businesses. White supremacists thereafter dominated political life in Wilmington and much of North Carolina, which did not elect another Black person to national office until 1992, when I was twelve. Statistics are enlightening, but insufficient for understanding this heritage. The qualitative fallout of 1898 is no less important for being more difficult to measure. We know that Black people lost life in 1898. Did they lose love? Lose touch? Lose hope, or muster strength? What did white people tally in pride, confidence, entitlement, shame?

To answer these questions, I have chosen principally to follow four Wilmington families, the Bellamy/MacRaes, the Moores, the Howes, and the Halseys. The first two are white families who contributed to the violence and its afterlife. The latter two are Black families who came through it. Their trajectories have diverged and sometimes overlapped in the 125 years since their forebears moved through the same dusty streets on one November day. Each family has developed its own strategies for explaining and remembering their ancestors' actions in 1898. Some of them have chosen to stay quiet for understandable reasons, but others have made courageous efforts over the course of many years to tell these stories. In collaboration with these living descendants, I have sought to create a more complete account of 1898 than that which can be understood solely from the archive.

1898 is often presented as "hidden history." It is true that the story was long subject to powerful taboos, but in recent years, public awareness has increased due to the work of filmmakers, scholars, writers, and musicians, along with a surge of interest in the subject of racial violence after the murder of George Floyd and the January 6 Capitol attack. Even if many people remain ignorant of 1898 and its seminal role in undemocratizing American democracy, its legacy is closer to a cipher than a secret. There are so many people, after all, whose relatives murdered or were murdered; whose fortunes prospered or failed; who *do* know what happened, because of the antique gun that they keep in a closet, or the New York address on their birth certificate, because of deathbed unburdening they've never forgotten, or how the ramifications of 1898 factored into their parents' 1960s divorce.

The historian Glenda Gilmore has written, "Murder's best work is done after the fact, when terror lives on in memory." This book argues that the damage of the Wilmington massacre and coup, already great, far exceeds the number of people murdered on November 10, 1898. It demonstrates that the white supremacists began their work long before 1898, and continued it long after with Jim Crow and the violently botched desegregation of schools in the 1950s and '60s; the devastating closure of Williston Senior High School, Wilmington's bastion of Black education, in 1968; and the wrongful convictions, in 1971, of the Wilmington Ten for arson and conspiracy. 1898 lives on in Wilmington today in persistently low rates of Black voter participation, homeownership, and business ownership. Among white people, intergenerational wealth, the monopolization of public memory, and an enduring sense of chauvinism—a locally tinctured strain of white nationalism—must be counted among the massacre and coup's consequences. Only with a full, encompassing inventory of 1898's harm can we seek appropriate repair.

1898 was a premeditated takeover that enabled the ongoing needs of white supremacy, not the spontaneous folly of a few local racists. Treating it as an idiosyncratic moment in an ever-distant past renders it spectacle to be wondered at from safe remove. In fact, as a case study in the sabotage of American democracy by revanchist politicians, aggrieved moguls, and a bullying right-wing media, it presents unignorable lessons for today. To avoid repeating 1898, we must acknowledge it for what it was: a successful effort by white supremacists to wrest power from Black people who had amassed significant amounts of it—murder's worst work, the crime of 128 years and counting.

THEY STOLE A CITY

Prologue

WILMINGTON, NORTH CAROLINA, SPRINGTIME, 1993

Cynthia Brown was expecting soup and sandwiches, but the ladies had made a fuss. They had set up card tables and dressed them with linens as heavy and smooth as cream. Each table had a floral centerpiece. Each seat had a calligraphed place card. A sideboard heaved with pitchers of sweet tea, platters of tuna salad, and pound cake dripping with peach preserves. In the sunroom, a boy played concertos on the violin, signaling to Brown that this was not an ordinary weekday lunch.

Brown wasn't quite sure what she was doing in the living room of a woman she'd never met. She was nearing forty and had just moved home to Wilmington from Chicago after almost twenty years away. A stylish dresser with a honeysuckle voice and a smattering of freckles, she had spent years in high-flying corporate jobs with the University of Illinois and Illinois Bell. House in the suburbs, corner office in a building that overlooked the Chicago River, snow boots and a parka, slushy commute.

On the most frigid days, Brown performed a mental trick, conjuring memories of mild North Carolina days until "my memories of home, so deeply present in my soul, broke the sting of the cold wind against my face." Her mother's sudden death from a heart attack, three years earlier, had deepened her longing for "that cozy feeling" she got in Wilmington, where she could trace her line back seven generations, where her family worshipped in churches that their forebears had raised with protractor and parallel rule, where her grandmother had created a garden and taught her that a can of beer poured into strategically placed saucers would stop the slugs from destroying dahlias, zinnias, daisies, hydrangeas, gardenias, and oleander.

Wilmington's own severities, chief among them a lack of professional opportunity for Black people, had sent Brown packing after high school. But she and her husband, Phillip, an engineer, were at the stage in their lives when the pull of family was greater than the force of their reservations. Brown had just accepted a job as the City of Wilmington's first-ever director of human resources. It was an important appointment, well suited to her knack for nurturing talent while fending off naysayers like slugs.

Her fifth-grade teacher, Mrs. Harris, had called to ask her to a meal at a friend's house. Brown was perplexed by the invitation, coming, as it did, from someone who'd been a mentor but never a peer, and involving a mysterious third-party hostess. But she was touched by her former teacher's solicitude, and the invitation piqued her curiosity. Anyway, it was effectively a summons.

At the luncheon, most of the other guests were women of Brown's parents' generation. Like her mother, many of them had been public school teachers. "I know your family," one guest told Brown. She figured that the woman was referring to the tight-knit world of Black educators. Then, Mrs. Harris, her old teacher, turned to her. "We want you to get to know us, and to know more about who you are," she said, fixing Brown with a bright smile and a dauntless look.

A part of Brown bristled at being thrust back into the classroom, involuntarily enrolled in this school of self-discovery. She was a grown woman with three children, who'd made efforts of her own at understanding where she came from. But a deep-seated sense of decorum made acquiescence a given. "My brain said, 'What's going on here?'" she recalled. "My soul answered, 'Sit back, relax, and be a good student.'"

After the meal, the ladies went through to the sunroom for coffee. As promised, they *did* know a lot about Brown. She felt her personal history solidifying as they supplemented her fuzzy girlhood memories with firsthand testimony, resurrecting beloved faces and reconstructing long-gone rooms. They remembered her maternal grandparents' white clapboard house at 802 Bladen Street, where Brown had lived as a child, with the lozenge-shaped upper window and the brick columns framing the wraparound porch; the living room with the leather nailhead armchair; the fine brown secretary with cabriole legs and the silver candlesticks holding tapers as tall as clarinets.

In one family picture, her grandmother and a friend posed by the fence in corsages and church hats. Other shots showed her parents' black-tie wedding there, just before Christmas in 1951, with nosegays of pink carnations and Southern smilax cascading from the mantel; her father on the front steps in plaid shirtsleeves, a few years later, lifting Brown's floppy toddler arms above her head so that she could try to walk. A pair of live oaks framed the front porch, reminding Brown, throughout life, of the importance of perseverance and deep roots.

Near the end of the luncheon, the hostess stood up, identifying herself as a distant cousin. "I have a gift for you," she said, handing Brown a spiral-bound booklet. It was titled "A History of the Howe Family." Brown knew

Cynthia Brown and father, circa 1955.

its late author, Nada McDonald Cotton, a cousin of her paternal grandmother and the longtime head librarian of the Wilmington Colored Library. As a girl, Brown had visited the library weekly, leafing through issues of *National Geographic* and admiring Swedish candle crowns in *Christmas the World Over*, her favorite book. Cotton had always slipped a second or third volume into her younger relative's hands, in keeping with the family's desire to instill in Cynthia an interest in the world outside the Brooklyn neighborhood, the city of Wilmington, the state of North Carolina, the United States of America.

Closer to home, however, certain questions were not encouraged. Brown's ancestry had always been a sensitive topic. Her father was a Howe, a member of one of Wilmington's most distinguished Black families, but questions about his line of descent had left their branch hanging at an uncertain angle to the rest of the family tree. At the luncheon, the elders addressed the issue head-on, walking Brown through her genealogy, restoring the "threads to our family tapestry that were never fully explained." She was the daughter of James Brown, who was the son of Louise Brown McCoy, who was the daughter of Athalia Howe Whitfield—Brown's great-grandmother, whom she knew as a child. Athalia was the daughter of William C. Howe, who, the women confirmed, was the illegitimate but acknowledged child of the construction entrepreneur Alfred ("Fred") Howe.

With his brothers, Pompey and Anthony, Fred founded a building dynasty that shaped Wilmington from the antebellum era to the turn of the twentieth century. "The Howes thrived as leading citizens and builders in an era of strong black community and economic life in Wilmington," one biographical dictionary declared, cataloging works such as their Italianate Mary Jane Langdon House of 1870, "supported by four tasteful & ornamental pillars or columns in front, and half antae in the rear." The spiral-bound booklet explained that the Howe brothers' father, Anthony Walker Howe, was born in present-day Nigeria. He had been kidnapped as a child by British traders, and enslaved on the Howe plantation, near Wilmington.

In addition to shedding light on some personal mysteries, "A History of the Howe Family" gave Brown insight into a historical event about which information was very hard to come by: the murder of dozens of Black citizens and the illegal takeover of the Wilmington city government by white supremacists on November 10, 1898. Brown had heard about 1898 for the first time as a child, in the mid-1960s. Her parents had taken her to visit her great-grandmother Athalia Howe Whitfield ("Grandma Thalia"), who was living in Pennsylvania. Brown remembers going into a bedroom, where Grandma Thalia lay dying. She began speaking to Brown in an agitated, almost hallucinatory tone. "Don't let them do this," she said, as though she had traveled far from the mid-century Pittsburgh suburbs. Brown wasn't sure what her great-grandmother meant. As her parents hustled her out of the room, Grandma Thalia caught her wrist and squeezed it: "*You have to know*," she whispered. "*If it ever happens—run*."

When Brown was older, she learned that Grandma Thalia had survived the 1898 massacre. She was a teenager when it happened, living with her parents and sisters in Brooklyn, just a few wide, quiet blocks from the Bladen Street house where Brown grew up. Looking out the front window of her house, Athalia witnessed a white man kill a Black man in the street. She ran with her mother and young sister to Pine Forest Cemetery, huddling with other refugees in the freezing rain. After several days, they returned to Brooklyn. Athalia lived there for the rest of her life, raising two children on the salary she earned as head cook at Live Oaks, the waterfront estate of Walter Parsley, one of the plotters of 1898.

THE WHITE SUPREMACISTS BANISHED DOZENS OF BLACK MEN FROM WILmington in 1898, and their relatives followed. Hundreds of other Black families tried to hold on under the new regime but ultimately found Wilmington untenable and moved north, joining a local exodus that prefigured the Great Migration. For those who stayed, Wilmington remained an insular place of recurring surnames and long-held addresses. You might move away, or you might move back, as Brown had, seeking to recapture the sense of belonging that eluded you elsewhere, but you were far less likely to move *to* Wilmington without any special connection, especially if you were Black. The city's Black population continued to shrink proportionally every year. From a high of 56 percent in 1898, it had dwindled to 34 percent by 1990.

In Wilmington, as Brown later wrote, memories of 1898 tended to be "quietly kept and held by family historians." Brown's father had imparted bits of knowledge over the years, but in general, the subject elicited private reticence and public omertà. As a high school junior, Brown had gone to the county library in search of more information. At the time, material regarding 1898 was literally kept under lock and key. White librarians meted out access sparingly, denying anyone they thought might "make a stink." When Brown asked to see the cache of papers, the librarian grilled her about her motives. "What do you need it for?" she asked. Brown left empty-handed.

Now, at the luncheon, the female elders were giving Brown the facts she needed to make sense of an event that had reverberated in her family for almost a hundred years, shaping generations in ways that history books failed to account for and even actively denied, if they mentioned 1898 at all. As educators, the women may have hoped that Brown, one of only a few Black people in a position of power within the local government, would be able to influence the way the event was remembered in the larger community. Or they may just have wanted to entrust their knowledge to someone they knew would recognize its importance, who felt the pull of keeping counter-history alive.

The young musician played a final concerto as Brown stole glances at Nada McDonald Cotton's neatly typed memoir, punctuated here and there with the penciled-in carets of a person who has thought hard about what she wants to say, and then thought about it even harder:

> We were saved from being slaughtered and our home was left intact. Many, many Negroes were killed, marched out of town, and their life-savings taken from them.
>
> This outrage, which resulted in rule by white supremacy, is called the Wilmington riot. It was really the Wilmington massacre.

As soon as Brown got home, she called her father.

"I just went to this luncheon, and I was given this document," she said.

"I have a copy, too," he told her. "I just didn't know when you'd be ready for it. But it's time now."

To move forward in her quest, Brown first had to go back. This would involve decades of investigation and reflection, a rewinding of the family tape back into the eighteenth century and the earliest moments of the Howe family's presence in America, which, as she later came to believe, was when the story of 1898 really began.

PART 1

FOUNDATIONS

1775–1898

Chapter 1

THE HOWES ARISE

It was sometime in the 1770s, September, hurricane season. A storm had battered Anthony's cabin, a simple structure with earthen walls and a thatched roof. His few belongings were drenched. He got to work, patching up the cabin with whatever materials he could find.*

His peers took notice of his skill and sought his advice on drying out their floors, straightening the planks that shielded their windows and had been blown awry. "The slaves under his instructions began repairing all the cabins to fortify them against the onslaught of another such disaster," Nada McDonald Cotton wrote in her family history. Even without the benefit of literacy, Anthony amassed stores of technical knowledge. He had a way of giving people confidence under the guise of lending them a hand. His fellow enslaved people spoke various languages, but he brought them together using gesture and example. Soon, he was leading an ad hoc crew in repairing all the damaged cabins at Howe's Point plantation, situated on a knob of land on the west bank of the Cape Fear River, about twenty miles south of Wilmington.

*A note about names: Because this is a story about families, and in particular Southern families, first names and last names recur through the generations. I have referred to characters by their last names when their identity is clear enough. In cases where confusion could easily set in, I have resorted to first names, first and middle names, or nicknames, so that the reader can distinguish among, for example, not only the many Howes in the story, but the many Alfreds.

Anthony was maybe fifteen years old. Before enslavers stole him from his family and brought him to America, he had learned from his elders to build shelters out of grasses, skins, and logs. His people were Igbo and lived in what is now the southern coast of Nigeria near Calabar. In the eighteenth century, enslavers, mostly from Liverpool and Bristol, exported approximately 1.2 million people from Calabar, cramming them into putrid ship holds. One Calabar cargo included 11,400 yams and 134 human beings, treated alike as perishables. Fewer than ninety African people were still alive when the ship arrived in Barbados.

Anthony—his birth name was said to have been Oboto—was only a child when he was abducted. The story he passed down to his children, who passed it down to their children, is this:

> He and his playmates were lured aboard the ship with the big, white wings. They were so curious about the parts of the ship that they did not notice that it was moving. As the sun began to sink, they decided that they had better start for home. To their surprise, the ship was surrounded by water. It was more water than they had ever seen. They knew that they could not swim home. They were terrified. They were carried down into the bottom of the ship. It was very dark. They did not see light again until they were being put in small boats to go to land in a strange place.

The strange place was North Carolina. Settler life there depended almost entirely on the labor and savoir faire of enslaved people. They spent the winter months sawing into longleaf pine trees to coax out sap that they distilled into turpentine, thousands of trees to a man. Or they hunched over the forest floor to gather branches that they burned in kilns for days on end. This process transformed the lightwood into tar and pitch, so crucial to the maintenance of the very wooden ships that had enabled their forced transportation across the Atlantic. Enslaved coopers made the barrels that housed the naval stores. Enslaved boat pilots who "knew every crook and eddy of the stream" ferried the barrels to the Wilmington wharves. Enslaved loggers ran the area's fifty sawmills, processing lumber, the area's other major export. Enslaved women did heavy labor, too, with enslavers often forcing them back to work only a week after childbirth.

On their own time, enslaved people reared hogs and grew vegetables. They knew how to use the leftover needles of a prickly pear as straight pins, and to fashion the skins of calabash gourds into button molds. Along with the remaining Native people of Cape Fear, whose ranks white settlers had nearly obliterated, they became the keepers of valuable ecological knowledge. They knew the best tides for finding clapper rail eggs and the best moons for turtle eggs, knew when the bluefish were running along the barrier islands so thick that the water glittered like silver.

After Oboto arrived in America, a man named John Walker bought him at the slave market, likely in Wilmington, and decided that he would be called Anthony. Walker died shortly thereafter and his widow, facing debts, put his human possessions up for sale. In 1775, around the beginning of the Revolutionary War, Robert Howe bought Anthony and took him to his plantation at Howe's Point. A low-country aristocrat, Robert descended from the area's earliest settlers, including the Moores, a clan so powerful they were known simply as "the Family." Robert inhabited a "palatial" three-story house, perched on a bluff above the river. He was purported to have been educated in England. An admirer wrote that he lived "in affluence, with his broad acres around him, his slaves, his library well stored with the best books of the day."

Robert's personal life was in some disarray. A high-strung man known for his "libertine" tendencies, he had recently mortgaged one of his properties, perhaps after a typically catastrophic outing at the horse races. George Washington had just appointed Robert as a colonel in the Continental Army; he would go on to become the highest-ranking officer in the South. Previously, he'd been a loyalist to the crown, and drawing rooms buzzed with talk that he'd embezzled money from the royal government before abruptly switching to the Patriot cause. "This Gentleman has the worst character you ever heard thro' the whole province," a female traveler complained.

Always a turbulent personality—he once threatened to tar and feather a woman over a drawing-room slight—Robert was in the throes of the most swashbuckling period of his life. Outwardly, he personified the complacent white supremacy of the enslaver class. But as he stormed around the Eastern Seaboard fighting the British, he stayed attuned to the threat of revolt at home. He was enough of a realist to warn, in a letter to John Hancock, "how numerous [are] the black Domesticks who would undoubtedly flock in multitudes to the Banner of the Enemy whenever an opportunity offered."* In 1776, British troops torched Brunswick Town, a neighboring settlement. They were said to have had help from local accomplices—people enslaved, like Anthony, at Howe's Point.

THE SEPTEMBER STORM THAT WRECKED ANTHONY'S CABIN MEANT WORK on top of work, but he approached the mess as an opportunity, building things up when he might have wanted to burn them down. "Colonel Howe noticed the work of the slaves and he took them out of the fields and had them repair the barns, storehouses, and the 'big house,'" Nada McDonald Cotton wrote. Anthony soon became the plantation's equivalent of a general contractor. Robert hired him out to supplement his income as he pursued a high-flying military and political career.

Enslaved people could not marry freely, but Anthony wanted a family. As a young man, he reportedly set his sights on a woman named Tenah. Her parents were Native Americans from the Tuscarora Nation. Shortly after her birth, they had participated in a raid on Howe's Point. During the chaos of battle, the baby was separated from her family. Someone found her and brought her to the Howes, who decided to take her in, entrusting her care to a housemaid.

Anthony appears to have acquired enough status at Howe's Point that he considered Tenah a plausible mate, despite her quasi-familial relationship to his enslavers. Having likely put aside some money from his building jobs, he made several proposals to "buy her as his wife," but the Howes turned him down. One summer, a Howe nephew came down from New

*Notwithstanding Howe's fears, some ten thousand Black Americans joined the Patriot cause, only to be deemed noncitizens in the new country they helped to found.

York and fell in love with Tenah, causing a scandal. The Howes sent him home and, at last, accepted Anthony's proposal.

Anthony and Tenah had seven children, five of whom—Anthony, Pompey, Polly, Isabella, and Alfred—lived to adulthood. According to family lore, Robert Howe supported the family's manumission and gave instructions for them to be "forever free" upon his death. Yet there is confusion about the circumstances of the family's emancipation, as written sources suggest that they remained enslaved long after Robert Howe died, in 1786. They may have been able to buy their practical freedom—striking a deal with Howe's descendants that enabled them to work, manage their own affairs, and move freely—while remaining technically in bondage, a not uncommon practice. It seems, however, that it was not until sometime in the mid-nineteenth century that Anthony and Tenah's descendants became free in the legal sense.

AT THE TURN OF THE NINETEENTH CENTURY, WILMINGTON WAS NORTH Carolina's second-largest city and biggest port—the obvious destination for a doer like Anthony. Naval stores, rice, indigo, tobacco, and the odd stowaway went out from its docks. Sugar, rum, coffee, news, and ideas came in. A European traveler might moan about ruining a silk shoe in the dusty, striving province, "trudging thro' the unpaved streets . . . by the light of a lanthorn carried by a black wench half naked." But, like all port cities, Wilmington was cosmopolitan in its way—a brown-water crossroads, a place of mixing and agitation where the larger world occasionally blew in with the wind.

By 1820, Anthony was living in Wilmington and working as a carpenter. He and his family would come to be mainstays of the city's small but prolific free Black community. As in other Southern cities, free Black people had a strong presence in the building trade, and free Black carpenters, painters, plasterers, and masons constructed many of Wilmington's most important buildings. They worked alongside white and enslaved Black people, often hiring out enslaved people and occasionally enslaving people themselves.

Free Black people occupied a fraught position in the antebellum racial hierarchy. "The status of these people, prior to the Civil War, was anomalous but tenable," one writer observed. Many were "mulatto," in the era's jargon, sometimes with white enslaver fathers who had helped to set them up in trade. The white elite, fearing the liberating influence of free Black people upon enslaved ones, tried to prevent the two groups from interacting.

Wilmington's free Black community was far and away the state's most prosperous. One of Anthony's fellow carpenters became the richest free Black man in the state, amassing a fortune of twenty-six thousand dollars, part of which he used to set up a clandestine school. In 1835, a white man named E. C. Bettencourt, kin to Anthony's former enslavers, executed a "deed of gift" awarding Anthony a half-acre parcel of land on Queen between Third and Fourth streets. The document stipulated that Anthony would be able to live on the property for life, giving the Howes a homeplace to call their own. Even after Anthony's death, "the same privilege to live on the same lot" would accrue to his children, his grandchildren, and his great-grandchildren.

NORTH CAROLINA WAS THE ONLY SOUTHERN STATE IN WHICH FREE PEOple of color had the right to vote from the end of the Revolutionary War until 1835, when the state constitutional convention disenfranchised them in the wake of enslaved people's rebellions and resistance. In the state's early days, the writer Charles W. Chesnutt explained, "the civil status of the inhabitants was largely regulated by condition rather than by color." In Wilmington, a tradition of Black political consciousness went along with political and economic opportunity. The abolitionist David Walker, author of perhaps the most incendiary document of the antislavery movement, was born into this fecund environment sometime around 1785.

Walker's father is thought to have been enslaved and to have died before his birth. His mother was free, as was he, per the principle of *partus sequitur ventrem*, a diabolical Virginian legal doctrine of 1662. The rule—decreeing that "that which is born follows the womb"—more commonly served to assign a person born to an enslaved mother to bondage, thereby increasing the enslaver's wealth. "I consider a woman who brings a child every two years as more profitable than the best man of the farm," Thomas Jefferson wrote.

As a young man, Walker watched as enslavers forced a son to beat his mother until she died. He vowed to escape Wilmington, and as soon as he could, he fled the South entirely, leaving "this Bloody land . . . where I must hear slaves' chains continually," to settle in Boston, where he kept a secondhand clothing shop and joined the abolitionist movement. In 1829, Walker published *An Appeal to the Colored Citizens of the World but in Particular, and Very Expressly, to Those of the United States of America*, calling on Black people to rise up against their "cruel and barbarous" white oppressors, using violence if necessary. "I tell you Americans! that unless you speedily alter your course, you and your Country are gone!!!!!!" he wrote. "For God Almighty will tear up the very face of the earth!!!" Per one historian, the work constituted "the first sustained written assault upon slavery and racism to come from a black man in the United States."

Walker seems to have been especially keen for his message to be heard in Wilmington, the city of his father's bondage and his birth. He arranged for bundles of *An Appeal* to be sent to the city, entrusting an enslaved man with the task of distributing them in secret. At the waterfront, authorities seized a shipment of two hundred pamphlets. Savannah, by contrast, received a mere sixty copies.

The pamphlet caused a sensation, "startling the land like a trump of coming judgment," Frederick Douglass wrote. Walker's message galvanized Black people, perhaps influencing Nat Turner's revolt, and terrified white ones, who passed laws banning seditious literature and forbidding enslaved people to read and write altogether. Wealthy white men in Georgia reportedly put a ten-thousand-dollar bounty on Walker's head.

Just ten months after the pamphlet's publication, he died in Boston. The official cause of death was consumption, but suspicion has lingered ever since that he was poisoned. Walker contributed to the flourishing of a Black intellectual culture in Wilmington that produced local activists such as Abraham Galloway, a brickmason who liberated himself from enslavement and became a Union spy. Later, Walker's work influenced Black radicals from Frederick Douglass to Malcolm X.

At least one historian has speculated that Anthony may have been David Walker's father. The dates don't line up perfectly for the theory to be entirely persuasive, but it is plausible when one accounts for the era's scant and muddled recordkeeping, particularly when it comes to the intimate lives of enslaved people. A more persuasive kinship between the two men is their shared defiance, manifested in careful deeds of leadership by the elder man and by the younger one in audacious words. Walker was fully aware that he would "be assailed by those whose greatest earthly desires are, to keep us in abject ignorance and wretchedness, and who are of the firm conviction that Heaven has designed us and our children to be slaves and *beasts of burden* to them and their children." Walker was no one's beast of burden. Neither was Anthony. Brought to North Carolina enslaved and alone, he died in 1837 a prospering patriarch. The foundation that he laid for the first American generation of his family, which would go on to build a dynasty, was as solid as that of a house.

CHAPTER 2

THOSE PESTIFEROUS MOORES

The Moores, who would become colonial North Carolina's largest enslavers and loudest revolutionaries, arrived in South Carolina sometime around 1675. That year, James Moore sailed from Barbados, settling in the Goose Creek area, near Charleston, to manage a plantation. James may have been the son of the Irish chieftain Roger Moore, as some descendants later claimed, or he may have been a headstrong young chancer of common origin. Whether he came from nobility or nowhere, he thrived in his new environs, marrying the stepdaughter of the governor of the Carolina colony and producing ten children.

Moore was an almost comically appropriate surname. James established himself in the Indian trade, "pursu[ing] wealth to the utmost limits of Carolina." He was so aggressive that he drew condemnation from the colonial authorities, no great defenders of Native American people, who complained that he had "contrived most unjust warrs upon ye Indians," all of this "in order to ye getting of Slaves." As he developed a political career, James continued to wield violence for profit. In the early 1700s, he led a series of raids into Florida, destroying Spanish missions and slaughtering Native people. His troops, according to one historian, "ran wild through the province, plundering, raping, and murdering at will."

The family accumulated more land, more people, more houses, more money, more connections, more swagger. Despite the family's stature in

South Carolina, most of the second generation migrated north in the 1720s, seizing the opportunity to colonize the Lower Cape Fear in what one historian called "a competitive, disorganized, and largely illegal rush to acquire land." Within a decade, a group of settlers led by James's sons Maurice, Roger, and Nathaniel controlled more than eighty thousand acres in the area.

The Moores brought more than a thousand enslaved people to the Lower Cape Fear; six of the area's ten leading enslavers were their kin. As their fortunes multiplied, so did their opposition to taxation without representation. "No creature sucks and teats of their dames, longer than they can draw milk from thence," Maurice Moore wrote, denouncing the Stamp Act. The family was so vocal in its opposition to the crown that King George III is said to have referred to them as "those pestiferous Moores."

James's son Roger (nicknamed "King") reigned from Orton, his plantation on the Lower Cape Fear. Built in 1725, with "thick brick walls loopholed for fire arms," the house came to stand as the embodiment of the Moore heritage of high living and brute force. The amateur historian Louis Toomer Moore, a direct descendant of King, later wrote that the estate was named "for the home of the Moores in the Lake District of England." For him, Orton substantiated a pedigree as fragrant as the plantation's famed camellia gardens. Conquest and luxury were natural companions, the master class's twinned pursuits. "When, at the outset, the Cape Fear Indians attacked his settlement, [Roger] annihilated them on 'Sugar Loaf,' the sand bluff just across the river from Orton," Louis wrote. He continued, "Orton rapidly became a famous plantation. Its rice fields and forests made Roger Moore a great slave owner and lavish host."

By the time the Revolutionary War began, The Family was synonymous with North Carolina. In February 1776, a scrappy Patriot force unexpectedly trounced loyalist troops near Wilmington by partially dismantling a river crossing's pine planks and greasing the remaining structure with tallow and soap. The battle was an early and significant victory for the Patriots, and it marked a turning point, ending British control of North Carolina, which, two months later, became the first colony to declare independence. The river was Moores Creek, the crossing was the Moores

Creek Bridge, and one of the commanders who won the day was James Moore's grandson.

In the new United States of America, John Adams would appoint Alfred Moore—a great-grandson of James, the first American Moore—to the Supreme Court. One of two North Carolinians ever to serve, he resigned in 1804 due to poor health after authoring a single opinion and returned home to Moorefields, his sprawling summer retreat near Hillsborough.

HIS OWN GREAT-GRANDSON ALFRED MOORE WADDELL—WHO, HALF A century later, would do more than almost anyone to incite white violence in Wilmington—was born at Moorefields in September 1834. His parents must have had a hard time deciding which forebear to honor as they carried the newborn from his mother's bed down the Chinese Chippendale staircase for which the house was renowned. In addition to descending from a Supreme Court justice, baby Alfred was a great-grandson of General Hugh Waddell, a colonial military hero, and of Brigadier General Francis Nash, after whom Nashville is named. Long dead by the time Waddell arrived, these illustrious ancestors nonetheless towered in the landscape of his childhood like "the tall sunflower plants spreading their noble glories" across Moorefields's expanses.

A lot was never enough for Waddell. Whereas his voracious ancestors amassed land, possessions, and wealth, he heaped exaggeration upon overstatement, trying to inhabit the sense of superiority his lineage presumed. His childhood of pomp and sadism pleased him greatly, if his memoirs are to be believed. He writes with sentimental relish of hours spent by the fireside of an "old slave," a white-bearded man he called Uncle Abel, "listening to his reminisces while he smoked the tobacco which it was my delight to give him." Once, his brother rode a large white hog through the streets like a warhorse, and on "red letter days for the school boys," Whigs and Democrats faced off in public brawls, spilling blood on the courthouse square.

After graduating from the University of North Carolina, which his grandfather helped to found, Waddell studied law privately. He had grown up listening to courtroom arguments, boasting later that "there was no Bar in the United States from Boston to New Orleans that was superior to the one which at that time assembled at Hillsborough." Despite his provincial upbringing, he already considered himself something of a sophisticate. And despite his maudlin streak, he was especially proud of what he considered to be a comic talent. He was a giver of jocular nicknames, a teller of lawyer jokes, a writer of doggerel—the type of man who could wax on about anything, sprinkling his speeches with classical allusions and French phrases, sometimes in the same breath, while complaining that "Hebrew" names were hard to pronounce.

In 1856, at the age of twenty-two, Waddell moved to Wilmington, "the old 'stamping ground' of my forefathers." The next year, he wed Julia Savage, the daughter of a well-connected attorney. Waddell opened a law practice, but his business seems not to have flourished, as he and his young

Alfred Moore Waddell, 1860.

family moved in with his wealthy father-in-law, rather than setting up their own household. In 1860, he told census takers he had no assets of any value. The deepening national crisis over slavery intensified this instability, yet the prospect of war held promise for an opportunistic scion looking to find his lane.

Chapter 3

THE BELLAMYS BUILD

As Waddell was building a law practice, Dr. John Dillard Bellamy was building a ridiculous house. Not eccentric ridiculous, but extravagant ridiculous. Located on a prime lot at the northeast corner of Fifth and Market, it would be Wilmington's finest residence, unrivaled by any building, public or private, save the newly completed City Hall, also known as Thalian Hall for the theater it housed.

The doctor and his wife had eight children by the time they would move in, in 1861, with another one on the way. At ten thousand square feet, spread over five levels, the mansion boasted twenty-two rooms—two for each family member and a couple to spare. Improbably, its design combined neoclassical, Greek Revival, and Italianate elements: twenty-five-foot-high Corinthian columns that wrapped around three sides, creating deep, shaded piazzas; arched windows with individual balustrades from which one might listen to a serenade or bark an order. A gabled roof culminated in a belvedere, with a view that swept the city. Up there, it was just the Bellamys, the birds, and the church steeples, straining toward the gods.

Such grandiosity seemed out of character for John Dillard, a teetotaling Methodist who, as one acquaintance noted, "dressed in plain old fashioned manner and always carried a blue umbrella." He descended from a French Huguenot, John Bellemie, who had immigrated to Barbados in 1665 as a grantee of the Lords Proprietors of England and, from there, to South Carolina. Like the earliest Moores, the first American John Bellamy settled at the Goose Creek colony. His sons and their sons fanned out across the South Carolina low country, acquiring cotton plantations, cultivated by people they enslaved. These beginnings would serve as the basis for an enduring sense of family pride. "These Bellamys were gentlemen of culture and wealth—leaving a splendid heritage to their posterity," one of their descendants, the seventh John Bellamy, boasted in the mid-twentieth century.

John Dillard was born in Horry County, near Murrell's Inlet. The family lived half a mile from the sea, and the deserted shore was John Dillard's backyard, "nothing upon it but sand, shells and pieces of wrecked vessels." His swimming pools were freshwater ponds filled with bulrushes. "You could ride the dry beach from Murrell's Inlet to the eight mile swash, a most delightful ride, at low tide on the strand, but sandy and heavy above the strand," he later recalled. Even in his burgher years, he retained a wind-bitten, thousand-yard look, as though he were staring out at the glinting horizon.

John Dillard's father died in 1826. With his toddler brother, Marsden, nine-year-old John Dillard inherited a sixteen-hundred-acre plantation at Winyah Bay, a second plantation on the Waccamaw River, and $9,076.13 in notes, silver, and furniture (not to mention a herd of fifty wild island goats). The boys also inherited twenty-one of the fifty-two people whom their father enslaved. The will named them—Big Scipio, Little Scipio, Nero, John, Peter, Ben, Byano, Mary, Hannah, Joe, Harriet, Betsy, Nancy, Lydia, Beau, Peggy, Stephen, Ben, Old Penny, Ephraim, and Tina—stipulating that the Bellamy boys would also inherit all of their children. The unacknowledged foundation of the family's "splendid heritage" was, in fact, chattel slavery. The Bellamys spoke airily of a patrimony of culture and wealth, but what they legally inherited were hundreds of human beings, living and yet to be conceived, or even conceived of.

In 1837, John Dillard moved to Wilmington to study medicine. Apprenticing with Dr. William James Harriss, a prominent surgeon who was active in Democratic politics, he learned to deliver babies, concoct medicines, and set broken bones. Once he had absorbed all he could from Dr. Harriss, John Dillard set off for Jefferson Medical College, in Philadelphia, where

Paul Revere's son instructed him in the "theory and practice of physick." As John Dillard pored over the mysteries of the human body, he received confirmation of its fragility: His fifteen-year-old brother had fallen ill on the road to boarding school, dying "in the springtime of his life," as his gravestone would note.

After graduation, John Dillard returned to Wilmington. He had become engaged to marry Eliza, Dr. Harriss's sweet, serious, and reasonably well-educated eldest daughter. Her interest in botany complemented his in medicine, and both had assumed responsibilities from a young age—he had become a functional orphan after his mother remarried to a man with whom he didn't get along; she was the eldest of seven siblings. In June 1839, the young couple married in a simple ceremony at the Harriss home, followed by a reception featuring cake, ice cream, and punch. They planned to set off for a honeymoon in Europe in a month. Eliza, still a few months shy of eighteen, was to be chaperoned by a female cousin.

Twenty-seven days after the wedding, Dr. Harriss suddenly dropped dead. The European honeymoon was off. John Dillard, at twenty-one, became responsible for his grief-stricken mother-in-law and her many children, all under the age of fifteen. He assumed his father-in-law's medical practice, while continuing to manage his own holdings in South Carolina.

The patriarch role seems to have suited John Dillard. In 1840, Eliza gave birth to the couple's first child, Mary Elizabeth ("Belle"). According to that year's census, the Bellamy household comprised twenty-three people, fourteen of them enslaved, including four young children. Feeding so many people cost a fortune, but money flowed abundantly from the outlying Bellamy plantations to their Wilmington urban seat. John Dillard and Eliza continued to expand their family, welcoming Marsden in 1843, William ("Willie") James Harriss in 1844, Eliza in 1845, and Ellen in 1852. John Dillard Jr., the legacy name-bearer, was born in 1854, followed by George Harriss in 1856, and in 1858, Kate Taylor, who lived only three weeks.

John Dillard's career in medicine fell by the wayside as his business interests multiplied. In 1842, he bought Grovely, a plantation just across the river from Wilmington, whose title traced all the way back to Maurice

Moore of the "pestiferous Moores." The larger his family grew, the more land John Dillard acquired. The more land he acquired, the more people he enslaved. An 1852 letter makes clear that he considered his human investments paramount to his agricultural ones. "My crop is not as good as I had anticipated it would be some time since," he wrote. "The copious rains have done it much damage. But to compensate for this my whole family black and white have been blessed with unusual health. We have abundant cause for thankfulness as Providence has been very kind."

The bulk of John Dillard's fortune came from pine forest plantations in Brunswick and Columbus counties. There, enslaved people extracted resin and converted it into "prime Virgin Turpentine." They also cultivated corn, oats, rice, sweet potatoes, hay, and peanuts. The naval stores they produced and the crops they raised generated capital that allowed John Dillard to invest in land, banks, and railroads. By 1860, with the country on the brink of war, he identified himself as a "merchant" and was a director of the Bank of the Cape Fear, as well as the largest shareholder in the Wilmington and Weldon Railroad. In North Carolina alone, his personal property was valued at more than two hundred thousand dollars. Included in this figure were 113 people he enslaved across three counties. Statewide, 70 percent of households counted no slaves at all. Only 0.5 percent of North Carolinians owned more land than John Dillard, and only 0.3 percent enslaved more people.

By the time John Dillard bought the lot for the mansion, he was, as a daughter later recalled, "just about the richest man around these parts." There was no question that he could afford a comfortable new home for his still-growing family, but he surprised his neighbors by abandoning his characteristic sobriety and splurging for every furbelow. He may have hoped to give his children a boost as they entered society: Belle had recently graduated from a Columbia, South Carolina, academy for women, while Marsden was studying at the University of North Carolina.

However strong his filial pride, John Dillard's vision for the mansion was likely even more deeply influenced by his politics. For generations, the Bellamys had shunned public life, exercising power behind the scenes as "independent gentlemen who held no important offices, and did not desire any." John Dillard broke with this precedent in the 1850s, stepping into the political fray as chairman of the New Hanover Democratic Association. Democrats of the time were fervent proponents of slavery, states' rights, and secessionism. As a right-wing, pro-secession extremist in the "fire-eater" mold, John Dillard stood apart from Wilmington's oldest families. Many of them, while defending slavery, had strong ties to New England; fearing that secession would harm interstate business, they aligned with the more moderate Whigs. From their point of view, John Dillard's politics carried a whiff of excess and populism. When he presided over a heated Democratic meeting that ended in a fatal duel, this stigma only intensified. According to one local historian, "despite his wealth, Dr. Bellamy lived under a certain cloud."

His response was to build out from under it. The Bellamy Mansion, as the house came to be known, was both a proclamation of stature and a tool of self-elevation, a means of one-upping the stratosphere of Wilmington society from which his politics alienated him. Other Wilmington families had fine estates: the DeRossets with their riverside terraced gardens, the MacRaes with their Scottish-inspired castle. But John Dillard chose to tack a romantic plantation veneer on an urban dwelling filled with the latest technology. The house practically shouted its admiration of South Carolina.

As hostilities heated up, Belle exchanged plucky fantasies of Southern invincibility with a South Carolina schoolmate. If Wilmington got too dangerous, the friend wrote, Belle could come to Columbia to stay with her and her family. She was assembling a makeshift arsenal, she boasted, of "spikes, knives, saws, & anything that will do to kill and cut the Yankees to pieces." The girls called themselves "secesh dames." The Bellamy Mansion was a secesh house—a house by slavery and for slavery; a prime example, with its idealized facade and internal contradictions, of what one scholar later called the "architecture of Southern nationalism." It reflected the Bellamys' belief in white Southern superiority and telegraphed the power that they were prepared to use to defend it.

One detects the same bellicosity in another strong choice that John Dillard and Eliza made around the same time, upon the birth of their ninth child in September 1859. While their other children carried family names, the Bellamys called this baby Chesley Calhoun, in honor of the South Carolina senator John C. Calhoun, the country's most fervent proponent of slavery and states' rights. In the stylized language of the Cape Fear plantocracy, the house and the boy alike delivered an elegant screw-you to John Dillard's political opponents.

"THE UNION DISSOLVED!" WILMINGTON'S *DAILY JOURNAL* PROCLAIMED in December 1860. "South-Carolina Seceded!!" With the city's best house almost finished, his family nearly complete, and South Carolina making good on its promise to break from the Union, all of John Dillard's dreams were coming to fruition. It was still unclear, however, whether North Carolina would follow suit. One observer recalled that "the people of Wilmington were deeply stirred by conflicting emotions" as their neighbors to the south blew up the nation in the name of preserving slavery.

While the Whig establishment urged caution, John Dillard lit up the town in jubilation. "He bought up all the empty tar barrels in Wilmington and had them strewn along Front Street from Campbell to Queen, and on Market from the river to Ninth Street, and had a great bonfire and procession at night," his son John Dillard Jr. recalled. A marching band played along the mile-long route as revelers whooped and hollered. Leading the parade was John Dillard himself, his wee namesake by his side, thrusting a torch toward the sky.

Three days after the secession fest, the Bellamys assembled for a lavish holiday dinner at 409 Market Street, the marble-trimmed redoubt of their close relatives John and Kitty Taylor. (Decades later, the house would serve as the headquarters of the Wilmington Light Infantry.) They arrived at midday. The porch was laid with cushions, in anticipation of the coming of the "Kuners," a holiday institution in North Carolina, thought to have evolved from the Junkanoo traditions of the anglophone Caribbean islands. "Every child rises early on Christmas morning to see the Johnkannaus," Harriet Jacobs recalled in her memoir of enslavement in Edenton, North Carolina. "They consist of companies of slaves from the plantations, generally of the lower class. Two athletic men, in calico wrappers, have a net thrown over them, covered with all manner of bright-colored stripes. Cows' tails are fastened to their backs, and their heads are decorated with horns." In the Wilmington version of the tradition, enslaved men disguised themselves in costumes made of brightly colored rags and donned "kuner faces" of phantasmagorical features painted onto buckram masks under great beards made of Spanish moss.

The Taylor party could hear the Kuners coming for blocks, rattling beef ribs and banging on triangles. *Hah! Low! Here we go!* went their song, as they roamed the city's sandy roads. *Hah! Low! Here we go! Kuners come for my lady!* They filed into the Taylors' front garden, delighting the Bellamys and their relations. "Faster and faster falls the beat of the flying feet, never missing the time by a space of a midge's breath!" one upper-class white woman recalled of a similar performance. Before moving on to the next house, a dancer held out his hat to "a shower of large copper pennies."

In some instances, the leader of the band dressed as a slave master, leading the troupe in skits that skewered white greed, hypocrisy, and lack of social conscience. Even so, the white upper classes were much enamored of the performances, whether for what one observer characterized as their "exotic grotesquerie," or because the day's inversions—paying for Black labor, for instance—only underscored the reality of the social order. Members of the Bellamy family retained warm memories of the Kuners throughout their lives, seemingly oblivious to the barbed subtext of the performances.

A grandfather clock struck two, and the clan sat down to dinner. Crystal decanters filled with amber spirits tossed rainbows around the holly-draped room. In the middle of the long dining table sat a pyramid that reached almost all the way to the ceiling, bearing tall glasses of syllabub and wine jelly. The menu, prepared by a pair of enslaved cooks, included turkey, fried oysters, duck, aged ham, roast pig, rice and gravy, sweet potatoes, relishes, pickles, brandied peaches, homemade bread, and "rutabaga turnips hashed with Irish potatoes with lots of butter." A dozen or so desserts, from sponge cake to snowballs, were followed by fortified wines. "We would almost gasp for breath after dinner," Ellen Bellamy recalled, "the grown up folks going up stairs and the children would play awhile."

During the late-afternoon lull, the Bellamys walked a block west to admire their new house. The main elements of the estate were shaping up, including the mansion and a freestanding, two-story "servants' quarters" of lime-washed brick, where nine enslaved people would live. The back of the lot had a barnyard feel, with stables, cow stalls, and a tin-roofed henhouse. The cost of the house, incredibly, exceeded the construction costs of the First Presbyterian Church, another of the architect's projects, by a third. Yet, according to John Dillard Jr., this amounted to "only one year's profit" at Grist, one of his father's turpentine plantations. As the country hurtled into chaos, and the South toward lean times, the Bellamys reveled in plenty, topping off their social aspirations, like buttered rutabagas, with lashings of money.

Chapter 4

THE HALSEYS ENTER THE RECORD

Joshua Halsey was born in Wilmington in 1852 to Eli Simon Halsey and Satyra Walker. Both were enslaved, Satyra likely by a wealthy lawyer, Thomas D. Walker, who served as president of the Wilmington and Manchester Railroad. Forbidden by law to marry, they were husband and wife nonetheless. Together, they produced four children: Caleb, Joshua, Mildred, and Chloe. Their lives were little recorded on paper. Only the broadest strokes of Joshua's childhood remain in the historical record—a before, a war, an after.

The year after Joshua came into the world, his future wife, Sallie Franklin-Jones, was born in Weldon, North Carolina, a railroad hub in the northern part of the state. Her father's name was William Jones. Sallie apparently did not know her mother, but her descendants, using DNA testing, have ascertained that she probably came from Fairfield County, South Carolina. Sallie's enslaver, William Lovejoy, ran a private academy for white boys in Weldon. According to family history, Sallie was a house servant, and from a young age, she served as a personal attendant to a white child who couldn't see. "She had to follow this little blind girl around," one of her granddaughters remembered.

Lovejoy, even as he held humans in bondage, had some unusual ideas about slavery. "Evidently, he wasn't like most of the slaveowners," Sallie's granddaughter said later. "He didn't believe in slavery that much." Though it was illegal, Lovejoy, perhaps out of religious conviction, taught his slaves to read and write. Sallie later recalled that he'd wake her and the other enslaved children for lessons in the middle of the night. She retained the memory of a makeshift schoolroom with "Chinese velvet curtains" all her life. "You're not going to be slaves all your days," Lovejoy told the tired children, as they deciphered the alphabet deep into the night. "When you get your freedom, you'll thank me for this."

One day, a merchant arrived at the Lovejoy house with bolts of luxurious fabric. "The person who was making the clothing saved some material out, and gave it to the little girl," Sallie's granddaughter recalled. "My grandmother thought that she should have had some too, because they always gave her whatever they gave the little blind girl." So, Sallie got a pair of scissors, went into the little girl's bedroom, located the expensive fabric, and snipped off piece for herself. She was "always doing little devilish things," the granddaughter recalled.

Lovejoy's wife wanted Sallie beaten, but he wouldn't allow it. Still, the precious fabric left a lasting impression. As Sallie's adult enslavers indulged themselves, she endured premature lessons in self-control, weighing her desires against the dangers to which they exposed her.

The documentary record holds far less information about Joshua's and Sallie's lives, particularly in their early years, than it does about many of their contemporaries—including the Bellamys, the Moores, and the Howes—but they are equally important. Their descendants have not been able to consult treatises or deeds, to pinpoint their ancestors' movements with perfect accuracy, or even to confirm how they met, but they have devised ways to know their patriarch and matriarch nonetheless, using science, creativity, and common sense.

In the absence of beeswax seals and fancy signatures, certain details about the Halseys have endured as marvels of individuation, as substantial as they are slight, because they were recorded and kept alive by people who loved them. The paper record says that as the Civil War approached, Joshua and Sallie were both children, both enslaved. The personal record, transmitted from generation to generation, says that Joshua was the "standout personality of his family"; that Sallie, the doer of "little devilish things," was getting an education to match her daring, just as the contours of their world were about to change.

Chapter 5

BREAKAWAY

In an 1861 speech rationalizing secession, Alexander Stephens, the vice president of the Confederacy, declared that the "cornerstone" of the breakaway republic rested "upon the great truth that the negro is not equal to the white man." John Dillard's slavery-financed castle was built on the same foundation of white supremacy. Nonetheless, he wanted the best labor he could get, and the best labor in Wilmington happened to be Black labor. And so, while John Dillard agitated for secession, a crew of Yankee architects and Black artisans raised a monument to his contradictions.

John Dillard hired James F. Post, a New Jersey–born architect who had just overseen the construction of City Hall and was enjoying a moment of popularity with Wilmington's white upper classes. He would receive credit for realizing the Bellamy Mansion, but Black contractors were responsible for every aspect of its construction, from raising the heavy yellow pine frame to joining the hips and valleys of the roof. "None of them could read, but give any plan an' they could foller it to the last line," a formerly enslaved person in Wilmington recalled. Rufus Bunnell, a young white architect whom Post brought in from Connecticut to assist with the project, struggled to reconcile his enslaved Black colleagues' professional mastery with their subaltern status. It "seemed strange to keep ever in mind," he confided to his diary, "that almost to a man these mechanics (however seemingly intelligent) were *nothing but slaves* and capable as they might be, all the earnings that came from their work were regularly paid over to their masters or mistresses."

John Dillard Bellamy Jr. later admitted, "It is remarkable that all the carpentry work was performed by negroes, chiefly free negroes." Decades after the house's construction, he could cite their names ("Howes, Artises, Prices, Sadgwars, and Kellogs") even as he strained to minimize their contributions. "As a matter of fact, in ante bellum days, white men generally refused to ply the trade of carpenters and masons, thinking it beneath their dignity," he wrote in his memoirs. "So the employment of negro carpenters and masons was not a matter of choice but one of necessity." The architect James Post's son, however, straightforwardly acknowledged the primary role that artisans like the Howes played in the mansion's construction: "Built by colored workmen. Was credit to them."

On March 20, 1860, Bunnell inspected the latest work and ascended to the cupola, where he "sat a long while talking with the negro contractor, 'Artis' about all the work." One can imagine them going over the specs, as Black workers such as Fred Howe—Anthony and Tenah's son, now a successful builder—came and went. It's interesting to think about where these conversations might have strayed, about what kinds of information might have been exchanged—Bunnell would have been a rare source of firsthand information from the North. His diaries reveal that he opposed the Confederate cause and was ill at ease with the racial oppression he encountered in Wilmington, but he was unwilling to challenge what he called "the Southern way of handling things."

Just as John Dillard relied on Black people to sculpt his intricate house down to the ornamental cornices, but still insisted on their inferiority, he looked to white Northerners to supply its materials, all the while bitterly protesting the industrial and electoral dominance that enabled the North to "wage a war on slavery." In 1860, with the secession debate at full tilt, he set out with his wife, Eliza, his eldest daughter, Belle, and the infant Chesley Calhoun on a shopping trip to New York. Fellow secessionists were urging Southerners to boycott Northern goods. "Let us have a civilization of our own and depend on our Yankee neighbors neither for refinement and elegance, nor Weathersfield onions and Connecticut cheese," one wrote. But practicing solidarity was less important to the Bellamys than procuring a new set of damask curtains.

The traveling family was accompanied by "Aunt" Betsy Kedar, an elderly free woman of mixed race. The Bellamys had hired her as a nursemaid specially for the occasion, Ellen Bellamy remembered, "thinking it unwise to take our regular slave nurse as the country was so excited just then on the slavery question." The Bellamys were afraid, in other words, that if they took one of the people they enslaved to New York, she might escape. So they paid a Black woman to do the work that they otherwise insisted Black women were born to do for free. With Aunt Betsy along, they traveled north to buy luxury furnishings, filling the coffers of their sworn enemies.

Even the mild-mannered assistant architect Bunnell couldn't help noting his patron's hypocrisy. Although John Dillard was a "'dyed in the wool' southern democrat," Bunnell observed, he insisted that the builders "order everything from the North that could be had cheaper than in Wilmington." Ultimately, John Dillard's desire to save a dollar was stronger than his sectional loyalty. And so went the commission to Jenkins and Porter of Canal Street in New York City for fourteen Corinthian columns to adorn the plantation-style mansion of the city's most ardently secessionist family.

FRED HOWE RUSHED AROUND TOWN, ORGANIZING HIS AFFAIRS FOR AN UPcoming trip. It was late January 1861, and he had much to do before darkness fell and the lamplighters appeared in the streets. He headed along Third Street, dodging pits and puddles, breathing in the acrid turpentine fumes that drifted across the river from distilleries on the opposite bank. The city was smartening up, but chickens still strutted around in muddy yards, bordered by backyard gardens in which people would soon be putting down seeds for green peas and lettuce. It was a straight shot from Howe's house, on Queen and Third, to the courthouse, eight blocks north.

Fred hustled past Market Street, where white schoolboys took their recess, chucking clamshells over the belfry of his church, St. James Episcopal. A mixed congregation worshipped there: The city's white upper crust attended services in the morning, followed by the Black upper crust in the afternoon. Nearby, the Baptists were putting up a two-hundred-foot spire, said to be the tallest in America. Farther down the street, the editors of *The Wilmington Journal* cracked jokes at the expense of William Seward, soon to be Lincoln's secretary of state. Seward had just declared on the floor of the Senate, rather optimistically, that "sedition and violence are only local and temporary," and that the union could be saved.

Down at the docks, schooners waited ninety at a time to unload cargoes from Rio de Janeiro and Demerara. The construction of what would eventually be known as the Wilmington and Weldon Railroad, finished in 1840, had cemented Wilmington's position as one of the crucial transportation hubs of the upper South. It was a volatile moment, demanding the hurried making of momentous choices, and, as at all such junctures, some people had a better sense than others for which way things were likely to go. "Gentlemen, your old customers are yet in market," a pair of slave traders, with a whiff of panic, promised in the advertising section of the *Journal*. "All you who have NEGROES for sale would do well to give us a call."

At forty-three, Fred had a wife and four living children, the youngest not two years old. He owned his house, which he had built on land that had been in his family for decades. The Howe settlement, as it was known, served as a sort of private talent incubator, facilitating the transmission of skills from one generation to the next. At the moment, Fred and his wife had two young relatives boarding with them—one of them was a carpenter, learning the ropes of the family business. Fred wasn't rich, exactly, but he'd managed to accumulate three hundred dollars in personal property. This was more than most anyone on the block, except for his oldest brother, Anthony, who lived next door and possessed precisely the same amount.

Fred stopped at the courthouse and tied up his horse. He was carrying two pieces of lined paper containing several handwritten paragraphs—a sort of laissez-passer, attesting to his good character. "Alfred Howe . . . a colored man who is the bearer of these papers is a carpenter by trade," the document read. "He has been raised in this community and he leaves here

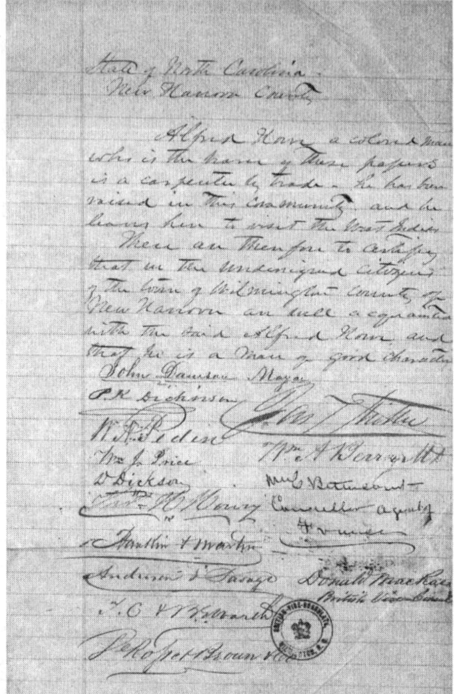
State of North Carolina
New Hanover County

Alfred Howe a colored man who is the bearer of these papers is a carpenter by trade. He has been raised in this community and he leaves here to visit the West Indies.
These are therefore to certify that we the undersigned citizens of the town of Wilmington County of New Hanover are well acquainted with the said Alfred Howe and that he is a man of good character.

John Dawson Mayor
P. K. Dickinson
Wm. J. Price
D. Dickson
Donald MacRae
British Vice Consul

Character reference for Alfred "Fred" Howe, January 24, 1861.

to visit the West Indies." Fourteen of Wilmington's most prominent white citizens had signed the pass, with Donald MacRae, the British vice-consul in Wilmington, adding a stamp featuring a bejeweled crown. At the courthouse, Fred presented himself to Samuel Bunting, the county clerk of court. Bunting wrote out an affidavit of the document's authenticity. Then, he scrawled his signature at the bottom in goose-quill pen and sealed the papers with saffron-colored wax.

Why was Fred undertaking such a journey? Did business call? Was he being sent away? Had his white guarantors charged him with an errand? Or did he smell violence in the air, on the eve of war, and figure he'd be better off getting out of town?

Certainly, Fred faced an increasingly repressive political climate. The Fugitive Slave Act of 1850 endangered all Black people, both enslaved and free, while the Kansas-Nebraska Act of 1854 set the nation on a course of bitter and bloody conflict over the expansion of slavery. Then, in a devastating decision in *Dred Scott v. Sandford* (1857), the Supreme Court ruled that members of "the African race" were not United States citizens, nor would they ever have the right to be. As white men mobilized for war, legislatures all over the South were cracking down on free Black people, fearing that they would encourage the enslaved to rebel. "For our part, we have always maintained the opinion that there should be but two classes in the slaveholding States the master white, and the subjugated black or colored race," the future North Carolina Governor William Holden declared in 1859, proposing to deport free Black people from the state.

In February 1861, just weeks after Fred buzzed around town soliciting signatures for his travel pass, the North Carolina legislature passed a law forbidding free Black people to "buy, purchase, or hire for any length of time any slave." The intent of the statute was not to ease the burden on enslaved Black people, but to discriminate against their free counterparts. It meant that a free Black carpenter like Fred was suddenly cut off from his industry's primary source of labor, while his white competitors could continue to employ whomever they wished. Another statute soon followed, stripping free Black people of the right to own guns. This marked them out as targets, unprotected by white enslavers and at a great disadvantage in defending themselves. The sense of escalating vulnerability was acute enough to lead several free Black North Carolinians to petition the legislature for permission to *reenter bondage*, "that they might select masters and become slaves."

Fred sailed for the West Indies sometime in early 1861. No record appears to remain of his departure from Wilmington, nor is it clear exactly where he landed or what he did once he got to the islands. But there is a record of his return trip—his name shows up on the passenger log of the *Empire*, a ship that departed from Gonaïves, Haiti, in late March 1861, arriving in New York Harbor on April 1. Fred was accompanied by an "E. Artest," a forty-two-year-old American man who, like Fred, listed his occupation as carpenter. Artest was almost certainly Elvin Artis, his Black colleague from the Bellamy Mansion, with whom the assistant architect Bunnell recalled chatting in the cupola.

While what Fred and Elvin did in the West Indies is beyond knowing, the possibilities are tantalizing. In 1791, enslaved Haitians revolted against French colonizers, and after thirteen years of struggle, they formally declared independence in 1804, soon establishing the world's first Black republic. Since then, Haiti had "enjoyed an unparalleled reputation" among Black Americans, as a shining exemplar of self-determination and self-governance. None other than David Walker, writing in his *Appeal to the Colored Citizens of the World*, had singled out Haitians as "brethren" who were "bound to protect and comfort us."

Haiti was, according to the historian William Seraile, the "main topic" of conversation among Black Americans in 1861. They debated whether to stay and "fight for human dignity" in what some hoped would be a war of abolition, or to try to get the hell out of a violent, imploding America. The exclusively white, enslaver-led American Colonization Society had long tried to persuade Black Americans to decamp for Africa, "repatriating" Liberia. But Haiti was a more attractive proposition. It was close to America, and its government was actively trying to recruit free Black Americans. When the United States government executed the abolitionist John Brown for treason in 1859, Haiti's president, Fabre Geffrard, gave him a state funeral. All over the island, flags waved at half-mast and houses were draped in black.

Throughout the early 1860s, Black newspapers carried advertisements promoting immigration to Haiti. In 1861, Geffrard announced a package of enticements for Black Americans, including free land and guaranteed employment. "Hayti is the common country of the Black race," his representative declared. "Listen, then, all ye negroes and mulattoes who, in the vast continent of America, suffer from the prejudices of caste, the Republic calls you; she invites you to bring to her your arms and your minds." The president even appointed an official to launch *The Pine and the Palm*, a newspaper dedicated to persuading Black Americans to immigrate to Haiti to create "a great Negro nation."

More than two thousand Black Americans heeded the call, setting sail for Haiti in 1861. Once they arrived, reality could be daunting. There was a new language to master and intense heat to endure. *The Pine and the Palm* counseled transplants to show up with their own supplies of such necessities as nails, shingles, dishes, candles, oil, and reading material, "for English books can seldom be had for either love or money." Most of the émigrés eventually returned to the United States, some only months after arriving.

It seems unlikely that Fred, a homeowner with a large family, would have chosen to leave behind the land of his birth and the flawed but known world of Wilmington to gamble on a new life in Haiti. But perhaps he did decide to emigrate, then quickly changed his mind and headed home. The possibility also exists that his trip was always intended to be a short one. He and Artis could have been hired for a building job there. Or if some portion of Wilmington's free Black community was considering emigrating en masse, the two men may have gone ahead to Haiti as scouts.

Intriguingly, the North Carolina–born abolitionist Abraham Galloway also traveled to Haiti in January 1861. Galloway had been an enslaved brickmason in Wilmington before freeing himself by stowing away in the hold of a ship, so it's probable that he and Fred were acquainted. Galloway arrived in Haiti just a month before Fred gathered his signatures in Wilmington. According to one biographer, Galloway was likely working on a plot to use Haiti as a base for an armed attack on the slaveholding South. Whether or not Fred and Galloway coordinated their journeys to Haiti, their departures coincided. They left the country on the same day, April 1, 1861, sailing back to America on separate ships. Whatever Fred was doing in Haiti, his choice to undertake the journey makes it clear that he was willing to take on significant risk for a chance at disrupting the status quo.

Chapter 6

DELIVER US FROM EVIL

John Dillard Bellamy did not like to go out in society, but occasionally he brought society home. In March 1861, he and Eliza hosted a "House-warming," honoring two newlywed couples, both Harriss relations. The occasion doubled as a rally for the brewing war. Inside the house, guests mingled beneath gas chandeliers adorned with horn-blowing Black cherubim and crossed pitchforks, "a not-so-subtle reminder that they were in the home of the planter gentry." A band played all evening on the back piazza, which the family had had tented for the evening. John Dillard was a teetotaler, so there was no alcohol, but coffee, tea, and chocolate fueled the crowd, as did fevered talk of the newly formed Confederate States of America. Their daughter Ellen Bellamy later recalled it as "the grandest party ever given in Wilmington!"

John Dillard was ecstatic when, a month later, Confederate troops fired on Fort Sumter. In May, he took the opportunity to express his approval directly to Jefferson Davis, as he passed through Wilmington with his entire cabinet en route to the new Confederate capital in Richmond. John Dillard Jr. later recalled, "My father being a warm and enthusiastic supporter of President Davis and Secession Democrat, was very prominent in the reception; he escorted me across the mall, and introduced me to the President, who put his hand on my head and said to me, 'Young man, you will live to be a good man and a valiant soldier, I know.'"

The Bellamy family geared up for a fight they believed they would easily win. Eighteen-year-old Marsden and sixteen-year-old Willie both enlisted, while at home Eliza delivered a tenth and final child, Robert, in her four-poster bed. When Christmas came in 1861, Uncle John Taylor's table heaved with delicacies: the wine jellies still jiggled, the glass pyramid still gleamed. Materially, life carried on much as before for the Bellamys and their kin, but the jolly holiday ambience had given way to melancholy. A year earlier, the Kuners had performed to the family's delight. Now, empty chairs at the table attested to wartime separations that threatened to become permanent losses.

In 1862 the war's realities began to set in for the Bellamys. That summer, seventeen-year-old Willie barely survived being shot in the shoulders and knees on the Virginian front. He came home to recover at the Bellamy Mansion, encountering a rapidly changing city. Staples such as coffee were scarce and a quarter of a lamb cost a hundred dollars. The homes of friends and neighbors were rented out to "rogues and desperadoes," whose arrival, one observer recalled, had turned "the staid old town of Wilmington . . . topsy turvy." Not infrequently, a random mutilated body floated up from the depths of the river.

At the outset of the war, Lincoln had ordered a blockade of the entire thirty-five-hundred-mile Southern coastline. Soldiers, sailors, speculators, brokers, and prostitutes flocked to Wilmington. They were joined there by blockade runners, proprietors of the quicksilver steamships of the same name that attempted to keep the South supplied in necessity and luxury alike. Wilmington—less than seven hundred miles from both Nassau and Bermuda—was ideally located for blockade running. Furthermore, the city's position between two inlets, one of them protected by Fort Fisher, made it almost impossible to cut off access to the port. Local mariners had a distinct advantage in navigating the treacherous waters. One Union officer wrote that patrolling Wilmington "was very like a parcel of cats watching a big rat hole, the rat often running in when they are expecting him to run out and vice versa."

As the Union's "anaconda plan" began to succeed in choking off key Southern ports, Wilmington became a lifeline for the Confederacy. Blockade runners there succeeded about 85 percent of the time in beating Union patrols. In 1864, the ships delivered six million pounds of meat, two million pounds of saltpeter (for gunpowder), and a million and a half pounds of lead (for musket balls) through Wilmington into Confederate hands. Once a cargo reached the harbor, it was loaded onto one of the city's three railroads. The trains delivered the imported goods to cities around the South, returning to Wilmington filled with cotton for export. "These were flush days in Wilmington, not withstanding its privations," John Dillard Jr. wrote, recalling a heady scene of cockfights and gold bars piled in the windows of brokerage shops. For a single successful round trip between Nassau and Wilmington, the owner of a ship could clear about a quarter of a million dollars, cash.

Mass death came to Wilmington in August 1862 alongside a shipment of bacon on the blockade runner *Kate*. The ship had departed Nassau, where a yellow fever outbreak was underway. By the time it reached the docks at Wilmington four days later, several crew members were showing signs of illness. The young attorney Alfred Moore Waddell, who happened to be passing through town, heard talk that a young German man, "a poor fellow named Swarzman," was holed up in his hotel, sick and alone. Serving in no official capacity, Waddell rushed to his side. "I called at his room, sat by his bedside and tried to cheer him, holding his hand in the meantime," he recalled. The man "died with black vomit within forty-eight hours," believed to be the city's first recognized casualty of the disease. Waddell seems to have emerged from the encounter persuaded of his own invincibility. Not long after leaving town, he cheated death again, surviving "a dreadful railroad accident" that killed two people. Everyone else was hurt, Waddell bragged, "while I crawled out with slight injury."

By September, the disease was spreading quickly to the rest of the population. Over the course of ten weeks, more than six hundred Wilmingtonians died, including five of the city's ten doctors. The Bellamys peered out the front windows of their mansion, John Dillard Jr. recalled, "watching wagon-loads of corpses go by to Oakdale Cemetery." As they made plans to evacuate, a railroad official rode by on his horse.

"Dr. Bellamy, aren't you afraid to be here while the fever is raging?" the man hollered.

"Yes, we are preparing to leave now," John Dillard replied. "Are you going to stay?"

"Yes, I am immune and not afraid."

True to their word, the Bellamys hurried out of town. The next week, they opened the newspaper to find the railroad president's obituary.

While the family fled, they left an enslaved cook named Sarah behind to look after the mansion. Many of their friends and neighbors did the same. "Pray in my bee half I am gitting better all But Bad Head," an enslaved man named William Henry Thurber wrote to the DeRossets, who were sheltering near Chapel Hill. Another woman they enslaved, Bella, reported that it was hard to find food. Learning of William and Bella's suffering, Eliza DeRosset was concerned, but not overly. In a letter to her daughter she reasoned, "I have heard that the fever seldom proves fatal to Negroes."

The unlucky souls who remained in Wilmington, out of duty or under duress, burned barrels of tar day and night hoping to contain the pestilence. To one inhabitant, the thick black pall that hung over the city "seemed more like fuliginous clouds of ominous portent, a somber emblem of mourning."

THE BELLAMYS SPENT THE DURATION OF THE WAR "REFUGEEING" AT FLORAL College, a shuttered Presbyterian women's college in Robeson County, farther west. The school advertised itself to deep-pocketed evacuees as a sort of gated community, "proverbially healthy; and in these troubled times as safe a retreat as can anywhere be found." Located in a village of about fifteen houses, the campus was relatively safe from both fighting and disease. The Bellamys waited out the war there with the Oscar Parsley family, hometown friends from another large, well-connected clan. While the world choked and burned, they retreated into a cozy compound of two connected residences, re-creating a microcosm of Wilmington society amid Floral College's quiet woods.

On the first day of 1863, as the nation approached a third year of war, President Abraham Lincoln issued the Emancipation Proclamation, decreeing that "all persons held as slaves . . . shall be then, thenceforward, and forever free." Lincoln's act confirmed that the war really was about slavery and made its abolition an explicit Union objective. The chances that things were ever going back to the way they were—that slavery would survive the war—were becoming slimmer than ever, but the Bellamys, like most white Southerners, ignored the proclamation and continued as before.

They had brought dozens of enslaved people with them to Floral College. They tried to maintain the style of life that they had enjoyed in Wilmington, sending for crates of fine furniture, porcelain, draperies, and art. The white children attended a little private school. There were picnics in groves, church socials, and a pair of roosters named Stonewall Jackson and General Lee. Ellen Bellamy, who was nine when her family relocated to Floral College, later remembered that "life was so sweet and different there." Deprivation was rare enough to seem like novelty. When gloves were unavailable in the latest colors, the girls bought a box of white ones and dyed them with green tea.

By the end of 1864, Wilmington was the Confederacy's only remaining Atlantic port, its last conduit to the wider world. Shutting down Wilmington, the secretary of the navy informed Lincoln, "would be almost as

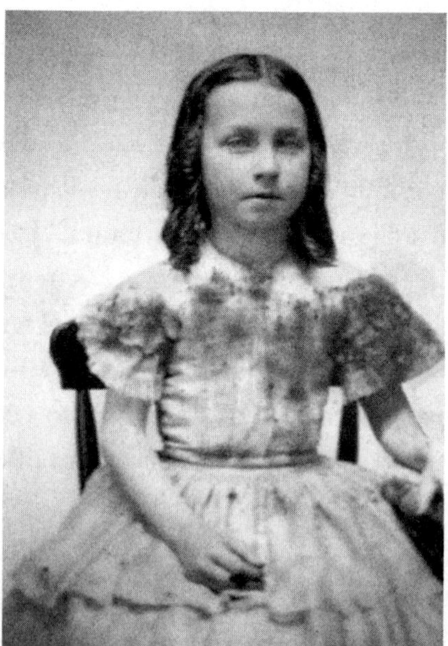

Ellen Douglas Bellamy, age nine.

important as the capture of Richmond on the fate of the Rebels." As the Union's anaconda squeezed the South ever tighter, the Bellamys, desperate to catch up with family and friends, decided to risk a visit home for the holidays. That year, Christmas fell on a Sunday. Eliza had planned a lavish dinner at the mansion—such was the Bellamys' conservatism that the more extenuating the circumstances, the less likely they were to alter their habits a whit.

On Christmas morning, Eliza and the children attended church at First Presbyterian, while John Dillard went alone, per his custom, to Front Street Methodist. Whatever their denomination, Wilmingtonians had ample reason to pray. Fort Fisher, the giant earthwork bastion that guarded the entry to the Cape Fear River, enabling the blockade runners to move supplies in and out of Wilmington, had been under attack since the early hours of Christmas Eve. With walls twenty-five feet thick and twenty feet high, the fort was known as the Gibraltar of the South. (John Dillard had donated the labor of men he enslaved to help build it.) The fates of Fort Fisher and the Confederacy were essentially one and the same. General Robert E. Lee admitted, "If Wilmington falls, I cannot maintain my army."

Union General Benjamin Butler had amassed some sixty-five hundred soldiers in a flotilla hovering off the coast. First, he tried to blow up Fort Fisher, packing the USS *Louisiana* with 215 tons of black powder to create a floating bomb. The scheme would likely have succeeded had an undertow not pulled the explosives-laden ship off course. Now he and his men were bombarding the fort. As the congregation at First Presbyterian recited the Lord's Prayer, explosions rumbled in the distance, jangling windows and rattling chalices. The worshippers knew that, barring divine intervention, the city would soon be full of those who would trespass against them.

Even a hostess as indomitable as Eliza perceived the danger. Calling back their dinner invitations, she and John Dillard hustled their children onto a ferry and fled across the river to their plantation at Grovely. As darkness fell, the sky lit up for miles around. The family huddled in stricken awe and watched shells exploding like rockets. Back in Wilmington, a lookout ascended to the cupola of the Bellamy Mansion and remained there for weeks, binoculars trained south.

ALFRED MOORE WADDELL SPIED OPPORTUNITY IN THE TUMULT. IN 1860, he pivoted from the law to the press, buying *The Wilmington Daily Herald*, a Unionist newspaper. For eight months, he used the paper to campaign for the preservation of the union. Then, as support for secession grew in Wilmington, he abruptly switched camps. This was an opportunistic choice, but Waddell depicted it as a bold stroke of romantic destiny. He claimed that he had gotten secret word of the impending attack on Fort Sumter and rushed to the depot, catching the train for Charleston just as it was pulling out. Looking out over Charleston Harbor from the cupola of his hotel, he witnessed "a sudden red flash, and a column of smoke, followed by an explosion, and opposite on James Island, a corresponding puff floated away on the breeze, and I realized with emotions indescribable that I was looking upon a civil war among my countrymen." From that moment, he claimed, "I was a Confederate soldier."

Despite this picturesque conversion, Waddell did not distinguish himself in the war. He enlisted as an adjutant in 1861 and rose to lieutenant colonel in the Third North Carolina Cavalry before resigning due to unspecified health problems at the height of the bloodshed in 1864. His distant cousin Roger Moore—a doer to Waddell's talker—took over the unit's command. Waddell admitted that he ended his military career "without any record worth mentioning," but for the rest of his life he used the title Colonel, lopping off the preceding "Lieutenant."

Now, a block away from the Bellamy Mansion at St. James Episcopal Church, Waddell was on his knees. He joined a large crowd of mostly women, many of whom were mourning a husband, a brother, a son, or some combination of the three. The booming of the guns from Fort Fisher added to the atmosphere of high anxiety in the sanctuary. The explosions came at irregular intervals; the second you let down your guard, a new broadside would shatter the peace. Nearby at Front Street Methodist Church, the pastor had sat down to write his Christmas sermon and, counting forty shells a minute, almost abandoned the task due to the brain-scrambling noise. Waddell thought the very air seemed to shake like jelly. As the congregation at St. James recited the Litany, the booms increased in frequency, until what had sounded like thunderclaps became an unbroken roar.

"From battle and murder, and from sudden death," the minister read.

"Good Lord, deliver us," the prayer went up.

FORT FISHER FELL IN MID-JANUARY, AND UNION FORCES ENTERED WILmington on February 22, 1865. Gray-cloaked horsemen streaked through the streets, rounding up the last Confederate stragglers. At nine thirty a.m., Union troops marched into the city, colors flying as they paraded into the heart of town, blowing bugles and pounding drums. "Leaving the main column at Market Street, heading a squadron of splendidly equipped men mounted on superb chargers—every horse a beautiful bay—[the general] dashed up to City Hall," one observer wrote. There, Mayor John Dawson formally surrendered the city. For many white Wilmingtonians, the procession amounted to an apocalypse. "The heathen have entered our land, they have spoiled our heritage," one elderly St. James parishioner wrote on a blank page of her Bible.

Alfred Moore Waddell joined the gawking crowds on Front Street. With characteristically cynical humor, he recorded the reaction of "an elderly citizen—a very quiet man—who stood on a street corner watching the column pass without a word or sign until the negro troops, beside whom streamed a shouting mass of ex-slaves appeared." Ever the anecdote artist, Waddell emerged from the scrum with a punch line that neatly encapsulated the horror with which the city's old guard greeted the change of regime. "Then he turned away," Waddell wrote, "and with both hands raised and an indescribable expression of mingled horror and disgust exclaimed, 'Blow, Gabriel, blow, for God's sake blow!'" The end of the world would have been better, in this view, than one in which Black people walked the streets freely.

Two years after the Emancipation Proclamation, many of the city's four thousand Black people were still living in slavery conditions. To them, the appearance of Union troops would have been a wondrous sight. The unit included some sixteen hundred Black soldiers, trailed by masses of Black men, women, and children who had joined them along the way. One of the Black regiments was composed largely of local men, many of whom had doubly risked their lives, escaping from plantations to join the fight. One soldier's mother, who had been separated from him for long years in slavery, emerged from the crowd as if by magic, ran to him, and hugged him tight. "How powerful it must have been to march back into the city with a US eagle on his buttons and a musket on his shoulder," the historian Thanayi Jackson observes.

At the Front Street Methodist Church, the words of Psalm 9 resounded through the sanctuary. "Thou hast rebuked the nations! Thou hast blotted out their name forever and ever!" a lay leader proclaimed, to glad amens. Today was a day of exultation, in Wilmington as it was in Israel. The Union Army had come marching into town, overturning the twisted moral order that had governed life since anyone could remember. Now the needy would not always be forgotten. The hope of the poor would not perish forever. The right-side-up world, so long awaited, must have felt surreal. "One week ago, you were slaves," a Black Union chaplain proclaimed, as dawn broke. "Now you are all free!"

Front Street Methodist had never experienced such a Sabbath. The congregation traced its founding to the early 1700s, and many of its first members were Black people, free and enslaved, drawn to the faith by the church's condemnation of slavery, "contrary to the laws of God, man, and nature." By the mid-1800s the Front Street congregation included white businessmen and planters, among them the city's largest enslaver, Dr. John Dillard Bellamy. At the onset of the Civil War, the commitment of such members to preserving slavery had led to the breakup of the national Methodist church.

Now, with the war coming to an end, Front Street Methodist faced its own schism. Eight hundred of the church's thousand members were Black. After Fort Fisher fell, the church's newly appointed pastor, the Reverend L. S. Burkhead, summoned prominent Black congregants to a meeting. Burkhead, a white man, was trying to get ahead of the social changes that would surely be sweeping into town alongside the Union Army. He focused not on freedom but on discipline, sternly advising his Black flock to "carefully refrain from all extravagance" and to "commit no depredations upon the whites." Should they be so "unwise" as to disobey their white superiors, Burkhead warned, they risked nothing less than "a good chance to be destroyed *as a race*."

Black parishioners chose their own course. Just a week after the arrival of Union troops, they wrote to General John Schofield, who commanded the occupying force. Elias Halsey, a relation to Joshua Halsey, was one of twenty-one Black church members who signed the letter. The signatories explained that they intended to join the African Methodist Episcopal Church, the Black denomination founded in 1816 in response to discrimination by white Methodists. They asserted that the church property was rightfully theirs, and they called for the white pastor to be dismissed and a Black pastor hired.

Pastor Burkhead tried appealing to Union authorities white man to white men: "I most respectfully submit that it is not best *even for them*, to grant what a portion of them now ask." But the authorities, unmoved, opted for a quite literally egalitarian solution, giving Black members the church "during one-half each day (morning or evening)," and white members its use during the remaining hours. Burkhead, outraged, struck more than six hundred Black members from the church's rolls. Six hundred and forty-two soon seceded from Front Street to found a new church, St. Stephen African Methodist Episcopal.

On the morning of the "never-to-be-forgotten" sunrise service, a United States Colored Troops chaplain ascended the pulpit after the reading of Psalm 9. His words to the Black faithful exploded the contingent version of freedom that Burkhead had been promoting—the one holding that Black people, though legally free, were still spiritually subject to white overlords. "You were not quite sure that you were free, therefore you felt a little afraid to say boldly what you felt," the chaplain preached. "I know how it is. I remember how we used to have to employ our dark symbols and obscure figures to cover up our real meaning."

Now they could raise a church. They could own the land, draft the plan, move the bricks, stack the stones, erect a house to a freedom-loving God, and put a pastor in the pulpit who would boldly say what they felt, instead of trying to bully them into submission. In 1866, Elias Halsey and a handful of others bought a plot of land on Fifth and Red Cross streets. Church members raised money to purchase 125 tons of stone and a hundred thousand bricks for "a substantial brick building" with space for fourteen hundred worshippers—the state's largest congregation, Black or white. The new church, designed in the Gothic Revival style, would take years to erect, but its founders, like so many Black Wilmingtonians, remained zealously committed to the task of building community and defining possibility on their own terms.

CHAPTER 7

CLOSER TO FREEDOM

Ellen Bellamy, twelve, was promenading through the woods with a trio of girlfriends. Pine cone, daddy longlegs, woodpecker, daffodil. Suddenly, an old major they knew came screaming for them to get inside the house: "*Run girls, the blue jackets are coming!*"

The Union Army had arrived at Floral College. Only a few minutes after Ellen made it home, a patrol rode up to the Bellamy compound. The soldiers searched the property from top to bottom, prodding the ground with bayonets. According to Ellen, "In a twinkling of an eye, the whole house was ransacked." Yet, the soldiers seem to have behaved with relative restraint. According to John Dillard Jr., they found his father's medical school diploma from Jefferson College in Pennsylvania, and an army surgeon, in deference to a fellow alumnus, extended protection to the family. This coincidence didn't strike the Bellamys as the little miracle that it was. Like many white Southerners, they seem to have felt that the clemency of a conquering army was simply their due.

Years later, Ellen still seethed at the way the troops forced her mother to taste the food they appropriated from her, in case she'd poisoned it. The women had managed to squirrel away a few valuables in strategic locations—a black silk dress in a hidden chamber of a bed; "the new silver cake baskets" amid piles of trash. Ellen was particularly proud of her mother's panache in stuffing some prized silver forks "down her stocking legs for several days, the prongs of one inflicting a painful little wound on the calf of her leg!"

The troops moved on, leaving the Bellamys scared, hungry, and bereft of enslaved labor for the first time in their lives. John Dillard Jr. interpreted this loss as a theft, a taking of passive human property, along with the silver, the horses, and the smokehouse hams. Ellen admitted that the people the family enslaved left of their own volition, yet she attributed their decision to emotion rather than reason. "Our servants—cooks, maids, nurses, and wash maids—were completely demoralized, and when the Yankees offered to bring them back to Wilmington, every one of them left us!" she admitted. "You could hardly blame them, ignorant creatures, who did not like it up here and were anxious to get home."

Ellen's account is opaque about her own emotions. She doesn't disclose how the absence of her "Black family" made her feel, whether the abandonment of people who had been obliged for lifetimes to perform loyalty and even love came, as it did to many enslavers, as a stinging shock. In any case, the Bellamys did not suffer for long. Wealthy friends of John Dillard soon sent "a load of meal, meat and other provisions, together with a negro cook, which relieved our terrible plight." The experience of temporary indigence seems to have done little to temper the family's materialism and, in fact, may have exacerbated it, as a means of counteracting their humiliation. Particularly in a rapidly changing society, snobbery can be a powerful weapon, a way of staying true.

The Bellamys believed that they had lost much because they were rich, not because they were wrong or weak. Later, Ellen recounted the story of the plunder of their home at Floral College with a pinched superciliousness. "By the way, I have heard my mother tell that those forks were the second set ever in Wilmington; steel forks with bone handles to match knives were used altogether," she wrote. The forks—and, by extension, all that they represented—were still in her family's possession, she declared, "the prongs much worn and sharp, but all the silver intact."

BACK IN WILMINGTON, THE UNION ARMY SEIZED THE BELLAMY MANSION. Its new tenant, General Joseph Roswell Hawley, had recently been appointed military governor of the region. Hawley was born in North Carolina but moved to Connecticut as a boy, becoming a lawyer, a newspaper editor, a Republican, and a fervent opponent of slavery. His wife, Harriet, was a writer and a cousin of Harriet Beecher Stowe. The Bellamys' house was inarguably the city's prime piece of real estate, but the takeover served, above all, a political purpose. Erected as a monument to the Confederacy, the Bellamy Mansion now stood as a cautionary tale: Secede from the Union and you'll be the one who gets kicked to the curb.

As the war drew to a chaotic close, it remained unclear what level of punishment the rebels would face and what form that punishment might take. Left to his own devices, Hawley opted for radical measures, decreeing that unoccupied Confederate land would be redistributed to "white and colored refugees." He seized Orton, Kendal, Lilliput, and Pleasant Oaks—the immemorial jewels of the Cape Fear plantation kingdom—and turned them over, along with the Bellamy estates at Grist and Grovely, "for the use of freedmen, and the destitute and refugee colored people." Unthinkably to the family, Black soldiers now patrolled their white-columned portico. "My parents came down repeatedly to try to get possession of their home—to no avail," Ellen Bellamy wrote. "They were stopped at the entrance by a guard, a 'n——' soldier!"

The family was hell-bent on getting the mansion back. Before Lee had even formally surrendered, John Dillard mailed off a petition to Hawley, seeking the restitution of his property. Hawley wasn't interested. "I have answered verbally that for having spent four years making his bed, he must lie in it for awhile," he wrote dryly to an aide. Hawley's mocking resolve must have infuriated the Bellamys, but it did nothing to diminish their determination. A few weeks later, Eliza traveled to Wilmington, enlisting a relation of the Hawleys to facilitate an introduction to the general's wife.

Eliza loathed the experience of visiting "her own dear house" as an importuning guest. When she and the neighbor arrived, Mrs. Hawley escorted them to the front parlor. There, according to Ellen, Mrs. Hawley "showed her raising by 'hawking and spitting' in the fire, a most unladylike act." The Bellamys were equally aghast at Mrs. Hawley's gestures at hospitality. Ellen recalled, “During the call she offered Mother some figs (from Mother’s own tree) which Aunt Sarah had picked—our own old cook, who had been left here in charge of the premises.”

Harriet Hawley found the encounter with Eliza mildly hilarious. “Mrs. General Hawley tells a piquant story of a visit from the wife of a runaway Rebel, whose showy but uncomfortable house the general has seized for quarters and private residence,” a journalist to whom she recounted the incident recalled. Eliza’s assumption that the matter could be settled between well-placed white people struck Mrs. Hawley as delusional. Even as the Bellamy matriarch attempted a show of charm and humility, her air of superiority burned through. She spoke, in Mrs. Hawley’s estimation, “much as people who had gone off to the seashore for the summer might speak of renting their town house til their return.”

By dwelling on personal slights, families like the Bellamys could avoid confronting the reordering of society that the Confederate defeat entailed. The problem, in their thinking, wasn’t that they’d lost a war and that the victors and their ideas would now prevail; it was that the Hawleys were uncouth. To the family, the situation was insupportable, a fairy tale about intrusion and violation made real. Yankee soldiers were sleeping in their bedrooms, eating their figs, and there was no hope of chasing them back to wherever they’d come from. The Bellamys said they were asking for pardon, but they sought something closer to expungement—an erasure of the entire conflict and its precipitating causes, so that everything could go back to the way it always had been.

IN APRIL, LINCOLN WAS ASSASSINATED BY JOHN WILKES BOOTH, AN OBSESSIVE defender of the South and slavery. “It may be abstractly wrong to be so jubilant, but I just can’t help it,” one South Carolina secessionist wrote in her diary. Despite her elation at the elimination of the man who would become known as the Great Emancipator, she feared that his successor, Andrew Johnson, was likely to be just as bad—“the railsplitter will be succeeded by the drunken ass.”

Wilmington’s Confederates were unlikely to have been heartbroken by

Lincoln's murder. They knew better, however, than to crow about whatever private satisfaction they might have felt. A week earlier, General Hawley had ripped the pews out of St. James Episcopal after the pastor had pointedly left Lincoln off his list of prayers, while continuing to pray for Jefferson Davis. Chastened, the white establishment in Wilmington performed what one historian termed a kind of "prudent grief," dutifully eulogizing the fallen president to head off their conquerors' wrath.

As General Hawley draped the Bellamy Mansion in black, white leaders called in Alfred Moore Waddell, their trusty balderdash artist, to headline a memorial service at Thalian Hall. Ever the performer, he mingled generic denunciation of "a most lamentable event" with a sly attempt at capturing Lincoln's political legacy for the Southern cause. Just before his death, Waddell ventured, Lincoln had been planning to pursue "a course of magnanimity which must have secured him the respect, and friendship, of those of his fellow-citizens from whom he has been estranged for the past four years."

Waddell's implication was that the president, had he lived, would have compensated Southern enslavers for the loss of their human property. Before the war, enslaved people were America's largest asset class, embodying more wealth than manufacturing and railroads combined. An entire economy—purchase loans, slave mortgages, insurance policies—conspired to transform their bodies into money. From the enslaver's perspective, emancipation without compensation was pure theft, as if the government had promoted homeownership for years and then suddenly abolished real estate. Like Waddell, the Bellamys publicly condemned Lincoln's murder, while hoping that they might benefit from its political consequences. John Dillard Jr. confessed, "The South thought, while not approving it, that Lincoln's death might change the course of the war to her advantage."

While the enslaver class sought an angle, Black Wilmingtonians channeled the pain of Lincoln's death into a pageant of civic pride. Exercising the newfound freedom of public assembly, they called a "mass meeting of colored citizens," as a newspaper ad announced, "to express their sorrow and grief in the death of ABRAHAM LINCOLN, their best friend." George Price, the marshal of the procession, rode on horseback at the head of a crowd of mourners that stretched half a mile long. Five years earlier, Price had been an enslaved artisan, smoothing plaster onto the walls of the Bellamy Mansion. According to one historian, the funeral parade "marked the birth of a Negro political movement on the lower Cape Fear."

Several weeks later, Salmon P. Chase, chief justice of the United States Supreme Court, arrived in Wilmington as part of a whistle-stop tour of the conquered South. By that time, John Dillard Jr. had resumed his studies in Wilmington. He was standing with classmates near City Hall "when a band struck up music" and proceeded down Third, up Market, "to the headquarters of General Hawley, our home." In Wilmington, freed people had already formed three Equal Rights League chapters, a third of whose members were women. Some three thousand supporters crowded onto the Bellamys' piazza to hear Chase deliver a speech supporting Black enfranchisement.

The occasion—and the reversal of the political order that it symbolized—was no less incredible to Black observers than to white ones. Decades later, John Jackson, a formerly enslaved man, claimed that federal authorities "told the colored people that any house in Wilmin'ton they liked, that was empty, they could go take it, an' the first one they took was the fine Bellamy Mansion on Market an' Fifth Street." He vividly remembered seeing "a lot of common colored folks . . . sittin' on the piazza an' all up and down those big front steps."* It's likely he was conflating the memory of Chase's speech with that of Hawley's occupation. The particularities of the scene

*Between 1936 and 1938, the Federal Writers' Project of the Works Progress Administration sent hundreds of interviewers fanning out across the former Confederate states to record the testimony of more than two thousand formerly enslaved Black Americans. The interviewers were mostly white. According to the historian John W. Blassingame, they were frequently "closely associated with the *ancien régime*; on occasion they were the grandsons of the blacks' former masters." Jackson's interviewer was Frances Latham Harriss, a Bellamy relation and amateur historian, whose husband, W. N. Harriss, played a prominent role in the 1898 white supremacy campaign. The "slave narratives"—as they were called when the WPA published them in 1941—were often heavily amended and even doctored, with editors inserting dialect and deleting references to such consequential subjects as cruel punishments, forced marriages, family separations, Black resistance, Black service in the Union Army, and Black political participation during Reconstruction.

are immaterial to the larger point: For a brief, astounding moment, the Bellamys' urban plantation became a palace of the people.

"Year 1 of American Independence," one abolitionist called 1865. All over the South, people—especially Black people—were in motion. Soldiers were returning from years in battle. Families that had been torn apart in slavery were searching for their missing relatives, trying to raise them from the tomb of forced separation in an era before long-distance communication. As freed people left plantations, they had to decide, according to a complex calculus of safety and opportunity, where to remake their lives. "Right off colored folks started on the move," Felix Haywood, who was enslaved in Texas, recalled of the massive migration that emancipation triggered. "They seemed to want to get closer to freedom, as they'd know what it was—like it was a place or a city."

The federal government had yet to devise a plan for reuniting the nation. Nor had it put forth a clear vision of what, concretely, emancipation would entail. The Emancipation Proclamation "frees the slave, and ignores the Negro," the white abolitionist Wendell Phillips argued, urging the government to provide formerly enslaved people with "substantial, practical common-sense protection," in the form of land and education. For the moment, in the spring of 1865, a hesitant form of Reconstruction was in effect under President Andrew Johnson, a white supremacist with little interest in punishing the Confederates or preventing them from reinstating racial subjugation.

Even the serfs of Russia were given three acres of land upon their emancipation, Frederick Douglass pointed out. The federal government had experimented, in a limited way, with the redistribution of confiscated Confederate property. General Sherman's Field Order 15, for example, allotted four hundred thousand acres along the South Carolina and Georgia coastline to Black people living in the area, most of them formerly enslaved. Meanwhile, at Port Royal, South Carolina, the government had allowed freed people to purchase seized plantation land at preferential rates. Given these indications, freed people widely believed that "forty acres and a mule" would be forthcoming, but in the absence of a firm directive, all they could do was wait. "Here we have toiled and suffered; our parents, wives and children are buried here; and in this land we will remain unless forcibly driven away," one group of North Carolina freedmen declared.

As soon as the war was over, Fred Howe threw himself into the struggle to define what Wilmington's postwar society would look like. Just weeks after the Confederate surrender at Appomattox, *The Christian Recorder* of the AME church, one of the most important forums for the exchange of information among Black Americans, published an appeal from Henry McNeal Turner, who was serving as a chaplain in the United States Colored Troops. COLORED MEN OF ENTERPRISE, the headline announced. READ THIS.

The letter touted Wilmington as a prime destination for Black Americans, inviting anyone with questions about the city to contact Fred. "Mr. Howe is for general advancement, not only in educational point of view but is exceedingly anxious to see colored men make this place a great commercial base," it read. "And as this city is very largely populated now, and is destined to become much more so, being the commercial base for an extensive interior, Mr. Howe, and several other influential gentlemen, regard the present time, the most favorable opportunity for colored men to take advantage of promising distinction."

For the moment, Wilmington teemed with displaced people: some seven thousand refugees, two thousand injured soldiers, and nearly nine thousand Union soldiers, freshly liberated from prison camps. In June, Johnson relieved General Hawley of his command and replaced him with a far more conservative district commander, John Ames, who had little interest in championing the rights of freed people. Charmed by the genteel "cake and wine" hospitality of Wilmington's white elite, Ames reversed many of Hawley's initiatives and quickly restored power to the same Confederate city officials who had been in charge before the arrival of the Union troops.

Still, Fred could envision a hopeful future. Secession had failed and slavery was over, those two things were for sure. Perhaps the "great Negro nation" that Haiti had once promised already existed, dormant in American democracy, and a flourishing community could be built here, rather than abroad. But the contours of the new order remained blurry. Had the bloodiest conflict America had ever known fundamentally changed things, or would postwar society simply perpetuate the old regime in new guises? Would Black people have land? Would they have the vote? Would the labor system allow real choice in whom they worked for and under what conditions, and when conflicts arose between white employers and Black employees, would the latter enjoy the full protection of the law? In the summer of 1865, these were open questions, and Fred, building society as he built houses, took it upon himself to try to answer them.

To get a feel for the situation in Wilmington, Fred went straight to Alfred Moore Waddell. Amid the political chaos of occupation, Waddell acted as the de facto spokesperson of Wilmington's conservative white elite. In June 1865, he wrote to the governor of North Carolina, bemoaning the "frequent and indeed daily outrages" perpetuated by Black soldiers stationed in the city. Black civilians, he complained, had been emboldened by their presence. "The negroes firmly believe that property is theirs of right," Waddell complained, and warned that "unless there is a change for the better, it will inevitably result in <u>massacre</u>." (The situation was not so desperate as to preclude Waddell from using it to angle for a job, pleading unctuously for the governor to "designate any one person with whom you would wish to advise with.")

Fred may have been aware that Waddell was lobbying Raleigh for a crackdown. More likely, he was simply acquainted with the younger man's reputation for long-winded indiscretion. In any case, he knew that Waddell wouldn't be able to resist an offer to sound off in public about the future of American democracy. On July 23, 1865, a paid "card" appeared in the Wilmington *Herald*:

> A.M. WADDELL, Esq.
>
> Sir: The undersigned on behalf of the colored citizens of Wilmington, request you to address us on the subject of our position in the

community, on Wednesday evening next, the 26th inst., at 8 o'clock, at the City Hall.

Yours, respectfully,
ALFRED HOWE
JAS. SCULL
J.G. NORWOOD
ALLEN EVANS

Waddell accepted publicly, stating that he hoped "that some good may be accomplished thereby." He signed the response, "I am, very truly, your friend."

Two Alfreds in a room—both grandees of their communities; one believing that Union victory had razed the racial caste system alongside Atlanta, the other committed to the reestablishment of a pyramidal society with the white man immovably sitting on top. One can imagine Waddell backstage, sweltering in his three-piece suit. A nod from the moderator and he strides to the lectern under a ceiling of gold rosettes. A red velvet curtain opens upon the hall, packed from floor to balcony, the seats upholstered in green Italian leather.

Before the war, Waddell had performed at Thalian Hall in amateur theatricals, in which "there was almost certain to be some mishap that put the house in a roar or laughter." Now, he plays the long-faced local statesman. Fred Howe watches from the front row in his own finery, magnanimous but wary. He cocks his head as Waddell takes the stage, alert to subtext as much as surface meaning, trying to gauge the wisest course for his family, friends, and the thousands of freedmen flocking to the city with his encouragement.

Flanked by the mayor and other white officials, Waddell greeted the crowd. "I am here to make known to you exactly your situation as members of the community, and to give you my best advice in regard to your new duties and responsibilities," he began, in the manner of a headmaster welcoming scholarship students to an exclusive school from which they might yet be expelled. After some throat-clearing denunciations of carpetbaggers and Northern missionaries, "your worst enemies, because they advise you to a course which can result in nothing but injury to yourselves," Waddell cut to the subject at hand: political rights for Black people.

Unsurprisingly, Waddell opposed the notion of universal suffrage. But while most former Confederates objected to Black enfranchisement under any circumstances, he argued for a form of limited suffrage based on either property or educational requirements. He made his case simply, his speech uncharacteristically shorn of antiquarian allusions and colorful foreign phrases. His words suggest that he may have considered limited suffrage a clever solution to the contentious issue of the Black vote, in that it purported to egalitarianism, while in practice perpetuating exclusion. "I believe that there are some colored men in this hall who could now vote with quite an intelligent conception of what they were doing as many white men," Waddell proclaimed, "but I believe also that a large majority of the colored people are not yet qualified to exercise this privilege."

In the meantime, he counseled Black people to demonstrate industry and obedience. Never mind that Waddell was emerging from his youth as something of a washout, having dropped out of the Confederate Army with nebulous health problems. Freed people ought not, he said, to "lounge about in idleness—this is the freedom of savages." He and his peers, he promised, would offer their "generosity and justice" to those Black people who accepted the natural and eternal superiority of the white race. His advice was not without a hint of menace. Toward the end of his disquisition, he warned, "I wish to impress upon you the fact that they are disposed to be friendly towards those of you who show the right spirit and only towards those."

While undoubtedly a drunk and definitely an ass, the new President Andrew Johnson proved relatively congenial to the interests of wealthy white Southerners such as the Bellamys and the Waddells. His weak form of Reconstruction required nothing more of Southern states than that they accept the Thirteenth Amendment (abolishing slavery), pledge loyalty to the Union, and honor their war debts. Most white Southerners had their political and civil rights restored by automatic presidential pardon.

As a former enslaver worth over twenty thousand dollars, John Dillard, however, was required to seek absolution directly from the chief executive. In the summer of 1865, he traveled to Washington, where he hired a fixer, who stole his money, and then another, who finally got him a personal interview with Johnson's secretary of state. After swearing never again to acquire slaves, John Dillard emerged from the meeting clutching a certificate. It acknowledged that he, "by taking part in the late rebellion against the Government of the United States has made himself liable to heavy pains and penalties," but it nonetheless decreed that "the circumstances of his case tender him a proper object of executive clemency." In other words, he was off the hook. Despite this astonishingly lenient treatment, the Bellamys, like many of their peers, would forever nurture a conviction that they had been ill-treated by the federal government.

Immediately, the family started to organize their Wilmington homecoming. On a Friday afternoon in September, Eliza wrote to Belle, at Floral College, on a sheet of paper bearing the typed inscription HEADQUARTERS DISTRICT OF WILMINGTON. Eliza had added "Bellamy House" to the letterhead in a firm cursive hand. "I expect you will be delighted & astonished when I tell you I am writing in *your own bedroom*," her letter began.

The Bellamys' greatest desire was the restoration of everything to its previous place, in their home as in society. Eliza orchestrated a frenzy of cleaning, shining, and scouring—"I have four persons hard at work & expect more tomorrow," she wrote—as John Dillard reasserted his authority as master of the house. Eliza proudly recounted to Belle that as the couple ventured upstairs for the first time, "a negro followed us & told us we could not go up without orders. Your Pa told him it was his house & he would go where he pleased, he walked off without saying a word." Eliza was "heartsick" over the dirt, the basement was a "hogpen," the white marble mantels were streaked with tobacco spit, and there were five panes of broken glass to be replaced, but she felt only "too thankful that Providence has so smiled upon us, so that we may once more enjoy our home."

Later, the Bellamys would characterize the postwar era as one of unrelenting abjection. It was true that many of their friends and relations had suffered deeply. Their holiday host, Uncle John Taylor, for example, lost his marble house and his plantation. His son lost an arm, and his son-in-law lost his life. But the Bellamys, incredibly, had all made it through the war alive. Their fortune also emerged intact, and in 1866, John Dillard was able to settle his account with the architect James Post for the extraordinary sum of $29,946.89. As the family "picked up the broken threads and began life again as it were," as Ellen wrote, there was even money for luxuries. Not six months after the cessation of fighting, they placed an order for an ornamental iron fence to enclose Eliza's garden of myrtle, candytufts, and five large magnolias.

"Everyone seems perfectly home & house crazy, you scarcely see any Yankees & very few negro soldiers & everything looks like old times," Eliza observed, brightly, at the end of her letter to Belle.

"Tell Georgy to remember his promise to be a good boy," she added, in

Members of the Bellamy family at the Bellamy Mansion, 1873.

a giddy PS. "Tell Ellen to tie Robbie's curl to keep out of his eyes." As postwar society took shape, the Bellamys reveled in the hope that their future would resemble nothing so much as their past, oblivious or unwanting to believe that the economic, social, and racial hierarchies that they had so cherished in "old times" were giving way to a new, more equitable order.

CHAPTER 8

ALDERMAN HOWE

The Republican victory in the national elections of 1866 enabled Congress to pursue radical Reconstruction, marking the beginning of what W. E. B. Du Bois would characterize as "seven mystic years"—the evanescent moment in which the majority of white Northern Americans "simply recognized black folk as men." With the Reconstruction Acts of 1867, Black men gained the right to vote and to run for office. Emancipated by the Thirteenth Amendment, made citizens by the Fourteenth Amendment, and enfranchised by the Fifteenth Amendment, they wielded their new political power with the aim of truly realizing the egalitarian nation that America had always claimed to be.

Fred Howe seized the multitude of opportunities that congressional Reconstruction opened to him with the unbridled energy of someone compensating for lost time. In 1869, he supervised construction work at the city courthouse, building an outdoor cowshed, a jury box, and a prisoner's stand; served as a city assessor; sat on the board of the Freedman's Savings and Trust bank; and stood bail for an acquaintance charged with voting twice. As if these responsibilities weren't enough to keep him busy, he supplemented them with a side job selling self-ventilating refrigerators, "justly pronounced invaluable to housekeepers."

He also took on his first political role, transposing the Howe tradition of informal leadership into the public sector as an elected member of the state penitentiary board. One day, he traveled to Raleigh with four fellow commissioners, all of them white, to tour a lunatic asylum. At the end of the day, the institution's superintendent, a doughty Confederate veteran, insisted that the commissioners join him for dinner. When Howe walked into the dining room, the superintendent rescinded the invitation. *The Raleigh Sentinel*, despite its white supremacist sympathies, denounced the incident, referring to Howe as the personification of "the new civilization itself."

The Howes believed in shaping systems by joining them. Fred and his brothers Anthony and Pompey, along with their various offspring, had been enthusiastic participants in the North Carolina Republican Party since its inception in 1867. Now, in 1868, of New Hanover County's 6,258 registered voters, nearly four thousand were Republicans—mostly white Northerners who had moved south and Black voters, like the Howes, loyal to "the party of Lincoln." Fred had a son on the police force and a nephew in one of the city's new Black volunteer firefighting brigades. His brother Anthony collaborated with him on the courthouse job while serving as a city alderman. Later, Anthony became a justice of the peace; when he was sworn in, a declaration was signed by the clerk and treasurer of the county Board of Commissioners, who happened to be one of his own sons. In 1869, Fred and Anthony ran against each other for alderman, representing competing factions of the local Republican Party. (Anthony prevailed in a large field, trouncing his more radical brother.)

The Howes were the quintessential "agents of change" of which the historian Eric Foner has written, striving during Reconstruction "to breathe substantive meaning" into the promise of Black freedom. They were everywhere, parading in a downpour to celebrate the passage of the Fifteenth Amendment, breaking up fights, and putting out fires (literally, in the case of Anthony, who passed by a smoldering house one morning and snuffed out what came "near being a serious conflagration"). White newspapers often mixed the brothers up. When they did identify them correctly, they didn't always know what to make of their public activity. In the space of a few months, the *Daily Journal* praised Anthony for restoring order during "a pugilistic encounter at the city clerks' velocipede ring," then denounced him as a "colored Radical fanatic" who was conspiring with carpetbaggers to ruin the city.

Wilmington was changing—that much was undeniable. Simply in demographic terms, it had become Blacker, with the slim white majority of 1860 giving way to a considerable Black one by 1870. The landscape of the city was in flux, too, and Black residents were staking claims to public space like never before. Pine Forest Cemetery, a new Black burial ground on fifteen acres, intended to "vie with Oakdale," the resting ground of the white elite, "in beauty and adornment." The Giblem Black Masonic Lodge, a three-story Greek Revival community center with a food market and library, boasted a black-and-white checkerboard floor with a red star painted in the center.

When the Freedman's Savings and Trust Company inaugurated its Wilmington branch in 1869, members of the Howe family were among its depositors. Clients of the Freedman's Bank often provisioned for their children, too. "Opening a savings account for one's one-year-old son or daughter reflected a sensibility that planned for economic security and generational improvement," Thanayi Jackson writes. The 1870 census showed that Fred had added seventeen hundred dollars' worth of real estate to his portfolio, for a grand total of two thousand. The family now owned the whole block at South Third Street between Queen and Castle.

Even in leisure, the Howes sought refinement. After the war, there had been a craze among the white elite for medieval-style jousting tournaments, in which mounted contestants battled for titles like "Knight of the Cape Fear" and "Knight of the White Plume." In 1871, fifteen Black knights held their own contest, parading through the streets in full costume. The winner went home with a silver watch and chain. Washington Howe, Anthony's son, "carried off, as the second prize, the privilege of a Champagne supper."

THE HOWES EXERCISED THEIR RIGHTS EVEN WHEN DOING SO REQUIRED DIrect confrontation with white racists. In 1870, Anthony appeared in court to testify as a character witness in a case against a white dry-goods store clerk named Charles Posner, who was accused of assault and battery. Only a few years earlier, Black people had been barred from testifying in white people's trials. Anthony, however, knew the courtroom as well as anyone, having built much of it with his own hands. At the witness stand, he sat down on an oak bench and prepared to tell the court what he knew. Posner's lawyer approached the stand for cross-examination.

"Anthony—" the lawyer began.

"I don't object to being so styled, but I do object to your tone and manner," Anthony replied.

The lawyer had called him by his first name, as though he were a boy, not an elected official. The plantation days were over now, not that Anthony had ever lived on a plantation.

The judge upheld Anthony's complaint and ordered the lawyer to address him in a proper manner—either "Mr. Howe" or "Alderman Howe."

The lawyer started his cross-examination again.

"Anthony—" he repeated.

"Ten dollars!" the judge interjected, fining the lawyer for contempt of court.

"Anthony—" the lawyer kept on.

"Twenty dollars!"

At this point, the judge called for a recess, sending Anthony home, even though he hadn't finished his testimony.

As the crowd broke up, the lawyer launched one last insult. "Stand aside, Anthony," he yelled, as he shuffled out. Ultimately, he garnered a fine of one hundred dollars to communicate his point: that the law of white supremacy reigned higher than the law of the land.

ALFRED MOORE WADDELL HAD A CATCHY ANECDOTE FOR EVERYTHING, and Reconstruction was no exception. Here is how he captured the feeling of incredulity that accompanied the dawning reality that his family—and white people, more generally—no longer sat alone at the top of the social and political hierarchy:

> I can never forget that my venerable father, being asked to go to the polls and vote . . . was confronted by a black fellow citizen who was

> recently a slave, and asked by him his name, and residence and so forth, as preliminary to the exercise of his right to suffrage. The old gentleman's face was a study for a moment, but he handed his ballot to the colored gentleman, and then coming out into the street and gazing for a moment across the river towards the plantations that had been the homes of his ancestors for more than a hundred years, he took off his hat and in an undertone said with upraised hands, "My God!"

Ever the maximalist, Waddell couldn't help laying on another detail to illustrate the grotesque "political degradation" to which he believed white North Carolinians were being subjected. During the same election, he claimed, "a poor wretched negro, who was idiotic and crawling on all fours, came up and was allowed to vote unchallenged."

This was 1867: the first time formerly enslaved Black men were allowed to vote in North Carolina. Their enthusiastic turnout helped to send more than a hundred members of the Republican Party, including thirteen Black men, to a state constitutional convention of 120 delegates. ("The N—— Convention," the *Daily Journal* called it. "The Gorilla Constitution.") Their passion for voting came as a shock to former enslavers like Waddell. As the historian William McKee Evans observed, "Their imaginary Negro had been too apathetic and ignorant to vote in a quiet election, while actual Negroes . . . buried them under a deluge of Republican ballots."

In the first three months of 1868, the delegates drew up a new state constitution, guaranteeing universal manhood suffrage. As the next set of elections approached, the Democratic Party was desperate to keep Black men and the white men who voted with them away from the polls, lest they ratify the new constitution or elect Radical candidates. The *Star* instructed readers on the first day of voting:

> Vote against the VAMPIRE-BOGUS-MONGREL-
> CAPE COD-NEW HAMPSHIRE-CARPET-BAGGER-
> SCALAWAG-AMALGAMATION-MONGREL-
> NEGRO-EQUALITY-GADFLY-NEGRO-MILITIA-

MIXED-SCHOOL-ALIEN-HYBRID-TOURGEE-CONSTITUTION!

IN NORTH CAROLINA, AS IN OTHER SOUTHERN STATES, EX-CONFEDERATES associated with the Democratic Party created the Ku Klux Klan to enforce white supremacy through terror. The commander of the Klan in Wilmington was thirty-year-old Colonel Roger Moore. The Colonel, as his descendants later knew him, was a great-great-great-grandson of "King" Roger Moore, of Orton Plantation. (Alfred Moore Waddell's great-great-great-grandfather Maurice was King's brother.) This heritage was a source of enduring pride. The Colonel would name his firstborn son Roger Jr. and another son Henry Roger. Roger Jr. died as a teenager, so the Colonel named yet another son Roger Jr., but he lived for only five months. For the first two decades of his life, Henry Roger went by Henry, but when he was twenty-one, the Colonel died, leaving the family Rogerless. The transmission of the name, and the heritage that it signified, was so important that Henry Roger went down to the courthouse and, in a gesture of patriarchal fealty, lopped off his first name. From then on, he was Roger.

After leading the Third North Carolina Cavalry during the war, the Colonel returned to Wilmington and went into business. Eventually, he ran his own company, Roger Moore Sons & Co., which manufactured brick and sold building materials such as cement, plaster, lime, and shingles, "made in the swamps by hand." His kilns produced twenty-five hundred bricks in a batch, for a total of forty-five thousand a day, allowing him to literally stamp his name on the foundations of Wilmington. In the moral universe of the white patriarchy, the Colonel (aristocrat, Democrat, veteran, businessman, devout Methodist*) was an exemplary citizen, the natural choice to lead the Klan. He was also a recruiting asset, because many of the men

*As a Bible study teacher at Front Street Methodist Church, Moore helped to organize the conversion and Christian education of a young Chinese man named Han Chiao-shun, or Charlie Soong, who would later make a fortune printing Bibles and become the father of the future Madame Chiang Kai-shek.

who would join the chapter had served under him in the Third North Carolina Cavalry—"the best blood of the South," according to one chronicler.

The Colonel went to Raleigh and took an oath to the Klan. Back in Wilmington, he and his men donned "hideous, ungodly" costumes—one involved a white flowing robe with a transparent headpiece that the wearer could slide on and "gown up about ten feet"—and set out on night rides around the city. "Now when one of these clans broke in on a gang of negroes as if they had just risen from Hell itself you can imagine what effect it had," one participant recalled of a raid that the Colonel led on "a favorite spot for Negroes to congregate at night," on the corner of Fifth and Market. As the election neared, signs printed in carmine ink went up around town, vowing vengeance upon traitors. Pliantly, the *Journal* claimed to have witnessed "frightened darkies" fleeing "a skeleton, with a winding sheet drawn about his dry bones, seated upon a snow-white steed, whose nostrils emitted streams of flame with a strong odor of brimstone." The warning went out: "*The Ku Klux Klan are abroad! The Avenger Cometh with the Night when man sleepeth! Beware! The hour is near at hand!*"

Around the South, the Klan tortured, maimed, flogged, raped, and murdered Black people and anyone who defended them. They torched their houses, burned their crops, stole their cattle, and drove them out of jobs and off the land. In just eighteen months between January 1866 and July 1867, the Klan murdered at least 197 people and assaulted more than five hundred in North Carolina and South Carolina alone. "On several occasions, they would capture some particular offensive[,] take him out of town, strip him bare, give him a sound cowhiding, turn him loose and tell him if he was ever taken again they would hang him," the Colonel's companion recalled.

As the Colonel raised a terror squad, the Black radical Abraham Galloway was mustering his own band of fighters. During the war, Galloway had served as a Union spy, recruiting Black men to Union ranks and risking re-enslavement by returning to the South to gather intelligence behind Confederate lines. He was known as a formidable personality—sarcastic, vehement, frank. When Lincoln invited him to the White House during the war, he made a point of entering through the front door. Now, back in

Wilmington, he was campaigning for a seat in the state senate, a pistol tucked into the front of his belt.

Wilmington's Black men followed Galloway's example of armed self-defense. For four nights, beginning on April 18, 1868, a Black patrol rode the city, "hooting and yelling," shooting off guns, and brandishing fence rails repurposed as weapons. While the Colonel's florid Klan relied on scare tactics, this informal Black militia seems to have made a concrete show of force. The *Star* expressed alarm at "gangs of negroes" that were setting up roadblocks around the city, posing "impertinent questions" to white men. The paper wrote, "We call on our authorities to put down at once this riotous parading at night in the streets."

In the nocturnal contest between the Colonel's Klan and Galloway's militia, white supremacy and Black resistance, the latter force prevailed. By the end of the month, Galloway's men overpowered the night riders, and the Klan in Wilmington effectively disappeared. The Colonel and his men seem to have thought that the mere intimation of white violence would be enough to keep Black people in line. They had failed to understand the depth of Black people's commitment to freedom—that the freed people had no intention of submitting to the former enslavers' methods of control and, in fact, would vigorously resist them.

Defying the Klan's threats, North Carolina voters approved the new constitution, making the state eligible for readmission into the Union. Galloway was elected to the state senate by a comfortable margin (and then elected again in 1870). In the face of racist abuse and physical danger—he almost died when a white man attacked him with a bowie knife—he asserted his claim on the land that his people had enriched. Black people belonged there, Galloway proclaimed, and they owed no explanation or fealty. He told a reporter, "If white people don't like their legislation, *they can leave*."

Chapter 9

A COMMUNITY OF INTEREST

Thaddeus Stevens, Radical Republican congressman of Pennsylvania, urged the federal government to assist formerly enslaved people. "We have turned or are about to turn, loose four million slaves without a hut to shelter them or a cent in their pockets," he warned. In one of the great betrayals of American history, no such measures came to pass. Freed people, nonetheless, set to helping themselves with astonishing resourcefulness. Impoverished Southern Black people, 90 percent of whom were illiterate in 1860, spent more than a million dollars on education in the first ten years of freedom.

In 1875, Black leaders in Wilmington organized an industrial fair, the first such exposition to be held in the state, to "show the world what our colored people can do." Thousands of visitors flocked to the Giblem Lodge on the first day, where they were greeted by a display of gleaming carriages. The breadth of Black Wilmington's talent was arrayed inside the meeting hall and the lots around it. There were pigs and fowl; crewelwork, cornice work, cart work, hairwork, and woodwork; jellies, pickles, and coconut cakes; and even "a sea monster preserved in alcohol." The Howes, of course, joined in. Fred and Anthony's nephew W. H. Howe contributed to an exhibit of quilts that showcased varying patterns (basket, diamond, puzzle, star, log cabin, US flag). Another nephew, John H. Howe, fourteen years old, displayed a mantel made in yellow pine.

On the fair's second day, Wilmington's Cape Fear Steam Fire Engine

Company—said to be the first all-Black steam fire engine crew in the entire nation—faced off in an exhibition against a squad of Black firefighters from Charlotte. Founded in 1871, the CFSFEC was already legendary. Every month, its members rode through the streets on plumed horses, performing drills and showing off their red, white, and blue uniforms, accessorized with white gloves. Fires were a near-constant plague in Wilmington, so the squad's presence was more than ceremonial. In three years of existence, the group had responded to twenty-six major blazes. Fred's nephew Valentine Howe served as the company's foreman. He was active in Republican politics, but firefighting was his first love.

At the "spirited contest" between the CFSFEC and the firefighters from Fayetteville, Valentine's company started strong but flubbed their exercises, handing the visiting company an unexpected victory. Colonel Roger Moore—the chief of the white fire department as well as, formerly, the Klan—was on hand to present the prize of $7.50 in gold. The Colonel, the *Wilmington Morning Star* reported, "took occasion in the course of his re-

Valentine Howe in his fireman's uniform.

marks to pay a very flattering compliment to the colored firemen, and also to the colored people generally for the success which has attended their first grand exposition, for which, he said, they were deserving of much credit."

Years later, in 1886, some bales of cotton caught fire on the lower deck of a steamship docked at Wilmington. The wind, "blowing a gale," sent the flames racing toward the wharves, yards, and offices on the nearby shoreline, where barrels of naval stores exploded, setting the whole riverfront aflame and destroying "a square and a half of wooden houses occupied by colored people." Within hours, the blaze had consumed a church, dozens of homes, and at least fifteen major businesses in the worst fire in the city's history.

After the fire, white men including the Colonel formed a relief committee, distributing aid to citizens who'd suffered, most of them Black. Valentine Howe and several other Black firefighters placed a notice in the *Morning Star* to express their thanks. They may have also wished to make the point that Black people were to be counted among the heroes of the fire in addition to its victims. "It is proper that we should all feel that there is a community of interest between those who live in the same place, regardless of color," they wrote, "and such trusts as those committed to your care and discharged in such an impartial and kindly manner tend to confirm and strengthen the belief on our part, and especially to confirm us in the opinion that those of the white race are always ready to alleviate suffering among those of the colored race."

This "community of interest" remained intact in times of Black suffering and was perhaps even strengthened by it. But the letter did not address the question of whether white fellow feeling could survive Black success.

PLING, PLING, PLING. FRED WAS, AT LONG LAST, BUILDING A HOUSE FOR himself, on the ancestral corner of Third and Queen. Business was booming, and the Howe brothers had got to the point in their careers where they were builders in name but architects in practice, even if they didn't have the formal credentials to prove it. The next generation of Black builders, keenly aware of this discrepancy between skill and status, was professionalizing.

Henry Taylor, a Black builder in Wilmington, was preparing to send one of his sons, Robert Robinson Taylor, off to the Massachusetts Institute of Technology (alma mater of the MacRaes, their white neighbors). Taylor would become the school's first Black student and, upon graduation, probably the first accredited Black architect in the country.

Fred had been elected to the city's board of education a few years earlier. He had already scored a major victory, pushing through a deal that allowed the board to purchase the Williston Graded School, a two-story white clapboard building that sat in the shade of an elegant live oak on South Seventh Street. Williston had come a long way since its inception in 1865, when teachers sponsored by the Freedmen's Bureau had started conducting classes in an old tobacco barn that someone had hauled over from across the river. For years, the school had been supported by the American Missionary Association, a group of Northern philanthropists that included the institution's namesake, Samuel Williston, a Massachusetts button manufacturer.

Fred's civic engagement was beginning to yield results. He persuaded his colleagues to buy Williston for three thousand dollars, making it the city's first Black public school. Under the missionaries, the teachers and staff had all been white. Now the school board appointed a Black faculty. Among the early teachers were two of his daughters, Isabella and Mary Washington, whom he'd sent to Philadelphia to be educated by the Quakers. Within a few years, Mary Washington would become the school's principal, a position she held for twenty years before dying young.

As the city's Black bourgeoisie solidified, the Howes expanded their empire. Recently, Fred had completed one of his highest-profile projects—an Italianate residence with a quadruple-columned central portico for a white woman named Mary Jane Langdon, the widow of a merchant. A white man was credited as the architect, but Fred had handled almost every aspect of the job. It was he who drew up the twenty-six-page contract. It was he who signed it. It was he who wrote the specifications for the house, which was to be "of neat and handsome appearance, with proper shaped roof, with gutter formed in the cornice and supported by four tasteful & ornamental pillars or columns in front, and half antae in the rear; to have neat siderails with turned balusters, and to have entrance steps in front of easy ascent, supported or flanked by neat side buttresses." You weren't going to get a shabby job with Fred Howe, and he wanted you to know, even if it meant repeating "neat" three times in a single sentence.

The choice to build a new house, rather than taking possession of an existing one, is a statement of social standing and financial vigor. But it is also a statement in the sense of a form of speech, articulating the deeply held and sometimes unexpressed aspirations of the person or people who are going to live in it. This was especially true for Fred, who had the technical ability to render his desires directly into doorframe and baseboard, unmediated by middlemen.

As he scaled a ladder to check that the shingles had been laid straight as typewriter keys, did he think of his father, Anthony, patching up his cabin after the hurricane at Howe's Point? Did he remember the obstacles he himself had patiently surmounted like rungs? Thirty years earlier, white builders in Wilmington had indulged their paranoia and jealousy with fire, torching the framework of a building that Black builders were putting up. The white builders had left a note at the arson scene, warning that "a similar course would be pursued, in all cases against all buildings to be erected by Negro contractors or carpenters." But Fred had persevered, constructing so many buildings that he was now able to create his own. To raise a house was, above all, a positive act, by which a person could shape at least a small patch of the world exactly as he liked.

Down Third Street, he was working on a grander residence. The clients were William B. McKoy, a white lawyer, and his Illinois-born wife, Katherine, whose brother Henry Bacon worked at a fancy architectural firm in New York City. Bacon, who would later design the Lincoln Memorial, had sent drawings over to the McKoys, but they had decided to go with a Wilmington architect instead. Fred was doing all the construction work, adapting plans the McKoys had selected from the October 1886 issue of *Carpentry and Building*.

The McKoys were going for drama, with deep porches, spindle railings, and vertiginous gables with undulating millwork that gave the house a theatrical personality, like a villain stroking his mustache. Fred could produce pretty much any effect, no matter how complicated or how cutting-edge. But for his own family he chose something fairly modest: one-and-a-half stories in the Second Empire style, with a mansard roof and the lightest frilling of ironwork on the front porch posts. The three dormer windows that poked out from the upper floor couldn't help but remind one of the three Howe brothers, their chests swelling with pride.

Chapter 10

I.O.U. WADDELL

Alfred Moore Waddell's situation was improving. In 1869, he bought his wife Julia's family home on Third Street, possibly using money that she had inherited upon her father's death. Finally the head of his own household, Alfred lived there with Julia, their children, his parents, his sister-in-law, and three domestic servants (one of them was only twelve years old). Life was a blur of commencement speeches, charity concerts, and legal pleadings. At the end of the year, Alfred lost a big civil suit on behalf of clients who owned a steamboat said to have started a fire that destroyed a local barn, but he planned to appeal to the Supreme Court.

Seventeen days before the 1870 elections, the executive committee of the local Democratic Party came to call on Waddell. Their candidate for Congress had dropped out of the race at the last minute, they explained. Would Waddell agree to take his place on the ballot? "My nomination . . . was wholly unexpected and was literally forced upon me against my earnest protest," he wrote later. In many ways, this was a classic Waddell moment: a confluence of availability and luck that thrust him, gabbling, into the center of the action.

Election Day arrived, and to everyone's surprise, including his own, Waddell won the contest. Off to Washington he went, arriving a month before the start of the legislative session. He recalled, "As an ex-Confederate Democrat was persona non grata in Congress, it seemed advisable to take time by the forelock and get acquainted with members prior to the assembling of that body." Waddell may have initially come off as something of a rube—on a visit several years earlier, he'd gone to see a spiritual medium who subjected him to such "extraordinary demonstrations of his peculiar gifts" that Waddell, very uncharacteristically, refused to discuss it further. But in his freshman term, a major assignment came sailing his way: a seat on a special joint committee that would investigate the Ku Klux Klan and its "alleged outrages in the Southern states."

Over ten months, the committee heard from nearly six hundred witnesses, including more than two hundred Black citizens. The historian Henry Louis Gates Jr. has argued that the hearings were the closest thing to a post-slavery truth and reconciliation committee that the United States has ever had. "It was extraordinary," he has said. "Congress was actually listening to Black people testifying about the atrocities committed against them."

Waddell had voted against the creation of the joint committee. Now, as a member, he did everything he could to thwart its proceedings. Not only was he on the record in support of the Klan, but in the district that he represented, its leader was his distant cousin Colonel Roger Moore. When the committee summoned Colonel William L. Saunders, the Klan's highest official in North Carolina, Waddell flung open his doors, welcoming him as a luminary. "Although myself a member of the Committee, he was my guest and shared my bed during his stay in Washington," Waddell boasted. Saunders defied the committee by taking the Fifth Amendment over a hundred times and repeatedly stating, "I decline to answer." (When he died, relatives had the catchphrase engraved on his tombstone.) Waddell marveled, "They recognized that they had now encountered A MAN."

Waddell was unmoved by the testimony of the Klan's targets. Along with every other Democratic congressman, he declined to join the majority report, which concluded that the Klan posed an existential threat to "the execution of the laws and the security of life and property" in the Southern states. The hearings ultimately led to the passage of the Third Enforcement Act, also known as the KKK Act, which allowed federal officials to be sent into violent areas and enabled mass prosecutions for terrorist conspiracy. Yet Waddell dismissed them as a useless exercise in Northern grandstanding, writing, "A greater waste of paper and ink was never perpetrated."

Whether one considered Waddell shifty or shrewd often depended on one's political orientation. He had a knack for showing up at the center of dubious affairs: In the immediate aftermath of the war, for example, he had delivered a thousand-dollar bribe so that a pair of white men who had lynched a white Union sympathizer could escape from jail. A decade later, he found himself at the center of yet another scandal that, this time, durably tarnished his personal credibility. It began when *The Wilmington Post*, the city's Republican paper, published a series of articles accusing Waddell of engaging in all manner of "vice and immorality."

Several years earlier, the paper reported, Waddell had sold off a grieving Black family's land, pocketing thousands of dollars and exploiting his connections to deny them legal recourse. The writer, Jesse Cassidey, characterized him as a drunkard and a gambler, with outstanding debts in Raleigh and in Washington. These were serious accusations, particularly for someone who was constantly touting his aristocratic lineage.

Cassidey went further, ridiculing the entire notion of the "true blue Southern gentleman." "Like the dog that returns to his vomit," Cassidey wrote, Waddell and his plantocrat peers continued to pursue "the grovelling, debased desires" they had indulged during antebellum days with little regard for the law or basic decency. Waddell, he would write, was hardly "the cultivated gentleman, the ripe scholar, the rare statesman" he made himself out to be.

On the first night of May, Cassidey was walking along the street with a friend. Suddenly, "without notice or warning," Waddell jumped out and began thrashing him with a hard object. This was a caning, the same form of abuse that Preston Brooks of South Carolina had meted out to Charles Sumner of Massachusetts on the Senate floor, nearly killing him, during the debate over slavery in 1856. Cassidey tried to fight back, but the Congressman, who had hurried back from Washington to avenge the insult, had brought along reinforcements. They hustled him into a nearby building.

The ambush was designed to inflict not only pain but also public humiliation. It left Cassidey with serious injuries, but it failed to shut him up. He continued to mock Waddell and the chivalric pretensions of his entire class, assailing him in print for resorting to "the method of the scoundrel, the assassin, the blackguard, the bully." Two weeks later, Cassidey traveled to Washington, where he showed up at Waddell's club and started bashing *him* over the head with a cane. Again, Waddell was surrounded by muscle. Cassidey left with a broken nose, but the *Post* continued to warn Wilmingtonians about the rickety character of "I.O.U. Waddell."

CONGRESSIONAL RECONSTRUCTION ENDED WITH THE COMPROMISE OF 1877. The deal resolved a contested presidential election by sending the Republican Rutherford B. Hayes to the White House in exchange for his agreement to withdraw the remaining federal troops from the South. In the 1870s, Republicans were the party of civil rights, federal power, and tariffs. Democrats stood for white supremacy, states' rights, and the free market. The Democratic platform of 1876 had promised to save the country from "a corrupt centralism which, after inflicting upon ten States the rapacity of carpet-bag tyrannies, has honeycombed the offices of the Federal Government itself with incapacity, waste and fraud." In plain language, the Democrats were promising to roll back Black people's civil rights and reinstate white supremacy.

For a white man, high birth was no longer the only way to get ahead in the world. With the plantation economy wrecked, the South was industrializing. In Wilmington, the MacRae family had amassed a fortune to rival that of the Bellamys. The Bellamys were synonymous with the Old South and Old Wilmington, while the MacRaes represented a new class of barons focused on money and machines. The families would eventually intermarry, in the way of medieval nobles, but in the post-Reconstruction era, the MacRaes were consolidating their own empire, with young and enterprising Hugh MacRae at the head.

Hugh's great-great-grandfather—a haggis-loving, kilt-wearing Celtic speaker—had immigrated to western North Carolina from the Scottish

Highlands in the 1770s. The family established itself in Wilmington fifty years later. When Alexander MacRae arrived in the city, he sought to work with his mind rather than his hands. He found employment in a printing shop, and then became a successful commission merchant, eventually making it big in railroads. One of Wilmington's earliest capitalists, Alexander helped to transform Wilmington from a sleepy seaport into a bustling city. A Northern journalist marveled, "Of all the places in the State, Wilmington has the most go-a-headity of the Yankees."

Alexander's money, ambition, and intelligence opened the doors to upper-class society. Although more a go-getter than a sybarite, he adapted easily to the plantocracy's mores when he saw an upside. He married twice, both times to women with Northern roots, and eventually had nine sons, who joined the city's socially elite military companies. By 1850, he personally enslaved eighteen people, profiting from the labor of another two hundred in his role as president of the Wilmington and Weldon Railroad.

The MacRaes were Whigs, Unionists, and above all, pragmatists. Despite their support of slavery, the last thing they had wanted was for hotheads like John Dillard Bellamy to drag the nation into a costly war that would cut them off from relatives and contacts in the North. Still, they took the notion of duty seriously. When the war broke out, Alexander volunteered for duty, becoming one of the Confederate Army's oldest officers. At least six of his sons joined him on the battlefield, one of them dying of typhoid fever. "Previous to the late rebellion, I was a man of no political importance, never having taken any part in politics," one son wrote, seeking pardon in the summer of 1865. "My proclivities were however decidedly Union until North Carolina formally seceded."

Alexander had been a successful man, but it was his son Donald—Hugh's father—who made the family grandiosely rich. In addition to serving as British vice-consul, he held interests in five blockade runners. By the time of his death in 1892, he had overseen two railroads, a bank, the Wilmington Cotton Mills Company, the Wilmington Gaslight Company, the Wilmington Compress and Warehouse Company, the North Carolina Insurance Company, the Linville Improvement Company, and the Navassa Guano Company (a highly lucrative venture that began by producing fertilizer from bird excrement). He had even served as president of the cemetery in which he would be buried.

Had it not been for the war, Hugh MacRae would have been born in a castle—his father's crenellated brick house at 713 Market Street, meant to evoke a Scottish keep. Instead, he came into the world in 1865 at the family's "up-country" place in the central part of the state. Upon his father's death, Hugh inherited the castle, along with a considerable estate, supplementing the fortune that he had created in mining and development after graduating from MIT. At twenty-seven, he presided over a diversified portfolio that spanned from the coast (where he controlled everything from cotton mills to utilities) to the mountains (where he owned sixteen thousand acres of land that, along with a consortium of Northern investors, he was turning into a first-class vacation destination).

If John Dillard Bellamy's home was a manor, Hugh MacRae's was a stronghold. A decade earlier, his sister, Agnes, had married Walter Linton Parsley, a son of Oscar Parsley, a three-time Wilmington mayor and the patriarch of the family with whom the Bellamys had lived in wartime exile at Floral College. The Parsleys were old-time enslaver-planters who had branched out into lumber, becoming very rich. The alliance between the two clans concentrated their influence in business, industry, politics, and society.

Hugh married Rena Nelson in 1891. Eventually, Agnes and Walter Parsley moved in directly next door to the newlyweds. The couples hired the same gardener to tend matching rear gardens of espaliered pear trees, saluting each other in mirror image across a neat alley. Reconstruction was over, and from the 1870s on, white Democrats across the South fought to "redeem" their states from Republican control, grabbing back political and social power. As the last decade of the century dawned, families like the MacRaes, ramrod alert as their trees, stayed vigilant for any threat to their interests.

Chapter 11

YOU WON'T PUT ME OFF

It was the thirty-first of July in 1892, the kind of stagnant deep summer day that made people "so eager for a change that they did not hesitate to say they wouldn't mind taking a little of that Montana frost 'straight,'" the *Wilmington Morning Star* joked. The markets overflowed with collards, corn, snap peas, butter beans, cantaloupes, and watermelon; sassafras and running huckleberry; red snapper at ten cents apiece and clams at fifteen cents a peck. A heat wave was on. Ninety-five degrees and hardly better in the evening. "There have been no deaths from sunstroke, but among those inquisitive wretches who are continuously gasping, 'Is-it-hot-enough-for-you?' the mortality has been awful," the *Star* continued. "This reporter has stabbed to death nineteen of 'em with his pencil."

Fred Howe got up in the morning and left his house around nine o'clock, likely to go to church. Twenty years earlier, Fred, now seventy-four, had helped to build St. Mark's Episcopal Church, where he served as a senior warden. It was ten crosstown blocks away, about half an hour away on foot. Fred's wife had died in March, so he was traveling alone. Rather than trekking across town in the heat, he walked one block north from his home on Third and Queen to the corner of Third and Castle, where he waited to board one of the city's brand-new electric streetcars, resplendent with brass fittings and white trim.

The car approached, moving west on Castle. Fred was standing on the east side of Third. He'd likely found a sliver of shade. He hailed the car, but it didn't stop. The motorman kept going across Third Street. It came to a halt a few moments later, on the west side of the block.

"Hurry up!" the motorman yelled.

Fred crossed Third and got on, rather irritated—here he was, trying to get to church to worship the Lord, and the young, white motorman was giving him a hard time?

Upon boarding, Fred complained to the motorman, James Kelly, who insisted that company rules required him to stop on the far corner of the street.

"Old man, I'm not responsible for the running of this car," Kelly said. "I'm running according to the conductor's orders."

The men continued to argue as the car trundled along the tracks. A couple of blocks down, a white passenger hailed the car and Kelly stopped promptly. Fred accused Kelly of discriminating against Black riders. Kelly replied that the passenger, unlike Fred, had been waiting in the proper spot. "Shut up or I'll put you off," he threatened.

"You won't put me off," Fred shot back. "You're a liar."

In the version of events that Kelly later told, Fred pulled out a pocketknife and tried to cut him. Fred, however, denied that he had started the fight and said that he had only got his knife out after Kelly attacked *him*. Neither party disputed what happened next: Kelly pulled Fred out of the car with the car's reverse lever in hand, approached Fred, and, per one account, "dealt him a terrible blow over the head."

Fred staggered off. A group of friends eventually found him on the corner of Castle and Front, bleeding profusely, and took him home. That afternoon, "upon information that Howe's wounds were of a very serious nature," the *Morning Star* reported, the police arrested Kelly. The next day, they served Fred, too, charging him with assault with a deadly weapon.

The white media acknowledged Fred's position as "a contractor and man of considerable prominence among his race," but defended Kelly. "Howe became insolent and, as stated by several witnesses, used abusive language," the paper claimed. The choice of the adjective *insolent*—the word that Wilmington's white officials had used in 1865 to try to goad the governor into cracking down on freed people; the word that white Southern lawmakers used to pathologize a range of banal behaviors; the word invoking a lineage of white grievance at the choice of a Black person not to submit to humiliation or violence—let the paper's readership know that the real issue at hand was race solidarity.

The following week, Fred and Kelly appeared in court for a hearing about "the streetcar fracas." Their lawyers were familiar figures around the courthouse: Alfred Moore Waddell represented Fred, and John Dillard Bellamy Jr. represented Kelly. Five witnesses, all white, backed up Kelly's assertion that Fred had initiated the conflict. Their accounts of the moment in which Fred had supposedly drawn the knife were vague, but they made it clear that, in their view, his expectation of being treated equally had itself been a provocation. The car's conductor, testifying for Kelly, complained that Fred "took his time in getting on the car." No one acknowledged that a slow start on Fred's part, if it occurred, might have been a function of his advanced age, rather than an attempt to irritate white riders. Instead, the conductor painted Fred as a known troublemaker, who "invariably quarreled over something every time he rode."

Fred testified in his own defense, with Waddell calling no additional witnesses. "Never drew a knife until Kelly had hit him twice" read the *Wilmington Messenger*'s coverage, written in an unfinished style close to transcription. "Wouldn't say that what the other witnesses had said was false, but this was his knowledge of the affair. Admitted having quarreled with the motorman on Capt. Whitted's car before, but it passed over without any hard feelings."

Sixty-five days later, with the case still pending, Fred was dead.

The Wilmington Messenger, October 7, 1892
Death of Alfred Howe.

Alfred Howe, a well-known colored citizen of Wilmington, who amassed a fortune of some $25,000 or $30,000, died yesterday at 11:45 o'clock. He was aged seventy-five years, and leaves a family of four children, two sons and two daughters. He was senior warden of St. Mark's Episcopal Church, and was an ardent churchman. He was a man of fine business quality and was a person of character and intelligence. He and his two brothers, Anthony and Pompey, were carpenters, and were slaves, but purchased their liberty when they were young men. He and his brothers all accrued property and gave their children good educations.

It will be remembered that on the twenty-first* of last July the deceased had a difficulty with Motorman Kelly on one of the electric cars of the street railway, and that he was struck in the head by a brass motor crank in the hands of the motorman. He was very seriously injured, and has not been able to leave his home but once since, and that was to attend a hearing in the case before Trial Justice R.H. Bunting, who bound both over to the Criminal Court for an affray. At the term of the Criminal Court ten days ago he was not able to appear in court, and the case was consequently continued. Since he was struck, it is learned from Dr. Bullock, his physician, that he has not been able to leave his room except for two hours at one time, barring his going to the Trial Justice court.

Solicitor B.R. Moore, of the Criminal Court, upon being apprised of the death of Howe, instructed Drs. Bullock and Thomas to make a *post mortem* examination in order to ascertain what the blow from Motorman Kelly had to do with his death, and such examination was held yesterday afternoon. The doctors made their report in writing to Col. Moore and from it we learn that the immediate cause of death was tuberculosis of both lungs. There was a small indentation where the lick was struck on the head, but the skull was not fractured and the examination by the physicians was such that Col. Moore did not deem it necessary to have a coroner's inquest held.

Both of the doctors were white. Their verdict meant that Kelly no longer faced serious charges. Fred died with more than twenty-five thousand dollars' worth of property to his name, the equivalent of more than eight

*The paper was mistaken; the incident actually took place on July 31.

hundred thousand dollars today. To a nephew he left "all my mechanical tools and mathematical instruments," along with his architecture volumes, "numbering about thirteen or fourteen." His four children were to inherit the rest of his library, "to be divided equally between them, share and share alike." These items were among the estate's least valuable, in monetary terms, but Fred chose to treat them first in his will. In doing so, he seemed to emphasize to his descendants the paramount importance of education, an inheritance that no one could plunder.

WITHIN A YEAR, KELLY WAS A FREE MAN. HE HAD GOTTEN OFF LIGHTLY, pleading to a minor affray charge for a ten-dollar fine, plus costs. Fred's murder, while officially refuted, was hardly unique, as white vigilantes across the country violently enforced the resurgent doctrine of white social and economic supremacy. In Tullahoma, Tennessee, they hung a Black teenager for being "saucy" to white people. In Memphis, they shot three Black owners of a grocery store that threatened the profits of a white-owned one. Across the country, they would lynch at least 161 Black people in 1892—believed to be the highest number in a single year ever. The South's "white citizens are wedded to any method however revolting, any measure however extreme, for the subjugation of the young manhood of the race," the investigative journalist Ida B. Wells wrote that June.

Kelly's brush with the law did nothing to temper his aggression. One late summer afternoon in 1893, he stopped in at a downtown drinking den called Croom's. George and James Smith, a pair of white thirtysomething brothers, were already there. They invited Kelly, an acquaintance, to join them for a drink, but the atmosphere soon soured.

Kelly called to James from the counter: "I understand you have something against me. If so, now is the best time to settle it."

James strode over to the counter and, according to a witness, "cursed him, said he intended to whip Kelly, and struck him with his fist." Spoiling for a hand-to-hand brawl, he had misjudged the situation. Kelly pulled out a knife and "tried to cut his head off," slicing the zygomatic bone clean in two and stabbing him in the jaw. He kept going, carving around James's right eye in a circle and twisting the blade until the wound was deep enough to stick a finger inside. Tate Croom, the barman, heard screaming and hurried into the back room, where he found James lying on the floor, his face in shreds. He tried to grab Kelly by the collar, but Kelly jerked free and ran out of the bar.

George Smith and Croom rushed out of the barroom with James in their arms, leaving the knee-high doors swinging behind them. They carried him down the unpaved street, blood gushing from his head and face. At last, they staggered into the office of Dr. William Bellamy—John Dillard's second-eldest son—and laid James on the table. He'd lost a tremendous amount of blood, but his eyes were miraculously intact. Bellamy sewed up the deepest wounds and bandaged the shallower cuts. He told a reporter, "It is not considered that Mr. Smith's wounds will prove fatal, as he is a very strong man and has a good constitution."

News of the attack was already circulating around town. The sheriff formed a search party and George led the group to the boardinghouse where Kelly lived. There, they managed to find Kelly's landlady, who said that her tenant had been there but had just left. He was said to be heading in the direction of the smallpox hospital. The search party tracked him for about an hour, before losing the trail and returning to town around nine o'clock.

The next day's papers carried detailed accounts of the "revolting cutting affray." Kelly, the reports established, was twenty-eight years old. He had come to Wilmington about two years earlier and was said to have a wife living in Richmond, Virginia. After the Howe affair, he had been let go by the streetcar company, and he had not managed to hang on to subsequent employment. He was currently applying for a job on the city's police force.

The final paragraph of the *Messenger*'s story about the bar fight entered into the record a crucial perspective on the Howe affair. "Kelly was once employed on the street railway and is the man who struck old man Fred Howe on the head with an iron crank, inflicting a wound which resulted in his death," the paper reminded its readers. Judging from the paper's casual tone, it must have been common knowledge in Wilmington—autopsy results notwithstanding—that Kelly had murdered Howe. The paper continued, "It is also stated that Kelly boasts of having killed two negroes in South Carolina or Georgia."

Kelly, it appears, had killed at least three Black people without legal consequence. But now he had committed violence against a white man, and the hunt was on. The sheriff's posse set out again the next day, but forty-eight hours after the attack in the bar, Kelly was still at large. He had run to the river, apparently never to be found.

Chapter 12

RETRIBUTION IN HISTORY

With Fred Howe gone, the next generation of Howes were branching out. One early November day in 1895, Anthony Howe's son John Harriss Howe stood in line at the post office, a portfolio under his arm. Imagine him reaching the front of the line, smoothing the brown paper around the parcel one last time. A dozen professional-quality photographs were inside. They depicted "twelve handsome residences"—his finest building projects from recent years. Among them were a house he'd built for his own family on Castle Street; a riverside country house for a railroad president; and a house on Nun and Third for an executive at the Wilmington Iron Works. There was even a house, likely a rental property, that he'd built for Colonel Roger Moore.

The photographs were headed to Atlanta, to be shown at the Cotton States and International Exposition (otherwise known as the Atlanta Exposition), a whiz-bang fair intended to promote the South's transformation, thirty years after the end of the Civil War, into an industrial force. The fair had opened in September and was set to run for a hundred days. Already, hundreds of thousands of visitors had flocked to the sprawling fairgrounds of Piedmont Park to witness such novelties as the phantoscope, an early motion-picture projector, and an eleven-acre lake with an electric fountain that pumped water skyward in rainbow-colored arcs.

John Harriss's contribution, coming in late, didn't feature in the exposition's official catalog. It may have been solicited by John Dancy, the

Wilmington customs collector, who served as one of North Carolina's Black representatives at the fair. Whatever the case, the photographs were certainly headed for the Negro Building, the exposition's designated showcase, according to the catalog, for "the capabilities of the Negro race in their present condition, as well as the progress that has been made since their emancipation."

The Negro Building stood just east of the entrance to the fairgrounds, between a grandstand where Buffalo Bill performed his Wild West review and a midway lined with popular concessions such as an ostrich farm, a vaudeville show, and various "international villages," many of them featuring human beings displayed as exotic attractions. At Dahomey African Village, for example, visitors were invited to look upon "40 cannibals" and to gape at "savages" pounding on drums. "The appearance of these racist representations at the fair," the scholar Mabel O. Wilson writes, "illustrated how the New South ideology resuscitated and mythologized Old South values, while also turning a handsome profit."

The Negro Building celebrated Black achievement against a backdrop of racial exploitation and discrimination. Two years earlier, the Chicago World's Fair had largely excluded Black Americans, leading Frederick Douglass and Ida B. Wells to denounce it in a scorching pamphlet. Now, after considerable campaigning, Black leaders, assisted by a large grant from Congress, had persuaded the event's white organizers to allow Black participation. Many of them would have preferred their contributions to have been integrated into the broader display, rather than crammed indiscriminately into one building. Worse, Black exhibitors were forced into segregated accommodations, and the Negro Building was the only place that they could get something to eat.

Still, the venue was a triumph—a twenty-five-thousand-square-foot neo-Romanesque temple to Black American ingenuity, built entirely by Black laborers, featuring a soaring central tower and four corner pavilions with pennants rippling in celebration. The exhibitions were organized by state and by subject matter: education, medicine, transportation; Potatoes, Tubers, and Unclassed Farm Products; Coffee, Spices, Etc. Even *The Atlanta Constitution*, no perpetual friend to Black people, was impressed: "The Paris exposition had its Eiffel tower, the world's fair had its Ferris wheel, but Atlanta has its negro building."

John Harriss Howe is thought to have attended the exposition and may even have heard Booker T. Washington deliver his famous Atlanta Compromise address at the opening ceremonies. He may have been invited by his old Wilmington friend Robert R. Taylor. After graduating from MIT in 1892, Taylor had gone to work for Washington at the Tuskegee Institute, and he was just starting to design the campus's buildings—a project he would continue over a four-decade career.* His Butler Chapel was memorably depicted by Ralph Ellison in *Invisible Man*: "the chapel with its sweeping eaves, long and low as though risen bloody from the earth like the rising moon; vine-covered and earth-colored as though more earth-sprung than man-sprung."

Taylor would likely have known that Washington was preparing a speech for the exposition that would cause a sensation. In the Atlanta Compromise address, he proposed a kind of bargain: Black Americans would drop the pursuit of social equality in exchange for white Americans' support of their economic advancement. For enthusiastic listeners such as the editors of *The Atlanta Constitution*, the compromise marked "the beginning of a moral revolution in America." But for others it represented a capitulation of everything Black Americans had been working for since emancipation. As Bishop Henry McNeal Turner argued, "social equality carries with it civil equality, political equality, financial equality, judicial equality, business equality, and wherever social equality is denied by legislative enactments and judicial decrees, the sequel must be discrimination, proscription, injustice and degradation."

One can picture John Harriss on the arena floor at Piedmont Park, peeking up from under the brim of his bowler, as Washington stood upon the risers "and delivered an oration that mark[ed] a new epoch." One can envision him nodding in agreement as Washington exhorted his Black brethren to "cast down their buckets" where they were, abandoning the no-

---

*The Obama adviser Valerie Jarrett is his great-great-great-granddaughter.

tion that they would be better off in some faraway place and committing to building their wealth in the South, as the Howes always had. It's difficult, though, to think that John Harriss—son of Anthony, who refused to be cowed in a courtroom; nephew of Fred, who spoke up against a racist motorman and paid with his life—would have shared Washington's belief that the pursuit of social equality was "extremist folly." Nor would he have been likely to agree that "the opportunity to earn a dollar in a factory just now is worth infinitely more than the opportunity to spend a dollar in an opera house." The factory and the opera house weren't mutually exclusive choices for a family that had been running a successful construction business for three generations.

DEMOCRATS FINISHED "REDEEMING" NORTH CAROLINA IN 1876, ELECTING Zebulon B. Vance as governor. A former Confederate official, he promised to roll back political and civil rights, rescuing the state from a Republican Party that, he claimed, had been "begotten by a scalawag out of a mulatto and born in an outhouse." The Democrats dominated North Carolina politics throughout the 1880s, using gerrymandering and "a liberal amount of 'judicious' cheating by election officials," per one historian, to maintain their control. But in the early 1890s, the agricultural economy faltered and lower-class white voters, particularly farmers, began to look for a political alternative. Many of them enlisted in the newly formed Populist Party, which sought to diminish the influence of big business. Then, in 1894, the Populists joined forces with the Republican party to form a ballot-box alliance based on class rather than color. "The interests of the black man and the white man are identical," one Populist politician declared. This unprecedented "Fusion" ticket swept the North Carolina elections of 1896, winning every statewide office and stunning the Democrats.

Fusion was an unprecedented adventure in interracial political cooperation. Once elected, the coalition penalized violence and bribery at the polls and repealed election laws that Democrats had passed after the end of Reconstruction, which made it difficult for Black men to vote. The Fusionists' most consequential reform undid a Democratic reorganization of city governments, returning control to local voters and thus restoring Black Republicans and their white allies to the political influence they had wielded during Reconstruction. The historian Helen G. Edmonds characterized the resulting "resurgence of the Negro in politics" in North Carolina as "a situation which obtained in no other state."

Naturally, Fusion threw North Carolina's white elite into a panic. In their view, the state was reverting to the social and racial anarchy that had characterized the bad old years of Reconstruction, when Black people walked and sat and voted as they wished, and Black politicians strode the halls of power. Across the state, Democratic papers sounded the alarm, calling for "the second overthrow of fusion, confusion, and negroism." The election of Daniel Russell as governor in 1896—the first Republican in the role in twenty years—particularly galled Wilmington's old regime. Russell had been one of them: a Cape Fear planter, a major enslaver, a Confederate captain. He was, in fact, the son of the same wealthy friend who had sent his cook to the Bellamys when the people they enslaved at Floral College ran away. But during the war, Russell had clashed with his superiors and rallied to the Republican side. In 1878, he ran for Congress, ousting Alfred Moore Waddell after four terms in office.

Russell "was hotly denounced as a scallawag and completely ostracized, and even hated," John Dillard Bellamy Jr. recalled. Russell returned his long-standing enemies' disdain with "pent-up fury," opening his inaugural speech with the vengeful line "There is retribution in history." Just two months before his election, the elder John Bellamy had died, leaving John Dillard Jr. and his brothers at the head of the family. Russell's ascent made things awkward for the Bellamys. One of John Dillard Jr.'s brothers had married Russell's sister, and they had christened their firstborn Russell Bellamy—the name, at this point, was basically a political oxymoron. Democratic papers equated "Russellism" with corruption and race treason. Heavyset and puffy-lidded, Russell was a sitting target for caricaturists. One cartoon depicted a ladder propped against Russell's corpulent figure. A Black politician perched on its top rung whispered in his ear: "Do this, do that."

Russell owed his political career to unwavering Black support of the Republican ticket, but he was not universally beloved by Black voters. His views on race were more convoluted than the white supremacist cartoonists made out. As a judge in Wilmington after the war, Russell had defended civil rights for Black people. Yet he wrote, "The Negroes of the South are largely savages. We with Northern aid and sanction kidnapped them, enslaved them, and with most monstrous wrong degraded them so that they are no more fit to govern than are their brethren in African swamps." Remembering this, many Black voters mistrusted Russell, yet most ultimately cast their ballots in his favor, preferring a merely racist candidate to an avowed white supremacist.

In 1897, Russell amended Wilmington's city charter so that the governor would appoint half of the members of the influential board of aldermen. John Dillard Jr. delivered a two-hour speech in protest, likening the maneuver to colonial oppression. A revolution, he suggested, was once again needed. In the wake of local elections, the Fusionist board jostled for power against various Democratic factions. At one point, Wilmington had three separate mayors and three boards of aldermen, all claiming legitimacy. After months of legal wrangling, a judge ruled for the Fusionist slate, and Silas Wright, a white Republican, took office. The board of aldermen now comprised three white Republicans, three Black Republicans, three white Democrats, and a white member of the Silver Party.

Fusion rule increased professional and social equality, which cut the white supremacists like jagged shells in the oyster-paved lanes. One day in 1898, Hugh MacRae was standing in the street near his home on the corner of Seventh and Market, chatting with a friend. A horse-drawn vehicle approached, and the driver, who was Black, stayed his course, leaving it to MacRae and his friend to get out of the way. The white men were furious. Echoing their forefathers' objections to Black "insolence" in the 1860s, they complained that they had been forced to "step up on the sidewalk to avoid being run down."

Hugh was so put out by the incident that he went to his uncle, Walter MacRae. A Harvard graduate, former mayor, and history buff, Walter was considered something of a local sage. When Hugh explained what had happened, Walter drew a parallel to the troubles of British colonialists in India. "If something is not done to put down this surly and rebellious attitude of the Negroes toward the whites," Walter warned, "we will have a repetition of the Sepoy Rebellion, which was ended only after the British authorities had shot some of the mutinous leaders out of the mouths of cannon."

CHAPTER 13

AN UNSAFE CONDITION

When the Civil War ended, Sallie Jones was around ten years old, newly emancipated from the Lovejoy plantation. She left the little blind white girl and the midnight lessons and the Chinese curtains behind and went to live with Ben Franklin, a Black teacher who had fought with the Union Army. Franklin raised her, continued her education, and gave her his surname. In 1869, he attended the National Colored Convention in Washington, D.C., gathering with hundreds of freedmen to organize for Black enfranchisement. Sallie's descendants believe it was there that Franklin got to know some Wilmington acquaintances of Joshua Halsey, and that the connection eventually led to the couple's introduction. Joshua and Sallie married in 1875, three days before Christmas.

By 1896, the irrepressible Sallie Halsey was a forty-one-year-old matriarch with a full household to manage. She and Joshua had been married for more than two decades. They were parents to three girls, the youngest only six years old. The Halseys lived in Brooklyn in a simple house on North Sixth Street, close to the railroad tracks. Joshua's mother, Satyra Walker, had acquired the property shortly after the war, perhaps from her former enslaver, who was president of the railroad.

The Halseys lived in the heartland of Black, working-class Wilmington. Among their neighbors were Alexander Manly, the gutsy editor of *The Daily Record*, and his family. Joshua cobbled together a living doing odd jobs. He probably didn't read the *Record* (according to census records, he didn't read at all, unlike his educated wife). Family lore suggests that he also may not have been able to hear.

Even as Wilmington attracted ambitious Black people from all over the South, not all Black Wilmingtonians were thriving. Many who flocked to the city after emancipation, for example, found themselves locked out of choice positions occupied by members of established Black families. John Dancy, the dazzlingly successful Black customs collector, contrasted the bright prospects of the Black elite with those of "the great majority," for whom "opportunities were pitiably few." Many of them, he recalled, hauled bales of cotton from the wharves to waiting ships. "This was all the work they did," he wrote. "They got a dollar a day, and the season only lasted about three months. Thus they made about $90 a year."

The Howes built houses; the Halseys kept them. Under normal circumstances, the latter family would have drawn little notice from socially prominent white people. A few years back, Sallie worked as a cook for the family of J. D. Munds, a white druggist, and his wife, Minnie, who gave watercolor lessons to local hobbyists. The Mundses ran with the establishment crowd and had a cottage on Wrightsville Sound, a pretty inlet near Wrightsville Beach, where Wilmington's white elite escaped from the summer heat to race yachts and gossip in wooden rockers. The Mundses had made a nice life for themselves specializing in remedies for consumption. One of their advertisements warned, "Women lose their beauty because colds undermine their life."

One day, the Mundses noticed some items missing from their sound house: fifty dollars, a blanket, baby clothes, three yards of cloth, "bracelets, cuffs, and sundry other articles." Another servant accused Sallie of having taken them, and a judge issued a warrant authorizing a search of the Halseys' house. "When the searching officer entered the house, a little 9-year-old girl was seen to throw a piece of cloth over the back fence," the *Wilmington Messenger* reported. The officer recovered a monogrammed cuff belonging to the Mundses. Sallie and Josh were arrested, as was their young daughter, Mary.

At their arraignment, the Halseys were represented by none other than

John Dillard Bellamy Jr., who requested "a continuance for want of witnesses for the defense." The Halseys may have hired Bellamy because he was the first person available, or they may have sought him out, hoping that his prestige or skill would work to their advantage. In any case, it was a banal encounter. Bellamy, for his part, took on the job like any other. It took several weeks for the case to make its way through the system, but Bellamy defended the Halseys successfully. They were ultimately found not guilty, on account of the prosecutors' failure to properly identify the stolen property.

BUT THEN, IN DECEMBER 1896, AN ACCIDENT PUT JOSHUA AND SALLIE squarely in the sights of the white establishment. Likely at one of the extremes of the workday—brisk dawn or sickly dusk, the sun going yellow-green-purple over the Cape Fear River—Sallie trudged over the Sixth Street Bridge, a wooden structure that spanned the railroad tracks, linking Brooklyn to the rest of town.

The texture was off: squelchy, slick. The second her foot hit the plank, Sallie must have known it was rotten, but by then it was too late to recalibrate her step. She fell through the hole, injuring herself badly. There she lay, stranded between her part of town and the other, waiting for someone to help.

Sallie knew that the bridge had been in bad shape for some time. Every so often, the city tried to close it down, amputating the neighborhood from the rest of town, but people would take down the boards as quickly as the authorities could nail them up. Without a functioning bridge, there was no way to get to work. Sallie and Joshua decided to sue, claiming that "the bridge was in an unsafe condition and that the city refused to repair it and left it open for traffic."

The Halseys were asking for five thousand dollars in damages—a life-changing sum, the equivalent of about two hundred thousand dollars today. There was no guarantee that the legal system would treat Sallie fairly, but in pursuing the award, she and Joshua demonstrated confidence that justice would prevail, or that at least they had a shot at securing it. "Black people poured out their family stories" in court, the socio-legal scholar Dylan C. Penningroth writes, chronicling the regularity with which ordinary Black people facing everyday problems approached the courts with "wary faith," holding up the law's "prism to the light to see what colors it would cast."

In 1883, the Supreme Court had overturned the Civil Rights Act of 1875, effectively legalizing racial discrimination in public places. Then just months before Sallie's fall, the *Plessy v. Ferguson* decision legitimized racial segregation under the "separate but equal doctrine," dismantling the last vestiges of Reconstruction's democratic reforms. It had only been a few years since Fred Howe had been effectively murdered in public by a white man. "The ground moved underneath African America," the historian Kidada E. Williams writes, continuing, "In the 1880s, the thin line dividing legal violence and extralegal violence collapsed under the consolidation of racism."

Yet the Halseys, humble though their circumstances, chose to assert

Toward the Sixth Street Bridge.

themselves as citizens. They knew Sallie's worth, and even as they risked unwanted exposure, they asked the law to protect them, to ensure that Sallie's body would not be wrecked without compensation, as those of so many of their ancestors had been through the years. Just five years earlier, they'd prevailed in a court of law, with a Bellamy as their advocate. But the political atmosphere was rapidly deteriorating, and whether they knew it or not, Black families such as the Halseys would soon no longer be able to rely on white institutions and individuals that they'd once considered, if not friendly, reasonably fair.

Chapter 14

WHITE VIOLETS FOR EVENING TOQUES

The promise that Fred Howe had made when he encouraged readers of *The Christian Recorder* to migrate to Wilmington had held up: By 1898, Wilmington was indeed a city of "promising distinction" for Black people. They made up about 60 percent of the city's population, working as dyers, pharmacists, lawyers, architects, wheelwrights, oystermen, washerwomen, hostlers, physicians, root gatherers, bill posters, boot makers, tailors, music teachers, confectioners, vegetable sellers, and ten of the city's eleven restaurateurs. Black and white families lived side by side in all five of the city's wards. Wilmington was arguably the most integrated city in the South.

W. E. B. Du Bois's "mystic years" of Reconstruction had lasted longer in Wilmington than almost anywhere in the nation. Even as Redemption undid the gains of Reconstruction elsewhere in North Carolina and in the nation at large, Wilmington remained a bastion of possibility. At St. Stephen, the politically engaged, outward-looking congregation welcomed lecturers such as Booker T. Washington and A. S. Ishida, a pastor visiting from Japan. Their collective labor was fruitful enough that they sought to share their blessings with those less fortunate, identifying South Africa as a particularly "inviting field" for mission work.

In early 1898, the belief persisted in Wilmington that a Black man could pursue power, dignity, and money all at once. The situation, however, hardly amounted to the "Negro domination" of the white supremacist imagination. The percentage of Black officeholders remained minuscule in proportion to the Black population. Those who attained power wielded it with an awareness that almost anything they did could incite resentment and even violence from their white constituents. The white police chief, for example, instructed his Black deputies never to arrest a white man.

Despite such concessions, the mere existence of Black authority enraged white supremacists. "A Dirty, Filthy Town Without Any Police Protection Worth Speaking Of, Thirteen Negro Policemen, with a Milk-Sop of a White Man for Chief," one newspaper headline read. In the accompanying story, a correspondent out of Charlotte reported that Wilmington's Black people were "saucy and overbearing." As evidence of their unfitness for office, he pointed to unsanitary conditions in the city: "During a short stroll on Market Street on Saturday morning, I counted six dead chickens and one dead cat, besides a dozen or more barrels of decayed cabbage leaves, beans, roasting ear shucks, and the like. Why all this? Is Wilmington without officers?" The city did, of course, have officers—the correspondent's goal was to paint them as woefully ineffectual.

THE DAILY RECORD WAS THE STATE'S ONLY BLACK DAILY NEWSPAPER AND, according to its slogan, "The Only Negro Daily in the World." Its proprietor and editor, Alexander Manly, was born in Raleigh in 1866, the unacknowledged son or grandson of Charles Manly, a white former governor of North Carolina. His mother, Corinne Manly, had been a maid enslaved in the Manly household. Alexander was educated at the prestigious Hampton Institute and moved to Wilmington in 1893, working as a painter before taking ownership of the *Record*.

Manly was a charismatic figure—a deputy register of deeds, a Sunday school teacher, and "goodly to look upon," according to his fiancée, Carrie Sadgwar. Carrie's family, the Sadgwars, were prominent in the community of civically active Black builders that, over the years, included Abraham Galloway, the Artises, the Taylors, and the Howes. She and Alexander had met shortly after his arrival in Wilmington. He was doing odd jobs to supplement his newspaper work and her father had hired him to paint a house. Passing by the site one day, Carrie smiled at her father, leading Manly to think, mistakenly, that she was smiling at him.

"Who's that?" Manly asked.

"My daughter," Sadgwar answered sharply.

"I'd like to meet her."

"If you prove yourself worthy you may meet her someday," Sadgwar replied. "But you had better to get painting that cornice up there, instead of gazing at every little petticoat going down the street."

Carrie continued obliviously down the block, having mistaken Manly for a white man. Manly was smitten, but, in deference to Carrie's "strict-hard" father, he pursued her from a distance. Three months later, he turned up to see her perform at a Friday Night Literary Evening at a local school.

"There's my girl," he whispered to his friend John Thomas Howe, as Carrie took the stage. The third son of Fred Howe, John Thomas worked as the newspaper's general traveling agent. "When this is all over, I want you to introduce me to her."

"What do you mean, *my* girl?" John Thomas replied. "I won't introduce you. Can't do it, man."

"Is she gold?" Alexander asked. "I am a gentleman and can prove it."

"Old man Sadg would see you smoked. She is gold, pure gold, and we don't let strangers meet our girls unless we know *just* who they are."

Alexander continued to court Carrie, finally appearing at the Sadgwar homestead with a letter of recommendation from his minister in Raleigh. Carrie went to college, and when she returned, she began setting type for the *Record*. By 1898, the young couple were deeply in love. The *Record*, for them, was as much a calling as a business. Acknowledged as "a very creditable colored paper" even by white competitors, it had gone from weekly to daily in 1897. Each day's edition was printed on a double-cylinder press that Alexander had bought secondhand from Thomas Clawson, the editor of the *Wilmington Messenger*, a white Democratic paper. Carrie worked alongside Alexander and his brothers Frank (co-owner and manager), Lewin (foreman), and Henry (also a compositor).

The *Record*'s pages reflected the sophistication and stability of Wilmington's Black community. A reader could educate himself on "the language of jewelry," or find advice about growing tulips, making croutons, and choosing cut glass. The paper covered fashion, preferring "white violets for evening toques," even as its editorial pages advised forgoing the latest trends in favor of lasting investments, as "every colored man should try to buy himself a little plot of land and erect a little house thereon." In the children's pages, poetry and stories gently inculcated moral lessons such as courage in the face of fear. White and Black merchants alike advertised in the paper's pages, promoting French-inspired wines and lace curtains. Mrs. Millie Heflin beckoned readers to her ice cream parlor, where "you can be served with the various creams: Pine apple, Banana, Strawberry, etc."

The paper's central mission was advocating for the interests of Black people. "The *Record* is of the Negro for the Negro and *by* the Negro," an early issue declared. It continued, "In North Carolina, the Negro holds the balance of power, which he can use to the advantage of the race, state, and nation, if he has the manhood to stand on principles." The Manly brothers took an optimistic stance, arguing for cooperation and tolerance, but they acknowledged that the atmosphere was growing ever more tense, with elections looming, and that the political chessboard was full of "clever traps." Wilmington's Black citizens were engaged in their city's civic life and using their voting power. At the same time, white families were determined to wrest back the influence they held before the war. As white anger over Fusion mounted, Wilmington's Black people found themselves in the dangerous position of having both too little power and—in the eyes of white supremacists—too much of it. With his good looks, civic stature, and daring pen, Manly was a prime target.

PART 2

HELL JOLTED LOOSE

1898

Chapter 15

WHITE MEN AND WHITE METAL

The campaign to reinstate white supremacy in North Carolina kicked off with a cannon blast on May 12, 1898. It was just after Confederate Memorial Day, the highest holy day on the Democrats' calendar. Staging any other political rally in conjunction with this sacred commemoration would have been considered blasphemy, but this one, in Laurinburg, represented an explicit continuation of the Confederate cause. The 1890s had been tough, with the economy sinking into a serious depression that hit small-time farmers especially hard. At the same time, the Populist movement had put hundreds of Black men into political office, providing the perfect scapegoat. As a band played, the state's top Democratic politicians assured the white people of North Carolina that "Negro domination" was responsible for their woes, and that it was only natural to feel "they were engaged in a righteous struggle, something far above politics, a sort of protection of home."

The Democrats' platform revolved around "white men and white metal." (The latter plank represented Free Silver, a political movement that advocated for money backed by silver, while handily conjuring up the image of a gun.) Furnifold Simmons, the party's state chairman, had begun calling for all-out assault on the multiracial, working-class coalition the Fusionists had built. The white supremacy movement, he declared, needed "men who could write, men who could speak, and men who could ride." Nothing less than the virility of American democracy, he implied, was on the line.

Chief among the men who could write was Josephus Daniels. He had been the editor and proprietor of the Raleigh *News & Observer* since 1894. Mocked by locals as "*The Nuisance Disturber*," the paper had been hemorrhaging readers, but Daniels entreated a hundred of North Carolina's most influential white men to help him buy it. He worked to make the sleepy broadsheet a political must-read, transforming it into "an aggressive exponent of Democracy." His primary backer was the Durham tobacco magnate Julian Carr, an ardent white supremacist who later publicly bragged of having "horse-whipped a Negro wench until her skirt hung in shreds."

Daniels had two complementary objectives: increasing his paper's circulation and delivering a Democratic victory. In its new incarnation as "a country paper, racy of the soil," his *News & Observer* instrumentalized white supremacy to achieve both goals. No headline was too sensational, no cartoon too crude, no story too far-fetched. Daniels later acknowledged that "whenever there was any gross crime on the part of the Negroes, the *News & Observer* printed it in a lurid way, sometimes too lurid." Black men assaulting white women "were few in number," he confessed, but made for unsurpassable propaganda. "Burned to Ashes, the Black Devil, Riddled with Bullets First, a Righteous Judgment, Ravished and Then Killed a White Lady, Paid the Penalty for His Crime, an Outraged People Chased the Fiend for Two Days and When They Caught Him Made Short Work of Him," one headline read.

Daniels came up with innovative ways of getting his product in front of as many white voters as possible. In concert with White Government Unions—local political clubs for white supremacist Democrats—he blanketed the state with newspapers, even sending them, spam-style, to people who had never subscribed. As the white supremacy campaign picked up speed, out-of-state newspapers joined in. The October 2, 1898, issue of *The Atlanta Constitution* carried a pages-long story claiming that Black people were plotting to colonize North Carolina, setting up a "sovereign Negro state." In Wilmington, even the "Negro children are impudent and aggravating," the paper claimed, warning that the situation was growing dire. "A little more than a month ago, Winchesters began to be shipped in here and there is no telling how many citizens have taken the precaution to arm themselves so that they may be prepared if a riot breaks out."

As North Carolina's white elite worked to turn back the clock on racial equality, the world was barreling toward modernity. In 1898, the telephone, the typewriter, the phonograph, the lightbulb, the elevator, the motion picture projector, and the Kodak camera were already in use. Wilmington braced for conflict; in New York, the Brooklyn Bridge was celebrating its fifteenth anniversary, while in Paris, Pierre and Marie Curie were weeks away from announcing their discovery of polonium. Just up the road, in New Bern, North Carolina, a pharmacist settled on the perfect name for a refreshing concoction of sugar, water, caramel, lemon oil, kola nuts, and nutmeg, calling it Pepsi-Cola.

On a nippy evening in early spring, Hugh MacRae's castle glowed from within. He was expecting people. Eight men, to be exact, all neighbors: J. Allan Taylor (wholesale grocer), Hardy L. Fennell (a dealer in horses and saddlery), W. A. Johnson (dry goods merchant), L. B. Sasser (druggist), William Gilchrist (fertilizer company owner), P. B. Manning (attorney), E. S. Lathrop (bookkeeper), and his businessman brother-in-law, Walter L. Parsley, who walked over from next door. The men weren't social equals, or necessarily close friends. But they were all fervent Democrats, united in their determination to secure victory in the November elections. As Furnifold Simmons kicked off the statewide white supremacy campaign, they huddled in Hugh MacRae's parlor, hatching a brash plan to deliver a winning result in Wilmington.

The group, who would become known as the Secret Nine, divided the city into five sections, following the contours of its electoral wards. In each one, they appointed an armed "citizens' patrol," led by a block captain and ready to mobilize upon command. Lieutenants compiled daily rosters of each man, woman, and child in their sectors for their block captains, as well as lists of armed men. Ostensibly, each unit was charged with protecting the residents of its jurisdiction, but the detailed lists were also helpful for herding votes. "Vigilance committees" whipped white Democratic voters in each neighborhood into line, while ensuring, through harassment and intimidation, that Republicans of both races dared not vote.

The Secret Nine effectively created a citywide paramilitary. Another shadowy organization called Group Six was also planning for a white supremacist takeover, aided by the Wilmington Chamber of Commerce and the New Hanover County Democratic Party Campaign Committee. As Election Day neared, the groups overlapped and merged, stockpiling weapons and transforming the city into what one Democratic official described as "an armed camp."

THE WILMINGTON LIGHT INFANTRY WAS A SOCIAL CLUB AS MUCH AS A MILitary organization. The company had produced sixty-five commissioned Confederate officers, and its members cultivated a gallant, antebellum-style insouciance. Its headquarters were located on Market Street, in the same marble-clad building in which Colonel John Taylor, in the years before the Civil War, had hosted the Bellamy family for lavish Christmas feasts. There, Wilmington's white sons of privilege drilled, networked, and preened, as well-born girls "walk[ed] by to silently flirt with boys on the porch." Aspirants applied in writing. Five black balls meant rejection. "To become a member one had to rate high in his profession; he had to act like a gentleman, and be acceptable into the best society of the town," a memoirist recalled.

In the spring of 1898, the mothers, sisters, wives, and daughters of these prominent white men were building a shrine to the Lost Cause. A new Confederate museum, housed in "two choice rooms" on the building's second floor, intended, the *Wilmington Messenger* wrote, to tell "the true history of the heroic struggles of the valiant soldiers and willingly imposed self-sacrifices and privations of the noble women of the South." Under the leadership of Mrs. William M. Parsley, volunteers from the local chapter of the United Daughters of the Confederacy gathered more than a thousand items: portraits, letters, photographs, uniforms, weapons, a piece of the smokestack of the *Merrimac*, "a minnie ball which passed through a portion of Colonel William L. DeRosset's body and he found it in his pants pocket." They were displayed in glass cases like religious relics rather than the detritus of defeat. As such, they invited veneration and communicated martyrdom, with a concomitant injunction to keep the faith.

All over the South, white women poured enormous amounts of energy into such memory-keeping ventures, understanding that they could shape the future by promoting their version of the past. Men grappled over the legacies of the war in the political arena; their female relations sought to shape the discourse through family, community, culture, and media such as *Confederate Veteran*, a magazine for which one of the Bellamy women posed in her antebellum skirts. "They built moats around their white tribe's castles to save children from false history and impure knowledge," the historian David Blight writes.

White Southerners' tenacious promotion of the narrative of noble victimhood was highly effective in encouraging a nationwide amnesia about the issues—slavery, particularly—over which the war had actually been fought. Privileging national reunion over racial justice, white Northerners effectively let go of the war, ceding public remembrance to the Lost Cause juggernaut. In the 1890s, as populist movements began to endanger the political hegemony of the white elite, this opportunistic forgetting was reaching its height. Drained of contentiousness, Confederate memories, Blight writes, "offered a set of conservative traditions by which the entire country could gird itself against racial, political and industrial disorder."

The Confederate museum at the WLI became the city's most active site of dismemory, with a library stocking "a number of schoolbooks printed for the Dixie children," promising "thrilling experiences of those stirring times." Attitudes that were often only implied in the public square found full expression in the domestic sphere, where mothers passed racial prejudice and caste pride on to their offspring. Imbibed on a mother's lap, this reverence could feel like a form of love. "They regarded their efforts to educate children as their most important work as they sought, in their words, to build 'living monuments' who would grow up to defend states' rights and white supremacy," the historian Karen L. Cox writes. Texts such as *A Confederate Catechism* inculcated in children ironclad confidence in the righteousness of the Southern cause:

> Q: What causes led to the war between the States, from 1861 to 1865?
>
> A: The disregard, on the part of States of the North, for the rights of the Southern or slave-holding States.
>
> Q: How were the slaves treated?
>
> A: With great kindness and care in nearly all cases, a cruel master being rare, and lost the respect of his neighbors if he treated his slaves badly. Self interest would have prompted good treatment if a higher feeling of humanity had not.

In 1898, the white supremacists' springtime celebrations of Confederate glory were really all about the fall election season. As the leaves turned from green to gold, the Democratic propaganda operation kicked into high gear. White men with typewriters pecked and pounded the white community into high umbrage, setting the stage for white men with white metal to realize their ultimate goal: forcing Black people out of politics, whether by the ballot box or at the barrel of a gun.

Chapter 16

SOWING THE SEED

On August 18, *The Daily Record* published an editorial attributed to its editor in chief, Alexander Manly. Its 606 words were the most consequential ever committed to paper in the city, setting into motion a chain of events whose consequences would reach across the nation and into the next two centuries. Manly was taking an enormous risk in publishing the piece, but he wrote from a place of perceived strength, given the intensity of his convictions and the practical fact that whatever happened in the upcoming statewide elections, on the city level a friendly Fusion government was in place. He began decorously: "A Mrs. Felton from Georgia, made a speech before the Agricultural Society at Tybee, Ga., in which she advocates lynching as an extreme measure. This woman makes a strong plea for womanhood and if the alleged crimes of rape were half so frequent as is oft times reported, her plea would be worthy of consideration." He was using epitrope—the rhetorical technique of establishing fair-mindedness by granting one's opponent a point or two before proceeding to rip her argument to shreds.

The Mrs. Felton whom Manly referred to was Rebecca Latimer Felton, an activist for equal rights for white women, from Cartersville, Georgia. Felton was an unusual character—a mother of five who had come to public life belatedly, after spending the early decades of her life as a slave-owning housewife. She got into politics alongside her husband, who served several terms in Congress, rising to prominence as a campaigner for temperance, education, and penal reform. She had been invited to Tybee Island to address the state agricultural society on the subject of "Woman on the Farm." In Felton's view, the most pressing problem facing rural women was the prospect of being raped by Black men. She declared, "If it needs lynching to protect women's dearest possession from the ravening human beasts—then I say lynch; a thousand times a week, if necessary."

A year had elapsed since the Tybee conference, but as part of the 1898 white supremacy campaign, Democratic papers around the state reprinted Felton's speech in advance of the fall elections, with the aim of working readers into a racist lather. The more outraged the white masses were, the more likely they were to go along with the political takeover that the Democratic bosses had been planning since the spring.

Manly felt that Felton's vile words, repeatedly diffused by the white press to inflame the political discourse, necessitated a response. He decided to take her on in the *Record*, answering her bloodlust with logic. Black men, he pointed out, surely weren't the only rapists out there. White women, moreover, weren't the only ones being raped. The subject was presumably one of special sensitivity for Manly, the son of a white enslaver father and an enslaved Black mother. He built up passion as he went along, coming to an obvious conclusion that would be taken as scandalous affront. "Every Negro lynched is called a 'big, burly, black brute,'" he wrote, "when in fact many of those who have thus been dealt with had white men for their fathers, and were not only 'black' and 'burly,' but were sufficiently attractive for white girls of culture and refinement to fall in love with them as is very well known to all." Worry about white *men's* purity, Manly urged Mrs. Felton. Then, he issued a bold warning: "Don't think ever that your women will remain pure while you are debauching ours. You sow the seed—the harvest will come in due time."

Death threats and nasty letters came pouring into the *Record*. White merchants withdrew their advertising, and the building's landlord kicked the *Record* off the premises, forcing the paper to scramble for a home. In Raleigh, the white Republican Governor Daniel Russell, ignoring the decisive role of Black Fusion voters in his election, publicly denounced "the Negro who edits the Wilmington paper." Even the local Republican executive committee unanimously disavowed Manly as "a mischief-making simpleton" at the head of "a kicking, disorganizing concern." Facing pressure to denounce Manly, a delegation of conservative Black leaders presented him with a prewritten retraction, but he refused to publish the document.

Manly pressed on, securing new headquarters for the *Record* at the Love and Charity Hall, a two-story wood-frame building on Seventh Street between Nun and Church, owned by a Black fraternal organization. There, he and his colleagues continued to publish their usual mix of lighthearted service journalism punctuated by resolute commentary on political and racial issues. In their coverage of the upcoming elections, the editors struck a cautious but calm note. "The Democrats are making extensive preparations for stump-speaking in all parts of the city, which will begin Monday night," they wrote. "It will be to the advantage of the colored people to avoid these places."

It may have seemed to Manly that he had survived the worst the Democrats could sling at him. He had spoken his mind and emerged relatively unscathed. Now that he had moved operations to a Black-owned building in a mixed neighborhood, the paper would be physically safer and his employees, such as John Thomas Howe, the *Record*'s traveling agent, could stop worrying that they might soon be out of a job. Yet, the hullabaloo over the Felton speech and Manly's rebuttal was merely an opening skirmish. The "race war" that the white supremacists had so long sought was kicking off, and soon there would be blood on the ground and guns at City Hall.

When the Spanish-American War broke out in April 1898, the Wilmington Light Infantry mobilized with gusto. Relaxing its membership policies (while remaining exclusively white), the company mustered more than a hundred men and reported for duty at the state capital, in Raleigh. There, they formed Company K of the Second North Carolina Volunteer Infantry Regiment, led by Captain Donald MacRae, Hugh's brother. But before Company K could get to Santiago de Cuba, the war was over—a ten-week rout that ended in August with Spain relinquishing sovereignty over Cuba and surrendering Puerto Rico and Guam to the United States, along with its empire in the Philippines.

The war had been a tease for the white soldiers. In the late summer of 1898, they were back in town, primed for action. Many wore the red-and-white pin-back buttons of the White Government Union as they disembarked from the train to the cheers of two thousand people. The naval reserves shot off a howitzer salute as a carriage parade set off en route to the depot. Colonel Roger Moore was serving as chief marshal. Impressed by his Confederate and Klan experience, the Secret Nine had recently appointed him to command their paramilitary block patrols. He led the returning soldiers through streets festooned with flags and flowers to the WLI Armory, where they were greeted by a display of incandescent lights spelling out "Welcome."

Alfred Moore Waddell was the day's orator. In 1878, he had lost his congressional seat to his Republican neighbor Daniel Lindsey Russell (currently serving as North Carolina's governor). After a few years, finding little to do in North Carolina, he set off on a five-month tour of the Northern states, putatively to drum up support for Democratic candidates. Traveling by horse-drawn carriage, Waddell subjected his companions to seigneurial monologues: "In my State, North Carolina, there are twenty-six mountain peaks that are higher than Mt. Washington, which you all think is the tallest mountain the world; but we don't have our mountains and lakes together, as you have," and so forth.

Now—two decades out of office but trying to keep a hand in the game—he climbed out of the last carriage and ascended to a balconet on the building's second floor, addressing the masses in the front piazza. "All hail! And thrice welcome!" he boomed. "Brave sons of brave sires!" After Waddell's speech, a band struck up "Dixie," and the men sat down to a roast beef banquet. The *Wilmington Messenger* immortalized the festivities the next day, beside a "sworn affidavit" from a white man who claimed that his fifteen-year-old daughter had narrowly escaped being molested by the "unholy hands" of two Black boys. The juxtaposition of the reports carried an implicit message: Now that they'd prevailed in one war, the white people of North Carolina ought to go win another.

For many white Americans, the victory in Cuba confirmed that Anglo-Saxons, as one senator proclaimed, possessed "the most masterful blood of history." Charles W. Chesnutt observed in *The Marrow of Tradition*, a novel inspired by the Wilmington massacre and coup: "The nation was rushing forward with giant strides toward colossal wealth and world dominion. . . . The same argument that justified the conquest of an inferior nation could not be denied to those who sought the suppression of an inferior race." With public opinion at their backs, the white supremacists of Wilmington turned their attention toward a local offensive.

Wilmington had also sent large numbers of Black men to the war, raising two companies for North Carolina's first all-Black battalion since Reconstruction. For many Black soldiers, the decision to enlist had been a difficult one, but the desire to aid their country had won out over hesitancy to serve a government that preached freedom abroad but practiced segregation at home. Like the Wilmington Light Infantry, the Black companies from Wilmington never left American soil. But unlike their white brethren, they were not quickly furloughed. As Wilmington's white soldiers came marching home, full of aggression and swagger, some of the city's most experienced Black fighters were stuck at a backwoods training camp near Macon, Georgia. Officially, they were digging water lines, but their absence from Wilmington meant the returning white militias faced no organized Black opposition, as they had back in the days of the Colonel's Ku Klux Klan. With a little help from the United States military command, the white militias now enjoyed a monopoly in Wilmington.

SATURDAY MORNING, OCTOBER 15, 1898—BODIES IN ROCKERS, FEET ON porch rails. The editors of the Democratic papers had timed the publication of their latest bombshell for maximum impact, when the white supremacists of Wilmington had time to sit back, relax, and work themselves into a state of hysterical affront that Josephus Daniels later described as "white heat." All over town, men were fuming over platters of calves' livers and corn muffins. Wives threw hands over the headlines, as though they were swatting flies, to hide the latest outrage from the children, or maybe they didn't. There, next to a story about "lustful black brutes" who had supposedly wanted to rape a farmer's daughter, the *Wilmington Morning Star* blared: "A HORRID SLANDER. The Most Infamous That Ever Appeared in Print in This State."

Manly's editorial had been out for almost two months, but Democratic leaders had decided to wait until just before the election to capitalize on it, knowing, as one of them later admitted, that "the article would make an easy victory for us" at the polls. Now, with a month to go, white papers ran Manly's piece in full. Politicians brandished his words as evidence for their argument that anything but a commanding Democratic win in November would mean the ruin of white womanhood and thus of white civilization.

The *Star* reprinted Manly's editorial fifty-four times. Each time it was followed by an affidavit signed by the county clerk, and testimonials signed by white men, attesting that Manly was "a Negro," a Republican, and "not regarded as a simpleton, or a nobody," as certain Fusionists, hoping to distance themselves from him, may have claimed. The paper went on to name Manly's colleagues at the paper, marking the whole staff out for retribution. It made special mention of John Thomas Howe, the paper's general traveling agent, noting that he had also served as a Republican representative in the state legislature of 1897.

Manly refused to back down. The *Record*'s issue of October 20 took a firm but placatory tone, urging trust in the democratic process. If white men could register and vote, "then surely it is no crime for their servants to register and vote," the paper argued. At a nearby military base, dozens of Black men had recently lost their jobs because they had done just that. Still, the paper counseled forbearance: "Don't get mad at all the white people because of the few who have forgotten, we have friends among them yet and they are not all in the Republican party either."

This unflustered attitude may have reflected an actual faith that peace would prevail, a desire to tamp down the increasingly febrile atmosphere in town, or sheer wishful thinking. "What Is There to Fear?" the *Record* asked, in the headline of a front-page editorial. The discussion that followed suggested, however, that there were ample threats to Black votes and to Black physical safety. "Who is there among the whole number [of white people] that would make of himself a murderer for the sake of carrying an election, which if it goes either way must give white men office?" the paper wrote. Toward the end of the article, this cool prognostication gave way to subtle pleading. The editors attempted to defuse the gathering mob by flattering white people's individual better natures:

> If the suggestions given out by the hostile papers were followed up, who can fathom the depths to which this fair community would be plunged? Make this matter a personal question! Ask yourself: "What have I against my neighbor that I would seek to destroy his life or happiness?"

The *Record*'s assurances only underscored the degree to which all was not well in Wilmington. The historical record shows that plenty of people knew that bloodshed was coming, but those who would stop it couldn't, and those who could wouldn't. George Henry White, a Black congressman from North Carolina, had gone to the White House several times during the summer, urging President William McKinley to intervene in "the unholy war that Democrats are making on the color line." In Washington, the *Evening Star* identified Wilmington as "the scene of a probable outbreak" in the Democrats' "reign of terror." As the elections neared, a group of Black clergymen went to see McKinley, alerting him yet again to "the farce that is about to be enacted in the state of North Carolina." The warnings were urgent and many, but McKinley did nothing.

The novelist David Bryant Fulton would later immortalize Manly's editorial as "the retort which shook the old State from the mountain to sea, and which enhanced the chances of the white supremacy advocates who were then planning for an uprising in November." As the statewide Democratic machine sought to crush Manly, and the Republican party abandoned him, local Black women stood in his defense. In late October, "An Organization of Colored Ladies" placed a paid advertisement in the *Record*, calling it "the one medium that has stood up for our rights when others have forsaken us." The women were clear in their mission to encourage turnout, intimidation be damned: "We have therefore resolved that every negro who refuses to register his name next Saturday that he may vote, we shall make it our business to deal with him in a way that will not be pleasant." They even vowed to instruct their daughters "to recognize only those young men who have the courage and manhood to stand up for the liberty which under God he now has."

If the *Record* believed that better natures would prevail, the women were not so sure. They left to linger the implication, far bleaker than Manly's vision of a soon-to-be-appeased city, that the freedoms that had allowed Wilmington's Black people to survive and prosper in the three and a half decades since emancipation were already almost as good as gone.

Chapter 17

CHOKE THE CAPE FEAR RIVER

The men who could ride—the White Government Union (WGU) and their Red Shirt paramilitary arm—worked on an intimate scale to deliver votes for the Democrats in the 1898 campaign. They acted as a local intelligence service, poking into people's private business and using what they found to control their political behavior. "The fact is this is a neighborhood fight," one leader said. "The victory for better government in North Carolina is to be won around the firesides."

In Wilmington, organizers shook off supervision, telling state chairman Furnifold Simmons, as the secret committees schemed and plotted, to "go to Hell, as we [are] going to run the campaign to suit ourselves down here." For much of the year, the WGU group had been meeting once a month, often at the law offices of John Dillard Bellamy Jr., who was locked in a contentious race against Oliver Dockery, a prominent Republican, for a seat in the US House of Representatives. In accordance with Article IX of the club's bylaws, members sussed out "the doubtful and floating votes in the township." The men were encouraged to submit lists of dissenters and undecideds to party higher-ups, so that they could "supplement the efforts of the Union" with special outreach "by sending literature, public speakers, etc." The group's constitution promised, "The work shall be constant."

Sending literature was a euphemism for applying intense, often intolerable pressure to any white man who didn't fall into line. The Republican postmaster William H. Chadbourn, for instance, spoke out against the Democrats' "gross libel" of "Negro domination and misrule" and endured a campaign of harassment, with the *Wilmington Messenger* suggesting that he "abstain from letter writing or otherwise meddling in politics, or he may have some very unpleasant things to consider." Unable to withstand the white supremacists' tactics, Chadbourn soon retracted his statement and switched camps, announcing that he had previously misunderstood the realities that white Wilmingtonians faced and that he was now *for* white supremacy. Eventually, he fled to Maine, "for his health." Black people faced even starker forms of coercion, such as being fired. "Imagine the uneasiness & here in free America & in this nineteenth century," a white woman wrote in a letter to a relative. "A great many of the businessmen turned off the colored men if they registered—that Stephen at Stevenson's had to go—Holmes & G. turned theirs off & have white drivers—nearly all did it."

As the WGU strong-armed white men to the polls, the Colonel's "vigilance committee" tracked their movements. Each night for six weeks, his men patrolled the city, locking down every block. Rumors abounded that Black residents were arming up, but a Black detective hired by the county Democratic committee, ostensibly to locate stockpiles of weapons, discovered "that they were doing practically nothing." Meanwhile, white residents were placing large orders with gun shops along the Eastern Seaboard. Members of the Secret Nine raised twelve hundred dollars from white business leaders to import a state-of-the-art rapid-fire Colt machine gun. After it arrived, they invited Black leaders out for a ride on a tugboat, obliging them to sit and watch a demonstration of the new weapon's capacity for destruction. Not only did the Colonel's men now possess hardcore firepower, but they also controlled the city's infrastructure. Should "any conflagration or outbreak" come to pass, they had arranged for both the city's telephone network and the street railway system to come under their command.

AT LEAST ONE WHITE MAN REFUSED TO BUCKLE. HIS NAME WAS BENJAMIN Franklin (B. F.) Keith Jr., a forty-year-old commission merchant. He traded anything he could sell—cheese, rice, deer tongues, leghorn chickens, hoe-cake soda—shipping cargoes from his Front Street warehouse as far as Boston in the north, Mississippi in the west, and south to the Caribbean. Keith did especially well with shingles, which he cut from timber that he raised on his own farm. Business was sufficiently profitable that in the spring of 1898, Keith purchased a "handsome naptha launch," a forty-foot boat that could carry a hundred people on pleasure cruises or fishing excursions.

A Baptist and a teetotaler, Keith had not grown up in luxury or leisure. His father, who owned property and enslaved several people, had opposed secession but fought with the Confederate Army. He was captured following the battle of Fort Fisher and held for months in a camp where food was so scarce that prisoners waded into a waist-high reservoir to scrape the bottom for officers' old bones. Keith, who became a lifelong pacifist, recalled that his father emerged from the war "wrecked in health, property, and ambition." Many ruined Southerners declared bankruptcy, but this was against the elder Keith's principles. At seven years old and "clad in only a shirt, bare-foot," Keith took up the hoe, toiling until he was nineteen to pay the family's creditors. Schooled in self-reliance, he later wrote, "[I] then started out to build my own castles."

When the Populist movement arose in response to the economic crises of the 1890s, Keith quickly rallied to the cause. He was concerned about issues dear to farmers, but his special passion was bimetallism—a cure for deflation, allowing unlimited amounts of silver to be put into circulation as legal tender, alongside gold. As a silver bug with a backwoods background, Keith stood apart from the financiers and railroad men of the Wilmington elite, who also objected to his proposals for bringing private utilities under public control. In 1896, he started publishing *The New Era*, a modest Populist newspaper devoted to agriculture, bimetallism, and "Government by the People."

In the fall of 1898, Keith was the Silver Party's only representative on the city's ten-member board of aldermen, and he had just been selected as the Populist candidate for a state senate seat. He later recalled that he tried to brush off the Democratic papers' sensational headlines as "poke-juice," but they "were large and red enough to frighten a blind man if he had been told what they looked like." In September 1898, the *Messenger* published an article accusing Keith of having met Manly's scandalous editorial with "pathetic indifference." Worse, the paper alleged, Keith had been heard on someone's piazza suggesting that "the ultimate solution of the negro problem would be the amalgamation of the black and white races."

In a rebuttal, Keith denied that he "was taking sides with the negro slanderer" and denounced the "uncalled for abuse." But the *Messenger* kept up the attacks. "On which side, Mr. Keith, do you draw your lance and couch your blade in this magnificent fight for 'civilization vs. barbarism'?" a second article asked. Should Keith choose the wrong camp, the paper implied, severe punishment would be forthcoming. The paper reminded its target that the clock was ticking: "The time may not be too late, if you act promptly and truly, to rehabilitate yourself in the respect of the white men of the city by action—not talk."

Keith was furious at the Democrats' bullying—if they wanted action, they would have it. Early on the morning of September 8, he walked over to the Fore and Foster mill and asked for its proprietor, James Fore, who he believed had started the amalgamation rumor. Keith caught Fore right as he was showing up for the day, walking into his office to open the mail. When he nonchalantly declared that the article accurately portrayed his views, Keith responded by punching him in the head.

"Murder!" Fore screamed, summoning his employees to the rescue. (He had recently replaced his Black workers with members of the Red Shirt brigade.)

The workers came running with boards and scantling, but Keith held them off with a pistol, telling them he would "blow their brains out" if they approached. Eventually, the workers pulled Keith away from their boss. The Democratic papers claimed that he had hardly landed a lick, but he was charged with assault and battery, and the episode cemented his status in the white supremacists' eyes as a traitor to the cause.

On the issue of race, Keith was hardly the radical that the Democrats made him out to be. Although he supported political and economic rights for Black people, he did not believe in social equality. In fact, his editorial had called *The Daily Record* a "dirty sheet" and Manly "a mischievous animal." Still, Keith dismissed "Negro rule" as a racist fiction, and he refused to join the white supremacy campaign, considering it a plutocratic power grab that would leave "innocent people killed, if they were Negroes (they, too, were of God's creatures the same as all other races)." As the frenzy mounted, the white supremacists rained down abuse on Keith. One handwritten letter, dated October 21, arrived, accompanied by a cut-out image of a Black baby boy sitting under an American flag. It read:

> Dear Sir:
>
> Are you going to vote with the Negro if you do it will be good bye for you . . . The Democrats are going to boycott you . . . so you won't dare open your shop to do business. Take note of this and be a white man. Remember you have a nice wife and how would you like to entertain a big buck Negro and his wife in your house along with your wife. This is a serious matter to think about.
>
> It's not too late to give this matter a deep consideration. . . . Take warning.
>
> A true Democrat & a white man

Discreetly, Keith tried to get the attention of high-placed people around the state, such as the Populist Senator Marion Butler, writing, "I look for a lot of innocent people killed here if things continue as they are now." His friends begged him to leave town, but he refused on principle, considering himself "too clean and brave to run." The white supremacists could bring it on, he declared, and "send their drunken red shirts to kill me, but if I left the city it would be feet foremost."

A few nights later, Keith heard a crowd gathering outside his house. His wife, Lillie—the daughter of German immigrants—was nine months pregnant. They both grabbed guns and crept down the staircase, planning to shoot at the gathering mob through a pair of glass panes. "When [we] were about halfway down, the butt of [my] gun struck one of the baluster supports with such force that it could be heard all over the house, as well as out in the yard," Keith recalled. The intruders took off running.

Keith had survived character assassination and held off a home invasion, but with every passing day, his continued presence grew more dangerous. He didn't care. He'd rather be ten feet under in Wilmington, he said, than abandon his property or his positions. But his exception proved the rule: The majority of his fellow white men were susceptible to blandishments, threats, and lies. They would follow the pack.

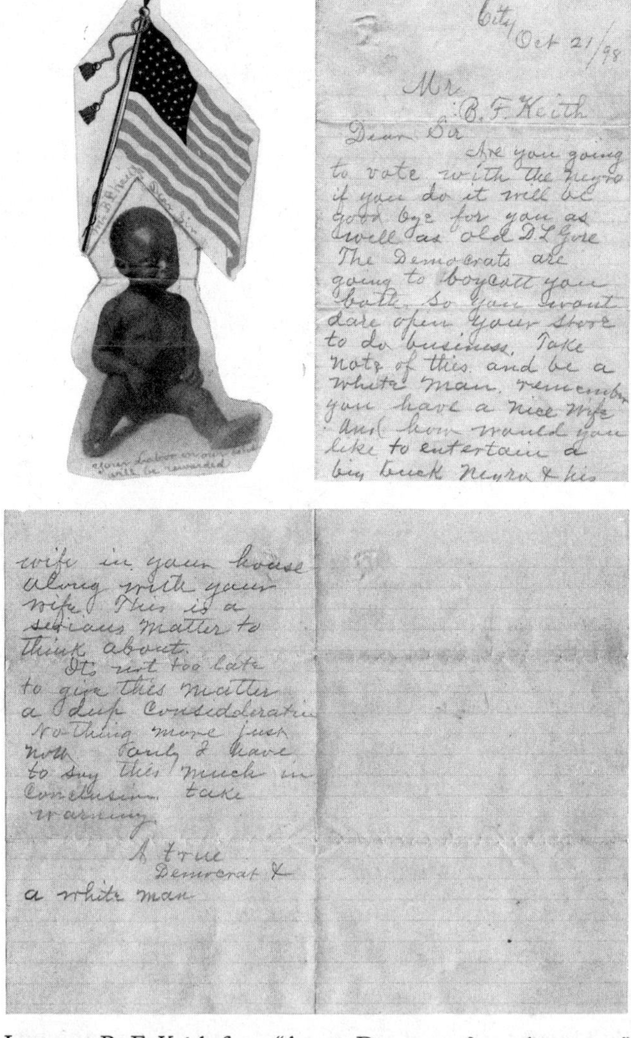

City Oct 21/98

Mr
B. F. Keith
Dear Sir
Are you going to vote with the negro if you do it will be good bye for you as well as old D L Gore The Democrats are going to boycott you both. So you wont dare open your store to do business. Take note of this and be a white man. remember you have a nice wife And how would you like to entertain a big buck negro & his wife in your house along with your wife This is a serious matter to think about.
It's not too late to give this matter a deep Considderation Nothing more just now only I have to say this much in conclusion take warning

A true
Democrat &
a white man

Letter to B. F. Keith from "A true Democrat & a white man," October 21, 1898.

ALFRED MOORE WADDELL STOOD BEHIND THE VELVET CURTAINS AT THAlian Hall. He'd always loved a stage, particularly this one—it was here that he'd trodden the boards before the war as the Invisible Prince, swooning over his brother-in-law, who played the Queen, as the audience guffawed; here, in the uncertain days just after, that he'd lectured Fred Howe and his comrades on the contingency of Black suffrage and citizenship. On the evening of October 24, the house was filling up fast. Tonight, Waddell was speaking on white supremacy, a subject on which he could expound with both flair and conviction.

With the political situation in flux, Waddell had finally elbowed his way back into the center of the fray. His renewed energy wasn't just attributable to the prospect of a career revival. His personal life had also evolved dramatically since the death of his first wife, Julia, and that of his second wife, her sister Ellen, in 1895. Now, at sixty-four, he had a new bride, thirty-five-year-old Gabrielle DeRosset Waddell.

Gabrielle came from one of Wilmington's oldest families, but her life had been tough, bordering on Gothic. Her father, Louis DeRosset, spent the first part of the war working in Confederate logistics before running blockades to the Caribbean. Meanwhile, her mother, Marie, partied. "Constant soirées of one sort or other engross her all the time," her disapproving mother-in-law wrote to a friend. In 1865, Marie made the rash decision to try to join Louis in Nassau, bringing along infant Gabrielle. As their ship attempted to slip out of Wilmington, Union blockaders opened fire. Marie wrapped Gabrielle in a blanket and tossed her off the boat into the arms of a sailor.

As Confederate prospects dimmed, the DeRossets fled to England. There, they attempted to penetrate high society without much luck. (They did manage to befriend the aging writer Edward Bulwer-Lytton, of "dark and stormy night" renown, who eventually used them as inspiration in his "silver fork" novels lampooning American parvenus.) Marie died of a laudanum overdose and Louis, penniless and severely depressed, sent Gabrielle off to live with an aunt. Orphaned at twelve, Gabrielle later supported herself as a governess in New England, but she was called home to Wilmington to nurse her grandfather through a flesh-eating cancer. She quit after several months and suffered a nervous breakdown. The next year, she married Waddell.

Now, past eight o'clock on a Monday night, white people made their ways to the opera house from all over town. The streets were loud with the commotion of sixty men "rigged out in red shirts"—white supremacist paramilitaries, who mustered at Sixth and Castle streets and proceeded downtown, passing within a block of the Howe homestead before turning on Front Street toward the theater. Inside, the house was packed, from galleries to parquet. At eight fifteen, the chairman of the Democratic executive committee of New Hanover County introduced Waddell, who appeared onstage surrounded by sixty of the city's most prominent white men. The crowd responded with "deafening cheers and applause."

Finally, it was Waddell's moment. For thirty years, he'd been regurgitating the same complaints about "Negro domination" and "insolence." This time, he would awe the crowd, inflame their passions, and earn his place in Furnifold Simmons's triumvirate of useful men. He began by uniting the audience across classes as proud Anglo-Saxons, beings of a superiority so evident that it was hardly more than common sense. To even discuss "the rightfulness and the expediency of maintaining the absolute supremacy of the white people in any part of the territory of the United States," Waddell observed, would be as ludicrous as questioning the Ten Commandments.

That settled, Waddell turned to the state of affairs in Wilmington. Black people had no capacity for self-government, he declared. It was a well-known fact that left to their own devices, they would descend into chaos and then cannibalism. Thus, Waddell thundered, it was "profoundly humiliating to be complied to acknowledge" that North Carolina was the only state in the union where "insolent" Black "savages" still exercised the full right of suffrage. Wilmington, furthermore, was the only city in the state where white people accepted the "insufferable evil" of "Negro domination." Cannily, Waddell was encouraging his audience to see themselves as victims by harnessing the power of social comparison: The grass was always whiter on the other side of the fence.

In Waddell's estimation, there existed a single remedy to these outrages: It must be made impossible for any Black person ever to hold office in North Carolina again. He built toward his climax, weaving his Moore forefathers' triumphs at Moores Creek and Valley Forge into an ongoing epic of heroism that encompassed the entire family of white man. The white men of Wilmington, he vowed, as the audience applauded wildly, "will have no more of the intolerable conditions under which we live. We are resolved to change them, if we have to choke the current of the Cape Fear with carcasses."

Waddell's words titillated white supremacists all over the state. His cousin Rebecca Cameron wrote worshipfully from Hillsborough, likening Waddell to his revolutionary forebears, "who said to the Magistry of England, 'No farther.'" She expressed her desire for a "thorough" bloodletting. "We are aflame with anger here," she wrote. "I wish you could see Anna, she is fairly rampant and blood thirsty. These blond women are terrible when the fighting blood is up. I hope it will not come to last resort but when it does let it be Winchesters and buck shot at close range." Her delectation recalled that of Belle Bellamy and her friend as they dreamed of tearing the Yankees limb from limb on the eve of the Civil War. But her words were clear-eyed prophecy, not schoolgirl fantasy. Across the state and with ample advance, well-placed white people could narrate with perfect accuracy the supposedly spontaneous riot that was about to take place. They had planned it for months to the smallest detail—now they would fire up the masses and watch them act.

Chapter 18

RULE OR DIE

Converging on the horizon with a blazing fall sunset, the Red Shirts were said to make it seem as though the entire world had turned scarlet. They were the enforcer caste of the WGU and the aristocratic cabals—poor white men who had abandoned the countryside in the late 1880s, when the price of cotton fell by half, only to learn that their prospects weren't much better in town. A Red Shirt's forebear was more likely to have been an overseer than an enslaver. Now, Charles Chesnutt observed, they performed "the dirty work of politics . . . for which the men of gentler breeding did not care." White supremacy promised to restore them to the position of relative primacy that they had enjoyed before emancipated Black workers entered the labor market and began beating them out for jobs.

The Wilmington Red Shirts made their debut at an October rally in Fayetteville. It was a family occasion, with "wives, daughters, sisters, and sweethearts . . . especially invited and expected," and a float featuring twenty-two maidens, all dressed in white. The show's headliner was "Pitchfork Ben" Tillman, a sadistic one-eyed senator from South Carolina who had proudly led a racial massacre at the end of Reconstruction and declared that he would rather his daughter be killed by tigers than be "robbed of the jewel of her womanhood by a Black fiend." Tillman challenged the seven-thousand-strong audience to make an example of Alexander Manly. "Why didn't you kill that damn n—— editor who wrote that?" Tillman yelled.

"Send him to South Carolina and let him publish any such offensive stuff, and he will be killed!"

Five days before the election, more than a hundred Red Shirts gathered again on the outskirts of Wilmington. They set off down Market Street, riding nearly all the way to the river, before they turned south on Front Street, toward the southside neighborhood. At Front and Castle—the corner where Motorman Kelly had bashed Fred Howe over the head with the reverse lever six years earlier—they turned east, heading right back in the direction from which they'd come. Their goal was not efficiency but exposure. The Red Shirts wanted to pass as many Black homes as they could. At Seventh Street, they made another turn, which sent them parading past the new offices of *The Daily Record*, before dipping down to Fourth Street, where they crossed over the railroad tracks and proceeded into the heart of Brooklyn.

For the moment, the streets were empty. Black people prudently stayed inside, but the threat of a climactic episode of violence—the thorough bloodletting so desired by Waddell's cousin—hung heavy in the air. The leaders of the white supremacy campaign were in Raleigh, hashing out an eleventh-hour deal with Governor Daniel Russell. The next morning's papers carried the news that Russell and the Republicans, hoping to avoid violence, had agreed to withdraw candidates from the local ballot. In other words, the Democrats' intimidation tactics had prevailed, and in Wilmington, certain Democratic candidates would run unopposed. Even so, the white vigilantes, armed and agitated, vowed to keep Black men from the polls. "You are Anglo-Saxons," Waddell had reminded them the night before. "If you find the Negro out voting, tell him to leave the polls and if he refuses, kill, shoot him down in his tracks."

Black and white residents braced for trouble when Election Day arrived, at last, on November 8. As the Colonel's militias locked down every block of the city, WGU members congregated at the polls, doing their best to scare off Republican voters and to facilitate a Democratic victory, whether fair or fraudulent. Never look a white voter square in the face, they were instructed, even if you know "that John Smith was voting as Willie James and the latter was dead and buried in Oakdale cemetery for lo many years."

In the Fifth Ward, one of the city's Blackest areas, white paramilitaries prevented Black residents from crossing from Brooklyn into the center of the city. Almost two hundred white men with white handkerchiefs tied around their arms stormed a polling station and started a fight, knocking out the light and throwing the place into chaos. A Black registrar who was there, counting ballots, later testified that he thought he would be killed. But despite intimidation and obstruction—or perhaps because of it—the violence that everyone anticipated never materialized. Republicans who did not wish to risk their lives stayed home, and the Democrats cruised to victory in what the *Wilmington Morning Star* celebrated as a "thoroughly peaceable" and "remarkably quiet" day of voting.

It was a landslide for the Democrats. The Wilmington congressional district, the *Star* boasted, had "covered itself with imperishable glory," electing a Democrat to every state Senate and House seat. That made fourteen Democratic representatives and six senators to the previous legislature's two and none. One white woman wrote to her daughter in New York with a sense of smug relief: "The white man to-day has gained his point, rule or die." But despite overwhelming success at the polls, the white men weren't finished.

THE ANNOUNCEMENT AROUSED THE READER'S CURIOSITY THROUGH A COMbination of brevity and portentousness. Thirty-seven words, in medium-size print, placed in a prominent box near the *Wilmington Messenger*'s masthead. As if Election Day hadn't been profitable enough for the Democrats, the notice—published the next day, on November 9—dangled the possibility that yet more spoils remained for the taking. "ATTENTION WHITE MEN," it read. "There will be a meeting of the White Men of Wilmington this morning at 11 o'clock at the Court House. A full attendance is desired, as business in the furtherance of White Supremacy will be transacted."

More than a thousand citizens, "from the minister to the merchant, the mariner to the mendicant," packed into the courthouse on a few hours' notice, whiteness and maleness their commonality and qualification. The

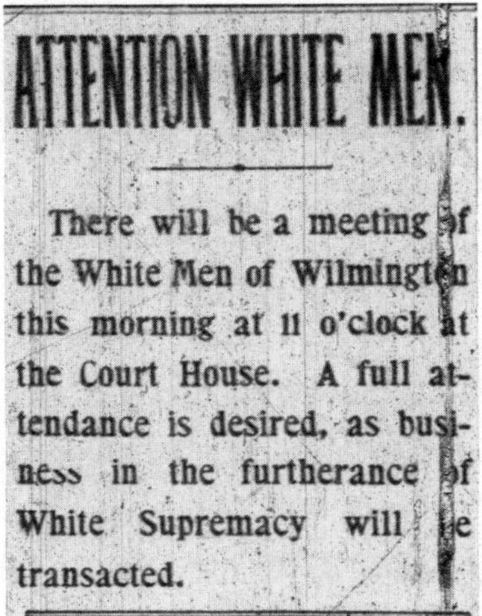
ATTENTION WHITE MEN.

There will be a meeting of the White Men of Wilmington this morning at 11 o'clock at the Court House. A full attendance is desired, as business in the furtherance of White Supremacy will be transacted.

Notice, *Wilmington Messenger*, November 9, 1898.

courthouse, which had been inaugurated six years earlier, was a redbrick building with a central tower, fitted out with every Victorian bell and whistle. Men packed the gleaming corridors, overflowing from the main room. There, Solomon Fishblate, Wilmington's former Democratic mayor—a committed white supremacist, despite being Jewish—presided from the rostrum. Fishblate called the meeting to order and immediately beckoned Alfred Moore Waddell to the front of the room, asking him to take over as chairman.

"I was entirely ignorant of the subject of this meeting," Waddell began, with false naivete. "But it's always a pleasure, as well as a duty, to accept the call of the people of Wilmington."

Just before his summons to the front of the room, he explained to the crowd, Hugh MacRae had pulled him aside and handed him some documents.

"When I arrived here this morning, a set of resolutions was placed in my hands," Waddell announced. "And I most heartily approve of them!"

A round of applause shook the hall as Waddell shuffled the papers. He began to read from them in a stentorian voice, hoarier now.

"Believing that the constitution of the United States contemplated a government to be carried on by an enlightened people; believing that its framers did not anticipate the enfranchisement of an ignorant population of African origin; and believing that those men of the state of North Carolina, who joined in forming the union did not contemplate for their descendants subjection to an inferior race—"

Waddell took a breath.

"—we, the undersigned citizens of the city of Wilmington and the county of New Hanover do hereby declare that we will no longer be ruled, and we will never again be ruled by men of African origin."

The shouts of hundreds of white men rattled the building.

For the white supremacists in the audience, Waddell's statement provoked a feeling that bypassed relief and went straight to a vengeful form of ecstasy. The authors of the document sanctified their forefathers, not their children. They weren't so much invested in the future as they were in trying to turn the present into the past. Victory aroused in them the urge to punish because, in their view, power was a stolen good that had been rightfully theirs all along. After years of encrypted, legalistic protestations against "misrule" and "corruption," the city's white bosses were now explicitly declaring that white people didn't have to share power with Black people. And after sweeping the elections, they had additional means to back up their talk.

The resolution that Waddell read out to the raucous crowd became known as "The White Declaration of Independence." The first of its seven articles pointed to the high proportion of taxes that white people paid as a basis for their sovereignty over Black people. The second treated "unscrupulous white men" who voted and associated with them; the third faulted the Black man for "antagonizing our interest in every way," mostly by voting; and the fourth contended that the strength of Black labor in Wilmington was inhibiting economic growth.

With the remaining amendments, the authors laid out the future they wanted to see. They promised to take Black men's jobs and give them to white men. They pledged that they would punish any Black person who challenged their authority. The declaration's final clause was the longest and contained two specific demands: the *Record* editor Alexander Manly, the white men declared, must "leave this City forever within twenty-four hours after the issuance of this proclamation." And his printing press had to go with him.

The courthouse buzzed as Waddell read out the document's final pledge: "If the demand is agreed to, within twelve hours we counsel forbearance on the part of all white men. If the demand is refused or if no answer is given within the time mentioned then the editor, Manly, will be expelled by force." Just as Manly's editorial had served as a convenient pretext for stirring white anger in the lead-up to the election, his continued presence in the city now provided the perfect excuse for any further violence the white men wished to commit.

According to one observer, the crowd "rose to its feet as one man."

With the multitudes behind them, the leaders went further. Solomon Fishblate moved to amend the declaration so that it would require the Republican mayor, Silas Wright, and the Populist chief of police, John Melton, along with the entire board of aldermen, to immediately vacate their positions. Now, with the city government in the crowd's sights, the White Declaration of Independence was a blueprint for a coup d'état.

A committee of five men—Solomon Fishblate, George Rountree, Iredell Meares, Hugh MacRae, and Walker Taylor—was hastily appointed to consider the resolutions. "For my part, I've recently had enough of committees," one of them said, proposing to skip the technicalities and just get on with things. But the crowd insisted that the committee adjourn, as though an adherence to the fine points of parliamentary procedure would legitimize the conspiracy. In their absence, Waddell kept the audience entertained, extemporizing as though he were back on the campaign trail.

"Judging from the feeling manifested here today, the pot needs no more fuel to set it boiling," he said. "Our duty is to quietly and firmly consider the question. It is not necessary to violate the law, nor is it necessary to adopt violent measures."

The White Declaration was already extremely aggressive, both in terms of the promises it made to lower-class white people and in its hostility toward Black people of all stations. On top of that, the white leaders had tacked on a pledge to depose the city government. Less than three weeks earlier, Waddell had threatened to choke the Cape Fear River with carcasses.

So, it wasn't decency or scruples that kept him from endorsing the plot with full-throated belligerence. More likely, it was the desire for plausible deniability in a scheme of such brash, unprecedented illegality that its success was far from guaranteed. Waddell, a gambler, knew to hedge his bets.

"The editor of the *Record* will be dealt with," he assured the crowd.

A voice rang out from the masses in the hall.

"Fumigate the city with the *Record*!"

After a few more speeches, the committee returned to the courthouse chamber. Their verdict: The White Declaration of Independence was pretty much perfect just as it was. The document was again read aloud, put to a vote, and unanimously adopted. Four hundred and seventy-two white men ratified it. For many, it was a family occasion. Alfred Moore Waddell, of course, signed, as did Colonel Roger Moore. Four Bellamys—John Dillard, John Dillard Jr., Marsden, and Robert—added their names, accompanied by several close relatives. Brothers Hugh and Donald MacRae signed alongside their uncle Walter G. MacRae and their brother-in-law Walter Parsley, who signed alongside *his* brothers Robert and George. The declaration was as much a guest book as a political circular—its endorsers wanted you to know they'd been there.

Before closing the session, Waddell appointed the Committee of Twenty-Five to "vigorously carry out the action of the meeting." He assumed chairmanship and appointed two dozen white men as members, including Hugh MacRae. The committee immediately got to work, meeting again that afternoon in the rooms of the Merchants' Association in the Seaboard Air Line Railroad headquarters. Together, the twenty-five white men composed a letter, which they sent out to thirty-three leaders of the Black community. In language as bureaucratic as its terms were brutal, it began, "The following named colored citizens of Wilmington are requested to meet a committee of citizens appointed by authority of the meeting of businessmen and taxpayers held this morning."

The white leaders targeted Black men whose stability and prominence rivaled their own. Among them were a pair of barbers, three ministers, two lawyers, two doctors, a mortician, an oyster wholesaler, a stevedore, and a drayman. Many were active in the Republican Party. Others—such as Fred

Sadgwar, Carrie Manly's father—had connections to the *Record*. T. C. Miller, who had started in saloons and built up a thriving real estate and pawnbroking business, owned property valued at ten thousand dollars and lent money to both Black and white people. Dr. Thomas Mask, a physician, had just come home from a stint with the North Carolina Third Regiment in the Spanish-American War. Isham Quick had started by selling coal, owned multiple properties, and had recently helped to charter Wilmington's first Black-owned bank. What they had in common was that they were, in one way or another, men of consequence, whose judgment held sway in their community and whose well-being affected numerous others bound to them by ties of blood, religion, politics, or business. In the white men's estimation, they were the conduits who would carry the message of white aggression to the Black community with maximum impact.

Among them were two Howes: the builder John Harriss Howe and his cousin John Thomas Howe, who had lost his father to white violence on the streetcar six years earlier and was working as a traveling sales representative for the *Record* while serving a term in the North Carolina House. The letter ordered the men to appear at the Merchants' Association offices at six o'clock, "to consider a matter of grave consequence to the negroes of Wilmington." It presented a slate of uniformly dangerous forced choices, obliging each man to spontaneously navigate a course of moral and political chutes and ladders. Ignoring the letter was impossible. Heeding it, possibly worse.

Most of the men whose names appeared on the list ultimately decided it would be wiser to show up. Perhaps they hoped for a fair hearing, but from the moment they arrived at the Merchants' Association, it was clear that no such dialogue would take place. Adjusting his glasses, Waddell informed them "in a very graphic and determined way" of the passage of the White Declaration of Independence. "He firmly explained the purpose of the meeting and announced that the ultimatum was an ultimatum, and that no discussion would be allowed," the *Messenger* wrote.

The Committee of Colored Citizens, as the attendees came to be called, as though they had voluntarily come together, were the mirror image of the white Committee of Twenty-Five that sat across the table. So much of

Wilmington's talent and clout gathered that day in one room. The men who sat there could have accomplished great things together, but rather than seeking coalition, the white leaders moved to crush their Black peers. White grocer Charles Spencer lived and worked in the racially mixed Brooklyn neighborhood. John Harriss Howe had built Committee of Twenty-Five member Gabriel Holmes's house. The men who sold them eggs now wanted to take their jobs. Their livelihoods and perhaps even their lives were being threatened by people over whose heads they had literally put roofs.

The Black men's response to the white men was conciliatory but noncommittal. Reverend I. S. Lee, of St. Stephen Church, promised he would counsel the Manlys to comply with the white men's demands. W. E. Henderson, a lawyer, offered to broker an agreement under which the *Record* would agree to move out of town.

"The committee will give you until 7:30 tomorrow morning to bring a reply as to whether the resolutions will be complied with without the use of strong measures," Waddell announced, declaring the conversation over before it had even begun.

The Black men adjourned to a nearby barbershop and tried to formulate a plan. They were in no position to speak for Manly, nor did they represent the city's eleven thousand Black people in any capacity other than in the white imagination. Still, it was clear that the white men were serious, and that they required a prompt response. Someone produced a pen and a couple of sheets of lined paper. Armond Scott, a young lawyer out of Shaw University, wrote for the group, addressing their reply to Waddell.

"Dear Sir," it read. "We the colored citizens to whom was referred the matter of expulsion from this community of the person and press of A.L. Manly, beg most respectfully to say that we are in no wise responsible for nor in anyway endorse the obnoxious article that called forth your actions." Nonetheless, they pledged to use their influence to see that the white men's wishes were carried out, "in the interest of peace."

The group appointed the young attorney Scott to hand-deliver the letter to Waddell, at home on Fifth and Princess. It wasn't a long journey, only about six blocks, but it was a treacherous one. White supremacists manned checkpoints all over the city. Near the First Baptist Church, a group of Red Shirts were plotting to lynch Manly the next morning if the Committee of Colored Citizens didn't comply. It was dark and many of the white men were drunk on liquor as well as the prospect of a fight. Scott set out on foot, alone. At some point along the route, he decided that the errand bordered on suicidal. "Please Deliver at House," he wrote on the front of the envelope, dropping it into a mailbox.

THE NEXT MORNING AT EIGHT O'CLOCK, WADDELL HAD STILL NOT RE-ceived the Committee of Colored Citizens' reply. So he grabbed his rifle and walked a block and a half to the WLI Armory, where hundreds of hopped-up white men awaited him. In fact, Waddell was aware that no correspondence would be forthcoming that morning—word had already come that Armond Scott had dropped the letter in the mailbox rather than hand-delivering it. But Waddell chose to suppress this information, using the putative lack of response from the CCC to further rile up the white mob.

The WLI brass knew it would look bad for the unit, which was part of the North Carolina National Guard, to destroy the *Record* under official command. Colonel Roger Moore would have been an obvious civilian choice to lead the men, but he was tied up with his paramilitary block patrols. He had asked Waddell to call for him if the men were going to attack the *Record*, but Waddell recognized that the momentary vacuum of leadership presented an opportunity and decided to take charge of the mob himself.

More than a thousand white men now filled the streets "as if by magic," forming columns as long as two city blocks. Waddell and representatives from the Secret Nine and the Red Shirts installed themselves at the head of the formation. They marched up Market, one of the city's main drags, and across Seventh Street heading toward the *Record*. The Populist chief of police reported that it took an hour for the entire procession to pass him by. "Flushed by victory, they hastened to emphasize their return to power," a sympathetic observer wrote, boasting that "they resorted to no secrecy or mask." He added, "What they did was done in broad daylight; and the entire proceeding suggested the stateliness of a Greek tragedy."

The mob arrived at the *Record* and Waddell, accompanied by a couple of men, marched up to the door. They knocked. No one answered, so they broke down the door. They trashed the place, pulling down kerosene lamps and smashing them on the floor. The building went up in flames as the ransackers threw trophies—a beaver hat, a crayon drawing of Manly—down to the crowd, which tore them to pieces. Later, Waddell claimed that the blaze was unintentional, but allowed, winkingly, that it was "possible that some fellow set it afire with a match."

BY THE TIME THE MOB CAME KNOCKING WITH THEIR GUNS AND MATCHES, Manly was long gone. He had fled Wilmington the night before after a visit from Thomas Clawson, the editor of the *Messenger*.

Clawson had sold Manly his printing press on credit some months earlier. On the evening of November 9, he had called at the *Record*'s offices to see about the machine, which the White Declaration of Independence had condemned to destruction. A white supremacist himself, Clawson was as concerned about the fate of the press as that of the man who operated it. But he knew that the Red Shirts were planning "a pre-arranged 'lynching' and burning party," and his visit, he recalled later, impressed upon Manly the seriousness of the threat to his life. Soon, Manly had slipped off into the night.

Later, Carrie Sadgwar Manly remembered the circumstances of her fiancé's departure from Wilmington differently than Clawson. In her telling, a white friend of Alexander's sent word to him that he was going to be lynched and needed to get out of town immediately. The correspondent enclosed aid for the road: money and a signal that would enable him to move through the checkpoints set up by Colonel Roger Moore's paramilitaries. Carrie wrote, "His friend gave him $25.00 and said, 'This is the pass word and May God be with you boy, you are too fine to be swung up to a tree."

Alexander and his brother Frank set out in one buggy, followed by another in which rode two other *Record* employees. They made it as far as the Fulton Bridge before a watchman called out, "Halt!"

The men furnished the password, leading the watchman to strike up a more relaxed conversation.

"We're having a necktie party tonight," he said. "Where are you gentlemen going?"

"We're going after that scoundrel Manly," the group responded, on cue.

The Manly brothers and their employees put on a convincing enough show of enthusiasm that they were able to pass through the checkpoint unperceived. "All four of them looked like white men and they didn't know the difference," Carrie recalled.

THE ALARM AT THE CAPE FEAR STEAM FIRE ENGINE COMPANY WAS SHRIEKing. Someone had triggered the alert from Box 51, at the corner of Seventh and Nun streets, and the company's firefighters, a few of them still bleary-eyed, rushed around the firehouse. Valentine Howe, the company's foreman, was likely among them. They ran out the door, throwing saddles on their horses and hitching up the engine in a blur. The alarm was coming from the next block over.

No sooner were they out the door than something bizarre happened. A brawny white man named Tuck Savage blocked the firemen at the corner of Sixth and Castle, explaining that he was acting on orders from the city's fire chief. At this point, Valentine Howe had been a volunteer firefighter for thirty-five years, earning citations of valor from white people with regularity. This was surely the first time they had tried to stop him from risking his life to save someone else's property.

As Savage held Valentine and his men back, they could see black smoke billowing from Seventh Street and hear the commotion of shouting men. At last, Savage let the Black firefighters pass: The fire was spreading, with sparks flying from the *Record* building onto the roofs of neighboring buildings, and they were needed to contain the damage. They proceeded up Castle Street and onto Seventh, where white men lined the sidewalks, firing their guns into the air in ominous greeting. Soon, Valentine and his crew arrived on the scene, where a kerosene fire was blazing on the building's second story. The firefighters were used to danger, but this time they faced human menace in addition to the natural threat.

The squad ignored the jeering crowd and fought the flames as the white arsonists looked on, but their skill was outmatched by the intensity of the blaze. By the time they had put the fire out, the building was in ruins. The roof and two of the second-floor walls were burned out entirely, leaving the two remaining walls teetering in the background. "We wrecked the house," Waddell boasted soon after. In the street out front, a hose coiled around a denuded tree like a dead snake.

Eventually, the firefighters managed to climb up to the second floor, where the remains of the *Record* lay soaked and smoldering. The only thing they could identify were the charred remains of Alexander Manly's printing press, still hot to the touch.

THE WHITE MEN PARADED BACK TO THE WLI ARMORY, WHERE WADDELL congratulated them on a job well done. The white supremacists would claim that they had simply wanted to put the *Record* out of business, that Alexander Manly was the sole target of their campaign, that the rest of the violence was reactive and spontaneous, rather than planned and predetermined. The plotters, in any case, had lost control of the action, and the city was erupting into chaos. The accounts that would be recorded in its wake are contradictory and often muddled by partisanship or panic, but one thing is clear: White men planned the violence, initiated it, and sustained it over a period of some hours, and Black people almost exclusively paid the price.

Down at James Sprunt's wharf, news of the arson at the *Record* reached several hundred Black workers. The employees, according to one newspaper, gathered near Sprunt's cotton compress "in a state of bewilderment, wondering what happened and what might eventuate." Something very strange was going on: Fire bells were ringing, the white bosses were whispering in each other's ears. Some of the workers' wives showed up, breathless. White people, they reported, had burned down the *Record* and Black neighborhoods would be next.

As the Black men stuck at work worried about their wives and children, white men zigged and zagged around the city. One group of Red Shirts peeled off from the WLI march and rode the streetcar around its Sixth Street route, giddily firing off their weapons. "They're fighting at Sprunt's, you better go get your gun," one white man yelled to another in the street as he walked to work. Meanwhile, Democratic heavyweights rushed down to the compress, where Sprunt was attempting to persuade the workers to stay at work, promising that he would keep them safe.

Soon, a crowd of white men had congregated at the wharf, guns slung over their shoulders. They had heard that the Black workers had walked off the job and that they were preparing to launch a retaliatory attack. Ready to "kill the whole gang of Negroes," the white mob looked to their higher-ups for permission. But when they tried to press Colonel Roger Moore into leading them, he declined, warning that he would have anyone who defied his orders placed under arrest. Captain Donald MacRae had arrived at the compress with a riot gun, two pistols, seventy-five pounds of cartridges, and "a bowie knife or two," but he, too, ordered the white mob to stand down. "I had very little stomach for it and as very few of the Negroes were armed, it was little less than murder that they proposed," he admitted. George Rountree got on the telephone and called the armory for the mounted machine gun, which he later admitted "was a fool thing to do."

"What have we done?" one of the workers asked him.

"I had no answer, they had done nothing," Rountree later recalled.

Sprunt was a paternalistic boss who prided himself on taking care of his workers. With the threat of immediate violence defused, he eventually began dispatching white chaperones to accompany his men back to Brooklyn and elsewhere in small groups. Some of them made it home, but others were turned back by paramilitary patrols. Jim Reeves, a cotton weigher, set out from the compress but ran into "guards, with their guns, on every corner." This so terrified him that he sprinted back to the office. When he arrived, he ran into a storeroom and jumped into a huge container. "That was ten o'clock in the morning, and I lay there til the middle of the afternoon," he recalled. "I never saw or heard a thing for I was fifteen feet deep in cotton."

AS MIDDAY APPROACHED, WHITE LEADERS STILL BELIEVED THEY WERE IN control of the situation. Amped-up white militias circulated around the city as hundreds of anxious Black men attempted to make their ways from the waterfront, on the city's western limit, to their homes farther inland. Sometime midmorning, the two groups converged in Brooklyn, at the intersection of Fourth and Harnett. The white group gathered near Heyer's grocery store, on the southwest corner, facing off against a Black group standing outside Walker's grocery store, catty-corner across the street. As insults flew back and forth, cooler-headed citizens tried to deescalate the situation. "For the sake of your lives, your families, your children, and your country, go home and stay there!" one Black man cried out. Aaron Lockamy, a white police officer, ran back and forth between both groups, begging them to disperse.

Then, a shot whizzed across the intersection. Black witnesses later claimed that the white crowd fired first; white witnesses claimed the opposite. (Lockamy, for his part, testified that only the white men had guns.) As soon as the shooting began, the white men unleashed a torrent of bullets, immediately killing three Black men. Several more wounded Black men staggered into nearby houses and others took off sprinting down Harnett Street, firing back at the white aggressors. "All hell broke loose," one witness later recalled. B. F. Keith said later that once the white men got started, they were uncontainable, "like striking a match to an old field of broomstraw on a windy day."

One of the Colonel's block patrol captains picked up the telephone and alerted him to activate the "riot alarm," summoning the WLI and the naval reserves to Brooklyn. Soon, white men—paramilitary volunteers as well as real soldiers, representing the United States government—were pouring into the neighborhood, inflamed by the news that several white men had been wounded. Word of the bloodshed in Wilmington was circulating fast on the telegraph wires: "Negroes Shooting and Killing Whites," one report read. Governor Russell sent a message to Colonel Walker Taylor, declaring that the military in the city was now under his command.

Chapter 19

MOTHER'S TATTERED SHAWL

On November 10, Athalia Howe, some eighteen years old, was at home in Brooklyn. Her father, William, had started work at the break of day down at the docks, where he was employed at the Sprunt Cotton Compress as "boss stevedore." William was Fred Howe's oldest son—born outside of marriage, but his existence was no secret in the family. Though William was acknowledged in a loose web of family relations, he had not inherited property from Fred, as had his half siblings. He and his family lived in Brooklyn, about thirty minutes' walk from the more impressive Howe homestead on Queen and Third. The physical distance between the branches of the family reflected a corresponding class difference. With the establishment of Williston, the entrepreneurial south-side Howes were entering the teaching profession. Meanwhile the Brooklyn Howes toiled as manual laborers, influential in their own working-class milieu, but lacking the same station and resources.

Athalia was the second of William's three daughters. Augusta, three years her senior, was likely out at work. Carrie was only three and may have been underfoot, buzzing around their mother, Mary. Athalia was likely in the middle of the morning's chores when terror came to her doorstep, confusing at first and then so clear that its memory marked her for life.

She had risen early that morning. Bustling around the house, she took a moment to watch a neighbor heading out to work. A few hours later, looking out the window of her house, she saw the same man running back toward his yard. Before he made it there, a white man on horseback stopped him and then shot him in the street as Athalia watched. They were dragging him somewhere. Athalia called to her mother, who quickly understood what was happening. Mary gathered her daughters and headed out the back door, toward St. Stephen Church.

The Howes ran west, darting between houses, gathering other women and children along the way. They figured they would be safe in a house of worship. But when they got there, more white men on horseback forbade them from entering the church. Their commander had primed them for maximum carnage as they neared Brooklyn: "Now boys I want to tell you right now I want you all to load and when I give the command to shoot, I want you to shoot to kill." Farther downtown, gangs of Red Shirts were detaining Black men at their workplaces, refusing to let them return to their homes. Women and children were left, a witness later wrote, "shrieking and crying in the midst of the flying balls and in the sight of cannons and the Gatling gun."

The white men aimed the machine gun at the front entrance to St. Stephen, threatening to "blaze away" if Rev. Lee didn't let them into the church. Standing in the doorway, Lee urged calm. But the men, who said they had heard that Black churches were "stacked with men and guns," stormed past him. Immediately they tore the place apart, transforming the sanctuary into a war zone. Then, they left as abruptly as they had come. They had found nothing, one member of the WLI later recalled, but piles of election flyers.

The WLI men told Lee that he would have to come with them. "The mob took the leading colored ministers and compelled them to go around the city with them and ask the colored people to be obedient to the white people and go in their homes and keep quiet," Rev. J. Allen Kirk, of the Central Baptist Church, later recalled. "This was a great humiliation for us and a shame upon our denominations." Seeing their pastor hauled off at gunpoint, Athalia and her mother understood that the white paramilitaries would stop at nothing. Their survival was in their own hands.

They ran northeast, back in the direction of their house, which they passed by without stopping, continuing until they had reached the damp, rustling expanse of Pine Forest Cemetery, where they had buried generations of kin. Hundreds of fellow refugees joined them there, seeking to preserve their lives amid a backdrop of death. Pine Forest had several advantages as a hiding place: It sat on the edge of town, it was densely wooded, and it was a place where few white people had ever set foot. Hundreds of Black people found each other there, sharing information and aid. Others waded through miles of treacherous swampland or stole away on northbound trains, staring straight ahead as the miles ticked by.

Pine Forest was a miserable and even potentially lethal place to pass a mid-November night, especially for the scores of hastily dressed children, "wrapped in mother's tattered shawl." As dusk approached, clouds rolled in and a freezing rain began to fall, drenching encampments of dazed families, as one magazine correspondent observed, "fearful to light fires, listening for chance footsteps crushing fallen twigs, shuddering and peering gray-faced into the darkness, wailing, waiting—they knew not for what."

Athalia and Mary had had no word from William. They had to find a way to keep Carrie warm. From the sodden darkness, an infant's cry mingled with a woman's singing:

When the battle's over we can wear a crown
In the new Je-ru-sa-lem

Athalia Howe's first cousin Nada McDonald lived across town at 301 Queen Street, in the house that Fred Howe, their grandfather, had built. He had left it to her mother, Rebecca. Now Rebecca and her husband, Robert McDonald—a Bahamas-born tailor, with a downtown shop catering to the white gentry—lived there with their children: Nada and her siblings, Alfreda, age two, and Edna, age one.

The atmosphere inside the McDonald house was more bookish than that of the Brooklyn Howes. Their neighborhood was also considerably whiter. On one side of the McDonalds lived the W. R. Halls—a white grocery salesman and his two teenage daughters. On the other lived the J. W. Grays—a white carpenter, his dressmaker wife, and their fourteen-year-old daughter. Another neighboring white family had eight children, and if they weren't in school, they worked at the cotton mills, like their parents, as carders, weavers, and spinners. As a result of their business dealings, in both construction and bespoke tailoring, the McDonalds also counted many of the city's prominent white people among their connections.

The McDonalds were almost certainly the senior homeowners on the block, their title to the property reaching all the way back to Anthony Howe's acquisition in the mid-1800s. On Election Day, they stuck close to familiar territory. Nada, like Athalia, was at home when the pogrom began. But because of her family's proximity to white people, she remained largely protected from the physical violence to which Athalia had been so harshly exposed. "We were the only Negro family in a white neighborhood," Nada later wrote. "The fact that our relationship had been friendly bore fruit that night."

Nada, who would grow up to become the head librarian at the Wilmington Colored Library, was a pedagogue to the core. Her account of her experience of 1898, written sometime in adulthood, was titled "A Historical Incident," and after several paragraphs of bland historical summary, she addressed 1898 directly:

> The Red Shirts paraded the streets and kept the Negro from the polls. Every able-bodied white was armed. They were to march into Negro homes, arrest the inmates, pillage the home, and then set fire to the house. The Negroes arrested were to be marched out of town. Those who resisted were to be killed on the spot.
>
> The home of my parents was one of those so designated. . . . Our neighbors kept vigilance all night November 10, 1898. The teenage boys and the men surrounded our home. They were armed with guns, bayonets, hatchets, and any tool that could be used as a weapon of defense. The women served hot coffee, hot bread, and sandwiches. They went on guard duty at sundown and remained until after sunrise.
>
> We were saved from being slaughtered and our home was left intact. Many, many Negroes were killed, marched out of town, and their life-savings taken from them.

The McDonalds weren't the only elite Black family with white protectors who shielded them from immediate physical harm. John E. Taylor, the deputy collector of customs, wrote to his brother Robert R. Taylor, the in-house architect at Tuskegee, in outrage at the "political murders" that had taken place in Wilmington. Because Taylor was a federal official, the white conspirators strategically exempted him from their summons to Black community leaders; even the marauding Red Shirts knew that an attack on him was out of the question. When the fighting broke out on November 10, Taylor was able to send a carriage to bring his children home from school. As at the McDonalds', white volunteers kept overnight watch at the family's home.

More than a century later, the preferential treatment accorded to her Taylor ancestors troubled Barbara Bell Coleman, a philanthropic consultant in Newark, New Jersey. "My husband raised the horrific question, which for me was just too much to take in," she recalled. "He asked me, 'Barbara, do you think they were complicit in some way, and that's why they didn't leave?' I was horrified, and of course I was angry with him, but, you know what, it has always been in the back of my mind." Coleman ultimately considered her nagging unease as a tertiary consequence of 1898: an event so painful that survivors refused to talk about it, leaving subsequent generations grasping to fill in the blanks. "They were very quiet, and I feel, in many ways, almost secretive about their pasts," Coleman recalled. "I think it had so much more to do with shame."*

The historian June Nash interpreted these vigils through the lens of class as well as race. Collecting testimony from Black survivors and their children in 1968, she found that many members of the Black upper crust remembered the mob as a poor-white phenomenon, "an outside rabble without leadership." One of the people she interviewed was Crummell McDonald, Nada's youngest brother, who gently defended the white elite, remembering that "it seemed that the aristocrats were beginning to lose

---

*Coleman served as an early reader for *The Human Stain* by Philip Roth, a Newark acquaintance. She told him about a light-skinned cousin's "blow hair," meaning hair that was fine enough to move around in a breeze, and he imported the expression into the book, using it in a passage about the racial anxieties of his white-passing protagonist, Coleman Silk.

control of the situation here to the poor what they call buckra, the people that they didn't even consider for many, many years." (If a white "buckra" called at an aristocrat's house, McDonald noted, he was forced to use the back door.) Nash also examined the influence of class on Black families' experiences, arguing that lower-class Black people were more likely to have been targeted for violence. Many of the people who were fired on, she surmised, "were not known to the 'old Negro families' of Wilmington but were sons of field slaves who had come from Georgia and South Carolina to work in the Sprunt cotton press."

Unlike the working-class Halseys, for whom proximity to white people equated to risk, the upper-class Howes had long-standing relationships with white people who saw them as deserving of protection. These ties kept them physically safe, but they didn't prevent them from experiencing 1898 as a singular trauma. For all her tendency toward dry exposition, Nada McDonald Cotton wrote with potent clarity about the white supremacists' murderous intent:

> This outrage, which resulted in rule by white supremacy, is called the Wilmington riot. It was really the Wilmington massacre.

Nada's Bahamian father, Robert, was a British citizen. Amid the mayhem, he went to see James Sprunt, who, in addition to being a wildly successful cotton merchant, then served as the British vice-consul at Wilmington. Sprunt gave Robert a "large English flag," telling him that he should wrap himself up in it whenever he went into town. His son remembered, "He wore that flag back and forth daily as long as that affair lasted."

Robert and his family had been spared bodily harm, but their world had decisively changed. Thousands of citizens remained shivering in Pine Forest. Robert's decision to swaddle himself in the English flag represented another kind of retreat, a symbolic withdrawal from the American grotesque and from a Black American identity that exposed him to the horrors of seeing his neighbors shot in the streets and his city illegally seized. Regardless of their background and status, Black Wilmingtonians knew that they would face excruciating choices in the coming days.

Chapter 20

IN TERROREM

Sometime after noon, the Wilmington Light Infantry came flying into Brooklyn in flatbed wagons drawn by "fiery big horses," trailed by members of the naval reserves. Almost immediately, they came across a group of Black men. Members of the unit would later claim that a sniper started shooting at them. Whether or not that is true, they opened fire. One Black survivor recalled that the soldiers were ready to blast away "for the least expression of manhood," as though they were "great sportsmen firing at rabbits in an open field."

Quickly, the white gunmen fanned out around the neighborhood. One unit went speeding over to Joshua Halsey's block at Sixth and Bladen, where, rumor had it, someone had fired at a white man from a shack. The gunman in the shack proved elusive, so the militia, led by Colonel Walker Taylor, decided to search a square just across the intersection, known as Manhattan Park.

The park housed several Black businesses, including a dance hall, enclosed by a tall wooden fence. The militia started shooting the machine gun straight into the park. Its .44-caliber bullets were so powerful that they sawed the planks of the fence clean in half. As craters appeared in the walls of the dance hall, a Black man who had taken shelter there went running out the back door.

"Halt!" the white gunmen called, still firing, as a crowd cheered. The man made a run for it but found himself blocked in on the park's far side. As he tried to fling himself over the fence, the white gunmen unleashed a fusillade, riddling the man's body with "fifteen or twenty bullets." One of the shooters thought the encounter was hilarious, boasting, "When we turned him ove', Mistah N—— had a look of s'prise on his count'nance, I ashore you!"

The militia hacked down the rest of the fence with axes and charged into the park, flinging open the door of the dance hall. Inside they found Joshua Halsey, along with a handful of Black men, one of them armed. When the militia ordered the men to surrender, Joshua darted out the door. Some people speculate that he may not have understood their commands, because of a hearing impairment. It's also possible that he understood them perfectly and decided to take his chances in the court of decisive action, rather than consigning himself to the kind of justice that the white men were meting out. The evidence suggests that Joshua just wanted out of there. Had he been a fugitive sniper, as the white men alleged, he could have easily disappeared into the neighborhood. Instead, he ran home, got into bed, and crawled under the covers.

The leaders of the militia dispatched a patrol to track Joshua down. One WLI member recalled that a detail was "lined up in front of Hill Terry's house and given orders to find this negro Halsey." (Hill Terry was Halsey's neighbor and a prominent Red Shirt.) Whether he knew it or not, Joshua was now a marked man. Did his wife Sallie's accident factor into the militia's decision to go after him? Did the white men, on account of the Halseys' lawsuit, consider him another one of the "insolent Negroes"—failing to yield on the sidewalks, falling through bridges and expecting white taxpayers to compensate them—that they'd been trying to quell for thirty years? Or was he just in the wrong place at the wrong time?

The militia tore apart every house in the vicinity. Finally, someone gave up Joshua's address. One of his young daughters saw the soldiers marching toward the family's home. "His poor little child ran in and begged her father to get up and run for the soldiers were coming after him," Jane Cronly, a white witness, wrote. A gauntlet of white men awaited Joshua.

"The poor creature jumped up and ran out of the back door in frantic terror only to be shot down like a dog by armed soldiers ostensibly sent to preserve the peace."

BY MIDAFTERNOON ON NOVEMBER 10, THE WHITE SUPREMACISTS HAD accomplished many of their goals. The state had been "redeemed" by Democrats, Manly was gone, the *Daily Record* was in ashes, and those they considered troublemakers were either dead or being rounded up. But the city government was still in Fusionist hands, with another year to go before the current mayor and board of aldermen were up for reelection. At four o'clock, members of the Committee of Twenty-Five gathered at City Hall, accompanied by more than a hundred armed men, who blocked the building's hallways. Their message was clear: Capitulation was the only way out. Behind closed doors, the self-appointed Democratic guardians of the city forced the mayor to resign and then turned their attention to the aldermen. Never mind that they had been democratically elected. Never mind that the overthrow amounted to a coup. "Under the form of law, but *in terrorem* [they] made each officer resign *seriatim*, filling his place with a reputable citizen and property holder," John Dillard Bellamy Jr. recalled, straining to bury bayonet law in courtroom Latin.

Six white men and three Black men went into the room as aldermen. They emerged powerless, having ceded their offices to members of the Committee of Twenty-Five, including Hugh MacRae and J. Allan Taylor of the Secret Nine, and their allies. The police chief was out, too. The mayor was replaced by a triumphant Alfred Moore Waddell. When the door opened again, an all-white board of aldermen, a white police chief, and a white mayor walked out. The most critical phase of the so-called 1898 revolution had been achieved, replacing an interracial coalition with a new regime whose singular goal was to make Wilmington white again.

Chapter 21

OMELETS

Alexander Manly's fiancée, Carrie Sadgwar, an accomplished soprano, was in Europe in the fall of 1898, completing an extended tour of the Continent with the famed Fisk Jubilee Singers. "The choir, led by Mr. F. J. Loudin is wholly composed of members of the coloured race from the Southern States of the American Union," one British paper explained, performing "sacred glees, part-songs, and hymns, which were composed by negroes of the plantations in the old slave days."*

On the morning of November 11, the group was preparing for an evening concert in London. Picture it: Sadgwar descends and takes her breakfast, picking up a copy of a London newspaper in a clattering hotel dining room smelling of rashers and beans. That day, *The Guardian*, the *Evening Standard*, and *The Telegraph* all gave prominent placement to a telegram report chronicling the "BLOODSHED AT WILMINGTON." In a foreign city, Sadgwar learns of the destruction of the tight-knit community to which she has belonged since birth, about the burning of her fiancé's beloved paper, *The Daily Record*. The newspaper notes that "eight negroes have been killed and two wounded." Her family is unaccounted for. Of her fiancé, the paper offers only, "Manly and his associates fled and cannot be found."

---

*Sadgwar's singing was so distinctive that, according to the writer John Jeremiah Sullivan, it inspired the Black British composer Samuel Coleridge-Taylor to write "A Negro Love Song." Musicologists point to the composition as the earliest surviving example of sheet music indicating the "blue note"—the flattened third, fourth, and seventh of the blues scale.

Sadgwar has to perform that night. She walks out on the stage, thoughts of "blood hounds" racing through her head as she stands under the hot lights. When she opens her mouth to sing, her voice wobbles—and then fades out entirely, like a music box winding down. "A doctor came backstage and said this child has had a shock," Sadgwar later recalled to her sons. "Do you know boys, my voice has never been the same since." Writing with fifty-five years' remove, Sadgwar still found the incident too painful to discuss at length. "The tears will blot this if I don't stop," she concluded, "so I will say good night."

BACK IN WILMINGTON, NOVEMBER 11 WAS UNSEASONABLY WARM—SEVENTY degrees under a clear sky. The Secret Nine set to ridding the city of anyone they didn't like who hadn't already left. A list went out: T. C. Miller, the city's richest Black man, was on it, alongside entrepreneurial Black men such as Salem Bell and Robert Pickens (who owned a fish and oyster business together), Ari Bryant (a self-employed butcher), and Carter Peamon (a barber). Politically engaged white men such as John Melton (the newly deposed police chief), G. Z. French (the "carpetbagging" deputy sheriff), and Robert Bunting (the United States commissioner in Wilmington, who lived with a Black woman and had spoken up for Black suffrage) were also targeted for banishment. When the Red Shirts found that Bunting and his common-law wife had already fled, they ripped gold-framed portraits of the couple out of their house and strung them up on Market Street, suspended between telephone poles, "with large black letters on the big pieces of canvas heralding their miscegenation."

WLI units scoured the city for their targets, snatching six Black men from a barbershop, for instance, and "toss[ing] [them] into Burkheimer's wagon like cordwood." Now, with their handpicked slate of candidates installed at City Hall, the conspirators controlled the police force as well as the paramilitaries. Almost as soon as he had taken oath, the new police chief went to T. C. Miller's home at Castle and Third, just a block down from the Howe homestead, and demanded that he surrender. Miller had a lot to lose. He had made a fortune flipping real estate, and he loaned money to both Black and white people, vying with white buyers for valuable lots at courthouse auctions. After being summoned by the Committee of Twenty-Five, he had decided to remain in the city.

Miller tried to resist the kidnappers, but his daughter was watching. "He was one negro we could not make keep quiet and he talked and talked until Ed McKoy's gun went 'click click' and when he told him to shut up, he kept a little quieter," one WLI member recalled. Fearing a violent scene, Miller eventually agreed to be taken to the city jail. As he pulled away, his daughter ran out into the street. "She followed the wagon that was conveying her father to the city jail, wailing and moaning all the way," one account recalled. "Enroute to the prison, Miller said he would rather be dead than to have to suffer such humiliation, whereupon one of his captors informed him that if he really had no desire to live, to leap from the wagon and his last wishes would be granted instantly."

Miller was tossed into jail and held overnight, "for safe keeping." Word of his detainment got around, and that night, a band of Red Shirts crowded around the building, clamoring for him and other prisoners. The high-placed white men who had ordered the arrests knew it would reflect poorly on the new regime if they allowed a rabble to lynch the captives. Subsequent accounts credited Colonel Roger Moore and Captain Walter MacRae—Hugh's uncle, who had just been appointed sheriff—with fending off the mob and keeping the prisoners alive until the next morning.

Just after daybreak, the prisoners were brought out of the jail and into the street. Members of the WLI "formed a hollow square around these . . . objectionable men," parading them through town as onlookers showered them with abuse and humiliation. A man wearing a "special police badge" jumped out of the scrum and thrashed Melton, the ousted police chief, with the butt of a rifle. The crowd taunted him with shouts of "White n——!"—per the *Star*, "the least of the insulting names." These expulsions were not random by-products of the coup; they were the cruel, culminating ritual of what one observer called "this war of purification." Ever conscious of appearances, the new board of aldermen reimbursed the Atlantic Coast Line Railroad $61.70 for fares that were overlooked in the excitement.

It was a point of pride for white supremacists such as the Colonel that the banishment phase of the coup was carried out according to their specifications, rather than left to the whims of the mob. In the same way enslavers often claimed that they treated the people they enslaved decently, without acknowledging the barbarous framework of the entire institution, the white orchestrators of 1898 pointed to these moments of comparatively restrained behavior as evidence of the honorable nature of the "revolution."

Over time, family members focused on these incidents, wringing claims to heroism out of their kin's ignoble acts by selectively forgetting the larger context. Sometime after the Colonel's death, his widow wrote a letter to the *Wilmington Messenger*, asserting that her husband and an associate—not Alfred Moore Waddell, as some claimed—were the "appointed and recognized leaders in that revolution." Mrs. Moore was at once proud of her husband's involvement in 1898 and keen that he be remembered as a moral exemplar. To resolve this paradox, she homed in on his performance at the jail, writing that he refused to succumb to pressure "to give the order to fire on the negroes." She asserted, "In his own words: 'I will do nothing of the kind, there will be no murder done today whatever else is done,' and so a great calamity was averted, not only in the way of preventing bloodshed, but the fair name of Wilmington was saved also."

White paramilitaries escort Black men marked for banishment to the city jail, November 11, 1898.

WHILE THE WHITE ELITE CHERRY-PICKED THE ASPECTS OF THE MASSACRE that they wanted to be associated with, the Black masses had few such choices. "If I had a job for Mrs. So-and-So, I just had to get up and go back to work," one Black woman said later. Thousands of Black residents did so, braving checkpoints and searches to deliver delicacies for celebratory white supremacy banquets and to launder their white employers' clothing, still encrusted with soot and blood and gun oil from the previous day's spree. Their friends and neighbors were still hiding in cemeteries and swamps, cold and starving. One federal official reported that "nearly a dozen infants were born and died, in many instances with their mothers the victims of exposure." Yet James Worth, a white railroad investor, wrote to his wife, Josephine, whom he'd sent away to a safer part of the state, that all was dandy in Wilmington. He assured her that George, a Black man in their employ, was "back at work again and is happy as can be[,] whistling at his work—I am quite satisfied that he as well as all the best darkies are glad the change has been made."

Overnight, professional opportunity for educated Black people disappeared, liquidated alongside the *Record*. Before the coup, for example, the city's four Black lawyers had vied with their white peers for clients and courtroom glory. Now at least three of them had been terrorized out of the city. W. E. Henderson, considered the most sparkling jurist of the group, fled to Indianapolis. There, seemingly shell-shocked, he recounted his experiences to a large crowd at an AME church, a local newspaper reported, "in a low voice, so low as at times to be almost inaudible."

Henderson had moved to Wilmington only a year earlier, after having successfully defended a Black man who was charged with murdering a white man during a corn shucking. Wilmington, he believed, was a beacon of Black progress. He decided to invest in real estate, putting four hundred dollars down on a house. Racing out of town, he was forced to sell his stake back to the original seller, for an eighth of its value. Henderson begged the man for seventy-five dollars to buy last-minute train tickets for his family of twelve. The man refused.

Armond Scott, the young lawyer who had dropped the Committee of Colored Citizens' letter in the mailbox instead of hand-delivering it to Waddell, also fled north. Notified via his father that "his presence in the city would not be tolerated," he had snuck onto a train, unnoticed by a horde of Red Shirts who were busy trying to lynch the white Republican deputy sheriff G. Z. French. "[Scott] has been entirely too pretentious to suit the tastes of our people—in fact, he is obnoxious," the *Messenger* wrote, announcing his banishment. "He has cause to be thankful that he had distance between him and the persons who were after him." The *Wilmington Morning Star* reported that five white citizens had put him on the train, with "specific orders never to return to Wilmington under any circumstance in the future."

William A. Moore, another Black lawyer, made it onto a northbound train only to find that it was swarming with Red Shirts. When he tried to get off the train—120 miles north, but still in North Carolina—they forced him back into the car. "This completely unstrung the most pitiful colored lawyer, for he had heard their threats, their determination to remove him from the earth," wrote Rev. J. Allen Kirk, of the Central Baptist Church, who was fleeing town on the same train. Kirk recalled a hair-raising journey throughout which the Red Shirts "sat gazing upon both of us like a lion watching his prey." As the train pulled into Wilson, Moore realized that he'd run out of money. He asked the white men if he might continue north to Rocky Mount. "Then they began to curse and swear and said they would rather send him down to hell," Kirk recalled. While the white men gathered in the first-class car to decide upon his fate, Moore leapt from the moving train.

WEEKS LATER, ALFRED MOORE WADDELL ASSURED THE NATION THAT THE violent overthrow of Wilmington's municipal government had, in fact, been a peaceful handover—voluntary and perfectly legitimate. "We didn't really have anything to do with it," he wrote, putting his case forward in an essay for *Collier's*. "They asked us whom we wanted. Successively they resigned, and our men were elected. The room was as quiet as a room in a private house."

Mayor Waddell: Like Colonel Waddell, it had a ring to it, even if its bearer had come by neither title honestly. Waddell, who had been waiting for a position commensurate with his self-importance all his life, sprang into action. In one of his first acts as mayor he sent emissaries to lure the refugees back to the city, promising that they would "not be harmed if they go quietly about their work and maintain an inoffensive deportment." He was less concerned with offering reassurance to the Black population than he was with placating white bosses, who had suddenly found themselves short of crucial labor.

The white supremacists had laid waste to the city's physical, political, and social infrastructures. Now the campaign began to reboot their businesses and sanitize their reputations. Waddell hired new white policemen, dissolved the Black fire department, and forced a few remaining Fusionists out of office. People who were unsure of their status and wished to stay in the city appeared at City Hall to seek his personal blessing, which he conferred or withheld, like the hereditary dynast that, in many senses, he was.

"We have taken a city as thoroughly, as completely, as if captured in battle," Rev. Peyton Hoge proclaimed from the pulpit at First Presbyterian, the Sunday after the massacre. "It has been redeemed for civilization, redeemed for law, and redeemed for decency and respectability." Across the city, white clergymen congratulated their flocks on their Christian bravery and resolve. "After this week, I feel that I really know Wilmington and love it," Rev. C. T. Blackwell, of First Baptist, told the *Messenger*. In Blackwell's view, the massacre was already yielding positive effects. Black people, "a childish race," were more obedient on the sidewalks. Even actual Black children were benefiting, Blackwell claimed: The "riot" had "put a lasting good . . . into their wooly heads." As a man of the cloth, Blackwell wasn't bothered by the taking of lives. "That a few Negroes were shot was a mere incident," he said with a shrug. "You can't make an omelet without breaking a few eggs."

Quickly, the state's white elite closed ranks around Waddell's government. "My dear Colonel, Just a few lines to congratulate you on your courage and the people of Wilmington on their nerve," the editor of *The Charlotte Observer* wrote, adding that he was enclosing a copy of the next day's paper, "in which I have endeavoured to give the public an idea of the character of Wilmington's new mayor." North Carolina expatriates sent tidings from Pueblo, Colorado, and from Baltimore, Maryland, praising Waddell for having "dragged the dear old state out of the slough of black mud and degradation, into which she was fast sinking."

Weeks earlier, Waddell had vowed to fill the river with carcasses. Now he maneuvered to lure Black workers such as William Howe, who had made it through the massacre unharmed, back to the factories and the wharves. With an eye toward public relations, he sounded notes of appeasement, proclaiming confidently that there was no possibility of further violence. "Gentlemen, I will patrol this city with six women, so quiet and peaceful and orderly it is," he declared. "It is like Sunday all the time."

NEARLY A WEEK AFTER THE MASSACRE, MILDRED CLINTON, JOSHUA Halsey's oldest sibling, went to claim his body. According to the papers—the white papers, because now there was no Black one—whatever had happened to him had been his fault. The testimony of witnesses before the coroner's jury, the *Star* reported, "will prove conclusively that the negroes were the aggressors in the unfortunate affair and that the white men were forced to fire as a matter of protection." This was a familiar projection, a transfer technique that has been used by everyone from enslavers and colonizers to patrollers, night riders, jailers, politicians, and police. The more violent they are, the more violent they accuse Black people of being.

Joshua lay dead on the coroner's table, labeled a "Negro aggressor." Clinton, called before the panel, kept her mouth shut. She told the men the body she had seen was indeed that of her brother, but that she didn't know how he had come to his death. Eventually, the coroner ruled that Joshua, along with five other Black victims, had died by gunshot wounds "inflicted by some person or persons to the jury unknown." A doctor who examined fourteen men—two white and twelve Black—who were wounded during the violence pointed out another commonality: Except for the pair of white men, all of them had been shot in the back.

With murderers ensconced at City Hall, survivors could hardly seek succor from local authorities. Nor would the shambolic state government be of any use. Desperate for help, they turned to the federal government, which was theoretically obliged to ensure their equal protection under the nation's laws. "Please send releif [*sic*] as soon as possible or we perish," one citizen wrote to President McKinley. Another correspondent, identifying herself only as "A Negro woman of this city," gave a detailed account of voter suppression, murder, and banishment, begging the president "from the depths of my heart" for protection against "lawless whites." She continued:

> I call on you the head of the American Nation to help these humble subjects. We are loyal we go when duty calls us. And are we to die like rats in a trap? With no place to seek redress or to go with our Greivances [*sic*]? Can we call on any other nation for help? Why do you forsake the Negro?

It wasn't as if a few frantic postcards from the provinces simply failed to land on McKinley's desk. Practically every national newspaper carried reports of the "bloody day in this one-horse town." The "fatal race riots" made the front page of *The New York Times*, while the *New York Herald* proclaimed, WHITES KILL NEGROES AND SEIZE THE CITY OF WILMINGTON. In an editorial, the editors of *The Richmond Planet*, a leading Black paper, expressed historic levels of shock. "The outrageous happenings at Wilmington almost surpasses comprehension," they wrote. "Never in this country have we heard or seen anything like it before." The paper's headline was stronger still: HORRIBLE BUTCHERIES AT WILMINGTON. THE TURKS OUT DONE.

Three deposed white Republican officials—the US commissioner and justice of the peace, the chief of police, and a policeman—got on a train and rode to Washington, D.C., where they demanded an appointment with the Justice Department, recounting their ordeal and demanding federal action. Judson Lyons, the register of the United States Treasury, published a "ringing letter" in the *New York Herald*, writing, "The record of those days immediately following the 8th of November makes me wonder if, after all, we are not mistaken and are not, in fact living in middle ages, with their racks and thumbscrews, instead of in the bright civilization of the closing days of the nineteenth century."

In Indianapolis, the exiled lawyer W. E. Henderson laid out the political stakes of the situation. Going into the election, he recalled, Black Wilmingtonians had been counting on backup: "We have a Republican sheriff, a Republican mayor, the governor is with us, and we have a Republican president. If we can't get protection now we can never get it." McKinley was their last resort.

People suffering in Wilmington could have reasonably assumed that McKinley would be sympathetic to their plight. He was the son of Methodist abolitionists, a former Union officer, and a reliable supporter of the Reconstruction Amendments—"the irreversible judgment of battle and the inflexible decree of a Nation of free men." In the immediate aftermath of November 10, his administration made faint noises of disapproval, with one cabinet secretary condemning the events in Wilmington as "a disgrace to the state and the nation." Booker T. Washington, who went to see the president late in the fall of 1898, recalled that "his heart was greatly burdened by reason of these race disturbances."

But McKinley, the last Civil War veteran president and "an inveterate conciliator," wished, above all, to do nothing that would disturb the fragile entente between the white people of the North and the South. With the Spanish-American War, the nation had at last come together to face a common enemy. Despite the contributions of Black soldiers, the war, the historian David Blight writes, "exacerbated racial antagonism," racializing American patriotism and solidifying the alliance between white supremacy and imperialism.

Under pressure from white supremacist industrialists such as the North Carolina tobacco magnate Julian Carr—"Don't do it," Carr wrote explicitly, jubilant over the victory of "men of white skins, sons of revolutionary ancestors"—McKinley chose to sacrifice equal protection on the altar of white unity. Leaning on a technicality, he claimed that he couldn't send troops to Wilmington because the governor hadn't requested them. Nor did he offer words that might comfort the afflicted or deter further vigilante violence. A group representing the "Colored People of Massachusetts" addressed the president in an open letter, questioning "your extraordinary, incomprehensible silence" in the face of innocent American citizens having been "butchered like dogs in the streets of that ill-fated town." *The Colored American* eventually concluded that the Wilmington massacre and coup "in one fell swoop throttled what was left of the sentiment of political equality for all citizens," with the "echoes of the wreck reverberating to the farther-most ends of the country." By declining to act in Wilmington, McKinley had sent a message to the whole nation: From now on, as far as the federal government was concerned, Black people were on their own.

Chapter 22

FLAMING MUTILATIONS

Democrats were jubilant that the Sixth Congressional District of North Carolina was in safe hands. John Dillard Jr. ascended to the United States Congress, having trounced the Republican candidate, Oliver Dockery, by nearly six thousand votes. "Bellamy Is Elected, Just as Expected," the *Wilmington Morning Star* reported, declaring that "there is not a real white man in the state who does not feel whiter."

John Dillard Jr. owed his victory in large part to the lower-class foot soldiers of the white supremacy campaign. On Election Day, he had supplied Mike Dowling and his band of Red Shirts with free liquor. In return, they delivered him an astonishing eleven thousand more Democratic votes than had even been registered in the district during the previous election. The next morning, the White Declaration of Independence meeting doubled as John Dillard Jr.'s victory party. "Wilmington has been rid of the vilest slanderer in North Carolina," he declared from the stage, cheering Alexander Manly's departure alongside his new constituents.

Less than a week later, John Dillard Jr. was entertaining again. This time, the recipients of his largesse were the members of the Second Regiment Band, from the same white volunteer unit that had missed action in Cuba, returned to Wilmington, and channeled its pent-up energies into activity with the WGU and the Red Shirts. "Mr. Bellamy invited the boys into his hospitable home and sat them down to a table laden with an abundance of good things to eat," the *Star* reported. It's unlikely that many of "the boys" had ever set foot in such a fancy household; if they had, it would have been as factotums, not guests. Now they were enjoying privileged access to the city's most rarefied circles. That the feast was meant as a form of social payback was obvious as John Dillard Jr. stood up and "paid the boys deserved compliments for their unswerving devotion to his cause during the recent campaign."

In December, Dockery filed a lawsuit contesting the results of the election. John Dillard Jr., he contended, had stolen the seat with the help of the WGU and the Red Shirts. "In pursuance of this plan they armed themselves with pistols, rifles, and other deadly weapons and interrupted and dispersed political gatherings and whipped and even killed citizens who dared stand upon their rights," Dockery wrote, asking Congress to prevent Bellamy from taking office. The election, Dockery declared, had been "a farce, a mockery, and a fraud."

John Dillard Jr. denied Dockery's charges. He could hardly have conspired with the WGU and the Red Shirts, he said, as he was out on the campaign trail and away from Wilmington in the months leading up to the election. With his November 8 victory, he had been elected an official of the federal government "prior to the riot"; therefore, as he later recalled, "he had to refrain from any active participation in the affair." In fact, according to Bellamy, the Red Shirts didn't even exist. "There was no such organization known as the 'Red Shirts' in any county," he told the court. Certain individuals in certain counties marked themselves out by wearing a red shirt, he admitted, "but it had no illegal object or purpose, but was simply a uniform for a legal political club."

Dockery v. Bellamy, as the case was known, dragged on for months, attracting intense publicity. Seventy-five witnesses testified for Dockery, detailing the full range of illegal tactics, from ballot tampering to murder, that the Democrats and their associates had employed. The proceedings brought back together many of the key figures in the violence, both perpetrators and survivors, the latter of whom were living all over the country in a diaspora of unresolved distress.

The witnesses' testimony, however precise or powerful, was of no consequence. As Dockery's lawyers argued their case, John Dillard Jr.'s old-boy network mobilized to protect his interests. Thomas Nelson Page—a best-selling writer of racist "plantation literature"—vouched for John Dillard Jr. in *The Washington Post*, reminiscing about his "charming home" and their glory days as classmates at the University of Virginia. Page spoke directly to moderate white readers' misgivings about "the Wilmington Revolution." They might be thinking of "some polite, respectable, kindly colored people they know," he granted, but to profess "horror at acts of bloodshed and tyranny" or to empathize with their victims would, in this case, be terribly naive. "It is impossible to convey to those not personally experienced an idea of life beneath the domination of Negroes such as those in Wilmington," Page wrote. His assurances helped to sway elite opinion in John Dillard Jr.'s favor, and the court ultimately ruled to seat him. With Page's endorsement and introductions, he made, by his own admission, "quite an entrée into Washington."

John Dillard Jr.'s fraternity brothers from Theta Delta Chi did their part to burnish his reputation, too, throwing a hotel banquet where they introduced him to influential officials. "The consequence was that my case was referred to the Committee on Privileges and Elections and the contest was never brought up," he wrote in his 1942 memoirs, proudly acknowledging that his confirmation was an inside job. For William E. Henderson, the exiled lawyer, John Dillard's rise to national power was almost unbearable: "[He] walks cheerfully to his seat over broken homes, broken hearts, disappointed lives, dead husbands and fathers, the trampled rights of freedmen, and not one word of condemnation is heard."

VALENTINE HOWE, WHO LOVED FIREFIGHTING, WAS NO LONGER A FIREfighter. Just two years earlier, his squad, the Cape Fear Steam Fire Engine Company, widely acknowledged as the city's most skilled, had celebrated its twenty-fourth anniversary with the inauguration of a brand-new firehouse. The city had paid Valentine a thousand dollars to design and build the new station. It was his masterpiece, with built-in cupboards for the company's collection of banqueting china, stalls for three horses, and private chambers for each of their drivers. Every detail had been thought of, down to the white blinds with red trimmings and a twenty-foot flagpole out front. In 1897, the city government had begun converting various volunteer fire squads into an official, paid fire department. Howe's company had already donated the firehouse and much of its equipment to the city, proceeding on the tacit agreement that once the consolidation was complete, their contributions would be honored with jobs.

On November 15, Waddell fired the city's fifteen Black firefighters, along with its ten Black police officers, Black janitor, Black messenger, and Black cattle weigher. "Wilmington's fire department is now composed of white men exclusively," the *Star* announced. Mike Dowling—the feckless leader of the Red Shirts, previously unemployed and with no firefighting experience—was appointed as foreman of Engine Company. "The new men will receive the necessary training at once," the *Star* assured its readers, "and the efficiency of the department will in no way be impaired by the addition of the untrained men."

In celebration, a group of women from the city's Fifth Ward presented Dowling with a monogrammed, gold-headed cane, "as an expression of appreciation for the efficient services rendered by Mr. Dowling prior to and during the recent 'race war.'" But Dowling's firefighting career didn't last long. Only a few months later, the city government sacked him, citing "incompetency, drunkenness, and continued insubordination." In fact, Dowling had run afoul of the Democratic power structure in demanding even more concessions for poor white labor. He soon left Wilmington, drifting through Norfolk to Washington, D.C. At one point, he was arrested for stealing four dollars and a diamond ring from a tourist after having forcibly poured half a pint of whiskey down his throat.

Barred from firefighting, Valentine continued to operate the family construction business with his brother John Harriss. The period just after 1898 was professionally fruitful for them both. Valentine secured the contract for the addition of a "colored wing" to the James Walker Memorial Hospital, while John Harriss renovated the First Presbyterian Church and repaired hurricane damage at the Carolina Yacht Club. Both were redoubts of the white supremacist elite, whose members praised "the beautiful and substantial manner in which he did his work."

In addition to being skilled builders, Valentine and John must have had a great capacity for compartmentalization. Months earlier, when the United Daughters of the Confederacy (UDC) were building their museum, Valentine had submitted a sheet of unused Confederate stamps—either an ingratiating gesture or a quietly acid joke. The brothers chose to resume work for white perpetrators of the massacre, whether because they felt they had no financial choice but to do so, because it was socially advantageous, or because of some more complicated sense of the interdependence that Valentine once described as the "community of interest between those who live in the same place, regardless of color."

Valentine died of illness in 1904, leaving the hospital wing unfinished. His only heir was a daughter, Cora, who worked as a maid and married a barber. John had died two years earlier, of heart failure. Three of his sons—James, Richard, and Henry—were by that time living in New York. As the white supremacists moved to institute total segregation, younger members of the Howe family began to see migration as a more attractive option than remaining in Wilmington, despite the prospect of guaranteed employment with the family business.

For several days after the massacre, Alexander Manly's whereabouts remained a public mystery. The white press fanned speculation, publishing accounts by witnesses who claimed to have spotted him in cities along the Eastern Seaboard. In Norfolk, a group of white men severely beat a Black man who had gone to the post office to buy a stamp, mistaking him for the Wilmington editor. On November 13, Manly resurfaced in Asbury Park, New Jersey. He had boarded a northbound train just outside Wilmington after escaping from the city in his carriage. He was staying in Asbury Park with his brother-in-law, trying to process the reality that his business had been incinerated, his city sacked, his family scattered, and his reputation destroyed.

In an interview with *The Baltimore Sun*, Alexander displayed uncharacteristic caution. He refrained from naming names and seemed quietly hopeful, even as he decried the "flaming mutilations" of truth that had led to the trouble, that his banishment might be revoked if he remained sufficiently discreet. "When asked if he intended to return to North Carolina, he replied that this was not a question he could answer at present," the *Sun* reported. "There were facts connected with that part of the case which might affect others, and he thought it best not to say anything as to his future prospects." Alexander declined to value his losses, except to confirm that "he had lost everything he owned in the world." He had purchased insurance on the *Daily Record* property, he added, but the policy made no provision for destruction by the fury of a mob.

The deed was done: The white supremacists had incinerated the *Record*, murdered untold numbers of men, banished dozens of others, and overthrown the city government. But the damage was far from contained. The violence of a few hours would persist well into the coming century, accumulating obvious casualties and other less predictable consequences.

PART 3

SUBSTANTIAL DENIALS

1899–1979

Chapter 23

A PERMANENT MEMORIAL

The white supremacists—so deliberate in their planning, so chillingly "stately" in their enactment of the massacre and coup—were suddenly in a hurry. The blood of their victims still fresh in the streets, the ink on their proclamations hardly dry, they raced to leverage the chaos they had wreaked in Wilmington into permanent change. They called the episode "The Wilmington Revolution of 1898," suggesting both glorious precedent and neat finality. Their storytelling transformed current events into capital-*H* History—done, over, and thus incontestable.

Taking a strangely elegiac tone, Wilmington's new mayor, Alfred Moore Waddell, wrote that the Revolution "was certainly the strangest performance in American history, though we literally followed the law, as the Fusionists made it themselves." If there were a formal, historical past tense in English, he would have used it. Still, his point came through clearly: "The crisis has passed" and the victors were moving on. "No one knows better than I that this has been a serious affair, but it has, like all such affairs, a humorous side," Waddell continued, launching into a jocular tale about "an old Negro" petitioning him for a jackknife he'd lost "during the fracas," while addressing nothing real or substantial about the violence.

The white establishment buried the truth under forward-looking generalization. They hustled the conversation along briskly by the elbow, away from atrocity and illegal seizure and toward an upbeat vision of Wilmington as a newly dynamized haven for white politics and business. At City

Hall and in the capitol, Waddell and John Dillard Jr. were striving to burnish their reputations and cement their wins. For families such as the Moores, the Bellamys, and the MacRaes, an honest accounting of massacre and coup, had they been intellectually and emotionally able to make one, would have risked damage to their image and to their cause.

With white people reclaiming a monopoly on power, Black families had their own reasons to keep quiet about what had happened. Fear, of course, was an effective muffler. After Joshua's murder, the Halseys remained in Wilmington. They knew firsthand that it could be lethal to speak up about injustice, to stick a head above the parapet in a period when facts were becoming ever more dangerous and disputed. The Howes had businesses to run and a dynasty to defend. They redirected the energy that they had poured into politics toward education, seeing it as the best chance for the next generation. Pride bred silence, too. Few Black parents wanted to weigh their children down with such harrowing memories, to dwell on darkest days as they sought to rebuild or to make fresh starts, seeking the light of self-reliance or migration.

Eventually, "The Wilmington Revolution of 1898" became, in common parlance, just "1898." It was a meager synecdoche, the part for a whole ensemble of interlinked causes and effects, reactions and counterreactions that reached back centuries and never stopped concatenating. The past was the past, not to be examined or reflected upon. But the past was patient, and it worked at its own pace, despite Wilmingtonians' efforts to confine the coup to a tick on a timeline. Whether or not people acknowledged or understood it, the past would play a signal role in the biggest conflicts of the coming century. And Wilmington would continue to embody an extreme version of the national pattern of Black progress and violent white backlash.

IN THE MONTHS THAT FOLLOWED THE COUP, THE DEMOCRAT-DOMINATED North Carolina General Assembly acted quickly to undo the Fusion movement's reforms, operating in what the historian Helen G. Edmonds called a "spirit of revenge." In 1899, the state legislature amended or repealed 153 laws, leaving intact little more than what one politician characterized as "some bills to protect fish in Hanging Dog Creek." With overwhelming numbers—ninety-four Democrats to twenty-three Republicans and three Populists—the majority had the will and the means to enshrine white supremacy in every facet of North Carolina life.

Before the 1898 elections, one judge had declared that Democratic political victories "will be but the getting in position for the most important work." Having eliminated the last redoubt of Black political power in Wilmington, white supremacists moved to intensify segregation statewide. The state legislature made good on the promise, mandating Jim Crow rules on the trains. "Separate Cars for the Races on the Railroad," Raleigh's *News & Observer* announced. "North Carolina Like Other Southern States Will Have Them." More oppressive measures followed: One required that even cadavers be separated by race.

The white supremacists' greatest ambition was the wholesale eviction of Black people from politics. To achieve this, they needed a legal mechanism that would strike Black voters from the electoral rolls without excluding poor white ones. Other states had instituted poll taxes and literacy tests, but North Carolina Democrats initially rejected both techniques on the grounds that they would disenfranchise a significant portion of the white electorate. The legislature appointed George Rountree, one of the leaders of the coup, to find a workaround method.

Rountree was a sort of juridical alchemist, transforming prejudices and preferences into hard-and-fast, official-sounding rules. Later in life, when he went to the movies, he would breeze past the ticket taker. "Sir, don't you want to buy a ticket?" the employee would say. "If I like the movie, I'll buy a ticket," Rountree would reply. As the legal consigliere of the 1898 coup, he had lacquered the white supremacists' crude plan with a sheen of legal respectability. Now the moment had come to consolidate the gains of the "revolution," inscribing its principles into law.

Rountree's solution was a constitutional amendment requiring any potential voter to "be able to read and write any section of the constitution in the English language." Crucially, the amendment included a so-called grandfather clause, inspired by a similar measure in Louisiana: Any person who had been eligible to vote in 1867 would still be eligible and so would all his direct descendants. In other words, almost every white man would remain able to vote, while nearly all Black men would be struck off the rolls.

In 1898, Rountree and his co-conspirators had imposed their will by machine gun and rifle; now they were codifying it in paper and ink. During debate on the house floor, one white lawmaker called explicitly for his peers to finish the job that the Red Shirts had started. "Every man who talks of white supremacy must show his faith by his works," he said, urging his peers to remember Wilmington. The events of 1898 were also on the minds of the voting bill's opponents. *The Richmond Planet* ably dismantled the twisted logic of disenfranchisement: "It has been argued that the ability to read and write carries with it a respect for the laws of the land. Is this true? If it is, how can you explain away the actions of the educated white men of Wilmington?"

The legislature approved Rountree's amendment in February 1899. One Black lawmaker called it "the great sledge hammer of political death," smashing the Fifteenth Amendment into virtual oblivion and knocking Black people out of the full citizenship that the federal government had guaranteed them some thirty years earlier. For white supremacists, the measure was a chisel, a means of putting the finishing touches on the long-term project of purging Black people from political life. The amendment, one historian concluded, constituted "a permanent memorial to the campaign of 1898."

In 1900, the bill passed handily in a popular referendum. That it did so even in each of the state's sixteen Black-majority counties demonstrates just how effective the 1898 terror campaign was in silencing Black voters. In Wilmington, just thirty of an estimated thirty thousand eligible Black voters registered for the election. The whole of New Hanover County recorded *two votes* against the grandfather clause amendment, the fewest of any county in the state. Now that Black voters were no longer useful, even the Republican party deserted them, promising to become "lily white." By 1902, fewer than 5 percent of Black North Carolinians remained on the electoral rolls.

As the twentieth century dawned, the white supremacists made little attempt to cover up the massacre, the coup, or the ideologies that motivated them. In the aftermath of 1898, Iredell Meares, a Bellamy relation and stalwart of the WGU, busied himself with writing valorous accounts of the "white men's revolution." Two years in, the so-called revolution, according to Meares, had yielded all manner of "beneficial effects," restoring Wilmington to comity and confidence. Capital was flowing into the city, yielding a new fertilizer plant and a $250,000 cotton factory. The city's finances were shipshape. "Sewerage (a new system) is under discussion and will be carried through," Meares reported, as though anyone would agree that a few murders were a small price to pay for getting a handle on the wastewater situation.

The white supremacists offered guidance to their peers in other states, branding their strategy the North Carolina Way. Yet the fact that conspirators were proud of what they'd done didn't mean they were honest about it. After the 1866 New Orleans massacre, the Louisiana state legislature commissioned an inquest. It established that white Democrats had initiated the attacks and discredited "the hollow pretext of a 'negro riot.'" In Wilmington, no such investigation would be initiated until 2000. In the absence of official reckoning, the perpetrators controlled the story. "That happened which will always happen when a lot of irresponsible half-savages talk themselves into a flame of passion," Meares wrote, passing off the white men's premeditated attack as a spontaneous Black spasm.

The Black writer Charles Chesnutt, a lonely voice of historicity, tried to push back against the conspirators' propaganda. In 1901, he published *The Marrow of Tradition*, a very lightly fictionalized account of the Wilmington murders and coup. Chesnutt hoped the book would "become lodged in the popular mind as the legitimate successor of 'Uncle Tom's Cabin,'" but it failed to find a wide audience. Of the white view of Black resistance, he wrote, "Every finer instinct would be interpreted in terms of savagery." He didn't need to spell out the corollary: When it came to their own actions, the white supremacists interpreted every savagery in terms of finer human instinct.

In 1900, Alfred Moore Waddell traveled to Montgomery, Alabama. He had been invited to speak on the question of Black voting rights on the basis of his "recent experiences in North Carolina." Waddell told the crowd that in his expert opinion, universal Black suffrage had been a colossal error. Not just an error—a punishment, inflicted on the South by spiteful Northerners as payback for the Civil War.

Waddell expected the grandfather clause to alleviate the immediate harms of "this greatest political crime," but in his opinion, state disenfranchisement bills didn't go far enough. The Black man, Waddell claimed, voted "with no more comprehension than the bob-tailed dog who goes with him to the voting place." The peace and welfare of society, he argued, could only be ensured by the repeal or overhaul of the Fifteenth Amendment of the United States Constitution, which guaranteed voting rights. "Fraud and shot guns have no place in this argument," Waddell proclaimed, with audacious hypocrisy.

While he was in Montgomery, Waddell visited the headquarters of the *Montgomery Advertiser*. Booker T. Washington, who was also attending the conference, was there at the same time.

"I expected to meet a Negro, but you're a much fairer-colored man than Frederick Douglass," Alfred said, when an editor introduced them. "In fact, you're about three-fifths white, which explains to me your history and corroborates the historical evidence that no pure-blooded Negro has ever attained greatness—although Toussaint L'Ouverture of Haiti came near it."

Eventually, Washington got a word in.

"Toussaint was a mulatto, according to my recollection," he said.

"That, of course, only strengthens the evidence!"

Waddell was on top of the world, spouting off pseudoscientific nonsense with a professorial air, lecturing the world's most famous race man on the literal color of his skin. It was a buoyant moment for Waddell and his fellow Democrats, yet their self-congratulatory narrative was a prelude, not a postscript. For the white supremacists, yet more action lay ahead.

Chapter 24

CUFFS

In 1900, Sallie Halsey was struggling. Grief was no solvent to responsibility, and with Joshua gone, the burden of nourishing and educating their two youngest daughters was hers alone. The bridge settlement would have changed her life—and potentially the lives of generations of Halseys—but with the white supremacy regime in charge, the lawsuit was a dead letter. In the years leading up to 1898, the case appeared frequently in the papers. After 1898, it vanished from the record.

Sallie was likely still dealing with injuries from the bridge fall. This left her in a dire position, as physical labor was more or less the only moneymaking opportunity for Black working women, 90 percent of whom were employed in domestic service in 1899. Even if Sallie was healthy, she may have struggled to find work with a white family due to the perception that she was a troublemaker after the Mundses' theft accusation, the bridge lawsuit, and the contention that Joshua had been an aggressor on November 10. Less than a year after his death, Sallie was facing legal issues again. In September 1899, she was accused of stealing an apron from a cook who worked for the aristocratic lawyer Iredell Meares.

Meares had strong opinions about Black people and criminal justice. According to him, the Wilmington "riot" was an inevitable consequence of "the demoralization of this county and city" by the flawed administration of justice in the area's courts. This problem, in his telling, was attributable to Black residents, who "packed and jammed the courtroom," and to Black lawyers, who "took possession" of the court, making it "impossible to convict a Negro of any offense when the Negroes did not want him convicted." This claim contradicted another of his opinions, which held that it was difficult to identify Black criminals: Black people, he believed, profited from a form of natural camouflage, "as 'all coons look alike.'"

This supposed advantage didn't shield Sallie from being blamed for an incident that took place in the Meares household on a Sunday afternoon in August 1899. When the crime occurred, the house was empty. Both its white inhabitants and its Black workers were away, worshipping or resting on a dog-day Sabbath. On Monday morning, Lucretia McDowell, a Black woman who cooked for the Meareses, returned to the kitchen to find "a quantity of provisions" and "several articles of raiment" absent. Per the *Wilmington Messenger*, she reported the theft to the Meareses, but "no trace of the robbers could be found."

One can imagine that McDowell was under pressure to name a culprit from her white employer, who believed in a conspiracy of indistinguishable "coons" covering up for each other's transgressions. One can imagine that Sallie was desperate, and that everyone knew it, because her husband had been publicly executed by the people who now controlled the city. One can also acknowledge that missing things turn up in the strangest places. But is it not perhaps too convenient that McDowell, according to the paper, went to visit her friend Sallie in her Brooklyn home and found her wearing the very apron that had gone missing from the Meareses' kitchen?

The rest of the account is even murkier. McDowell "identified the apron by several peculiar marks and demanded of the wearer where she obtained it," according to testimony. "The Halsy [*sic*] woman informed her that she got it from her married daughter, Mary Fonville, who resides on the sound." Even if Sallie confessed, why would she have given up her daughter? When questioned, the paper continued, Mary admitted giving the apron to her mother but denied stealing it, saying she'd found it in the woods.

The story has a hypnagogic unity: the hearth, the apron, the little girl who once threw the cloth over the fence changed into the woman stumbling across a garment in a forest. From the Chinese velvet curtains of Sallie's childhood, fabric runs through the stories of the Halsey women as a motif of desire and its thwarted fulfillment. Sallie and Mary were both charged with larceny—the mother-daughter band back together again, supposedly magicking away items of negligible value in the shadow of ultimate loss.

No record remains of the Meares case's disposition. The next year, Sallie was arrested again, for entering the home of a local grocer and making off with a basket containing napkins and a butter jar. "Woman Sneak Thief Caught," one headline boasted. Her first hearing, the next morning, was presided over by Mayor Waddell—one of the men responsible for her husband's murder. Several months later, the case went to trial. This time, a jury convicted Sallie. Her lawyer pleaded "for mercy for her," explaining that "she had some small children depending on her for support and that she was a widow, her husband, Josh Halsey, having been killed in the riot in the city on the 10th of November, 1898." Ultimately, the court reserved sentence.

The white supremacists used a range of techniques to make people disappear like aprons on a Sunday afternoon: murder, exile, exclusion, prosecution, incarceration, harassment, attrition, making a person's life so materially difficult that no one would believe she wasn't a thief, whether or not she actually stole. Sometime around the turn of the century, Mary and her husband had had enough. They seem to have left Wilmington, entrusting the care of their toddlers to Sallie—two more dependents to care for.

THE COLORED AMERICAN CONSIDERED 1898 "THE BLACK MAN'S WATERLOO." One of the most immediate and visible consequences of 1898 was the diminution of the city's Black population. Dozens and perhaps hundreds of Black citizens were, of course, eliminated by murder. Others were expelled and warned on pain of death never to set foot in Wilmington again. In the years just after the massacre and coup, Black people chose to leave North Carolina in unprecedented numbers, anticipating the Great Migration by about a decade. These exiles sought refuge and rebuilt their lives across the country, driven from a city that had ceased to be a viable place for them to live. Oral tradition holds that some of the city's "most fair-skinned Negroes just walked out of their houses and closed the doors behind them," never to be heard from again as they pursued new lives, passing as white.

Armond Scott, the young lawyer tasked with the doomed job of delivering the letter, migrated to Washington, D.C., where he tried to make a go of things from a grim rented bedroom that doubled as his office. Even four hundred miles away from Wilmington, he wasn't sure he was safe. He felt obliged to take out a newspaper notice, stating, "I am here in no official capacity whatever and have no intention of saying anything to the President or taking any action in the matter at all." Clearly, he felt that he was still in the sights of his Wilmington persecutors.

Scott's law practice failed, and he had to leave Washington. The 1900 census shows him living in New York City, working as an "elevator man." At some point, he found a job as a bellhop in a hotel in Saratoga. One day, a guest ordered a bucket of ice water. Scott brought it to his room and put it down on the table, turning to the elderly guest in anticipation of a tip.

"Hell, this isn't Scott?" the guest said. It was a former chief justice of North Carolina, who, in what seemed like another life, had sworn Scott into the state bar. "Is this what we gave you a license to practice law for? I don't care if you have had bad luck. Go back and try again." Scott was so chagrined by the encounter that he eventually returned to Washington to resuscitate his legal career.

He succeeded, and in 1935, at the age of sixty-two, he was appointed to the municipal court of the District of Columbia, making him the first Black judge in the Roosevelt administration. (Surprisingly, Scott became a Democrat at some point.) In twenty years on the bench, he earned a reputation as a "colorful, often fiery" jurist, "deal[ing] justice not from the law books but from the heart." He helped to establish clinics for alcoholics, philosophizing from the bench that "every dog is entitled to one bite, and every man is entitled to one drink." His lively personality made him an in-demand guest. According to a profile of Scott that appeared in *Ebony*,

"He probably has attended more White House functions than any other Negro."

Despite his stature and his sociability, Scott heeded the injunction against returning to Wilmington for more than half a century. "I will never forget the day they put me on the train," he said. In 1945, nearly fifty years after his banishment, he finally went back to his hometown. A reception committee greeted him as he stepped off the train "in triumph," and he delivered a keynote speech at a dinner meeting organized in his honor.

Despite this warm homecoming, Scott never forgot the heartbreak of his Wilmington youth. When he died in 1960, at the age of eighty-seven, he left an estate valued at $140,000. It included real estate, jewelry, cars, and cash for each of his three grandsons, accompanied by an autobiographical manuscript. He called it "Up from Hell."

"Returning to hometown, Wilmington, N.C., in triumph, Judge is met by reception committee." *Ebony*, September 1958.

BY 1900, WILMINGTON'S BLACK POPULATION HAD CONTRACTED FROM A pre-1898 high of 56 percent to 49 percent, giving the city a white majority for the first time since the Civil War. Almost a thousand fewer Black people appeared in the listings of the city directory. Black workers who chose to stay in Wilmington saw their professional prospects dry up, as white employers brought in white replacements in accordance with the White Declaration of Independence. (White boys even took over the Kunering tradition, donning red bandannas and "Cooner-face" masks.) Black property ownership remained stable in the years just after the violence, according to one study, but Black businesses withdrew from the city center, many of them retreating to the relative safety of private homes in majority Black neighborhoods.

Some Black residents moved to the city's outlying areas, where they hoped to be left in peace. Others went much farther. One of Alexander Manly's brothers crossed the color line and trained as a trans-Atlantic steamboat captain. Thomas McKeller, another Wilmington exile, moved to Boston, where he met John Singer Sargent while working as an elevator attendant. McKeller became the painter's model and muse, now known as "the Boston Apollo."

Racial violence stretched Black people to their limit and propelled them to the North, the elastic relationship between the two regions quivering for years after. School principals in Philadelphia were said to be able to deduce where bad things were happening just by looking at where the new Southern kids were coming from. In New York City, trains arrived from Wilmington on Wednesdays and Saturdays, unloading "fresh consignments" to "join the Brooklyn or Manhattan colonies of refugees until they can find employment either in the city or near by." This "influx of colored people" from Wilmington was significant enough that churches orchestrated a special series of revivals for the newcomers. "The movement is thought to be on a permanent basis," *The Brooklyn Daily Eagle* declared.

In 1899, the paper reported that an "intelligent colored man belonging in Wilmington, N.C." had come to town "on a curious mission." He had been sent by his employer, the cotton tycoon James Sprunt, to try to entice "several hundred refugees of last winter's race war" to come home. A full half of Sprunt's hands, many of whom had worked for him their whole lives, had fled north. As cotton-pressing time approached, Sprunt found himself facing a labor shortage. Despite his good reputation and the promise of five dollars a day, few of the migrants could be persuaded to return. "Some of the refugees owned houses in Wilmington which they can't rent and can't sell," the *Eagle* noted. "Many of them had just lost all their savings in the Wilmington bank troubles and are beginning life over again here. There aren't many of them that want to go back after all their troubles, not if they have to live on scraps."

Years later, the son of a Sprunt employee recalled a conversation in which his father tried to persuade a brother who had migrated north to return home.

"George," the brother replied, "I'm not going back to Wilmington. I don't intend to go back to Wilmington. They are the meanest white folks I ever seen is in Wilmington, North Carolina. Ain't no place worse than Wilmington, North Carolina. Oh no, I ain't going back to Wilmington. I rather be a lamppost in New York than a man in Wilmington."

T. C. Miller, formerly the city's richest Black man, felt differently. He had survived a lynch mob, but he was desperate to return home. In 1902, he wrote from exile in Norfolk to John D. Taylor, the clerk of the superior court. The letter was theoretically about a land transaction, but Miller poured out his soul to Taylor, a well-connected white Democrat:

> I have been treated not like [a] human but worse than a dog and someday the Lord will punish them that punished me without a Cause. I am Well and doing Well the only thing that worries me is just to think that I [will not be] allowed to come to my Mothers funeral she being 95 years of age and the oldest Citizen on Wrightsville Sound. Just to think of it will last me to my grave. If I were guilty of any Crime or was a Criminal it would not worri [*sic*] me in the least but oh my god just to think it is enough to run a sane man insane.

Miller seems to have been discreetly trying to feel out Taylor to see if the banishment still held, but a homecoming was not to be. Miller never set foot in Wilmington again. The next year, he died, and only then was he allowed to reunite with his relatives, who arranged for his remains to be brought home and buried him in Pine Forest Cemetery.

GEORGE HENRY WHITE, THE BLACK CONGRESSMAN WHO HAD URGED McKinley to prevent the 1898 violence, declined to seek a third term in 1900. "George H. White, the insolent negro[,] . . . has retired for office forever," one white congressman crowed, as the statehouse clock struck noon on the final day of his term. (White's successor, a Red Shirt organizer who had openly called for election fraud and lynching, served another eleven terms, running each time unopposed.) The last Black congressman before the Jim Crow era, White knew well that, as the historian Glenda Gilmore has observed, the political exclusion of Black people amounted to "a civil death sentence." He told reporters that he was moving out of state: "I cannot live in North Carolina and be treated as a man."

White moved his family to Washington, D.C. He had every reason to be bitter, but he was determined to make something positive out of the horrors he'd endured. In 1901, he and his wife hosted Alexander Manly's wedding to Carrie Sadgwar at their Washington town house. The Manlys, too, approached the next chapter of their lives with fortitude and vim. Undaunted by their losses in Wilmington, they resurrected the newspaper, calling it the *Washington Daily Record* and using it to condemn American imperialism in the Philippines and highlight the work of Black writers. Eventually, they moved to Philadelphia, where Alexander worked as a painter and was active in the Armstrong Association, securing jobs for Black migrants from the South.

The same year, White and investors including Paul Laurence Dunbar and Booker T. Washington paid fourteen thousand dollars for a two-thousand-acre tract of land in southern New Jersey. The land was fertile, perfect for growing vegetables and raising poultry. Crucially, it occupied an undeveloped, unincorporated slice of the Cape May peninsula, free of neighbors for miles around. White, according to a history of the area, "had a dream to buy as much land as he could in southern New Jersey and build a black city."

If Wilmington was hell, Whitesboro—as the town came to be known—was conceived as a kind of paradise, a sanctuary of Black safety, freedom, and self-determination. The founders advertised in publications to recruit settlers of "good character" and "steady and industrious habits" to "Progressive Whitesboro, Industrial Whitesboro, an Educational Center, a Haven for the Negro." In exchange for a five-dollar down payment and a pledge to cultivate the land, each inhabitant received a lot of about a sixth of an acre.

Heeding White's call, hundreds of Black people left Cape Fear for Cape May. The 1910 Census shows page after page of Black families whose members were all born in North Carolina, like their mothers and fathers before them. Wilmington surnames appear in abundance: Sadgwar, Telfair, Bell. In the 1940s, one young couple from the Cape Fear area followed the migratory trail and settled in Whitesboro, raising six children. (One of them was Stedman Graham, entrepreneur and partner to Oprah Winfrey.

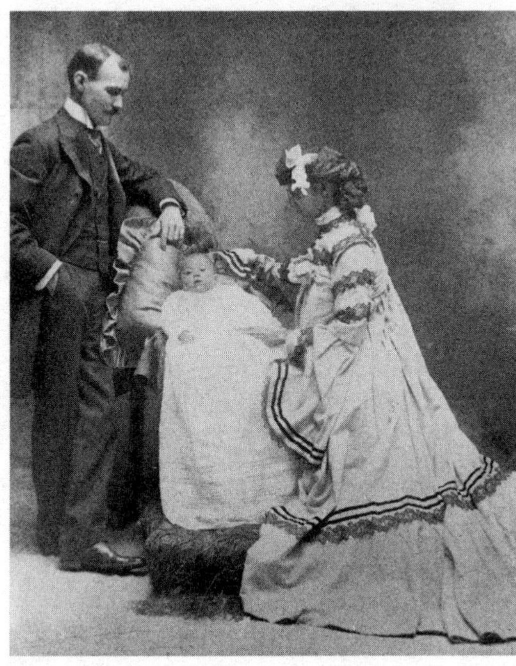

Portrait of Alexander and Carrie Manly with their infant son, Milo, July 14, 1903.

He goes back to Whitesboro most summers to attend the town's annual Labor Day reunion, often accompanied by Winfrey, who, in 2008, donated a million dollars to a Whitesboro scholarship fund.)

As Black Wilmingtonians tried to rebuild, Whitesboro offered real advantages of climate and community. But its ultimate attraction was intangible: the peace of mind of knowing that your neighbors wouldn't one day attack you or send you packing because of your race.

Chapter 25

A CHILD'S BOX OF LETTERS

In 1899, John Dillard Bellamy Jr. purchased a sprawling Queen Anne–style house on Sixth and Market, just a few hundred feet from the white-columned family seat. "Both the interior and exterior decorations will be on an elaborate scale, but those on the interior will probably be unsurpassed in the whole state," one observer wrote, rhapsodizing over such details as an onyx fireplace and a mahogany newel post carved to resemble acanthus leaves. Four decades earlier, the elder John Dillard had raised his secesh mansion as the South threatened to withdraw from the Union. As he prepared to go to Congress, John Dillard Jr. needed his own stately residence, a post-1898 power seat. The house offered room for him, his wife, Emma, and their many children. Their most conspicuous improvement was the addition of an enormous metal cupola with a spike protruding from the top. Thanks to this feature, which lent a martial air to the place, the house would become known as the German Helmet.

At the start of the congressional term, John Dillard Jr. invited a colleague, Frank Wheeler—Republican of Michigan, a rich shipbuilder—down to Wilmington for a visit. Except for their wealth, the two men couldn't have been more different, but they had common ground in capitalism and were working together on a business deal through which Wheeler would buy a tract of local forest and John Dillard Jr. would manage the legal end of the transaction. The attorney sought to entertain his guest in style.

"While in Wilmington, we spent a night at my summer home on Wrightsville Beach," he recalled. "The next morning, I sent for Henry Brewington, a negro valet, to serve us at the cottage."

Brewington was a familiar figure around town. An enthusiastic outdoorsman, he made the paper one summer for gathering 152 turtle eggs from a single nest. He was also known for his skill as an oyster shucker. One caterer considered his presence as critical to an event's success as that of the warming sun. "I am prepared to offer fifty Oyster Roasts on twenty minutes' notice," the caterer advertised. "Henry Brewington will serve them. Cold, rainy weather will not interfere. You will be comfortable."

Before 1898, Brewington had been active in Republican politics in Wilmington. At the time of the coup, he was serving as a magistrate; like every other Black official, he was forced to resign. Scrambling to make ends meet, he got a job on Wrightsville Beach, working as a watchman at a cottage owned by Governor Daniel Russell. In October 1899, a powerful hurricane made landfall at Wrightsville, demolishing more than twenty houses and subjecting Brewington to yet another traumatic experience, nearly a year to the date after the coup. He was forced to weather the storm alone, "the only living soul that spent the night on the beach."

What happened to a Black man who stayed in North Carolina and hoped to be treated as a man? What happened to a Black man who stayed in Wilmington and had to work for the very people who had murdered his neighbors, taken his job, and stripped him of the rights the Constitution guaranteed him? Brewington's experience suggests he would have to be tough and persevere, swallowing taunts alongside loss of station.

At the cottage, John Dillard Jr. instructed Brewington to shine his and his guest's lace-ups.

"This man, polishing your shoes, was once a Republican magistrate," John Dillard Jr. bragged to Wheeler. "I have tried many cases before him and always addressed him, 'May it please Your Honor.'" He prodded Brewington. "Isn't that so, Henry?"

Once the valet had duly confirmed the tale, John Dillard Jr. turned again to his guest, ticking off the positions of influence that Brewington had held before the coup. For Bellamy, Brewington was a sort of human attraction, a circus freak of political humiliation, and he offered as enticing an advertisement of the Wilmington area's charms as its glassy waters and white-sand beaches. His downfall served as an irrefutable parable of the common interests of white people, triumphing over sectional or political difference. According to Bellamy's memoirs, Wheeler was easily charmed:

"Well, Bellamy," Wheeler said, "I am a Republican, but I can't blame your people for ridding yourselves of ignorant negro domination. If I lived in the South, I would be as strong a Democrat as you are."

AS THE FIN DE SIÈCLE RUSHED TOWARD THE AMERICAN CENTURY, THE white supremacists grew even bolder in their manipulation of 1898's meaning. In their lexicon, 1898 served as a shorthand for the entire bundle of racist strictures they were striving to enshrine in law and practice. It was the Lost Cause remade for the hydroelectric era, a do-over of the Civil War untainted by submission or surrender. And like the war, 1898 served as an eternal source around which white people could gather, grow misty-eyed, and launder their aggression into grievance.

The United Daughters of the Confederacy had done more than any other organization to promulgate white supremacy via the Lost Cause, likely surpassing even professional historians. In 1901, the group held their national convention in Wilmington. Alfred Moore Waddell addressed the delegates, praising their relentless efforts to "record the truth . . . as to the causes which impelled [the Southern people] to assert their rights and as to the battles in which they maintained them." If a bystander had closed her eyes, she would have had a hard time guessing whether she was hearing a contemporary orator or one from decades earlier. Waddell's words could have applied as easily to 1898 as to 1865.

While the ballads of the Lost Cause and the "Wilmington Revolution" differed in their particulars, they forced the same conclusion: White prosperity and Black freedom were incompatible pursuits. Waddell knew the power of conflation, of fungibility and juxtaposition. He was also open about the advantages of telling lies of omission and otherwise. History, he once declared, quoting the English historian James Anthony Froude, is "like a child's box of letters with which we can spell any word we please. We have only to select such letters as we want, arrange them as we like, and say nothing about those which do not suit our purpose."

Every time he cut a ribbon or laid a cornerstone, Alfred placed 1898 on a continuum of white dominion that spanned back to the nation's founding. At one public ceremony, he was meant to honor a Revolutionary War hero, but he invoked the "Wilmington Revolution" so incessantly that a visiting journalist understood 1898 as a sort of local AD/BC, from which those who "participated in . . . the suppression of black supremacy in the city date events." You couldn't go a day in Wilmington, he wrote, without hearing the word *revolution* mentioned many times.

In 1906, a hotly contested race for the governorship roiled Georgia. In the Democratic primary, Hoke Smith, the former publisher of *The Atlanta Journal*, faced Clark Howell, the editor of *The Atlanta Constitution*. Smith centered his campaign around the notion that Black people needed to be kept "in their place," at the bottom of the heap. The best way to accomplish this, he believed, was to deprive them of the right to vote. Seeking practical advice, he looked to North Carolina, consulting Furnifold Simmons, now a United States senator, and other 1898 conspirators. They happily shared their playbook for fabricating a race war that the white man was predestined to win. *Use violence*, they counseled. *Let the Black blood flow.* Smith careened around his state, promising white voters to "handle them like they did in Wilmington," turning the woods "black with hanging carcasses."

Smith got the riot he ordered. On the twenty-second of September, the white media brimmed with stories about "black devils" and "the extreme insolence of the Negro." The *Journal* led with the case of Monroe Wellborn, a young Black man who had been asked to deliver a piece of ice to a white shopkeeper's home. While his daughter was loading the ice into the refrigerator, he supposedly kissed her hand. Like Alexander Manly's editorial, Wellborn's "fit of Negro passion" served as a pretext for a bloodbath. That afternoon, five thousand white people streamed into Atlanta's Black neighborhoods, killing at least twenty-five Black people, including a pair of men huddled under a porch.

Yet again, the plan worked: Hoke was elected and the grandfather clause imposed. "And all this was to sate the greed of greedy men who hide behind the veil of vengeance!" W. E. B. Du Bois, who survived the attacks, wrote. The *Journal* shrugged the massacre off, reasoning that even if a few people had died, the violence paled in comparison to that at Wilmington eight years earlier.

TWO YEARS LATER, IN 1908, THE INDUSTRIALIST HUGH MACRAE, ESQ.—AS he was listed in the program—was promoting the North Carolina Way on Broadway, addressing the North Carolina Society of New York's annual white-tie gala at the Hotel Astor. MacRae was in the midst of a prodigious career streak, reaping the benefits of the regime that he and his 1898 co-conspirators had instituted. Unconstrained by Fusion and Populist regulations, he now controlled the railway, power, and gas systems for all of New Hanover County. Each of his investments fed the others. He extended the city's trolley lines, creating lucrative real estate opportunities: new white neighborhoods, Wilmington's first suburbs; Lumina, a twenty-five-thousand-foot pavilion and dance hall with a movie screen that seemed to rise out of the ocean on pilings. It was situated at the terminus of the city-to-sea line, drawing crowds to Wrightsville Beach, most of which the MacRae family owned. Lumina was lit by a thousand incandescent bulbs—a clever advertisement, in turn, for MacRae's electricity company, at a time when many residents were still using candles and coal.

It was nearly Christmastime, and the city was abuzz. The North Carolina Society had been founded ten years earlier, in 1898, by five prominent North Carolinians living in New York. All of the club's members were white men. (In Brooklyn, Black emigrants launched their own group, the Sons and Daughters of North Carolina.) They had obvious reasons for wanting to burnish their home state's image. As they found their places at the hotel's long banquet tables, excitement coursed through the room. Several distinguished guests—chief among them William Howard Taft, the president-elect of the United States—would join MacRae in expounding on the theme of "Southern Progress."

Hugh MacRae, businessman.

The band struck up "America" as the toastmaster raised a glass. The jolly atmosphere belied that fact that serious influence was gathered in the room. The function served as an unofficial policy workshop, where regional players could pitch their pet causes to the nation's power brokers. MacRae's speech, titled "Bringing Immigrants to the South," dealt with his passion: agricultural reform. "What are we going to do with that land, Hugh?" his father had asked when he was a young boy, waving his hand toward the family's tens of thousands of acres of virgin fields. Now, in 1908, MacRae was several years into a project by which he hoped to transform southeastern North Carolina's rural economy, and eventually that of the entire South. "Diversify, diversify," he urged, preaching the merits of science-led, small-scale farming.

MacRae spoke the zippy language of progressivism, but, when it came to race, his project was regressive to the core. As the South industrialized, white men were flocking to the mills, leaving Black men to work the land as tenant farmers and sharecroppers. Many white landowners were content with the situation, which allowed them to exploit a politically unempowered workforce. MacRae, however, considered Black labor inferior, and so he came up with a scheme that would compensate for the defection of white Southerners from agriculture, the "constant withdrawal of brains from the cultivated areas of the South." His idea, inspired by the euthenics movement—a cousin of eugenics that purported to promote "race improvement" through bettering environmental conditions—was to import white European workers to Southern farms. This, he believed, would end reliance on Black workers and create a new class of self-sufficient white citizens.

"The South has everything to gain and nothing to lose in this movement, because we would replace the lowest type of labor, that is labor originally retained from the lowest race on earth," MacRae wrote to his old 1898 ally, the newspaper editor Josephus Daniels. He explained that he aimed to "so decrease the proportion of blacks to whites" that race would cease to be a problem. To achieve this racial rebalancing, he sent agents to recruit settlers from Europe. The goal, as ever, was the dilution of Black power, but this time, MacRae turned to capitalism rather than murder and seizure.

As George H. White was creating a Black utopia in New Jersey, MacRae was luring white settlers to North Carolina with the promise of the American dream. In 1905, his Carolina Trucking Development Company finished St. Helena, a planned community twenty miles north of Wilmington. Thirteen homesteaders, the *Wilmington Messenger* reported, "came direct from Italy via New York and all of them are practical farmers." Some white locals objected to their presence, but MacRae assured them that the Italians were of decent stock. "The South has no cause to fear the people who were the builders of Rome and Venice, and of Florence and Milan," he proclaimed at the North Carolina Society gala, citing no less an authority than the famously racist senator "Pitchfork Ben" Tillman. The senator, MacRae said, had toured Italy and concluded that the Italians would "make good citizens and help in every way to assist the white race in solving the race problem."

MacRae provided the settlers with seeds, fertilizer, and technical supervision so that they could get off to a successful start. Each household received a ten-acre plot and an attractive three-bedroom house, which it could rent to buy over several years. To promote family values—and, not

Two girls, probably Dutch immigrants, holding daffodils in a farm field near Castle Hayne, North Carolina.

incidentally, white population growth—MacRae gave a present of five dollars in gold to every new bride. The prize doubled for the "parents of each child brought by the storks to St. Helena."

The location was optimal, "in the most fertile belt on the Atlantic Coast, the winter garden for the Northeastern states," the journalist Ida Tarbell wrote. More planned communities followed. MacRae eventually brought over some three thousand Dutch, German, Polish, and Hungarian farmers to grow beans, lettuce, corn, and potatoes. (Later, during World War II, he helped to bring Jewish families to the area to escape Nazi persecution.) "The Italians at St. Helena will ship each day more than one solid refrigerator carload of strawberries to the northern markets," he boasted at the North Carolina Society gala. The villages were company towns, equipped with churches, schools, and community centers. One observer lauded the quick adoption of "fried chicken, American flags, layer-cake, cars, and ice cream cones" by people who had first set foot on American soil just a decade earlier.

From the Hotel Astor dais, MacRae celebrated the success of the scheme.

"The ownership of land appeals strongly to the hardy, industrious peasants of Europe, who have eked out existence on farms, but have never been able to accumulate sufficient [capital] with which to buy land," he explained. Black people had been doing the same thing for generations, but MacRae did not extend them figurative or actual credit. In fact, he had hired local Black people to ditch, clear, and fence the land at the Pender County colonies. Then he gave it, ready and arable, to European newcomers, offering them generous mortgages.*

The North Carolina Society closed the evening with entertainment by the choir of the Hampton Institute, Alexander Manly's alma mater, singing "old plantation melodies." MacRae stepped into the Broadway chill, the plangent harmonies of "Steal Away to Jesus" mingling in his mind with worldlier concerns. As he had mentioned in his speech, he was urging the United States Department of Agriculture to begin relocating Europeans on a national scale. "We feel certain that the race problem of the South will either be solved by immigration," he declared, "or will be so greatly minimized that its solution will not be of supreme importance."

THE FINEST HOUSE SINCE THE BELLAMY MANSION WAS COMPLETE. IT WAS called Live Oaks, for the magnificent trees that presided over its grounds, trailing Spanish moss in perfect evocation of Southern cliché. Its owners were the Parsleys—the lumber company owner Walter Linton Parsley and his wife, Agnes, Hugh MacRae's sister. As members of the Secret Nine, Walter Parsley and Hugh MacRae had both been deeply involved in planning the 1898 takeover. They had taken a city, as their minister had bragged, and now, in 1913, they continued to shape it to their advantage.

To design the house, the Parsleys had called on the architect Henry Bacon, who had just received the commission for the Lincoln Memorial.

---

*In the 1930s, with the "race problem" still unresolved, MacRae opened the colonies to Black farmers. J. Vincent Lowery writes, "Whereas he once imagined the region freed from the necessity of Black labor, he adopted a more gently paternalistic position two decades later: 'I do not blame the negro in the least: but taken as an important factor in agricultural conditions, it does not make a bright picture when we realize just how badly we have handled him.'"

He delivered an octagonal house built in the Italian Renaissance style, with coquina walls made from local seashells, and white-columned, wraparound porches. For the ultimate view, one could ascend to the cupola, topped with a pineapple finial, to look out over three hundred feet of private waterfront. The sound-side cottages of Wilmington's white elite had always been beautiful in a rustic, understated way. Live Oaks, however, was a true estate—the Cape Fear equivalent of the Breakers or the Biltmore. The Parsleys moved in on Thanksgiving Day.

"On moonlight nights the sound was full of white sails, the boats filled with ladies and men singing and chatting and sometimes a guitar or banjo playing," Walter Parsley remembered, later in life, of his days on the Masonboro Sound. These idyllic moments were achieved with the help of much work behind the scenes. In a 1910 letter written from Bide-a-Wee Cottage, the Parsleys' earlier summer residence, Agnes Parsley was largely preoccupied with the undertaking of "moving [back] to town" after a busy summer. "Betsy and Annie have almost finished with the house cleaning," she wrote, in a tone of cheerful efficiency. A personnel matter remained to be settled. Agnes added, "I am hoping that my new cook will be a good one—if so, things may be very comfortable this winter."

This cook was likely Athalia Howe Whitfield, who, as a teenager in Brooklyn in 1898, had eluded the Secret Nine and their rampaging foot soldiers by hiding in Pine Forest Cemetery. Her father, William, survived, too, but by 1900 he was working as a cooper, seemingly having lost his position as "boss stevedore." Now nearing thirty, Athalia had spent her working life tending to white people's households. The 1910 census listed her as a laundress, living with various family members in her parents' residence. Around that time, she went to work for the Parsleys, and by 1920, she was the head of her own household. She was successful enough in the job that the Parsleys promoted her to head cook, an accomplishment that has endured as a source of family pride.

The position with the Parsleys gave Athalia a steady living and a measure of prestige, but it required a near-total devotion of her talents and time. She had her own family—James, born in 1907, and Louise, born in 1912—whom she was raising as a single mother. The more sacred a moment, the more given it was to gathering loved ones around a laden table, the more Athalia was expected to be on hand. She worked holidays. She worked Saturdays, producing such delicacies as frozen custard, animal cookies, and angel food cake for the second birthday party of a Parsley grandson, with "a color scheme of pink and white." On New Year's Eve 1920, she almost surely found herself at Live Oaks, creating a buffet for an oyster roast "for about thirty of the younger set," including various Bellamys and MacRaes. As a bonfire flickered, tables set up under the oaks groaned with her handiwork: sandwiches, pickles, cheese straws, beaten biscuits, and bunny cake.

Athalia worked for the Parsleys over the course of decades. In 1939, for example, she worked all fifty-two weeks of the year. She made a total of $468 (around $10,000 today): more than most neighbors employed in private homes, but less than a woman who worked as a seamstress or a man who worked as a janitor at an art museum. In 1935, Congress had passed the Social Security Act, but it intentionally excluded agricultural and domestic workers, the majority of whom were Black. Athalia, therefore, was not entitled to unemployment or retirement benefits. (It wasn't until the

Athalia Howe Whitfield and Cynthia Brown, circa 1958.

1970s that Congress extended to most domestic workers the right to a minimum wage.) Theoretically, she had Sundays off, but the Parsleys sometimes asked her to stay through the weekend. They would send a chauffeur to Brooklyn to collect her children and, later, her grandchildren. Cynthia Brown recalled these occasions as thrilling excursions for Athalia's young offspring: "They would go down to the Sound and catch fish, and she would cook for them."

Wealthy white women such as Agnes Parsley didn't concern themselves with cooking and cleaning. But Agnes was far from idle. As Live Oaks was being built, she was wrapped up in another construction project: the erection of an eight-foot-tall, five-and-a-half-ton monument to George Davis, the attorney general of the Confederacy. Davis, who was born in neighboring Pender County, was a special hero to white Wilmingtonians because of his local ties. He was of particular interest to Agnes because one of his nine children, Monimia, had married her brother Donald. Another Davis daughter had married George Rountree, the Secret Nine leader and grandfather clause mastermind.

Since the end of the Civil War, the Parsley women had carved out a powerful sphere of influence with the United Daughters of the Confederacy. Agnes's sister-in-law was the president of the state chapter. Both women were members of the George Davis Committee, which had raised the $5,010 required for the erection of the statue. Its dedication, on April 20, 1911, began with a parade from the Wilmington Light Infantry building to the site of the statue, wreathed in flowers donated by the UDC. As one ladies' association reminded its members, "A land without monuments is a land without memories."

Although women had done the work of creating the monument, men dominated its public inauguration. Four of Davis's grandsons—including the young Masters Donald MacRae Jr. and George Rountree Jr.—whisked away a drop cloth to reveal Davis's bronze likeness. The statue depicted him in a prophet-like posture, his right hand raised in grandiloquent defiance. According to an inscription on the monument's granite base, Davis represented "the true heart of chivalry in Southern manhood." With Walter

MacRae presiding as the city's mayor, the ceremony resembled a family reunion. The day was a tribute to the white elite's continuity and power, to the living monument to white supremacy that these overlapping families comprised, from the antebellum days to the Civil War, Reconstruction, Redemption, and now, the consolidation of the Jim Crow regime.

Chapter 26

THE HERB THAT FLOURISHETH

In 1912, one of John Dillard Bellamy Jr.'s oldest friends was elected president of the United States. His name was Woodrow Wilson, but John Dillard Jr. knew him by his nickname, "Tommy." Their relationship went back to 1874, when the Wilson family moved to Wilmington so that Tommy's father, Dr. Joseph Ruggles Wilson, could accept a new job as head pastor at First Presbyterian, the Bellamy family church. The families quickly became close, with the Bellamy doctors looking after the Wilsons' health and Dr. Wilson tending to the Bellamys' souls.

Tommy found Wilmington boring and mostly stayed aloof, but he and John Dillard Jr. were inseparable. Down at the riverfront, they admired nautical riggings and quizzed each other on the differences between the schooners, sharpies, barques, brigs, brigantines, and corn crackers. On fine days they set out for "reading raids": long walks into the pine forest, where they would sprawl at the foot of a particularly fine tree, reading aloud from the novels of Sir Walter Scott. "We are like the herb that flourisheth most when trampled upon," Scott assured them as the Lost Cause germinated, holding that white Southerners were both the war's gravest victims and its noblest heroes.

Linked by a mutual sense of destiny, the two young men, according to one Wilson biographer, "haunted each other's houses." One of their favorite pastimes was discussing the great men of history. The Wilsons' butler recalled, "When I wanted to find Mr. Tommy in those days, I would go to his room, and generally there he would be sitting with his elbows on his knees and his nose in a book. He had just two friends in those days—John Bellamy and the old Doctor. If he wasn't reading a book with one, he was talking about a book with the other." Tommy particularly enjoyed spending time in the upholstered grandeur of the Bellamy Mansion. "It was the Old South at its apex," the biographer observed. "This home must have influenced the youth, must have given him something of that ornate and festal languor that brocaded the patterns of Irish lace over his somber and implacable soul."

Occasionally, the companions loosened up, attending church picnics and steamer excursions. "Together they went girling," the biographer writes, "after the fashion of sheep-killing dogs, always in pairs—for safety." Years later, John Dillard Jr. recalled his friend as "a raging social lion," perhaps jokingly, as the pair seem to have been less interested in flirtation than in chaste pranks. At the Bellamy Mansion, they purloined Eliza's much-cherished edition of *Godey's Lady's Book* and drew glasses on all the women pictured inside.

TOMMY WILSON'S EARLY INTERESTS IN SHIPS, GIRLING, AND DOODLING ON women's faces gave way to a career in politics. After stints as the president of Princeton and the governor of New Jersey, he ran for president in 1912, defeating the incumbent William Howard Taft and the third-party candidate and former President Teddy Roosevelt. Wilson garnered just 42 percent of the popular vote but an overwhelming share of the electoral college. He was the first Southerner to hold the office since before the Civil War. He was also the first Democrat to win the Black vote, such as it was with Southern disenfranchisement. On the campaign trail, he had pledged to be "the president of all people," garnering the tentative support of Black luminaries such as W. E. B. Du Bois.

Yet, almost as soon as Wilson took office, it became clear that he was no friend to Black people. A Lost Cause diehard, he filled his cabinet with fellow Southern racists, including the *News & Observer* publisher Josephus Daniels, media cheerleader of the 1898 white supremacy campaign. Daniels served as secretary of the navy for all of Wilson's tenure, sending Marines to occupy Haiti, where they perpetrated "tortures, destructions, humiliations and misery" and introduced Jim Crow to the world's first Black republic.

Before Wilson's election, Black people made up about 10 percent of the federal workforce, which served as a critical pipeline to the middle class. One of Wilson's first moves was to authorize the segregation of the civil service. Prospective hires were required to attach photos to their applications, and many Black workers were dismissed from their positions. For those who remained, impossible conditions stymied productivity and morale. One clerk, Du Bois reported to Wilson, "could not actually be segregated on account of the nature of his work [and] consequently had a cage built around him to separate him from his white companions of many years." Researchers have found that this "unique episode of state-sanctioned discrimination" damaged Black workers' careers in ways that redounded for generations, reducing their earnings by 20 percent and causing declines in homeownership and even in the rates of education, earnings, and social mobility of their descendants.

Meanwhile, Wilson was turning the White House into a Bellamy Mansion on the Potomac—a white-columned shrine to Southern righteousness. In 1913, the elderly sisters Ellen and Eliza Bellamy visited him there, drawing attention with their florid accents and "old-fashioned poke bonnets." Less than two years later, Wilson hosted the second-ever film screening to be held at the residence, inviting guests to watch D. W. Griffith's white supremacist epic, *The Birth of a Nation*. The screening came about due to North Carolina connections: Wilson's old friend Thomas Dixon Jr., from Shelby, had personally persuaded him to show the film, which was largely based on *The Clansman*, his 1905 novel of Ku Klux Klan worship. Dixon's work, while wildly popular, had drawn criticism in the past. Worried that local authorities might ban the film, he and Griffith turned to Wilson, hoping his endorsement could shield it from censorship.

Dixon was explicitly inspired by Wilmington. His first novel, *The Leopard's Spots: A Romance of the White Man's Burden, 1865–1900*, published in 1902, reimagined Wilmington as Independence, a little city dominated by "insolent and incompetent Negroes." The white men of the city are forced to take action to protect white women and children. They pack the town hall and issue a declaration of independence, demanding "the overthrow of the criminal and semi-barbarian regime under which we now live." Just as in Wilmington, they demand the immediate removal of "the negro anarchist who edits a paper in this city." Just as in Wilmington, a Committee of Twenty-Five summons prominent Black men, who fail to reply to their ultimatums, so the white men burn the paper. (In Dixon's version, they get the editor, escorting him away "with a rope around his neck.")

As the lights went down at the White House, Wilson could not have helped feeling flattered. The film approvingly cited his five-volume survey of the country's history, *A History of the American People*. A title card carried a quote from the book:

> Adventurers swarmed out of the North, as much the enemies of one race as of the other, to cozen, beguile, and use the Negroes. . . . In the villages the Negroes were the office holders, men who knew none of the uses of authority, except its insolences.

The perpetrators of racial terror were Wilson's trusted advisers and treasured friends. One can almost hear the grandees of the Secret Nine and the Committee of Twenty-Five whispering into his ear, recounting their exploits in gilded drawing rooms rendered even grander by the spoils of the coup. Like the makers of *The Birth of a Nation*, the Wilmington gentleman-terrorist class considered Wilson's *A History of the American People* a foundational text. The book was published in 1902, just four years after their killing spree. They lived it; he wrote it, with fidelity to their memories.

In *Chronicles of the Cape Fear River: 1660–1916*, the Wilmington cotton baron James Sprunt characterized Wilson as a sort of bard of 1898. He particularly appreciated Wilson's view of reluctant, benevolent white vigilantism: "The white men were roused by a mere instinct of self-preservation," Wilson wrote, praising the "great Ku Klux Klan" as "a veritable empire of the South." Conditions in Wilmington, Sprunt argued, had required the same kind of violent intervention. To prove his case, he was able to cite no less an authority than a president of the United States.

In *The Leopard's Spots*, Dixon depicted the federal government's indifference to Black pleas for help as the coup's crowning moment. "For the first time since 1867," he wrote, "it fell on deaf ears." For Dixon, this marked a turning point—Reconstruction well and truly over. "The Anglo-Saxon race has been reunited," he wrote, adding that the event "made a tremendous impression on the imagination of the people." This melodramatic view of history clearly resonated with Wilson, who praised *The Birth of a Nation*'s emotional impact, reportedly likening it to "writing history with lightning."

Wilson may have also taken some practical insights from Dixon's work. In the summer of 1919—so called the Red Summer as racial terrorism resurged in the wake of the war—white mobs in at least twenty-eight cities attacked, shot, burned, and lynched thousands of Black people. Many of them were veterans returning from the war in Europe, singled out for "disproportionate abuse and assaults" by white people bent on denying them the freedoms that they had fought for abroad. The violence was the worst since Reconstruction, and just as in the Reconstruction years, the Klan, emboldened by the popularity of *The Birth of a Nation*, was rising again. Wilson was in Paris, deep in peace negotiations. Civil rights groups urged him to do something—"We call upon you, in the name of justice, to use every method within your power to stop this carnage of blood now raging," the National Association of Colored Women wrote in a telegram.

"A boy never gets over his boyhood," Wilson once declared, explaining that the only place "where nothing has to be explained to me is the South." His training showed in his response to the violence. Just as in 1898, Black people were asserting themselves. Just as in 1898, they encountered lethal white anger. Wilson could have sent troops to protect Black citizens, he could have pushed for federal anti-lynching legislation, he could have addressed the nation and told the terrorists that he would spare no effort to make them stop. The moment called for decisive federal action against racial terror. Instead, Wilson did nothing, insisting, just as McKinley had in 1898, that the violence was a local problem, to be dealt with by local authorities—or not.

Chapter 27

MRS. HALSEY

In 1913, Sallie Halsey's eldest daughter, Mary, fell ill and died. She and her husband were back in Wilmington at the time, and after her death, her widower decided it was time to leave town for good. He packed up for New York, with Sallie and some other relatives in tow. It had been fifteen years since Joshua's murder. Sallie was fifty-eight—living in a huge Northern city for the first time in her life, trying to keep the family together even as the centrifugal forces of sickness, poverty, and plain bad luck spun them into difficulty.

Tragedy struck the family again in 1916, when Sallie's youngest daughter, Bessie Halsey Cato, who had remained in Wilmington, died of pulmonary tuberculosis, likely brought on by syphilis. Her husband, also suffering from the disease, was committed to an asylum and died soon thereafter, as did two of the couple's young children. Their remaining children, Wilhelmina ("Annie") and Juanita, were left parentless, so Sallie sent for them and brought them to New York.

By this point, Wilmington was a void more than a homeplace for the Halseys. For years, Mildred Clinton, Joshua's sister, had managed to hang on to the house on Bladen Street, but in 1918, she had lost control of the property under troublesome circumstances. What, exactly, happened is unclear, but a sale notice indicated that she forfeited the property under some kind of legal duress. "Under and by virtue of the power vested in me as Commissioner in a decree of the Superior Court of New Hanover County,

N.C., in the matter of the City of Wilmington against Mildred Clinton, I will offer for sale for cash, to satisfy the judgment therein, to the highest bidder," the notice read. The notice was signed by the assistant city attorney, Chesley C. Bellamy—John Dillard's grandson, christened after John Calhoun, the patron saint of slavery and secession.

Soon after bringing her orphaned grandchildren north, Sallie moved to Summit, New Jersey. In 1920, Sallie is sixty-five—still working, doing white people's laundry, raising a six-year-old and a thirteen-year-old by herself. She is the head of the household; matriarch and patriarch; roots, trunk, and unshakable, ever-reaching branch of a family tree that has been stripped of too many leaves. She stretches herself to cover the bare spots. She makes sure her granddaughters have the shade of love and stability. She makes enough money to rent part of a cute brick house on a street called Orchard Street. The neighbors are butchers, shoemakers, gardeners, machinists, freight men; Black and white, many of them born in Italy. A little iron eagle over an archway that covers the entrance serves as a reminder of the wages of flight, but also its possibilities.

Annie and Juanita grow up. The women's household expands—the three of them move to another house in Summit, joined by Juanita's husband, Grady Starks, and their infant son, Grady Jr. Annie marries, too, but the relationship doesn't last long. She and her infant daughter, also named Juanita ("Needa"), live in the Summit house with their relatives. Starks works at a shipyard. Juanita stays home with the baby, while Annie works as a maid at the local hospital.

With the family back on its feet, Sallie can finally rest a bit. She goes to church. She gets to know her great-grandchildren. When she dies, in the summer of 1940, her obituary reveals no trace of her tumultuous past, of the travails she's survived and surmounted. Her funeral services bear respectful mention in the newspaper. She has the proper send-off that Joshua never got, and she is laid to rest in a suburban memorial garden, where her relatives can visit her grave.

"Mrs. Halsey, who was the widow of Joshua Halsey, was a member of the Fountain Baptist Church, and a member of the Missionary Circle," the notice reads. "She has been a resident of this city for some thirty years."

Once shunned as a "woman sneak thief," she is now a valued citizen, Mrs. Sallie Halsey. Sallie took a great risk in leaving Wilmington, in reinventing everything so that peace and stability, rather than the upheavals of the past, would be the last words of her life. Horrible things happened to her, but she outran them. She just kept going. In the end, her descendants will see her as a great success.

Chapter 28

VISIBLE WORK

Once they had settled questions of politics to their liking, by disenfranchising Black voters at the turn of the century, the white supremacists turned their attention to the schools. Charles Aycock, one of the leaders of the 1898 statewide white supremacy campaign, rose to power in 1900, positioning himself as "the educational governor." Aycock argued that white North Carolinians, having eliminated Black men from political life, should now embrace universal public education. "I believe in the education of everybody," Aycock declared. "Yes, and I believe in the education of n——s. You believe in the education of a mule; you train your setter pups and fox hounds."

In Aycock's view, schools could serve as a sop to Black people, a consolation prize for the loss of the Black ballot. They were also an effective means of social control. White North Carolinians' interest, Aycock argued, lay in extending education to "the Negro in our midst" rather than leaving him vulnerable to outside influence, particularly that of Northern philanthropists. It was better to educate Black people on limited terms, he warned, than to risk the total alienation and possible exodus of "that race which does a very large proportion of the actual hard labor in the state."

In 1915, Wilmington's school board was all white, as it had been since 1898, when coup leaders forced its one Black member (along with two white Republicans) to resign. The current board included several 1898 ringleaders. Even the officials for the Williston district, serving Black students, were all white; one of them had been a member of the Committee of Twenty-Five. The chairman of another district was John D. Bellamy Jr., serving a thirteen-year term.

Many of the 1898 conspirators had made or multiplied fortunes since the coup. Now, in their benevolent paternalist phase, they shaped the city's educational institutions with gifts of cash and land: two and a quarter acres from Hugh MacRae; eleven hundred dollars from James Sprunt for cement and piping; another lot acquired "through the generosity of Mr. and Mrs. W. L. Parsley," after whom an elementary school would eventually be named. Meanwhile, B. F. Keith, the white man who had refused to go along with the white supremacists in 1898, contended with social ostracism and sabotage. "I gave my best years to Wilmington although the mob ruined my business, one of the best in the city, by organizing all the crooked traveling salesmen in the city to lie on me throughout the Carolinas, telling all the merchants that handled my goods that I believed in social equality and intermarrying of the races," he wrote in 1921, petitioning the new Republican president, Warren Harding, for compensation for the "dirty treatment" he'd received "simply because I was straight and fair to all alike."

In the half century since emancipation, the New Hanover County public school system's expenditures on Black education had been "so insignificant," a report by the board acknowledged, "that we ought to be ashamed to mention it." Wilmington's Black citizens paid taxes like their white counterparts, but they didn't receive the same benefits: If they wanted to improve their schools, they were obliged to use their own money and labor. In fact, the public school system had not put a cent toward a Black school building since 1873, when Alfred Howe had persuaded his school board colleagues to allocate three thousand dollars to purchase the Williston schoolhouse from the American Missionary Association.

The 1915 opening of Williston Industrial School, then, represented an unprecedented public investment in Black education. Twenty thousand dollars from the school board paid for a new, three-story building with a grand central staircase, constructed on a spacious campus at Tenth and Church. According to a white official, the school was intended to "enable the colored people to better equip themselves for the duties of life in their own homes and to render more valuable services to their employers."

Male students spent the initial weeks of the term clearing "an undergrowth of years' standing, and full of stumps, roots, and other obstructions." They cultivated vegetables on five acres of adjoining land, in keeping with the Booker T. Washingtonian emphasis on agricultural and industrial training. "We have not seen in the county a finer growth and yield of Irish potatoes," the school board boasted. Female students perfected their laundering, cooking, and sewing, one year producing no fewer than fourteen gingham aprons, ten children's dresses, and five ladies' corset covers. Their Black teachers, among them Howes and Sadgwars, received a base salary of thirty-five dollars a month to their white counterparts' seventy-five.

Despite its inferior budget and straitened curriculum, Williston was an impressive facility—a commodious, modern institution in a traditionally Black neighborhood. "So located that it is not desirable for use by the white race for school purposes, but it is convenient to the colored people and extremely well adopted for the purpose for which it is intended," the school board explained, straining to congratulate itself on the school's opening without arousing white jealousy. With political strife lying dormant for the time being, education was emerging as the primary arena of conflict between white supremacy and Black autonomy.

ALFRED MOORE WADDELL SERVED TWO MAYORAL TERMS AND WROTE SEVeral books in semiretirement (surely he would have said "penned"). When he died of a heart attack in 1912, at the age of seventy-seven, the flag on every municipal building was lowered to half-mast. For almost a decade, Wilmington's mayor had not been a Waddell or a Moore. Then, in 1913, the election of Parker "Quince" Moore—one of the Colonel's sons—put the Family back in charge at City Hall.

Quince wasn't a political animal in the mode of the 1898 generation. Though he had been twenty-two in 1898, he didn't play a notable role in his father's paramilitaries, nor did he sign the White Declaration of

Independence. (He may have been mourning his four-month-old son, Roger, who died in his crib at the Colonel's house on Christmas Eve of 1896, smothered by a pet cat.) Once elected, he sold his interest in the brick firm and governed as a modernizing booster, largely sticking to unobjectionable issues like infrastructure. When Quince appeared at a Black church, it was to discuss the topic of "Good Roads."

The outbreak of World War I united the nation in a common cause. Black men enlisted in droves—including some twelve hundred from Wilmington—even though they were largely assigned to segregated regiments and many faced harassment and violence upon their return. Two decades after 1898, the country's social fabric was changing, but North Carolina's good-old-boy network remained formidable. John Dillard's twenty-two-year-old grandson, Lieutenant Hargrove Bellamy, demonstrated "extraordinary heroism in action" fighting near the Hindenburg Line, remaining with his soldiers even after sustaining a wound. At the end of the war, upon Hargrove's release from a German prison camp, his father, Robert Rankin Bellamy, appealed to Senator Furnifold Simmons for help bringing him home. "Through the efforts of Sen. Simmons, Lieut. Bellamy has been supplied with whatever money he needs and is expected to sail for home shortly," one newspaper reported, adding that the young soldier was "prominently connected in the state."

The war meant that the factories desperately needed labor. White business owners, when it suited them, selectively loosened the racial restrictions that had been put in place with the White Declaration of Independence. The Carolina Shipbuilding Company, for example, counted Black carpenters, blacksmiths, and riveters among its eight-thousand-man workforce. After the armistice, however, white workers protested management's plans to keep on skilled Black workers, and fighting broke out at the plant. This time, white capitalists saw an interest in keeping Black workers at the hangars and furnaces. Ignoring "howls of ridicule and abuse," Hugh MacRae's Tidewater Power Company continued to allow Black workers to ride its unsegregated trolley cars to the factory.

Quince served as mayor until a commission form of local government was instituted in 1921. He receded into the business world, but a decade later, he burst back onto the scene as part of a wild scandal involving the Wilmington heiress Jessie Hargrave Kenan Wise. A daughter of William Rand Kenan, who led the machine gun squad in 1898, Wise had inherited an ungodly amount of money from her sister, the widow of the Palm Beach industrialist Henry Flagler, a founder of Standard Oil and developer of Palm Beach. (At Flagler's Florida hotels, Black men pedaled white tourists around on wheeled chairs called "Afromobiles.") Quince and an accomplice, the city's former police chief, sent Wise a letter threatening to kill her unless she dropped nearly fifty thousand dollars at a countryside filling station. According to reports, they paid "four Negroes" a dollar to fetch the bag, but the scheme quickly unraveled.

Curiously, the Wilmington papers hardly covered Quince's trial, which resulted in his conviction on blackmail charges in 1933. Some Wilmingtonians believed that Quince's scandal was part of a larger pattern of dire fates visited on the plotters of 1898 and their kin in the years after the coup. In 1900, for example, at the height of his authority, the Colonel was getting into his pajamas after a busy day when "he dropped upon the bed and died without a word." Not long after, his co-conspirator Solomon Fishblate contracted an excruciating kidney disease and went blind. The 1898 leaders were aging, of course. A new generation was taking over. Yet, in the absence of legal sanction, people who had suffered at their hands couldn't help but hope that some spiritual justice was being done.

Alfred Moore Waddell's line ended when his son, Alfred Moore Waddell Jr., shot himself at his home in the Carolina Apartments. But the Colonel's descendants went forth and multiplied, regarding him as a role model even after his death. Eugenia, his widow, so longed to see him one more time in his wartime grays that, at some point, she asked her son Roger to try them on and pose for a photographer. "Mama wanted a picture of Papa in his Confederate uniform," Roger wrote, adding that the suit "fitted as though it had been made for me." Whoever created the portrait clipped an image of the father's head from another photograph and pasted it onto the son's body: the Confederacy and the Colonel rising again, together. The

Composite portrait of a Confederate soldier, created using Roger Moore's body and his late father Colonel Roger Moore's head.

expectation that each generation would bear his ancestors upon his shoulders has rarely been so emphatically conveyed.

After Alfred's death, his much younger widow, Gabrielle, stepped into public life, devoting most of her energy to historical preservation with the Colonial Dames and the UDC. In 1919 and 1920, as North Carolina debated whether to ratify the Nineteenth Amendment, she threw herself into the fray, lobbying against women's right to vote. The logic of anti-suffragism had little to do with gender and everything to do with race. Activists such as Gabrielle reasoned that if white women could vote, then it might open the door for Black women, and if Black women voted, who could stop Black men?

The suffrage debate presented a direct contest between a white woman's gendered interests and her racialized ones. Gabrielle chose the latter, serving as vice president of the Southern Women's Rejection League's North Carolina chapter, whose male supporters included many of her late husband's associates from 1898. Together, these women and men diverted the question of female suffrage into a referendum on white supremacy. "God grant that North Carolina has enough men with the spirit of the Old South left in them to go down with their backs to the wall," one anti-suffragist prayed. This battle cry, though perpetual, was urgent enough to ensure the amendment's narrow defeat. (White women got the vote in 1920 anyway, but North Carolina did not formally ratify the Nineteenth Amendment until 1971.)

The Waddells and their contemporaries preferred a fixed, passive image of Black womanhood. In 1923, the UDC and Congressman Charles Manly Stedman—Alfred's brother's wife's sister's husband—nearly succeeded in erecting a so-called mammy monument near the National Mall. Stedman had practiced law in Wilmington before being elected to Congress, serving ten terms as the last Civil War veteran. When the Jefferson Davis chapter of the UDC came up with the idea to honor "the faithful slave mammies of the South" with a statue, he volunteered to sponsor it in the House.

Just weeks earlier, the Senate had allowed an anti-lynching bill to die by filibuster. But the chamber acted quickly on the mammy monument, appropriating two hundred thousand dollars for its construction. With the atrocities of Red Summer having recently laid bare the nation's elemental hypocrisies, and Black people streaming out of the South, raising fears of a sectional labor crisis, the mammy monument offered an idealized picture of a consensual racial hierarchy. Of the Black women it ostensibly honored, Stedman declared, "No class of people held in bondage could be found anywhere who lived more free from care of distress."

Proposed designs for the monument trafficked in the same fiction. One depicted a stolid Black woman in a kerchief tenderly cradling a white baby, his older siblings clinging nearby. An inexhaustible font of milk and absolution, the mammy demanded nothing of white people, only gave. Her own children were nowhere to be seen. This non-transactional, chaste version of interracial intimacy denied the realities of sexual violence and economic exploitation. Even in her moment of honor, the mammy was, of course, on her feet.

The mammy statue was really a monument to white women. The UDC president general later admitted as much, stressing the value of such memorials as "*visible* work" bringing the Confederate daughters "publicity and acclaim" for decades of labor behind the scenes. Black people saw through the ploy. "Democracy is the monument that the noble 'black mammy' wants erected to her, and not this marble shaft which can only be a symbol of servitude to teach white and black alike that the menial callings are the Negro's place in the scheme of things," one activist wrote. The *Washington Eagle* issued a fierce challenge: "Let the daughters of Confederacy erect a monument to the 'Black Mammies of the South,' and we will put a bomb under it."

Confronted with their near-unanimous rejection of the statue, the House let the bill languish in committee. But in Wilmington, well into the twentieth century, the Confederate mentality was still going strong.

Chapter 29

I WANT IT ALL EXACTLY

It was late April 1937, the seventy-seventh year that eighty-four-year-old Ellen Bellamy had seen the magnolias bloom behind the filigreed iron fence that her father had bought with profits from his turpentine plantation. Dwindling money and deteriorating health meant that she was now confined to a few rooms on the Bellamy Mansion's top floor. A literal Confederate in an attic, she navigated her ever-shrinking domain in a high-backed wicker wheelchair, passing out ginger biscuits to young relations on their visits.

One described Ellen as "an unreconstructed rebel." She had never married or had children. Eight of her nine siblings were gone, including Eliza, her lifelong roommate. As the historian John Haley has pointed out, Ellen's life "coincided with most of the significant events in the history of the United States during the late nineteenth and early twentieth centuries." She'd witnessed the advent of the New South, the Frontier Wars, the Spanish-American War, the Populist and Progressive eras, World War I, and the Great Depression. Yet only the Civil War—the War, as she called it—fundamentally mattered. Those years were "so vividly impressed on my memory," she wrote, "I often go over them during the wakeful hours of the night."

Broom corn that the family had planted in the lean wartime days still grew in the front yard, the *Wilmington Morning Star* reported, "shooting forth lusty shoots even today, as it helps to keep alive the spirit of Ante-Bellum days." The damask draperies that John Dillard had purchased in New York in 1860 still hung from the windows. They had never once been taken down, even to be cleaned. Before her physical confines shrank to match her mental world, Ellen would walk to the downtown shops, taking special care to cross the street when she came to the WLI Armory in a show of disdain for the American flag that now hung in front. She sat alone in her turn-of-the-century topknot and solemn black clothes, polishing the family silver in the palace of her memory. Surrounding her were framed engravings of Confederate generals, whom she referred to as "my sweethearts."

The Bellamy name was still synonymous with aristocratic privilege, but the family no longer ruled alone over Wilmington society. More than ten years earlier—in the "most brilliant wedding of the entire winter," per the *Star*—John Dillard Jr.'s youngest daughter, Marguerite Grist Bellamy, had married Hugh MacRae's only son, Nelson MacRae, uniting the city's two most powerful families in a profusion of pink roses and snapdragons.

John Dillard Jr., Ellen's last remaining sibling, was in the emeritus phase of his career. In 1927, he found time for his first trip abroad, securing passports so that he and his wife could travel to Fiesole, Italy, where one of their daughters was living. This was a very Bellamy thing, a very old-Wilmington thing—to be the richest people in town but to bother with a trip to Europe only if you could count on being received by one of your own. In Rome, John Dillard Jr. encountered Mussolini, but he declined to be introduced, he recalled, "because of the unfavorable opinion given me by the Count at Genoa, and other prominent Italians I had met who could speak English." He reserved his greatest enthusiasm for various infrastructural wonders, such as the paraffin, naphtha, and benzine house paints that he encountered in Wimereux, France, which he was told "lasted as long as the best linseed oil paints in America."

John Dillard Jr. never stopped promoting the idea of governance by force. He and his old pal Woodrow Wilson had fallen out during the 1912 election, when John Dillard Jr. supported another candidate for the Democratic nomination. They never mended their relationship, but John Dillard Jr. did venture to send a letter to Wilson, once elected, on a matter of utmost importance. "As an old friend and associate of yours, I would like to make a suggestion," he wrote, urging the president not to withdraw American troops from Mexico, where they were occupying Veracruz. John Dillard Jr. continued, "The American mining and agricultural interests are very great and valuable in Mexico and now is the opportune time to annex this country, as we did Texas." In other words, he was lobbying the president to push aside the legitimate government and seize Mexico for America's own—to take a country, just as he and his cohort had taken Wilmington in 1898. Even to Wilson, the suggestion was outrageous. His reply was so "curt and offensive" that John Dillard Jr. tore up the letter and threw it into the trash.

When John Dillard Jr. died in 1942, *The New York Times* carried his obituary, calling him "the dean of the North Carolina bar." The article mentioned his election to Congress in 1898 but said nothing of the brutality that secured it. For most white people, the era's events had faded into oblivion. To the extent that they were mentioned, they were presented as ineluctable and preordained—hand-of-God stuff, rather than the willing work of scheming men.

"Since that time Wilmington has greatly prospered," *A Child's History of North Carolina* declared of the 1898 "revolution" that restored the government of "competent white men." Another textbook assured students that "the menace of the dark cloud was removed from the life of Wilmington and the state of North Carolina," quickly moving on to the great snowstorm of 1899. The lesson was that 1898 was effectively political weather—an event that came and went, without antecedent or lingering effect—and that no one was to blame. The last of the 1898 conspirators died as grandees, remembered for their accomplishments in law, politics, and business, rather than for the violence that had purchased their success.

ELLEN, HOWEVER, WAS STILL LIVING IN THE MID-NINETEENTH CENTURY. She decided to write a memoir, calling it *Back with the Tide*—an allusion to her hope for the restoration of the world order that Scarlett O'Hara feared had gone with the wind. The document opens in 1865, with the "burly Yankee soldiers" sacking the Bellamy-Parsley refuge at Floral College. Ellen's development seems to have been arrested the day that the Union Army threatened her bone-handled forks and carried off the people her family enslaved. With undiminished, adolescent anger, she recounted the saga of her father's quest for a pardon that would allow him to get his house back. "For what?" she writes. "For being a Southern Gentleman, A Rebel, and a large Slave Owner!"

Like many white Southerners, Ellen avoided substantive engagement with the issues that had provoked the war and precluded closure, preferring to focus on perceived crimes of manners. The slaughter of World War I was fewer than twenty years past, and it was already clear that another bloody conflict loomed, but for Ellen, no horror surpassed that of the "terrible" days of Reconstruction. "Not an easy matter with the city under the rule of 'Carpet-Baggers' and n——s!" she recalled, adding, "No real recovery till the 'Riot,' in 1898." (Her highly selective use of the N-word, a slur then as now, leaves no doubt that she knew the word's violence and wished to inflict it. She referred to Black people that she approved of as "Negroes.")

The writer Isabel Wilkerson likens America to an old house, with a caste system serving as its unseen framework, as fundamental to its functioning as studs and joists. "Caste is the infrastructure of our divisions," she explains. "It is the architecture of human hierarchy, the subconscious code of instructions for maintaining, in our case, a four-hundred-year-old social order." Race and, to a far lesser degree, class are the caste system's soft furnishings—the visible, changeable means of expressing its underlying design.

The archetypal caste enforcer, Ellen clung to her place at the top of the American hierarchy as stubbornly as she did her rooms in the heights of her falling-down mansion. In 1937, the pear trees and strawberry plants whose fruit she'd gorged on as a girl were gone, as were the Black workers who had tended them, forcing her to buy "by the pound at a ridiculously high price." To Ellen, this went against the natural way of things. "None of these generations of slaves is left and the descendants of our old overseers and neighbors—the very plain and common folk are now occupying important places in State and society," she wrote. To call out the origins of these people was to perpetuate her position of perceived superiority—over Black people and among white ones.

By the 1940s, the Bellamy Mansion had fallen into disrepair. But because caste is not money and it's not power and it's not beauty—although those things, or the perception of them, accrue to people at the pyramid's top—Ellen could receive guests in a "great, gray apparition" of a house and feel like she was doing them a favor. Part of an upstairs floor had been subdivided to accommodate a rental apartment, and the mahogany furniture sat shrouded in tarps. Still, an observer noted, callers "use all social leverage to have a visit with one of the most interesting 'ladies of quality' of this lovely old city by the sea." They were rewarded with the chance to encounter "a dainty, aristocratic lady of the old school," who gave "the delicate impression of 'lavender and old lace.'"

IN 1942, AS HIS ELDERLY RELATION CLUNG TO APPEARANCES IN HER CRUMbling downtown mansion, Hugh MacRae II was in his final year at St. Paul's School, the elite New Hampshire boarding school. Unlike the Bellamy side of the family, which crossed the Mason-Dixon Line reluctantly, the MacRae family had a tradition of sending its scions to Northern institutions. Hugh's grandfather, the first Hugh MacRae, had an engineering degree from MIT, and his father, Nelson, had also attended St. Paul's. "St. Paul's school was the first boarding school in America and is often considered today to be the finest single school in the world," Hugh II boasted. Even if his accent set him apart from his classmates—"*skoo-wel*," he said, rhyming the word with *jewel* and stretching it to two syllables—he fell in easily with the nation's sons of privilege, playing football and hockey for Isthmian, a school club, and captaining the crew.

One evening, just as the spring term was getting underway, Hugh II was working in the library. Someone came and summoned him to the school office. His father had fallen ill, he was told, and he needed to get himself to Wilmington as quickly as possible. Hugh got a car to Boston. Then he made the overnight train ride from Boston to Wilmington, worrying about his father the entire way. When he arrived, he went straight to his Bellamy grandparents' house, just down the block from the family mansion on Market Street.

Hugh II burst in the door: "Where's Dad?"

"What do you mean, Where's Dad?" a cousin replied. "Come here, I'll show you where Dad is." Hugh II walked into a bedroom and saw his father lying in an open casket. His cousin didn't know that no one had told him that Nelson was dead.

"Your father killed himself," she said.

Nelson, forty-eight, had shot himself in the chest with a .32-caliber pistol. He was found in a bathroom of his home in Oleander, a sparkling suburb that he had helped to develop as vice president of Hugh MacRae and Company. His death was as inexplicable to his family as it was shocking. (Later, members of the family would attribute it to depression.) He died without a will, so his property went to his wife, Marguerite Grist Bellamy MacRae, and their children, Hugh II and his thirteen-year-old sister, Marguerite.

Hugh II had been taught to take things stoically—never to show vulnerability or to project weakness—so that's what he did. At seventeen, he was now the head of the family. He went back to St. Paul's, graduated, and turned himself into the man of starch and enterprise that he was expected to be. He continued to Princeton, interrupting his studies in 1943 to join the Aviation Cadet Program of the U.S. Army Air Force. When the war was over, he returned to Princeton, where he allowed himself the tiny liberty of majoring in economics instead of his grandfather and father's discipline, engineering.

IN 1945, THE WRITERS TALBOT AND JESSICA HAMLIN, CRUISING THE EAST Coast in their sailboat, stopped at Wilmington to tour the historic district. They were drawn to the Bellamy Mansion, which, they wrote, "stood out from all the rest because of its magnificence of scale as well as its almost complete absence of paint." Visiting turned out to be as easy as walking up the front stairs and ringing the bell. Lina Stallings, Ellen's "companion, secretary, nurse, errand boy, and friend for five decades," opened the door, bundled in a thick sweater against the cold. The high-ceilinged entry hall, the Hamlins noted, was thick with dust. In the dining room, they noticed cabinets full of immaculate porcelain, but the vast kitchen was nearly empty, except for a cheap gas stove and a little table littered with dime-store plates. Stallings, still working at seventy-three, complained about "the whims, caprices, exigencies of her still more ancient employer." She told the Hamlins that Ellen forbade anyone to clean or paint the house, or to touch the gardens, insisting, "I want it all exactly as it was when I was young."

Ellen died at the Bellamy Mansion the next year. The last time the house had changed hands was upon her father's death, nearly half a century earlier. More than fifty heirs, a complicated mishmash of nieces and nephews and cousins, had some claim to the property. Ellen's will revealed that she had neglected to pay property taxes on the house for more than a decade. As negotiations over the estate dragged on, Lina Stallings refused to vacate the premises, tearfully telling the *Star* that she had nowhere else to go, and that "Miss Ellen" had promised her she could stay as long as she was alive.

With the mansion's future in limbo, Ellen was laid to rest at the First Presbyterian Church. Nearly half a century earlier, the Reverend Peyton Hoge had proclaimed from the same pulpit that the men of her generation had taken a city. Ellen had dug in her nails and hung on to it as tightly as she could. As the mourners sang hymns, her nephews and nieces approached the altar, adding red and white carnations to a floral arrangement. It transformed the surface of her casket into a Confederate battle flag—a final statement of ultraconservatism from beyond the grave.

Chapter 30

FLEAS IN A JAR

Summit, New Jersey, was getting too expensive for the Halseys, and the growing family needed more space. In 1941, the year after Sallie's death, her granddaughter Juanita and her husband, Grady Starks, welcomed another baby. Two years later, they had their third and fourth children—twins Joan and Jean, the latter of whom died just after birth. Grady and Juanita started thinking about the Bedford-Stuyvesant neighborhood of Brooklyn, where the rent was cheaper and some of their Wilmington kin already lived. In 1944, the Starkses—accompanied by Juanita's sister, Annie,

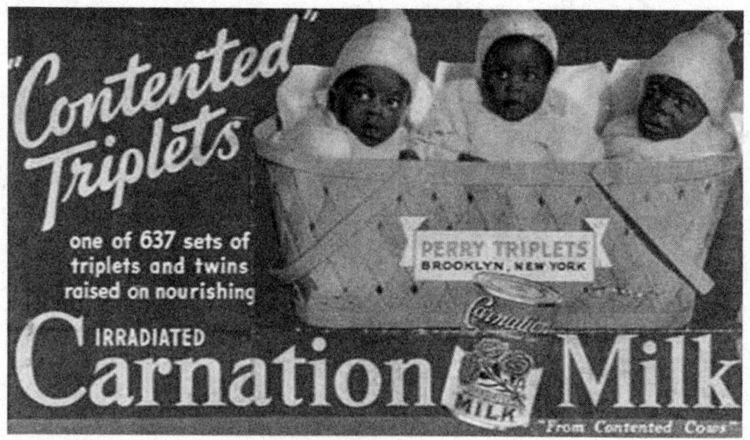

The Perry triplets in an ad for Carnation Milk.

and her daughter, Needa—moved into rooms in a converted auto body shop at 143 Jefferson Avenue. They laughed about the way their new environment felt like a kind of homecoming: "From Brooklyn to Brooklyn!"

North Carolina faded from memory as the Starkses reinvented themselves as New Yorkers. The baby triplets of their Brooklyn cousins, the Perrys, appeared in an ad for Carnation Milk. In 1963, Grady was the subject of a *Look* magazine report about Black life in "'the Box,' the huge Bedford-Stuyvesant ghetto in Brooklyn." The magazine photographed him at home, where he minded a grandson during the day, and at work, manning the door of an apartment building in a middle-class white neighborhood in a livery coat, bow tie, and cap. "The job doesn't pay anything, but it has a certain air of dignity," Grady said.

Across the country, racist federal policies such as urban renewal and redlining were cheating Black communities and the people who lived in them. The Blacker the neighborhood, the more resources the federal government denied its inhabitants, creating far-ranging inequities that endure today. The government-run Home Owners' Loan Corporation, for example, awarded its worst rating, "D," to Bed-Stuy, branding it as an area where it would be "hazardous" for a lender to offer a mortgage. In deciding upon a rating, the agency considered the presence of Southern Black people like the Starkses an explicit defect. "Colored infiltration a definitely adverse influence on neighborhood desirability," an assessor declared.

Grady was well aware that he earned less than a white man would have for the same labor, and that his dollar didn't go as far. Black people, he pointed out to *Look*, paid rent just like his white employers. Yet that rent entitled white people to a doorman, parquet floors, and laundry facilities, while he and his neighbors got tenement conditions and spotty trash collection. Worse, some white people attributed these disparities to laziness or a lack of ambition. Starks recalled that he had once lost a job at a gas company after applying for a promotion. "When I brought up the fact that Negroes couldn't get better jobs there, the union told me that Negroes didn't want those jobs," he said. "That's what white people do—they tell us what we don't want."

Look reported, "On the job, Starks is courteous, says little, is liked by the white tenants." Off the job, he was more outspoken, and his critical mindset created tension with his wife and some of his neighbors, "who feel he is trying to put himself above them with his talking, his analyses, his 'differentness.'" The reporter had no idea that sixty-five years earlier, Starks's wife's grandfather Joshua Halsey had been murdered by a white supremacist mob, yet he detected the family's habit of keeping their heads down, of living with silence. If some survivors found purpose in remembrance, the Halseys coped by letting go. Sallie had persisted by staying quiet, blending in, and moving on. This tendency manifested itself in her descendants in an easygoing stoicism. Sallie's great-great-grandson Nate Brown would later describe it as "never really showing the pain or bitterness that most of us feel when life hits us that hard." With few resources to work through what had happened to them, and still fewer means of redress, the Halseys chose a form of strategic forgetting.

The Colored American had prophesied that "Remember Wilmington" would be "a drumbeat that will carry [the Negro] out of the mire of im-

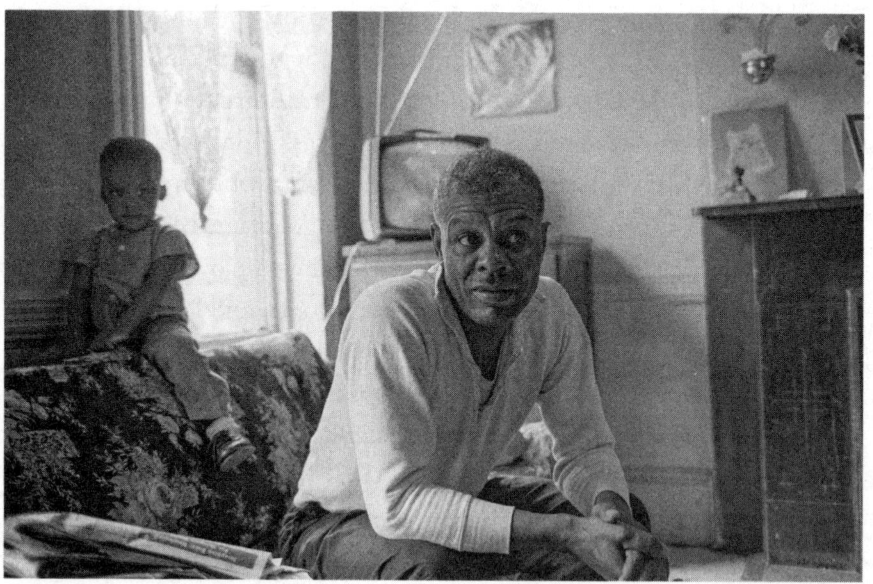

Grady Starks and his grandson Bryant, photographed for *Look* magazine. Brooklyn, 1963.

pending defeat to racial glory and honor," and that the memory of the massacre would be kept alive to motivate Black success, the best revenge. But in many Black families, memories of 1898 had been hushed to a whisper. "You ask them questions, they clam right up," one Black man said of his parents' generation. People like Sallie kept quiet because they didn't want to subject their children to sadness and anger, because they didn't want to be denied a loan or lose a pension. Another Black man likened this reticence to a science experiment in which "you put fleas in a jar, and you put a top on it, and you can remove the top and they never jump higher than the top." He continued, "And similarly here in Wilmington, you have a conditioning that you just don't talk about it. And if you look at 1898, and think about it, if you look at the names on the White Declaration of Independence, you can look in the Yellow Pages, they are here."

THE 1898 COUP HAD SUCCEEDED SO THOROUGHLY IN ELIMINATING BLACK people from public life in Wilmington that by 1950, the city still didn't have a single Black policeman, fireman, city councilman, county commissioner, or member of the board of education. In November of that year, letters appeared on the desks of county officials, signaling the first significant public challenge to the white power regime in over half a century. On cream letterhead, lawyers from Virginia informed the administrators that concerned Black citizens of New Hanover County had retained their firm "to investigate whether or not the colored school children are being afforded an education inferior to that being provided for white children." The lawyers requested permission to tour several schools as part of a fact-gathering mission.

The leader of the concerned citizens was the physician Hubert A. Eaton. A native of Winston-Salem, he trained at the University of Michigan and moved to Wilmington several years earlier upon marrying Celeste Burnett, the daughter of a pioneering Black doctor in Wilmington. Unable to find a house to rent or buy due to residential segregation, the newlyweds initially lived with Celeste's parents. After two years, they bought a place on the outskirts of a mostly Black neighborhood. "Because several white families lived in the block, the real estate agent agreed to sell me the property only through a dummy intermediary owner," Eaton recalled.

The first thing Eaton did was put in a tennis court. He had discovered the game as a child and quickly became an accomplished player, winning the American Tennis Association's national junior title in 1933. Black players were barred from city courts, but everyone was welcome at the Eatons'. The house rules were simple: If you dropped a set without winning at least one game, you had to go buy sodas for everyone at a nearby superette.

In 1946, Eaton arranged for Althea Gibson, a promising young player from Harlem, to come to Wilmington. The plan was for her to finish her schooling at Williston while boarding with him and his family. Eaton remembered that she showed up "carrying two cardboard suitcases fastened with leather belts," with "a wad of dollar bills secured inside her blouse by a large safety pin." At Williston, Gibson played basketball and joined the marching band. Eaton served as her mentor and subsidized her career on the youth tennis circuit. Gibson went on to become the first Black American to win a Grand Slam tournament. "It was in Dr. Eaton's home, while completing high school, that I received love and encouragement," she said in 1957, just after accepting the Wimbledon trophy from Queen Elizabeth.

Analytical and self-contained, Eaton played a long game in tennis and in life. His aloof nature masked a fierce desire to triumph in seemingly hopeless situations. The more outmatched he was, the harder he played. Early in his career, Eaton's father-in-law had gently criticized his stiff bedside manner. So the young doctor literally taught himself to smile, forcing a friendly expression for so many hours that his facial muscles ached at the end of the day. He wrote, "I found it necessary to place a towel over my face and hold my head under the warm water as I took a shower before bedtime."

Arriving in Wilmington, Eaton was shocked by the "exceedingly strong" peer pressure by which the city's white people enforced racial solidarity. He was equally discomfited by what he perceived as local Black people's resigned acceptance of second-class status. He attributed this state of affairs directly to 1898, writing, "The terrorism applied by Wilmington whites in the ensuing turmoil frightened the colored community into pitiful docility." Eaton was impatient with the folkloric staying power of 1898, suggesting that "years of telling" had perhaps "magnified" the event's significance. In his desire to free his neighbors from the trauma narrative, he seems to have ruled out the inverse possibility—that over decades of transmission, some of the event's horrors had been lost, repressed, or diminished.

Many Black residents shied away from Eaton's campaign for equal schooling, fearing they'd face retaliation from white employers. Eaton came to believe that only a well-resourced outsider could risk disrupting the status quo. "We did not have the pervasive fears of native Wilmingtonians," he wrote, of himself and a colleague who joined the fight, pointing out that "as doctors who did not depend on referrals from white practitioners, our income was fairly reprisal-proof."

The board of education denied the group's request to examine local school facilities, claiming that Black and white students enjoyed "substantial equality of treatment." Furthermore, the board blamed out-of-state attorneys for proposing an investigation that "we feel . . . would be disruptive of the friendly relationship which has existed for many years between the colored and white people of this community." For anyone who knew Wilmington's history, the letter's subtext was deafening. Eaton observed, "The reference to 'friendly relations' between colored and white people was without doubt veiled intimidation based on the race riot of 1898."

At one public meeting, the county's attorney explicitly referenced 1898, warning that Eaton's lawsuit could jeopardize "fifty-three years of good race relations" in the region. Descendants of victims of racial or ethnic violence often urge remembrance as society grows complacent, believing that such an event could never happen again. In Wilmington, the descendants of perpetrators reminded the community never to forget that they could do it again at any second.

After months of legal skirmishing, the concerned citizens secured permission to inspect every school in New Hanover County. One of the four representatives chosen by the board to escort them was Hugh MacRae Morton—a grandson of Hugh MacRae, and Hugh MacRae II's first cousin. Eaton and his team documented a panoply of inequalities. White students had lockers, gymnasiums, and cafeterias; Black students ate lunch at their desks. Two Black schools, both unpainted wooden shacks, were still using outhouses for toilets. Eaton found that the white schools' total property value amounted to more than $3.5 million, compared to just over $700,000 for the Black schools, attended by 34 percent of the district's students. If the schools were indeed separate but equal, the Black facilities' value should have been close to $2 million.

Eaton's schoolhouse tour persuaded him that it was "exceedingly urgent" to get a Black person elected to the school board. He decided to run himself—the first Black person to seek election to the board of education since 1898. In 1952, Black people comprised just under a third of the county's population. But fewer than two hundred of its twenty-three thousand Black citizens were registered to vote. "My first task was to persuade other colored citizens that the tenor of politics had changed in the past 50 years, and it was now possible to vote without fear of reprisal," Eaton explained.

His candidacy marked a trailblazing foray into political life, but he did not enjoy an immediate groundswell of support from the Black community. Accommodationist Black leaders objected to his disruption of the tacit agreement of peace for passivity that had prevailed since 1898. Black people who had grown up under its strictures feared that they would somehow be made to pay for his audacity. "Especially among older members of the community, the belief that 'the white man can't be fought' at times went with gloomy pronouncements that Hubert Eaton would soon be driven out of town, just as Alexander Manly and Armond Scott had been more than fifty years before," one historian noted.

When Election Day came, Eaton placed seventh, failing to win a seat by 252 votes. Still, his showing alarmed the all-white school board, who immediately switched to staggered elections, making it more difficult for a Black candidate to win. Eaton ran again in 1952, 1954, 1956, and 1958, losing each time. "Although victory eluded me, my campaigns were not without success," he recalled. After his first campaign, the number of Black people registered to vote doubled, continuing to rise with each run.

Armed with data from the inspection tour, Eaton's group filed suit against the school board in 1951. His seven-year-old son, Hubert Jr., served as the lawsuit's lead plaintiff. "We believed it was important that someone stand up and be counted so that other colored citizens would have the courage to join the cause," Eaton recalled. Just as the case was about to go to trial, the school board yielded.

To afford the renovations, the board proposed a bond issue, pitching it to white voters as a boon for their children's schools with some incidental benefits for Black ones. The bond issue thus passed, allocating nearly $1 million to Black schools. Despite the concrete gains that the lawsuit brought about, Eaton recalled, "our success in court did little to change attitudes." After signing Eaton's petition, a Black substitute teacher named Glotherine Everett never received another assignment in the New Hanover County school system. She eventually got a job in Brooklyn, New York, and moved there with her four children—the latest 1898 exiles, half a century after the fact.

ANY OTHER GLORIOUS MAY SUNDAY, HUBERT EATON SURELY WOULD HAVE been on the tennis court, whacking forehands down the line and dispatching an endless procession of challengers to the corner store for sodas. May 14, 1954, however, was an exceptional occasion. As a crowd slowly filled the auditorium, dress shoes squeaking on the glossy floor, Eaton waited on a dais in a coat and tie. Along with other dignitaries, he was there to participate in the dedication of the new Williston Senior High School, the gleaming product of his separate-but-equal lawsuit.

The new Williston had been worth the fight. Housed in an "ultramodernistic" brick building with two rows of louvered windows gridding the length of a low-slung facade, the school boasted educational and extracurricular conveniences to rival those at New Hanover, the white high school. In addition to the new auditorium, there was a gym with three thousand seats, a library, showers, "a two-way intercommunication system and equipment of the latest design," facilities for physics, chemistry, biology, home economics, arts, music, and drama.

Change was coming to Wilmington more slowly than in other places with a long-standing tradition of civil rights organizing, but Eaton and his collaborators were beginning to succeed in loosening the post-1898 white stranglehold on public life, public funds, and public space. In 1954, the city hired its first Black police officers since the turn of the century. (By contrast, Black officers had joined the Charlotte, Richmond, Savannah, and Atlanta forces in the 1940s.) The same year, Eaton and a group of golfing buddies integrated the municipal golf course, out of principle more than any real interest in putting. "I didn't even know the difference between a wood and an iron," Eaton recalled. "Nevertheless, I was determined to avail myself of the tax-supported facilities."

Despite its initially grudging attitude toward funding the county's Black schools, the school board seized the moment of Williston's dedication. The new school was the fruit of a form of tactical beneficence, upholding the "North Carolina Way" of opposing desegregation through legal maneuvering rather than overt, bombastic defiance of the "massive resistance" strategy that many Southern states would adopt. The white political class's position was, essentially, that Black people ought to be glad that they had it as good as they did in North Carolina, in terms of the relatively generous funding that the state had supplied since the era of Charles Aycock (the "education governor" who, fifty years earlier, had likened Black education to that of setter pups and mules).

The board had brought in Dr. Rufus E. Clement, the president of Atlanta University, to serve as keynote speaker. After a musical introduction by Williston's top-rated marching band, the school's principal, Booker T. Washington—named after the Tuskegee Institute president—opened the ceremony by welcoming the gathered dignitaries and guests. At some point during the proceedings, Clement was mysteriously summoned from the stage. He returned several minutes later and leaned over toward Eaton, whispering an urgent message in his ear:

"The Supreme Court has just issued a ruling overturning *Plessy vs. Ferguson* and has ordered the desegregation of public schools in four states and in Washington, D.C."

Clement swore Eaton to secrecy, as the ruling wasn't to be announced until after the weekend. The irony of the decision's timing wasn't lost on either man. Eaton recalled, "Just as we dedicate a new high school to the Negro community built to comply with the separate-but-equal law, the Supreme Court rules that separate-but-equal violates the Constitution." There they sat on the dais, silently united in the knowledge that their cutting-edge Black high school was already an anachronism on its opening day.

Chapter 31

VERY PERTINENT FACTS

In 1951, Helen G. Edmonds, a Black historian at North Carolina College, a historically Black institution, published a bombshell. *The Negro and Fusion Politics in North Carolina, 1894–1901*—published, amazingly, by the University of North Carolina Press, after careful political maneuvering by white male members of the faculty who supported Edmonds—presented the first major revisionist look at 1898. Edmonds used cautious academic language, but her findings were radical. "This account of the riot has been given with such regularity and with such slight variation that it has become 'standard' and thus generally accepted," she wrote. "A more careful investigation of the available information, however, renders it somewhat unreliable and requires some substantial revision of the generally accepted story."

Edmonds took apart the lies and tropes that served as the foundation for the prevailing version of the history of 1898, offering, in the words of one scholar, "a sweeping challenge to the moral, social, and political basis for white Democratic rule." She demonstrated that neither Manly's "slander" nor "Negro domination" were to blame for the bloodshed, and she dug into its real causes: competition between Black and white labor, meretricious journalism, and violent white opposition to Black political participation. Above all, she called the government takeover a "coup d'état," exposing it for the shabby, thuggish thing it was, rather than the glorious revolution of which its perpetrators had long boasted.

Louis Toomer Moore, the perpetually bow-tied chairman of the New Hanover County Historical Commission, was apoplectic. Now in his sixties, Louis was the Colonel's youngest son and a UNC alumnus. Three days after the *Wilmington Morning Star* carried a review of the book, he fired off a letter to the university's president:

> The assumption is that this Dr. Edmonds is a Negress. . . . If she is of the Negro race, certainly that is nothing to her discredit. Whether she is colored or white, however, doesn't excuse her references to the Wilmington event of 1898. It was distinctly a REVOLUTION and not a race riot as she terms it. Her general statements are inflammatory, not in accord with real facts, distorted and sensational. They certainly are of a caliber to disturb the present pleasant and agreeable racial relations which exist in North Carolina.

Louis cataloged eleven "very pertinent facts" that he claimed Edmonds had neglected. He didn't mention his personal connection to the events, yet his list couldn't help but bring to mind the White Declaration of Independence that his father had signed fifty-three years earlier. In 1898, Louis contended, "a misguided Negro majority" had conspired with "some men whose skins were white but whose hearts were black" to dominate Wilmington. "Power-drunk" Black people strode the streets, arresting white men, slapping white children, and pushing white women into gutters. Alexander Manly's "filthy" editorial, meanwhile, had obliged the good white men of the city to demand an apology.

Louis was an expert at working the levers of power in North Carolina. Since 1921, when he took over the Wilmington Chamber of Commerce, he had been a tireless advocate for what he believed were the best interests of the community, championing the construction of a new post office and a deepwater port. Where others saw a backwater, he saw a well of interest. Over decades, he took more than a thousand photographs of local life, documenting everything from baby parades to seafood markets and automobile dealerships. At one point, he secured a weekly spot on the airwaves on

KDKA radio, in Pittsburgh, touting Wilmington's charms to prospective vacationers. HELLO MR. MOTORIST & PARTY, read a jaunty sign his chamber of commerce erected near the ferry.

His passion for local history led him to cofound the Lower Cape Fear Historical Society. He was active in Confederate causes, presenting a Fort Fisher battle flag to local authorities on January 19, 1933, "anniversary of the birth of General Robert Edward Lee, the revered and immortal leader of the Confederate forces of The War Between the States," and he contended that "in those not-to-be-forgotten times, the relation of slave, master, and mistress was one of sympathetic understanding and friendly interest." Long before historic preservation was a fashionable cause, Louis spent long hours hunched over a manual typewriter in a study stuffed with old newspapers and magazines, "piled so high as to block out the strong summer sun" as whatever baseball game was going blared from a transistor radio. His grandson recalled that he saw himself as a "warrior" for the Wilmington area, "its long-range protector against shortsighted pursuits and commercial interests." Every year, he easily exceeded the meager honorarium that the city allotted him on postage costs alone.

Louis had long positioned himself as the legitimate gatekeeper of Wilmington's past. Less than a decade earlier, he had donated the newspaper editor Thomas Clawson's eyewitness account of the massacre to UNC, vouching personally for its accuracy. It was a shame, he now observed, that "this female writer" had failed to grasp "the simple truth" that "white men properly got control of their government state, county, and municipal, paid for with their taxes." She would not, he continued, "be able to comprehend the infinite harm which may result from the publication of her book." In case the point was lost, he copied the editors of daily newspapers in Wilmington, Raleigh, Charlotte, and Greensboro, along with Edmonds's boss at UNC. Like the treasured Moore family photo with the father's head pasted onto the son's body, Louis's protest was a composite job: the justifications of the Colonel's generation pasted onto the letterhead of a mid-century professional.

Louis campaigned against Edmonds for months, baldly urging UNC's president to use his position to complete "a restoration of the thoughts, ideals, and aspirations of a half century ago." Ultimately, the university brushed him off, with one official dismissing his complaints, in an internal memo, as "an appalling combination of ignorance, prejudice, carelessness and unwanted interference."

The feeling that history as he knew it was being eclipsed may have factored into Louis's decision to write his own book, *Stories Old and New of the Cape Fear Region*, a compendium of local arcana published privately in 1956. The book was charming in ways that both cloaked and revealed its function as a rebuttal to competing interpretations of Wilmington's history. Louis devoted four pages to Wilmington streets that had the same names as streets in Liverpool. Another six covered "the elephant that turned Wilmington topsy-turvy." Curiously, for all his investment in the historiography of 1898, he mentioned the event only in passing, as part of a list of Oakdale Cemetery's notable graves, including his father's. Colonel Roger Moore, he wrote, "was placed by his fellow citizens in overall command of the community prior to, and during, the political troubles which culminated

Louis Toomer Moore at one of his favorite graves in Oakdale Cemetery.

in a racial conflict, November 10, 1898, in Wilmington, as a result of which governmental control was wrested from radical elements and restored to a higher and better class of citizenship."

Louis and other members of his class played a long game, and they played it relentlessly. In 1964, for instance, Mrs. Isaac Bates Grainger was living on Park Avenue in New York City with her husband, who had retired as president of Chemical Bank. His sister had married the son of Walker Taylor, who led Group Six and took military command of the city on November 10, 1898. One day, Mrs. Grainger attended a lecture given by the renowned historian John Hope Franklin at the Madison Avenue Presbyterian Church. In it, Franklin asserted that "the murder of twenty Negroes in Wilmington, North Carolina, in the riot of 1898 was a mere suggestion of what lay ahead." Mrs. Grainger took issue with this, complaining to the pastor that Franklin had exaggerated the number of casualties. She instructed the pastor to transmit to him an excerpt of a work by William L. DeRosset—an uncle of Gabrielle DeRosset Waddell, Alfred's third wife—estimating that "seven to ten" Black men had been killed, so that Franklin could "make a correction" to his speech.

Franklin found Mrs. Grainger's suggestion risible. "What kind of historian is it who talks of a 'carpetbag regime' in 1898 or who would speak of 'darkies' as 'insolent and impudent'?" Franklin replied, dismissing DeRosset's work. He advised Mrs. Grainger that he had no intention of revising his lecture. If ever he did, he added, it "would be on the basis of objective facts, not on the polemical tirades of a white supremacist."

Black scholars such as Edmonds and Franklin were starting to speak up about 1898, but many white Wilmingtonians clung to cherished lies and convenient interpretations. One elderly woman associated November 10, 1898, not with terror or guilt, but with baked goods, because it had happened to fall on a sister's birthday: "Even now I never smell or see donuts that I do not see that kitchen on that far-off day," she wrote in 1961. Others cherished Woodrow Wilson's maxim that it was better to fail in a cause that they knew someday would triumph than to win in a cause that they knew someday would fail. The "Wilmington Revolution" was an undying fight, a local Lost Cause straining toward the same oxymoronic conclusion that upper-class white people were born masters and eternal victims all at once. White descendants kept the faith, whether that meant engaging in public confrontation, working back-channel connections, or coating their memories in the powdered sugar of obliviousness.

Chapter 32

THE GREATEST SCHOOL UNDER THE SUN

Cynthia Brown—great-great-great-great-granddaughter of Anthony Walker, great-great-great-granddaughter of Alfred Howe, great-great-granddaughter of William C. Howe, great-granddaughter of Athalia Howe—entered the world at the reasonable hour of nine forty-five p.m. on September 8, 1955. In the coming decades, she would move away from Wilmington and then come back home. After a pivotal lunch of tuna salad and pound cake with a bunch of retired schoolteachers, she would become a matchless keeper of memory and teller of truth about 1898. But for now, at her grandparents' white house at 802 Bladen Street, she was a perfect doll in pressed linen and butterfly sleeves, propped up on a leather nailhead armchair with a frilly white pillow in broderie anglaise.

"An American Citizen is Born!" her birth certificate announced. It listed seminal events in the American "fight for freedom": the Declaration of Independence, the Constitution, and seven wars, including the Spanish-American War of 1898. This vision of American history as a continual forward march toward freedom didn't acknowledge the methods of political, social, and economic exclusion that made Black Americans less free than their white peers and, in some cases, less free than their ancestors of half a century earlier. Cynthia's mother gave birth in the segregated wing of the James Walker Memorial Hospital. Valentine Howe had built the wing, and generations of Howes had paid taxes to maintain it, but Black doctors were forbidden to practice there or to use vital equipment. To read patients' X-rays, Dr. Hubert Eaton had been forced to install a darkroom in his house.

Cynthia was her parents' first child. At the time, they were both teachers. Her mother, Gladys, taught outside the county, traveling during the week. Her father, James, taught math. He had been a baseball star at Williston, and he dreamed that his daughter would attend his alma mater. As a younger man, he had turned down a contract with the Kansas City Monarchs to enlist in the air force. Now he spent part of his summers playing with the Negro Leagues.

On the hottest summer days, the Brown family would pile into the car, roll down the windows, and drive fifteen miles down Highway 421 to Seabreeze and Freeman Beach, Black resorts at the tapering southern tip of the county, known colloquially as "Bop City." Seabreeze boasted dance halls, a fishing pier, and an amusement park with a Ferris wheel. A day-tripper could visit a snake exhibit or rent a bathing suit for a day, sleeping over at a vine-covered bungalow if he'd had too much to drink. The resort stood on land that the Freemans, a Black family, had owned since 1876. People who loved it said that part of the joy of the place was that it really belonged to Black people, who could do what they wanted to there, away from white strictures and judgments.

Cynthia's mother's sister worked at a restaurant called Monte-Carlo-by-the-Sea. Cynthia was wild for its clam fritters, flavored with chopped onion and bell peppers—as famous "as McDonald's hamburgers." The owners of the restaurant were a couple named Frank and Lulu Hill. Lulu was a Freeman. Frank's father, Lincoln, had been James Sprunt's butler and chauffeur, the first Black man to drive in Wilmington. Their granddaughter, JoAnne, sometimes helped out at the restaurant. "For me, the beach was a wonderful place, and to this day there is no place on this earth that I love more," JoAnne wrote later, lamenting local authorities' decision, in 1952, to dynamite a new inlet to serve commercial fishermen from a white beach nearby. The move, followed by Hurricane Hazel in 1954, left Seabreeze "a pale shadow of what it used to be, most of it destroyed by erosion."

With her parents carving out careers, Cynthia spent much of her time with her maternal grandmother, Nana, who suffered from heart disease and was mostly housebound. Nana taught her phonics, and by the time she was three, she could read the headlines in the newspaper that sailed between the two live oaks every morning, landing on the front porch with a thwack. Despite her illness, Nana kept an extraordinary garden. Her crape myrtles were as fluffy as angora sweaters and her yellow roses looked as though they'd drunk gold. Nana was adamant about weeds, impressing upon Cynthia the importance of wrenching them out entirely before they could take root. Cynthia took lessons in vigilance from "I Come to the Garden Alone," a favorite hymn in the family. She explained later: "You go to the garden alone, while the dew is still on the roses, and, while you talk to God, you rip out the ragweed and the crabgrass with all the strength He gave you."

During college, James Brown had worked as an orderly at the Duke University Hospital, an experience that awoke in him a fascination with medicine. After working at Maryland's Naval Ordnance Laboratory, where he became the institution's first Black senior mathematician, he enrolled at Howard's medical school, graduating in 1963. For years, he commuted to Wilmington from Maryland, where he practiced family medicine. When her mother got sick, Gladys lobbied James to move home. "We don't put our family in a nursing home," she said. He refused to go, arguing that a Black doctor could never prosper in Wilmington, given that the White Declaration of Independence had never been overturned. Gladys and the children stayed in Wilmington and the couple divorced, another uncounted casualty of the long hand of 1898.

Cynthia couldn't wait to get to Williston, known to generations of Black Wilmingtonians as "the Greatest School Under the Sun." It wasn't just her father's stories that made her so excited about high school. Everyone talked about Williston, giving it a mythical aura. The teachers there wore pearls—a choker for Mrs. L. S. Williams, an English teacher; a double strand for Mrs. Boykins, of the language laboratory. Latin was, in the latter's estimation, "a ray emitted from the eternal flame of knowledge" that, with the addition of French or Spanish, would ensure the success of Williston graduates, "bound to travel far and wide." The class of 1954 counted among its members twenty-five aspiring nurses, eighteen stenographers, ten engineers, five lawyers, three cosmetologists, two psychiatrists, a mortician, an interior decorator, and a private detective. Before graduating, each pupil memorized the prologue to Chaucer's *The Canterbury Tales*.

Williston was more than a school. It was Black Wilmington's unrivaled incubator of elegance, erudition, and ambition—"our village," according to one alumnus; "a grand example of collective community life." Many teachers and administrators lived close to campus, and their relationships with students and their families extended far beyond the school grounds. One longtime assistant principal ran a photo studio out of his house, three blocks from the school, immortalizing prom dates and proud graduates, who knew him as the Picture Man. The school mascot, a pouncing tiger, was a fitting tribute to Williston's vitality. The school even had its own pastry, the cinnamon-dusted Williston Bun.

Williston's wealth of tradition, folklore, and pageantry contributed to a sense of social cohesion that held together the entire community. Day and night, the school flung open its doors for concerts, symposia, lectures, teas, raffles, debutante balls, and fish fries. For the annual fall homecoming festivities, students, alumni, and no small number of hangers-on donned mink coats and filled the parking lot outside the football stadium teeming with hand-waxed Cadillacs. Inside the stands filled with spectators in Afros, "like fields of huge black dandelions," as the famed marching band riffed on the "Batman" theme. Awash with maroon and gold, the crowd chanted an ode to "the bone-deep, heart-deep, pride-deep—love-deep—place Williston Senior High occupied for generations of us in Wilmington's African-American community."

I would not be a Gold Bull
I'll tell you the reason why
I've been a Tiger all my life
I'll be a Tiger till I die

The Williston Senior High glee club, 1963.

A decade had passed since the *Brown v. Board of Education* decision, and the Civil Rights Movement was in full swing. Yet Wilmington's schools remained effectively as segregated as they had been the day Hubert Eaton got news of the Supreme Court ruling, up on the Williston dais. After *Brown*, the school board had implemented the Pearsall Plan, a statewide foot-dragging scheme. When the Pearsall Plan was struck down in court, the board switched to a plan known as "freedom of choice," which off-loaded the burden of desegregation to Black students. If a Black student wanted to go to a white school, he could apply for reassignment on an individual basis. So far in New Hanover County, a single Black student had availed himself of the option.

In March 1964, Eaton launched another lawsuit, filing the papers at the federal courthouse, a grand marble building overlooking the riverfront. This time, he'd had better luck persuading local families to join him. In *Eaton et al. v. New Hanover County Board of Education*, as the case came to be known, Eaton and the parents of twenty-five other Black students, working with NAACP lawyers, sued the school board for violating the equal protection clause of the Constitution by maintaining racially segregated schools.

Even compared with cities such as Birmingham and Nashville, which integrated in 1957 and 1963, respectively, the pace of desegregation in Wilmington was glacial. Black activists tried to nudge things along with dialogues and petitions, but at every turn white officials feigned a sort of hapless good faith, as though they were really trying to get this integration thing done and their efforts unaccountably just kept failing. Faced with their disingenuity, one exasperated Black lawyer communicated as though he were speaking to simpletons: "While we appreciate your prompt answer, we are concerned over the Board's failure to understand the basic problem which prompted our petition, school desegregation."

ONE MORNING NOT LONG AFTER FILING THE LAWSUIT, THE EATONS WERE eating breakfast when a drunk white man, a local newscaster, barged into their house, not even bothering to remove his trademark fedora before subjecting the family to a racist tirade. A few months later, Eaton received a letter from the Internal Revenue Service announcing that he was being audited. An IRS agent showed up at his office, requesting his receipt books and canceled checks. At one point, he insisted that Eaton must be underreporting his income because he couldn't furnish a record of his expenditures on tennis balls. Eaton later recalled, "He left no stone unturned in his effort to obtain sufficient information to indict me for fraud, but his time and efforts were fruitless." Tiring of the aggravation, Eaton eventually agreed to pay additional taxes, concluding that he had likely been targeted for his activism.

Then, on August 11, 1964, at 9:35 A.M., the kitchen telephone rang. It was a Tuesday, and Eaton was again at the breakfast table, lingering over the newspaper. The front page read "Soviets Hint Gal Next Space Pilot." Ann Landers was fielding questions about an under-eating toddler. A month earlier, Congress had passed the Civil Rights Act of 1964, which Eaton and his wife had celebrated by taking themselves out to one of Wilmington's finest formerly white restaurants. The school board's attorney, meanwhile, had marked the occasion by writing a letter to Sam Ervin, North Carolina's staunchly segregationist senator. "Like you, I am deeply disappointed by the civil rights bill," Senator Ervin replied, invoking the eternal threat of a return to the "dark days" of Reconstruction. "I did everything in my power to defeat it."

Eaton picked up the phone. "This is Dr. Eaton."

"Dr. Eaton, this is Chief Deputy Sheriff R. A. Jarrell down at the sheriff's office."

"Good morning, Mr. Jarrell. What can I do for you?"

"Dr. Eaton, the New Hanover County Grand Jury indicted you this morning in the death of the patient who died in your office in July of last year, and you have been charged with murder."

THE MURDER INDICTMENT RATCHETED UP THE PRESSURE ON EATON TO a nearly unbearable level. The patient in question was a thirty-year-old schoolteacher who had lived with her brother in a neighboring county. She had visited Eaton's office in July 1963, complaining of abdominal pain. Eaton had examined her and gone over her medical history, then written her a prescription for antibiotics. To ease her immediate symptoms, he gave her a shot of penicillin, a common remedy at the time. The patient had told him she was not allergic to the medicine, but she went into anaphylactic shock and quickly died.

Eaton reported what had happened through the proper channels. His report satisfied the coroner, who requested no further examination. Yet Eaton was deeply shaken by the incident, even if he dealt with it in his typically undemonstrative fashion. "In the process of health care, few occurrences can make a doctor feel more helpless and cause more emotional trauma," he later wrote, allowing himself the rarest whisper of vulnerability.

After hanging up with the deputy sheriff, Eaton went out to his front porch and waited. The officer picked him up and drove him downtown to the county courthouse. When Eaton got out of the car, a photographer from the *Wilmington Morning Star* was waiting to snap his picture. In the resulting photograph, Eaton, shown from waist up, walks toward the camera, filling the left side of the frame against a background of lush summer trees. The rumpled deputy sheriff follows in his wake, jangling a set of keys.

Dr. Hubert Eaton with Chief Deputy Sheriff R. A. Jarrell, after being indicted for murder, August 11, 1964.

Less than half an hour earlier, Eaton had received the shock of his life. Still, he managed to present himself sharply, in brow-line glasses, a pressed shirt, and a plaid suit. In the photo, his expression is contemplative—gently furrowed brow, solid gaze into the middle distance. Deep creases frame his mouth's slightly upturned corners. Twenty years earlier, he had trained himself to look friendly. Now he was smiling for his life.

EATON WENT ON TRIAL IN NOVEMBER. THE GRAND JURY INDICTMENT HAD allowed for a first-degree murder charge, carrying the possibility of a death sentence, but the prosecutor decided to seek conviction in the second degree. One of Eaton's three lawyers was Robert Bond, the city's only Black attorney and his frequent partner in civil rights litigation. To round out his legal team, Eaton hired attorneys George Rountree Jr. and John Burney Jr., members of the city's white old guard.

Rountree was a grandson of George Rountree, the Secret Nine adviser who, in 1900, wrote the grandfather clause to the state constitution, disenfranchising Black voters. He bore his ancestor's name, practiced his profession, and shared many of his views, including a belief in the righteousness of the 1898 takeover. Burney was an old boy, too—an avid segregationist and canny sealer of deals over quail hunts and billiards tables. As a young lawyer, he had soaked in local history at the knee of Marsden Bellamy Jr. Initially, he had declined to represent Eaton. "Dr. Eaton, I don't like you, and you and I have always thought opposite about this civil rights stuff," he reasoned. But Eaton knew that white lawyers and judges had their own ways of talking to each other, and that the successful use of this racial code language could make or break a case. (A white lawyer might, for example, tell a judge, "This man's employer went to Carolina," to indicate "This man's employer is white.") Eaton pressed Burney to reconsider, and eventually he accepted the job.

The prosecution alleged that Eaton had killed the patient while performing an abortion.

"Are you sympathetic to the Ku Klux Klan or have you ever been a member of the Klan?" Burney asked a prospective juror as voir dire got underway.

"I used to be a member of the Klan," the juror replied.

Burney wanted to keep the man: If nothing else, he was honest. Eaton was appalled, telling Burney, "If you left a Klansman on the jury I'd never sleep again as long as I live." They struck the man from the list, but the incident was a harrowing reminder that Eaton was up against the weight of racism in addition to the burden of evidence. His activism had made him more enemies than he could count. The star witness for the prosecution, for example, practiced at James Walker Memorial Hospital, which Eaton had sued over its failure to extend staff privileges to Black doctors.

The trial proceeded quickly. Refuting the state's assertion that Eaton had injected "foreign material" into the patient's uterus, the defense argued that she was an asthmatic, and that she had suffered a previous pneumonia. The foreign substance was, in fact, a mass of red blood cells. As the scientific evidence showed, the state's case was exceedingly flimsy. On November 26, 1964, the judge dismissed the charges in their entirety. Eaton was fully cleared.

The trial had been a nightmare—an unpredictable torment that receded as suddenly as it had come on. Eaton remained puzzled at the ordeal's mysterious onset and its abrupt resolution. Where had the charges come from? Who had made them go away? *The Wilmington Journal*—the area's leading Black paper since 1927, led by the mercurial T. C. Jervay—called the trumped-up trial the "work of the Devil" and suggested it might be attributable to an internecine traitor in the Black community, "a low-down ungodly individual who would bring so much worry, sorrow, and inconvenience into the lives of members of his own race."

The suggestion that a Black person might have denounced him, while unproven, left Eaton particularly unnerved. "I had been alert for reprisals of all kinds, including attempts at physical harm," he later wrote. "I always thought attacks on me would emanate only from the white community. That such vicious allegations leading to a criminal charge would come from a person of my own race is more than I ever imagined. I still have no idea of what was behind it."

Years later, on a trip to San Francisco, Eaton suffered a serious cerebral bleed. After weeks of bed rest, he went back to work, recovering his full physical capacities, but "a previously unexpressed aspect" of his personality, as he termed it, came to the fore in an unexpected way. So strategically guarded all his life, Eaton lost control of his emotions. Thinking about the struggles of the past, he started to weep.

Chapter 33

WHY IT WAS THE WORST

The successes of the Civil Rights Movement triggered violent counter-reactions, among them the rise of a so-called Third Klan. In March 1965, Alabama Klan members murdered Viola Liuzzo, a white housewife who had driven down from Detroit to help organize marches for voting rights. The crime prompted Congress, at the urging of President Lyndon Johnson, to launch an investigation into the Klan. The hearings—the first of their kind since those in which Alfred Moore Waddell had participated in 1871—began in October 1965. During more than a month of questioning, witnesses testified to the resurgence of the Klan in at least nineteen states. "North Carolina is by far the most active state for the United Klans of America," the committee concluded.

At rallies sponsored by some two hundred North Carolina klaverns, supporters gobbled hot dogs and drew lots for cake raffles as a prelude to sunset cross burnings. Speakers blared songs with titles like "They're Looking for a Handout" and "Move Them N——s North." At one gathering, Grand Dragon Bob Jones proudly posed with a Cadillac that the state's ten thousand members—more than all other Southern states combined—had chipped in to buy. Daytime parades on city sidewalks demonstrated that the group had "nothing to hide" and, it seemed, little to fear in terms of arrest or ostracism. According to the North Carolina State Bureau of Investigation (SBI), Wilmington's klavern was among the state's most powerful and "boasts of members from nearly all walks of the county's business and civic life."

On October 26, Marion Millis, the sheriff of New Hanover County, was called to testify before the congressional committee. Many of the Klan leaders who appeared stonewalled the legislators, just as they had in Waddell's time. The United Klans of America's imperial wizard, for instance, stated his name, age, and birthplace and then took the Fifth Amendment 156 times. But Millis, a pinkish forty-nine-year-old with a whispery voice, proved to be a jaw-droppingly voluble witness, confirming not only that the Klan was alive and thriving on the Lower Cape Fear, but that he and at least six of his nineteen deputies had joined the organization. He claimed that they had done so for investigative purposes. Yet, he admitted, no one from his office had produced any written reports, nor had they informed the SBI about their supposed infiltration.

Only months earlier, Millis had publicly denied that any member of his department had ever been a member of the Klan. The exposure of his lies didn't seem to bother him any more than the mild drubbing he took from liberal members of the committee. Yes, he knew that his deputy sheriff had become the state organization's klaliff, or vice president. No, he hadn't fired him. Yes, they had paid dues to the Klan. Yes, they had received a copy of *The Fiery Cross* at the office address, where they filed membership cards in a little gray box. Yes, they had sworn an oath that they would rather die than give up a fellow Klansman accused of any crime other than treason, rape, or murder. No, they didn't have any suspects in the recent burning of a six-foot-high cross right in front of their headquarters.

"Were any other public officials in the county members of this Klan?" one investigator asked.

"I don't have any knowledge," Millis replied.

"Were any close relatives of public officials members of the Klan?"

"Yes, sir," Millis said.

"Would you care to name them?"

"My son-in-law," Millis responded.

Amid the parade of terrorists, demagogues, and bigots called to testify before the committee, Millis stood out for his audacity. Responsible for upholding the law in a community of nearly eighty thousand people, he was content to tell Congress that he'd joined the Klan, that his office had practically doubled as its local headquarters, and that its adherents included members of his own family. "Sheriff Says He and 6 Deputies Joined Klan to Keep an Eye on It," read the incredulous headline of a long story in the next day's *New York Times*.

Far from ending his career, Millis's performance bolstered his image with some of his white constituents, particularly those who were determined to prevail by any means in the mounting battle over school desegregation. As Millis embarrassed the city on the national stage, the *Star* offered little more than a tepid piece announcing that local officials were deciding to "wait-and-see" whether he should face any sanction. (It bears noting that press cards were issued to the local media at Millis's discretion.) One county commissioner praised Millis for running "a mighty clean county." The chairman of the board declared, "If a man does a good job, what church or organization he belongs to is not my concern." Millis, in his estimation, was doing a good job.

IT WAS EARLY APRIL 1968, AND DR. MARTIN LUTHER KING JR. WAS COMING to Wilmington. The board of education had signed off on the use of Williston Junior High School's gymnasium. A host committee was in formation. Dr. Hubert Eaton, who had been instrumental in arranging the visit, aimed to capitalize on the occasion to "get as many Negroes registered as possible." Despite the passage of the Voting Rights Act of 1965, still only about a third of New Hanover County's eighteen thousand Black people appeared on the electoral rolls.

Dr. King planned to swing through the state, lending support to Dr. Reginald Hawkins, a Black dentist who was running for governor. The fifteen-city tour would culminate at Williston, where King would address a crowd of thousands. The symbolic potential was surely not lost on King of choosing Wilmington, site of the "elimination of the Negro" from North

Carolina politics, to throw his weight behind Hawkins, the first Black man to seek statewide office in a Southern state since the end of Reconstruction.

As Black people reentered political life, white voters, not coincidentally, were moving right. The Republican party pursued its "Southern strategy" of promoting white resentment of Black equality in Wilmington as across the nation. In 1964, a Republican gubernatorial candidate won New Hanover County, breaking the Democratic monopoly that had held since 1898. In the same year's presidential election, local voters chose the Democratic candidate, Lyndon Johnson, over the Republican one, Barry Goldwater, by only 450 votes. The area's demographics were changing, too—manufacturing concerns brought new jobs, along with newcomers from all over the country. Wilmington was growing whiter, more suburban, and more prosperous, but its Black citizens reaped few benefits of the growth.

In advance of King's visit, the propaganda arm of the far-right John Birch Society arranged for a competing lecture to take place at John T. Hoggard, one of the city's two majority-white high schools. A hand-drawn flyer went around, alerting white citizens to the threat of the "Negro block vote." It could just as easily have circulated during the 1898 white supremacy campaign. BEWARE! it read. DO NOT BE FOOLED AGAIN! VOTE WHITE! On April 2, as the Birch Society sounded the alarm that civil rights activists were planning to install a "Soviet Negro Republic," King postponed his Wilmington appearance. He needed to remain in Memphis, he explained, where a sanitation workers' strike was entering a critical phase.

King, of course, never made it to Wilmington. On April 4, James Earl Ray shot him in the jaw as he stood on a second-floor balcony at the Lorraine Motel in Memphis. He was pronounced dead at 7:05 P.M., approximately the same time he was to have started speaking at Williston. Violent protests broke out in dozens of American cities, but Wilmington remained peaceful, its streets blazing only with freshly bloomed azaleas. The white police chief, H. E. "Fats" Williamson, congratulated Black citizens on their composure. One group of students from Williston, singing "We Shall Overcome," marched to the county courthouse, where they held a prayer service for King before returning to school. Sheriff Marion Millis, still in office, kept an eye on things from the building's porch, where he sat drinking a Coca-Cola.

Instead of speaking at Williston, King was eulogized there. Like many Americans, Black people in Wilmington were heartbroken and angry; on top of their grief, they felt as though they'd missed a moment of specifically local catharsis. They filed in to mourn King in the same auditorium where they'd hoped to hear him deliver a message of defiance, strength, and victory.

OVER THE WEEKEND, DEMONSTRATIONS OF GRIEF TURNED CHAOTIC. ON Saturday night, according to the *Star*, a "full-scale riot" broke out in Brooklyn, leading Mayor O. O. Allsbrook to call in the National Guard, "to aid beleaguered police groups facing roving bands of stone-throwing Negroes." In reality, the police far outmanned the protesters, who, according to the *Star*, eventually numbered around a hundred. The police presence, by contrast, included the entire city police department, the highway patrol, the sheriff's department, and 150 National Guardsmen, equipped with helicopters, fixed-wing aircraft, armored personnel carriers, .30-caliber machine guns, tear gas, and chemical Mace.

As violence escalated, Allsbrook placed the city under a midnight curfew. The next day, protesters threw bricks into cars. Allsbrook moved the curfew to three p.m., and the board of education shut down the schools. Over five days, more than two hundred people—mostly Black, ages thirteen to sixty-three—were arrested, mostly for curfew violations. They were said to have injured twenty-one people, set thirty-eight fires, shot at three cars, and burned down several grocery stores in what the *Star* referred to as "racial outbreaks."

The paper's imprecise language reflected white people's surprise and even bewilderment at the amplitude of the violence and, moreover, at the sheer fact that it could happen in Wilmington, just as in Washington and Detroit. One elderly white woman's husband was knocked unconscious by a rock that a member of a group of Black people threw into the couple's car. "Beats all I have ever seen," she told the *Star*, sobbing.

Many of the Black protesters interpreted King's assassination not as a freak event but as a reprise, the latest entry in the long annals of white violence. They sought "black retaliation," the local historian Larry Thomas later wrote, both for the global tragedy of King's death and for the specific injury it inflicted in Wilmington. According to Thomas, King's death constituted "a double disaster for most black Wilmingtonians" because "they not only considered themselves personally responsible, but because it also marked the second time in their history that they were robbed of strong, black leadership."

A Wilmington city official characterized the riots as "guerrilla warfare," telling reporters, uncomprehendingly, "There has been no looting to speak of, just plain and simple destruction." The Associated Press classified Wilmington's violence as the state's worst, writing that the police used so much tear gas that extra supplies had to be trucked in from neighboring cities.

Thomas contended that this was no accident and looked to history to explain the intensity of the protesters' anger. "Why it was the worst is best answered by its black participants," he wrote. "It was the worst because they wanted it to be. They wanted the public to know that they were tired of being at the bottom of their city's ladder and that they considered themselves part of a new black breed who, unlike their ancestors of 1898, were not afraid to retaliate. But most of all, they wanted white Wilmingtonians to know it."

Chapter 34

A NEST OF COILED SNAKES

A month after King's death, the superintendent of schools resigned. To replace him, the school board appointed Heyward C. Bellamy, a forty-three-year-old former high school chemistry teacher with years of experience as an administrator in the New Hanover County system. He took over the role in the summer of 1968, becoming, for the moment, the most consequential Bellamy in Wilmington.

A native of Horry County, South Carolina, Heyward descended from the same distant Bellemie ancestors as the Wilmington Bellamys. His great-great-grandfather fought with Francis Marion during the Revolutionary War, and his great-grandfather fought with Stonewall Jackson in what Heyward was taught to call the War Between the States. His great-great-grandfather's 1846 will shows that he held thirty-eight people in bondage, among them "the boy Scye" and "the girl Tyre," whom Heyward knew in his childhood. "I am a product of the South," Heyward wrote, in a 2009 memoir. "I remember former slaves and Civil War soldiers."

Heyward wasn't really a Bellamy, though. Not in the Wilmington sense. Unlike the rich North Carolina branch of the family, Heyward's forebears had lost their land and thus their wealth in the aftermath of the Civil War. By the 1930s, his father was working as a police chief in Loris, South Carolina. During the Depression, as the family struggled to make ends meet, he tried to farm beans and tobacco. Heyward had to drop out of fourth grade to help. The same year, he contracted malaria. Doctors treated him with a medicine called atabrine, which turned him yellow for the better part of a year.

When Heyward was eleven, the family moved to Wilmington, seeking economic opportunity. His father opened a grocery store on Eleventh and Fanning. The shop was a modest concern, operating out of a corner of a house owned and occupied by a widowed Black woman. Most of the customers were Black—teachers, railroad workers, mill workers, civil servants, and artisans, buying oil sardines at five cents a tin or candy from a Victorian-era display case. The family lived in the neighborhood, too, renting a small house at 721 North Fifth Avenue. Heyward delivered ham and flour on his bicycle. Seven blocks south, at the corner of Fifth and Market, Ellen Bellamy was living out her last days in the mansion that caused all of Wilmington to equate wealth, power, and a certain strain of white dominance with the family name. The Bellamys of 721 North Fifth, however, possessed no moldering Persian carpets or long-suffering retainers. In fact, the two branches of the family had never even met.

Heyward thought he knew what he was getting into when he accepted the superintendent job. It had been nearly fifteen years since the *Brown* decision, and while many white people in Wilmington, including some of his colleagues, hadn't accepted the mandate, he saw desegregation as inevitable. After *Brown*, one principal said he was leaving Wilmington for the mountains, where there weren't any Black people; others threatened to quit teaching altogether. Heyward's own feelings were relatively, perhaps naively, simple: "When the time comes to place black students in the school I will be at my door to welcome them and will do my best to teach my subject well."

In May 1968, the United States Supreme Court ruled that local school boards had an "affirmative duty to take whatever steps might be necessary" to achieve the desegregation of schools and that further delays were "no longer tolerable." The decision rendered "freedom-of-choice" plans, such as the one New Hanover County was using, illegal. Three months later, a local judge ordered the school board to heed the Supreme Court in effecting "a transition to a unitary, nonracial system of public education." An attorney for the school board admitted that "the jig was up."

Hubert Eaton had won a critical legal victory, but the rulings created new problems. The school board had been counting on continuing its program of half measures in the coming school year. Now, rather than outsourcing the task of desegregation to individual Black students, it was required to come up with a viable mechanism for bringing the schools into racial balance. Officials had had fourteen years to acclimate parents and students to the idea of togetherness, fourteen years to put together a plan best suited to the local landscape, fourteen years to come up with a constructive approach. Instead, they had stalled and deflected. Now, with the start of the 1968–1969 term fast approaching, they scrambled to accomplish in less than a month what should have been the steady, thoughtful work of years if not centuries.

The county had three high schools: Williston, with some nine hundred Black students; New Hanover, traditional alma mater of the white elite; and John T. Hoggard, which had opened less than a year earlier and whose students came predominantly from the new, mostly white suburbs. Under the "freedom-of-choice" plan, nearly 90 percent of Black students in the system still attended entirely segregated schools. Not a single white student had elected to transfer to Williston. To achieve the racial balance required by the courts—72 percent white and 28 percent Black, in New Hanover County's case—the school board had three obvious options: (1) divide the county into three zones for three schools; (2) build a new high school; or (3) assign white students to schools that had been predominantly Black.

Some white parents formed a group called Save Our Schools. Its leadership included a nurse at the public hospital, a deputy from the Klan-ridden sheriff's department, and a locally famous amateur puppeteer. Trying to stave off the third option, the group threatened massive resistance if the school board sent white kids to Williston. "The SOS is a non-political, non-racial organization," the sheriff's deputy told a reporter, winkingly. "We invite anybody, but so far I can't say any Negroes have showed up."

Heyward Bellamy tried to get a handle on the mess he'd inherited. (Across town, Hargrove Bellamy, his distant relation, had his own problems: Someone had stolen a Gainsborough painting valued at $150,000 from a plantation he owned.) It did not help matters that his predecessor, H. M. Roland, who had held the superintendent job from 1935 to 1960, was going around town distributing race-science pamphlets. "It is inhuman to inculcate in the Negro mind hopes for academic equality which so few will ever obtain," one of them read. Heyward denied Roland use of county Xerox machines, but he continued his campaign, later testifying to Congress that integration was responsible for a "startling increase in VD" in white girls. (A Wilmington middle school bears his name to this day.)

For different reasons, many Black people were also skeptical about the wisdom of immediate desegregation. Some feared the loss of the nurturing, Black-centered environment that their schools had traditionally provided, the erasure of traditions, and the dilution of community spirit. They had already lost institutions such as Seabreeze, the beloved Black beach, where Cynthia Brown gorged herself on clam fritters at the Monte-Carlo. It is likely that JoAnne Byron, the granddaughter of the restaurant's owners, drew on her experiences in Wilmington when she decided to join the Black Liberation Army and to change her name to Assata Shakur. "The rulers of this country have always considered their property more important than our lives," she wrote from prison several years later, where she was awaiting trial for the murder of a New Jersey state trooper. (She was convicted, escaped from prison, and fled to Cuba, where she lived until her death in 2025.)

Others questioned the wisdom of seeking proximity to a hostile white population, as if, as Zora Neale Hurston wrote, deploring the *Brown* decision, there were "no greater delight to Negroes than physical association with whites." This feeling was particularly strong in Wilmington. The violent suppression of the Fusion movement still served as a cautionary tale about interracial proximity and cooperation. The 1898 massacre had destroyed Black Wilmington's political power and severely diminished its economic might. Now the community's greatest remaining asset, its excellent if not equal educational system, was at risk. "It seemed that our track record of throwing in with whites hadn't been so good going all the way back to the riot of 1898," one Williston supporter recalled, explaining that Black hesitation over desegregation, in its local particulars, carried with it a profound aversion to getting twice bit.

ON JUNE 26, 1968, THE SCHOOL BOARD HELD AN EMERGENCY MEETING. Turnout was so large that organizers had to change venues, from a courtroom to the New Hanover High School gym. Days earlier, the board had unveiled its integration plan: Williston Senior High would be converted to a middle school, and its former students would be bused to Hanover and Hoggard. The school board claimed that this had to be done, because bringing Williston up to code would require two hundred thousand dollars that the county didn't have.

More than a thousand people showed up at the gym, the *Wilmington Morning Star* reported, to register "hot and loud protests" to the board's proposal. The preponderance of students and parents of all races wanted Williston to remain open, whether they treasured the school as a haven for Black students or saw it as a convenient way to cordon them off from white ones. "Ironically, both Negro and white speakers appeared to be pleading with the Board of Education for essentially the identical move which would retain Williston Senior High School in operation," the *Star* observed.

Even in the rushed, sweaty chaos of the meeting, the speakers projected the past on to the present moment. They were eager to link the implications of the decision at hand to their sense of historical victimization, real or imagined. The conflict of reference was not the ongoing war in Vietnam, nor the Second World War, in which many of the people present had served. Rather, attendees invoked the Civil War and its aftermath in Reconstruction—the eternal touchstones, conscious or not, of any American discussion about racial equality.

Under the weight of unresolved history and contested memory, the meeting nearly tipped into mayhem. One hysterical citizen shook a walking stick across the table at the members of the school board, while a county commissioner denounced the folly of trying "to force the type of social relationship in 60 days that hasn't been developed in 100 years." The father of the first Black child to attend a white school in New Hanover County stood up and reminded the crowd that white kids were just as capable of integrating Black schools as Black kids were of integrating white ones. "Too long we have waved a rebel flag for a backward and decadent society," he said.

The school board, in the end, ignored public sentiment, voting unanimously to close Williston Senior High. The board called the move a "consolidation," but it was really a shutdown, not a merger. Only months after claiming that it couldn't afford to keep Williston open, the county turned around and spent a million dollars on improvements at Hoggard.

Overnight, nine hundred Williston Tigers became New Hanover Wildcats and Hoggard Vikings. Their teachers were reassigned, almost uniformly in inferior positions, inflicting yet another blow to the city's Black middle class. The Williston yearbook was discontinued, its PTA disbanded, its class president deposed, its clubs and organizations dissolved. Ultimately, the school was shuttered so heedlessly that its cups and banners were taken out of trophy cases and simply thrown in the trash.

"We were in a cocoon bathed in warm fluid, where we were expected to excel," one Williston alumnus observed. "And then something called desegregation punctured it." Another likened the sensation of being ripped away from a beloved neighborhood institution and plunked down into a school in the white suburbs to "falling face first into a nest of coiled snakes."

Even after closing Williston, the school board continued to defy the law, filing a last-ditch lawsuit so frivolous that the court ordered the board to pay costs of more than twenty-three thousand dollars. Still wrapped up in eleventh-hour maneuvering, officials did nothing to prepare the public for the reality of desegregation. On the first day of school, in August 1968, Black students boarded buses to Hoggard or hiked over to Hanover instead of walking the familiar route to Williston, showing off the platform shoes and floppy caps that they'd worked to afford over the summer. On one bus, the atmosphere was "somber, like we were crammed into the family's limo headed to the cemetery to bury grandma." Twelve-year-old Cynthia Brown, who had been expecting to start at Williston the next year, never got to eat a Williston Bun.

Feeling like "the black refugees from Williston Senior High," the students arrived to "cold, foreign schools teeming with hostile, white students, teachers, and administrators who hardly concealed their disdain." Their own principal, Booker T. Washington, had been forced into early retirement, while their assistant principal, the beloved Picture Man, had been demoted to an elementary school. (Similar fates awaited their colleagues across the state: Of 227 Black principals in 1963, only eight remained in 1970.) One teacher was reassigned to a white elementary school, where she was the only Black teacher. She later recalled that she was so nervous that she couldn't stop sweating, so she blotted with a tissue, leaving little bits of paper all over her face.

White students were left to their own devices, too, having received no guidance as to how to welcome or relate to their new classmates, whose presence their elders had for years presented as a cataclysmic fate. Raised under apartheid conditions and thrown together abruptly, Black and white students clashed at Hanover and Hoggard throughout the 1968–1969 and 1969–1970 school years. Clubs, sports teams, and student organizations were frequent sources of discord. At New Hanover High, leading student clubs refused every Black student who applied. To run for student office, candidates had to pass an examination about the Constitution—a kind of poll test for extracurriculars.

In 1970, five Black girls at Hanover tried out for the twelve-person cheerleading squad; none were chosen. An attempt by Black students to protest their exclusion by blocking the front steps of the school turned into a campus-wide melee, involving students, teachers, and, according to one eyewitness, "a group of whites [who] came towards the front of the school with chains and started hitting blacks." The county hospital reported that it treated nine students and one adult for injuries including cuts, black eyes, contusions, abrasions, and stab wounds in the back.

Another recurring conflict involved public space: who got out of whose way, who ceded the right-of-way when faced with traffic in the schools' buses, lunchrooms, and corridors. One group of white students complained that "there are Blacks who carry combs made of metal prongs which could be used as lethal weapons" and that "large groups of blacks" in the halls made it "impossible for a white person to walk through." Wayne Moore, a Black student, expressed similar frustration:

> One school day when the fellas and I were hanging out in the hallway between classes at Hoggard, a white boy came walking through like we were invisible or worse yet, inconsequential. As he came close to me, he barked, "Get out of my way, n——." Then he pushed my skinny ass aside.
>
> Before I had time to respond, my boys were all over him, stomping him into the hallway's freshly waxed tile floor. The next thing I knew, I jumped in and started stomping him, too. I had never been so angry. Words gurgled up and out of my throat, words I had never dared even think before.
>
> "I'll kill you, you white muthafucka!"

As these standoffs continued, a group of white adults, "concerned citizens," threatened action if the school board didn't put an end to "the constant agitation, riots, property damage, filthy language, beating and cutting of our school boys, and the molestation of our school girls." These parents saw white children as victims of racial violence, never its perpetrators. In their view, the volatile atmosphere in the schools was not a predictable consequence of a plan that Black people viewed as inequitable and white people viewed as undesirable, causing different kinds of distress for both groups, but rather a one-sided threat to "our way of life."

That way of life, as ever, was white supremacy. "The next time we hear of a riot, through any media, we must leave our jobs, our businesses or whatever we are doing, and assemble at the trouble spot in such numbers that there will be no doubt that we mean for order to be kept," the parents wrote.

"We will use whatever means necessary to restore order to our campuses and streets." They may have been consciously evoking 1898 or they may simply have inherited their predecessors' language and stratagems, perfectly intact after seventy-two years.

AS WHITE PARENTS THREATENED VIGILANTE JUSTICE, A WHITE SUPREMACIST paramilitary was organizing in Wilmington. The organization, incorporated in 1969, called itself the Rights of White People Party—ROWP, pronounced "rope." Its leader was a thirty-nine-year-old ex-marine named Leroy Gibson. Most of the group's members, like him, had served at nearby Camp Lejeune and believed that the Civil Rights Movement had caused "law and order" to be sacrificed to "black demands." The county's top law enforcement officer was still Sheriff Marion Millis, who had admitted that he and many of his deputies had joined the Klan; the local school board, meanwhile, had defied *Brown* for nearly two decades. Yet for ROWP, local authorities were insufficiently racist. "If necessary, we'll eliminate the black race," Gibson told a reporter. "What are we supposed to do while these animals run loose in the streets?"

The operation was unpolished, but many of its members had been professionally trained to kill. The FBI rated ROWP as more dangerous than the Klan, which, for its part, wanted nothing to do with the group, likening them to Nazis. Supporters passed out cards around town, listing reasons to join: "ROWP will see that we WHITE people stay white—and your children's children," "ROWP will do everything in its power to keep your housing area a WHITE one," "ROWP does not believe in mixing the races." In addition to rhetorical violence, the group offered free target practice to white teenagers.

Gibson revived the practice of night riding in Wilmington. His most active followers were young men drawn from the lower ranks of white society, just as the Red Shirts had been. Armed and highly motivated by the cause of preserving the racial caste system, they sped around the city looking for Black people to intimidate. One police report read:

> Hilton Murdie Jones, WM, Age 36, Rt 2, Box 361-L, Wilmington, arrested for being dangerously armed and brown-bagging, Robert Gregory Farrow, WM age 46, Rt. 5, Box 93, Wilmington, arrested for being armed to the terror of the populace. (1) .12 pump shotgun, (5) shells, (1) pint "Early Times" whiskey.

ROWP promised to finish the work of racial terror that the Red Shirts had begun in 1898. Like the white supremacists of that era—and of ours—the group was adept at using the media to disseminate lies, depicting Black people as "Communist-inspired black revolutionaries" and incorrigible criminals. At one rally, at Hugh MacRae Park, Gibson regaled a crowd with his plans to send armed caravans into Black neighborhoods. Failing the imminent resegregation of schools, he said, he wanted to secede from the Union. Calling a meeting for the same time and place the following week, he urged his supporters to come armed. The echoes of 1898 were unmistakable. "If the black people won't abide with law and order, we'll have to take matters into our own hands," he said. "We have as many as two thousand white men in Wilmington who are ready to settle this trouble right now. If it weren't for Wilmington police, the blacks in there would have been destroyed by now."

The writer Tim Tyson, a junior high school student at the time, happened to be at the park, practicing with his baseball team, on the night of a ROWP gathering. As he and his teammates huddled in the dugout, they heard the revving of engines and the slamming of doors. The diamond filled with white men and women, toting guns and Confederate flags. Tyson recalled:

> Their paramilitary leader, Leroy Gibson, walked up to the makeshift microphone and began bellowing about how the "n—s" and "n— lovers" had all the rights and white working people had none. "The n—s keep talking about how Waddell said in 1898 that they were gonna clog up the river with carcasses," he jeered. "I don't know if they did or not. But if this integration and rioting business doesn't

> stop, we're going to clog that river with dead n——s this time, and I mean it.'"

Like the Red Shirts, ROWP drew from the humble ranks of white society, fanning the aggression and anger of white people who felt that if they had less than they wanted, it must be because Black people had taken it. ROWP, however, was operating without the patronage or protection of the white elite. Taking up Waddell's mantle for "white working people," Gibson brought the threat of racial terror to its highest pitch since 1898.

Chapter 35

DO NOT CALL OUR BLUFF

The Bellamys—the school superintendent Heyward, his wife Mary, their three children, and Heyward's ailing eighty-one-year-old mother—were sitting in the living room of their split-level house on Lynnwood Drive after dinner on a Wednesday night. The curtains were drawn, but light seeped through a crack.

"Doesn't it seem like it's brighter than usual?" Heyward said.

Mary got up to check.

Looking out the window, she saw that their usually quiet street was jammed with traffic.

"I think the traffic's for us," Mary said.

Sedans and pickups disgorged entire families onto the Bellamys' front lawn. Several hundred white people congregated there: older women in cat's-eye glasses, Brylcreemed men in striped shirtsleeves, a mother with a bouffant and a toddler on her hip. A little boy in madras shorts, his tummy poking out from under his T-shirt, raised a sign with a simplistic drawing of a bus. Next to him, another boy raised a sign that read "Save Your Self / Save Your Children / Stop Bussing / BOYCOTT."

"Mama, there are babies out there!" cried the Bellamys' sixteen-year-old daughter, Mary Louise, edging in at the window for a look.

As he ushered in the final phase of the court-approved desegregation plan, Heyward Bellamy drew contempt from every corner. Black parents

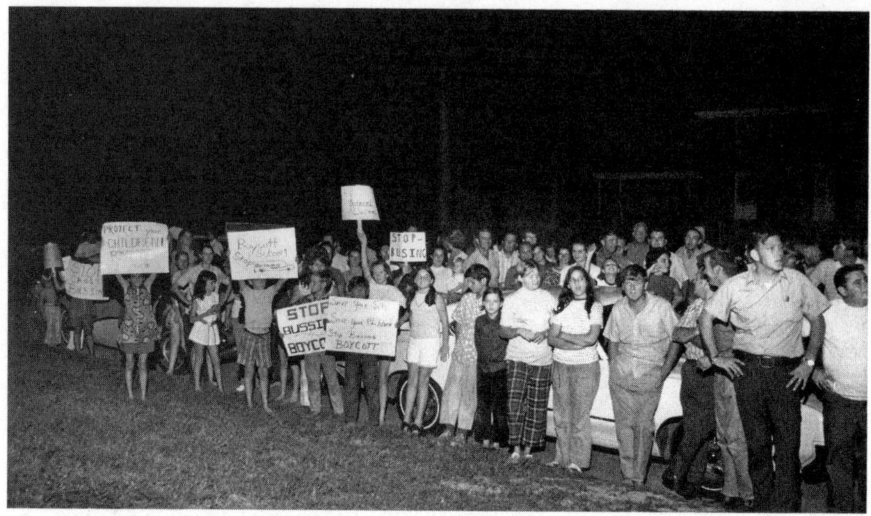

Protesters on Heyward Bellamy's front lawn, September 1, 1971.

and students remained distraught over the closure of Williston. White parents and students blamed him for busing their kids. "Bellamy has to go," the arch-conservative *Hanover Sun* wrote. Most everyone was unsettled by the febrile ambience in the county's high schools.

Heyward was a complex figure: "a New Deal / Great Society liberal, but certainly not a radical," according to his son. He had been raised in a macho culture and expected to come home to a roast in the oven. His way of dealing with work stress was to go out in the backyard and start sawing boards. But when Mary won a Fulbright scholarship, he encouraged her to take the eight-week fellowship in Spain, leaving him at home with three young kids. And as the children got older, he encouraged them, in a land of sports mania, to play string instruments.

Heyward idolized Franklin Roosevelt and the New Deal but, like many Southerners, detested the "arrogant" officials that the federal government had sent to Wilmington to monitor desegregation. He believed in the moral necessity of dismantling educational inequity but was patient with white prejudice, speaking in careful euphemisms about "what this town is ready for" and "what is possible in the community." Despite a hippie streak that led him to oppose dress codes and corporal punishment, he could be patronizing. The Black person he knew best was Flossie Harris, the family's longtime housekeeper. "She was like a second mother to all of us," he recalled, even though they were essentially the same age.

Heyward believed that his early years of living and working among Black people in the Brooklyn neighborhood made him singularly suited to guide Wilmington through its latest period of turmoil. At one public meeting, he gestured toward two Black women he'd known as a boy at his father's store. "I think I have a unique insight into Black America because of my childhood experience with people such as these," he declared. "I hope I can continue to use it for the betterment of this community."

SOME OF THE SHOUTING WHITE PEOPLE WHO CONGREGATED IN THE BELlamys' front yard on the evening of September 1, 1971, had come armed. Mary ran upstairs with the kids and had them lie down on the floor. Not too long ago, someone had written "N—— LOVER" in shaving cream on the side of Heyward's van. Just before the first day of school, a vandal had broken into the school board parking lot and poured sand into the gas tanks of thirteen buses. Tonight, Heyward's opponents were trespassing on his property and threatening his family.

Incensed, Heyward called the police. Two officers arrived quickly, urging him to keep his cool. In previous months, as the fight over desegregation had escalated, Heyward had amassed an arsenal: a Remington .12-gauge shotgun that he sometimes used for hunting, along with pistols and an M-1 carbine that his brother, a highway patrolman in South Carolina, had furnished. Heyward told the officers that although he was a pacifist, he would not tolerate the crowd getting any closer to his home.

"The first person who comes in the house gets his head blown off," he declared.

One of the officers went out and relayed Heyward's message. The hecklers stayed in the street most of the night, but no one approached the house. By morning, they were gone.

THE PREVIOUS WINTER, JUST BEFORE CHRISTMAS BREAK, HEYWARD WAS at Hemenway Hall, the board of education's imposing redbrick headquarters, lingering over a final preholiday lunch with his staff. A secretary rushed in with urgent news: There had been a fight—a "street disturbance" pitting Black and white students against each other—at New Hanover High. Several students were hurt. Bellamy later wrote, "There had been isolated incidents before, but this one was more serious, involving rock and bottle throwing. This incident ushered in a period of about 18 months when there was little peace to be found in New Hanover County."

History is supple, and our interpretation of it varies according to how we choose to handle time, compressing or expanding events. White people in Wilmington took the long view when it suited them, linking their resistance to desegregation to what they saw as the overstepping policies of the federal government during Reconstruction. Heyward Bellamy was no nostalgist, but he acknowledged the elasticity of white memory—stretching time when it serves, snapping it tight when it doesn't. "As I look back on the mid 60s, I am more sure than I ever have been of the need to study the history of an area if a person is to understand it," he wrote later. "In the case of North Carolina, one needs but study the 1860s and 1870s to get some understanding of the reasons certain legal patterns were established. This does not make a practice right, but it could have, I believe, made people a little more understanding and patient as a School Board struggled to obey the law, provide for the education of the children, and maintain the support of the citizenry in the process."

Many people believed the conflict that would come to engulf New Hanover County's schools, and then the entire community, had a crisp, contemporary genesis in a single street disturbance. *This incident ushered in a period of about 18 months when there was little peace to be found in New Hanover County.* Was New Hanover County peaceful before then? Did the trouble begin with rocks and bottles, or with mounted machine guns and Colt .44 revolvers, or did it go back to siege and bombardment and secession, slavers and their ships with the big white wings?

After Christmas break, the scraps and clashes escalated into a full-on crisis. The immediate cause was Dr. Martin Luther King's birthday, which Black students had hoped to honor with a memorial service. Even in Charleston, South Carolina, school administrators had recently approved a Black history syllabus, but New Hanover County administrators rejected the students' request. In protest of their decision, seventy students staged an impromptu sit-in over milk cartons and brown-bag sandwiches in Hoggard's cafeteria. The school responded by expelling fifteen students.

The following weeks brought more drama: At the end of January, Black and white students brawled at a café near Hanover. The fight spilled onto campus, and several students were injured, including a Black teenager, who was cut on the leg by a bottle thrown by a white boy. She reported her injury to the principal, but instead of finding and punishing her assailant, he suspended her, along with four other Black students.

The incidents spurred Black students to act on the ambient sense of injustice that had troubled them since the closure of Williston. On January 26, eight student leaders, representing both high schools, drew up a list of grievances and delivered them to Heyward. They were concerned over practical matters: the reinstatement of expelled classmates, the discriminatory behavior of the principal, "who only gets one side of the story when there is a Black student involved." The document made clear that they felt not only disrespected but unsafe—vulnerable to white adults, including ROWP members, "who have been coming onto campus provoking fights with Black students," and to "attacks from male faculty." (After one fight, a driving instructor at Hoggard admitted to a reporter that "he made a flying tackle on the blacks and dispersed them.")

The students wanted to be able to invite speakers to campus and they wanted Black coaches on the faculty: "To function as a coach and not a call boy!" Black studies, they argued, should be added to the curriculum—why were they taught that Fort Fisher was the last port of the Confederacy, but not about the colored troops who liberated Wilmington? "We believe that we as a people will not fully understand ourselves until we are allowed to learn about our history and our heritage," they wrote. Until officials addressed their proposals, they announced, they would be boycotting their classes. For the moment, the boycott seemed like a small-time threat, but it would turn out to be a historically consequential decision.

The teenage protesters were hardly seasoned activists. The summer before, one of them had traveled to Washington for a march and been repulsed by the slovenliness of his fellow protesters—"bologna and apple cores everywhere," he recalled, complaining that "a few of the people were wearing nothing but dirty underwear." Seeking a place to set up headquarters, student leaders solicited Black churches. The first three turned them down, as did the Boys Club.

Like Hubert Eaton, the students encountered a distinct lack of support from established Black leaders. Their tactics, however, could not have differed more from the careful doctor's. He had been prepared to pursue a long fight through the courts. The students were making it up as they went along. "We were a restless, isolated group of black, urban Southerners coming of age on the trailing edge of the modern civil rights movement," Wayne Moore, one of the student leaders, recalled. "Whole generations of effective black leadership had been wiped out by the Massacre of 1898. Much of what was left of established leadership in black Wilmington cringed in fear in the face of power. We had few mentors."

This lack was not coincidental. The massacre had annihilated the infrastructure of Black leadership in Wilmington; in rebuilding, Black leaders, mostly drawn from religious ranks, had erred on the side of appeasement, not wanting to provoke white aggression once again. While white adults advocated for what they perceived to be white children's best interests, Black students were largely left to fight for themselves. Wayne Moore recalled, "We were a new generation of black Wilmington and we were finding our legs and testing our muscles. We hadn't been around a lot of white people before. Maybe we didn't know any better. Nevertheless, we were standing up. And it felt good."

A FEW WEEKS AFTER THE SIT-IN, THE BOYCOTTING STUDENTS FINALLY found a headquarters at Gregory Congregational United Church of Christ, a small brick chapel on Nun Street between Sixth and Seventh. The church stood close to the former site of *The Daily Record*'s offices, next to where the *Daily Journal*, the city's current Black paper, was now published. The grandfather of one of the students was a parishioner. Others knew Eugene Templeton, the church's young white pastor, from an after-school volunteer program.

Most of the church's 150 members were Black working people: longshoremen, civil servants, technicians at the DuPont or General Electric plants that city boosters had lured to town after the departure of the Atlantic Coast Line Railroad, in the late fifties. Generally, job opportunities in Wilmington had increased considerably, but the Black population, decreasing since the turn of the century, stagnated economically, while white workers profited from the growth. In 1966, 42 percent of the city's Black families received some form of public assistance, and the median income for Black families fell below the poverty line.

The students' request was an easy yes for Templeton. Figuring that organized religion was "supposed to correct the wrongs of society," he offered them the use of the church's sanctuary. On January 28 and 29, around forty students reported there for "freedom school," studying Black history in the morning and trying to get their movement off the ground in the afternoon. By the third day, the crowd had grown to over a hundred students. "We're not getting an education anyway," one of them reasoned, "so why shouldn't we stay out?"

Templeton quickly sensed that he was in over his head. He had arrived at Gregory two years earlier, directly from the Union Theological Seminary, in New York. The Congregational church had a strong tradition of social justice, but at twenty-seven, Templeton was far from the stereotype of the crusading young white reverend determined to make a difference in the inner city. Born in Maine, he had spent much of his childhood in the North Carolina mountains, in the overwhelmingly white western part of the state. Before coming to Wilmington, he admitted, he hadn't given race much thought. The job at Gregory, in fact, was the only one he'd been offered after graduation.

Templeton and his wife, Donna, a nurse, lived in a parsonage next to the church. They had married there the year before, in front of a small crowd of congregants. Neither of them knew Wilmington well, and their acquaintances were largely limited to people they'd met through Gregory. Templeton later recalled that the other white people they crossed paths with seemed to view them with "somewhere between disapproval and disgust." He continued, "It was kind of like I was totally isolated from the white community."

The students' greatest assets—their willingness to challenge white authority and their refusal to back down—were also their biggest vulnerabilities. It is probably not coincidental that Templeton, a newcomer and the sole white person they approached for support, was the only one to volunteer it without hesitation. By his own account, he did not fully grasp the implications of signing on as the student protesters' sponsor. "I knew a lot about the history and theology of the church, and I knew very little about community organizing," he said later.

As the school boycott gathered momentum, Templeton called the UCC's Commission for Racial Justice to ask for help. The commission dispatched Ben Chavis, a twenty-three-year-old field organizer, to Wilmington. Chavis had already led successful campaigns under intense conditions. Recently, in his hometown of Oxford, North Carolina, an all-white jury acquitted two white men in the murder of a close Chavis family friend, despite overwhelming evidence that they were guilty. In response, Chavis had organized a boycott of white businesses, ultimately helping to force the town to integrate its public facilities.

Chavis came from one of North Carolina's most intellectually distinguished families. His great-great-grandfather, John Chavis, a minister and teacher, was reported to be "during his lifetime probably the most learned Black man in the United States." Free at birth, John studied at what later became Princeton and, returning to North Carolina, established a school where he tutored the scions of the state's white aristocracy in Latin and Greek. After they had gone home, he taught Black children late into the night. In 1832, in response to Nat Turner's rebellion, North Carolina outlawed Black education. John lost his academy and fell into poverty, but continued teaching Black children. In 1838, he was clubbed to death in his home by an unknown assailant. Tim Tyson writes, "The Chavis children grew up hearing that white opponents bashed in his skull because he refused to stop educating Black children."

Ben Chavis arrived in Wilmington at the beginning of February, "stepping tall, lean, and brown from his blue, sunroofed Cadillac El Dorado, a full-length fur coat draped over his square shoulders." One observer ventured that "he looked more like a pimp than revolutionary." His appearance on the scene immediately upped the stakes of what had been, until then, an essentially parochial conflict. With a glamorous, battle-hardened activist in the mix, Wilmington authorities scrambled to save face. The students started to wonder, for the first time, whether they might just win.

WHITE AUTHORITIES DENOUNCED CHAVIS AS AN "OUTSIDE AGITATOR"—A politically motivated manipulator of a local population that would otherwise have remained content and acquiescent. (A staple denunciation during the civil rights era, the trope has recently resurfaced to cast doubt on the motives of protesters in such places as Ferguson, Charlottesville, Minneapolis, and Los Angeles.) The police chief blamed Chavis for stoking hostility, claiming that "after [his] arrival . . . in our city, the tension got real tight and we started having more violence." The city's problems, of course, long predated Chavis. But his leadership indeed posed a threat to the status quo of Black deference. Chavis was more than conscious of the depredations of white supremacy, but he was unburdened by the specific belief that, as some locals feared, Wilmington's white city fathers would "wipe out the Black community again."

The first thing Chavis did was to advise the students to hold a press conference. On February 2, they addressed the media from Gregory's sanctuary. The boycott committee comprised six high school juniors and seniors, all male, seated at an antique wooden desk that looked like it might have been hastily grabbed from the church office. They were boys on the bottom, the laces of their high-top sneakers tied in floppy bows, and revolutionaries on top, in berets and the odd pair of sunglasses.

Chavis announced that if the students' demands were not met by noon the next day, the group would shut down the schools. "We intend to close up the whole system—one through twelve," he warned. Their delivery had clearly benefited from the tutelage of Chavis, who, with a showman's flair, denounced Heyward Bellamy as "a lie." (The comment so irked Heyward that he jotted a teacherly quibble in the margin of his meeting notes: "not liar, but lie.") By the end of the conference, it was apparent that what had started as a localized dispute over contemporary issues was intensifying into something that encompassed a far more historic sense of injury.

"Any more questions?" Chavis asked, closing the event. "Do not call our bluff!"

The noon deadline came and went without a response from Heyward. This was not a surprise—at earlier meetings, he had told student leaders that, in keeping with the proper chain of command, they should address their complaints to their school principals. Heyward said that he was ready to readmit anyone who returned to school with a note from their parents, but warned that any student who kept on with the boycott would be suspended.

The students and many of the adults opposing them had little knowledge of the historical context in which they were operating. This was to be expected, given the conspicuous absence of key events from their classrooms and the textbooks from which they learned. According to Harcourt Brace's *North Carolina*, for instance, all had been well in the state since the white supremacy campaign of 1898 had restored Democrats to power. "Beginning in Aycock's time the whites and the negroes became more friendly and learned to work together for their own and the state's good," the book claimed. "There was less and less occasion for trouble between the races." Had various players in the conflict been better versed in Wilmington's past, they might have recognized alarming congruencies: ultimatums; missed rendezvous; a flagrant lack of communication between Black people and white people, exacerbated by performative public encounters. This wasn't 1898—for one thing, Black people were the ones issuing demands, even if their daring to do so exposed them to reprisal—but familiar patterns of mistrust, bad faith, and escalation were creating a combustible situation.

As the standoff continued, no one in power seemed inclined to do anything to protect the students, who were at greatest risk of harm. The school board remained obstinate, while the *Wilmington Morning Star*, fanning the flames of conflict as in 1898, called for a hard-nosed approach to "the utter illogic of a handful of people presuming to dictate public school policies here." With armed ROWP members prowling Black neighborhoods in their pickups, some of the students, rather than walking home at night, started sleeping over at Gregory. On February 3, a white-owned furniture store in a Black neighborhood burned to the ground. One city council member declared, "It's a bunch of youngsters who have been stirred up by outsiders—we've had a wonderful relationship between blacks and whites before this."

Soon, Templeton received information from a detective that ROWP was planning to firebomb the church. Alarmed, he asked Mayor Allsbrook to instate a curfew. The mayor declined, offering instead to install a wooden police barricade. It proved ineffective at stopping ROWP members, who managed to drive through and shoot at the church.

"We then agreed that the church could and should be defended," Templeton later recalled. Students scrounged up old guns from their garages. A ragtag assortment of better-armed adults gravitated to the church, including servicemen from nearby military bases and "brothers of the street," characterized by Larry Thomas as "high school dropouts, ex-convicts, winos, heroin addicts or former students who had been expelled for discipline reasons." Thomas recalled in a lightly fictionalized account, "Most of them were not afraid to say they hated white people and that they loved the idea of 'blasting some Cracker Klansmen in they white asses!'"

"HI, DADDY," SIXTEEN-YEAR-OLD MARY LOUISE BELLAMY SAID TO HER FAther as he walked in the door.

Heyward didn't smile.

"Hi," he said, blowing past her. "Where's your mama?"

"Upstairs."

Mary Louise listened—hurried footsteps, a door closing, anxious voices. She climbed the stairs gingerly, as though one of them might explode the second her foot touched the carpet. Heyward came charging back down the staircase, yelling to his wife, who had been cooking a roast, to turn off the oven. Mary Louise's mother called her to the room. "We can't stay here tonight," she said. "Pack your clothes and take your schoolbooks so you can do your homework."

The family threw their belongings into bags and loaded two cars with math books and violins. Over dinner at Lum's, a chain restaurant famous for its hot dogs steamed in beer, Heyward explained that opponents of desegregation were threatening to burn their house down. After dinner, the Bellamys drove to Heyward's sister's apartment. Heyward parked the cars far from the house in case anyone might recognize them. In the kitchen, the Bellamy kids tried to do their homework.

The night after the Bellamys had paid their check, Lum's went up in flames. Police blamed the fire and several others on Black arsonists, although later evidence suggested that the owner of Lum's had torched his own restaurant to collect on an insurance policy. As the week went on, firefighters battled conflagrations across the city, sniper fire was reported at a downtown intersection, and bomb threats were called in to several schools.

Mary Louise didn't go back to school. Her parents pulled her out of Hoggard and enrolled her at Vardell Hall, a preparatory academy for girls more than an hour outside Wilmington. (Her brothers, who were in third and ninth grades, remained at home.) The irony was painful: A school superintendent, presiding over desegregation, encounters such alarming pushback that he ends up sending his own daughter to a private school. Moreover, the school was a "segregation academy," founded as a racial fortress for white families hoping to escape the very measures that he was trying to put into effect.

Mary Louise confided to her diary that she was "vaguely aware of a pervasive, nameless fear of some unyielding, totally evil power." A product of New Hanover County schools, she wasn't able to identify it more precisely than that. Off she went, another exile, as Wilmington burned again and white supremacists prepared to uphold the racial hierarchy by whatever means it took. But this time, Black residents knew what to expect.

Chapter 36

JR. BABYLON

By February 5, 1971, around 80 percent of the county's Black high school students had joined the boycott, heeding the call "to walk out of the slave master's classrooms." That day, some four hundred of them marched on City Hall to protest the school board's policies. There, in 1898, Alfred Moore Waddell had riled the white supremacist mob with visions of a carcass-clogged river. Now two students climbed the steps of the same building and unfurled a black flag.

Ben Chavis raises a fist on the steps of City Hall as student protesters look on. February 1971.

That night, once the sun had set, the area around Gregory lit up with flames and gunfire. The students had been holed up in the church for days. Some drew comfort from the sacred atmosphere, channeling a higher mission as electric candles shone against its smooth, pale plaster walls. Others blasted party tunes on 8-track players and sent pot smoke curling up into the sanctuary's high ceilings. Outside, armed sentries fended off screeching caravans of white vigilantes. The church's facade was full of bullet holes. What had begun as a boycott had effectively turned into a siege.

Around seven o'clock, a young man burst through the church door yelling a code word that the group had agreed upon to indicate trouble.

"Rabbit!" he screamed. "Rabbit! Rabbit!"

Before he could explain, a student stumbled in behind him, bleeding from the chest. The boy had been shot and needed medical care, but the group at the church felt that taking him to the hospital, where another Black gunshot victim had been arrested in the emergency room, was too great a risk. Donna Templeton laid the student out on a table and tended to the wound as best she could with the materials at hand. The next day, a Black minister was shot in the leg as he stood on the sidewalk near Gregory, trying to persuade the young people to lay down their weapons and go home. Even the most idealistic students were disillusioned and enraged. "It even moved some to vow that 1971 was not going to be a repeat of 1898," the student leader Wayne Moore recalled. "Some blacks ran into the streets promising to destroy everything the white man owned."

Around ten o'clock, Mike's Grocery, a wood-frame corner store about three hundred yards from Gregory, went up in flames. Mike's was close enough to the church that the Gregory lookouts could see it from their positions. Steve Mitchell, a Hoggard senior, went running in the direction of the store. At the same time, police rushed to the scene. One of them shot Mitchell, killing him with three shotgun blasts to the throat.

A white-owned store with a mostly Black clientele, Mike's was not universally beloved in the neighborhood. Some people accused its owner, Mike Poulos, of price-gouging in an area with limited food access; others resented his reportedly "nasty" manner with customers and his refusal to sell

Firefighters battle the blaze at Mike's Grocery as gunfire rings out, February 7, 1971.

alcohol to minors. For several nights in a row, arsonists had tried to burn down the store. While many observers assumed they were driven by animosity toward Poulos, others have suggested a tactical motive. According to one student organizer, the church had been taking sniper fire coming from the direction of Mike's.

In the aftermath of Mitchell's death, police claimed that Black protesters had shot at emergency personnel as they arrived at the scene. The officer who killed Mitchell said that Mitchell had pointed a shotgun at him, but the gun had misfired, so he shot Mitchell instead, in self-defense. White officials all the way to the top backed the officer. The mayor remarked, in a particularly inhumane aside to the *Wilmington Morning Star*, "I see the shooting of Steve Mitchell as a deterrent. I think we have the situation in hand now."

Mitchell's peers told a different story. They said that when he saw from his lookout post that Mike's was aflame, jeopardizing nearby homes, he handed his weapon off to another guard and went running to pull a fire alarm down the street. Neighbors testified that Mitchell hadn't died immediately after being shot, as the police claimed. According to them, officers roughed him up and then threw him into a patrol car. It took them ninety minutes to make the three-mile drive to the hospital. Mitchell was dead on arrival. His comrades memorialized him as "the FIRST BROTHER to give his life for us in our very indigenous struggle here in 'JR. BABYLON.'"

Despite the mayor's assurances, the violence was far from being under control. On the morning of February 7, less than twelve hours after Mitchell's death, a white man named Harvey Cumber was shot and killed in front of Gregory. At first, white officials presented Cumber, a retired roofing contractor, as a random, unlucky victim. "He was struck in the temple with a bullet from a sniper as he was returning to his home from a trip to a store to get a carton of soft drinks," the *Star* reported. It quickly emerged, however, that he had blown through the police barricade in his pickup truck and started shooting up the church before an unidentified gunman shot back.

Cumber's grieving relatives enacted a dramatic public spectacle of martyrdom. The next week, two of his sons carried his casket out of the family home and loaded it into the same pickup truck that he had driven to Gregory, its rearview window still shattered by bullets. Newspaper photographers followed as the family drove the makeshift hearse to the local state prison unit, where a third son, Benjy, was incarcerated. Prison officials had yet to issue Benjy a pass to attend his father's funeral, so the family brought Harvey to him. Cumber's widow, Leona, trailed the pickup in a black Cadillac.

At the prison gates, the cortege came to a halt. Flanked by her sons, Leona Cumber emerged from the Cadillac and stood on the grass, raising a hand in the air in the manner of an evangelist receiving the spirit.

"Let Benjy come out and see his daddy!" she cried.

When Benjy failed to materialize, the Cumbers began unloading funeral wreaths from the truck, signaling their intention to camp out on the

Leona Cumber and sons at the state prison unit with makeshift hearse, February 13, 1971.

lawn until prison officials conceded. Next came the casket. Someone opened the lid, and Leona Cumber crumpled into one of her sons' arms. "Mrs. Cumber Faints," the next day's *Star* declared. Her sons laid her out on the trunk of the Cadillac to recover.

In the end, the Cumbers got their way and officials gave Benjy a dispensation to travel to his father's funeral, more than an hour's drive from the prison. They were aided by a sympathetic media: The *Star*'s managing editor admitted to having lobbied the authorities "in the capacity of a private citizen." In an interview with the paper, the eldest Cumber son, Byron, radiated pride. He had done some bad things, he said, but in "taking Daddy to see Benjy," he had fulfilled his filial duty.

"I think Daddy would have wanted it that way," he said.

The death of Cumber, a white vigilante, moved the intertwined communities of law enforcement, government, and the press in ways that Mitchell's hadn't. Now that a white man was dead, city administrators began treating the Gregory standoff as an urgent problem. Within hours of Cumber's killing, the mayor finally imposed a curfew on the cold but smoldering city, and the governor dispatched six hundred members of the National

Guard to Wilmington "to regain control of the situation." One commander made a point of telling his unit that their duffel bags would not be searched—an enticement to fill them with illicit weapons.

The publication of an article in *The New York Times* brought Wilmington's problems to national attention. Clearly irked by the prospect of unflattering publicity, Luther Cromartie, the mayor, explained to the *Times'* reporter that "outsiders stirred everything up." This complaint ignored the fact that Wilmington already possessed one of the country's most ignominious records of racial violence. It also elided the contemporary reality that the city's students had a plethora of reasons to be upset, independent of external influence. As the guardsmen arrived with machine guns and "million candlepower" infrared scopes, the mayor still had not made contact with Eugene Templeton, the pastor at Gregory. "He looks like a hippie, but I don't let that influence my thinking," Cromartie said. "I haven't been able to talk to him yet. I can't get in touch with him. I sent word through a Nigra preacher but I haven't gotten any answer."

The National Guard stormed Gregory on the morning of February 8 with a warrant permitting them to search for "weapons of mass death and destruction." No one was inside, except for a custodian and a woman who had nothing to do with the fighting. The adjutant general of the guard admitted that the raid had turned up nothing. Other law enforcement officials, however, claimed they had found "sniper nests" filled with empty shotgun shells, empty wine bottles, and sticks of dynamite.

At a press conference, Ben Chavis sounded a defiant note, promising that "the struggle has just begun," but the boycott was effectively over. The students stood down, their commitment to the cause finally outweighed by the immediate threat to their lives. They went home, showered, ate their moms' bacon, and listened with incredulity to the "rumbling, clanking, crunching metallic sound" of Sherman tanks rolling through their neighborhoods. "All I could think was, *Has it come to this?*" Wayne Moore recalled.

Despite the lockdown, Byron Cumber, the eldest of Harvey's sons, was still roaming freely around the neighborhood. As the National Guard arrived at Gregory, he showed up on the church's doorstep, vowing "to avenge my father's death." Cumber told reporters that he had been in the area earlier to pick up his father's truck. Someone, he claimed, had fired at him from a green house near the church. He had wheeled around and opened fire with a .12-gauge shotgun. "I don't know whether I hit anyone or not, but I hope to my God I did," he said.

The siege had amounted to a near-death experience for almost everyone inside the church. Two people had lost their lives. Twenty-seven buildings had been incinerated. To student organizers the transformation of their nonviolent boycott into a "small war," as one lawyer later described it, seemed surreal. "Had this been a different time before there were national television and radio news, national daily newspapers quick to print, we would have been slaughtered like our predecessors had in the Massacre of 1898," Wayne Moore later wrote. "Our slaughter would eventually come, but it would be largely bloodless, and done in the light of the day with a public veneer of the just and lawful."

Chapter 37

THE HAPPIEST DAMN POLICE CHIEF

On a Sunday night in May, three months after the Gregory fiasco, a fire consumed Hemenway Hall, the New Hanover County school district's brick-and-wood Greek Revival headquarters. By two thirty a.m., a quartet of Ionic pillars that framed the building's front entrance were, according to a news report, "burning like Roman candles, flaring up to lick the lintels." The pillars soon collapsed, sending flaming rubble flying into the yard. By the time the fire department arrived, the whole building was in flames.

As firemen hosed water onto the ruins of the complex, police estimated that the damage would amount to hundreds of thousands of dollars. The most serious loss was that of seventy-five years' worth of documents: nearly every report card, diploma, registration form, disciplinary file, personnel record, and payroll record created since 1897. When officials could finally get into the building, the only things they were able to salvage were an old safe and thirty-five "soaking, rusting typewriters."

With the school district plunged into administrative chaos, Heyward Bellamy remained preternaturally calm. The system would be able to reconstruct the payroll records with the help of state documents, he told reporters, and academic activities would proceed as usual. Lacking offices, he set up a temporary "nerve center" in the auditorium of a middle school. "I arranged for a telephone to be installed in the stage area, borrowed some pencils and legal pads, and started to work," he recalled. Perhaps it was comforting to feel as though he were just playing the role of besieged superintendent in a student production.

Behind the scenes, Heyward was working to tamp down speculation about the fire's cause. Shortly after it broke out, he visited the site with Fats Williamson, the city's police chief. Williamson had no doubt that the fire had been an arson. He was able to show Heyward exactly where the perpetrators had entered the building. There was no shortage of people with grudges against the New Hanover County school system—the one thing that almost everyone, Black or white, agreed upon about the desegregation process was that they had gotten royally screwed. But Heyward needed the fire *not* to be an arson. Even if all the evidence was pointing in that direction, he explained to Williamson, he didn't want to give the "wannabes" who had set it the publicity they craved. And he worried that after all the recent tumult—the rolling violence after Martin Luther King Jr.'s assassination, the fights at the schools, the bomb threats, the Gregory siege and its disastrous consequences—more bad news from the schools would simply be too much for people to handle.

Williamson turned to Heyward:

"What are we going to do about this, Doc?"

"As far as I'm concerned, we had a fire start in a building that was a fire trap," Heyward said.

"Thank you very much," Williamson replied. "That's what I was going to suggest."

A week later, Williamson announced that a team of experts had concluded an investigation of the fire. They had combed through all the available evidence, he said, and found nothing to suggest that the blaze had been deliberately set. Officially, the cause of the fire would be of "undetermined origin." Maybe it had had something to do with the open stairwells, or the oiled floors. "We're at a dead end at this point," the police chief told the *Wilmington Morning Star*. "We've done everything in our power to bring the facts to the public." The paper concluded, "The sudden fire which destroyed Hemenway Hall in Wilmington over a week ago will probably remain a mystery forever."

FOR MONTHS, THE POLICE HAD BEEN UNDER HEAVY PRESSURE TO HOLD someone responsible for the loss of white life and property during the February riots. From the bench, a district court judge publicly accused the police chief of leniency during the Gregory standoff: "Maybe we should have brought in Lt. Calley to go in and clean the place up," the judge said, referencing the army officer who presided over the civilian massacre at My Lai, in Vietnam.

The National Guard lockdown had ended the fighting at Gregory, but it only diverted the conflicts that had caused it. Black activists and white supremacists both continued their activities, adapting to changing conditions. In the months following the church siege, bullets continued to fly around downtown Wilmington, and more than forty Black people were shot, their attackers never to be found. After Ben Chavis and others opened the First African Congregation of the Black Messiah, a storefront church dedicated to Black liberation, ROWP set up a headquarters one block away. New organizers began to arrive in town, connecting young people in Wilmington to wider Black Power and Black nationalist movements. One, taking an absurdist approach, threatened to unleash chickens at the Azalea Festival, a beloved springtime rite of white society. He said, "They can't arrest the chickens, all they can do is eat them."

In 1969, the FBI had named Ben Chavis as a "Key Extremist" in its Agitator Index. According to the historian Kenneth Janken, law enforcement spent the better part of 1971 using "police surveillance, petty harassment, court injunctions and arrests on serious federal and state charges," in an attempt to bring Chavis down. The authorities knew that the more people they leaned on, the better probability they had of turning something up that they could use against him. "Except for Chavis, who exactly would be caught up in the dragnet seemed to be arbitrary," Janken writes.

In December, the police charged Chavis as an accessory in the murder of a Black man who was shot while playing cards at the home of a woman whose daughter was involved in the school protests. Chavis insisted publicly that the murder had been a racially motivated "assassination" and that a white man had done it, which turned out not to be true, infuriating authorities even further. In March 1972, more than a year after the church standoff, police officers executed a series of "lightning raids" in connection with the violence at Gregory. Announcing seventeen arrests, Fats Williamson declared, "I'm the happiest damn police chief in the country."

Prosecutors eventually whittled the list of defendants down to eleven: Ben Chavis; the student organizers Reginald Epps, Jerry Jacobs, George Kirby, James McKoy, Wayne Moore, Marvin "Chili" Patrick, Connie Tindall, Willie Earl Vereen, and Joe Wright; and Ann Shepard, a thirty-three-year-old white social worker who had supported the students during the school boycott. They charged the group with various crimes relating to the firebombing of Mike's Grocery on February 6, 1971. None of the students' parents could make bail, so they sat in jail for months, losing jobs and the opportunity to complete a GED program that the school system had set up. Eventually, the group became known as the Wilmington Eleven.

From the start, Black activists argued that the arrests were politically motivated. At a press conference after the raids, Irv Joyner, a young lawyer with the Committee for Racial Justice, called for "the dismantling of the present illegal Government of Wilmington," referring to the regime that was installed by the 1898 coup and never repudiated. "Wilmington is a symbol of all that is wrong and ugly in America," he proclaimed. Joyner helped to organize a vigil outside the New Hanover County courthouse, where the Wilmington Eleven were appearing for an initial hearing. The marchers' signs placed the trial within the larger context of the struggle for racial justice, expressing skepticism at the possibility of a fair trial.

"African Power," one placard read.

"Judge Burnett Would Hang His Own Mother."

"We Shall Avenge 1898."

The next month, the Wilmington Eleven published a letter from jail. It set forth a genealogy of Black oppression that, they wrote, had "been institutionalized" in Wilmington since 1898. They attributed their harsh treatment to the white desire to hold on to ill-gotten power. "Clearly we are now held prisoners in Wilmington, N.C. not because of accused criminal activity or rhetoric," the letter concluded, "but rather as a result of our continued political action against the most racist and repressive local governmental regime in America today."

Chapter 38

ISN'T THIS BEAUTIFUL?

The Wilmington Eleven trial opened at the Pender County courthouse, in Burgaw, about thirty miles from Wilmington, in June 1972. Due to extensive publicity, the defendants' lawyers had petitioned for a venue change. Each day, prison buses deposited the ten men and one woman at the courthouse, a picturesque Georgian Revival building in the middle of a square shaded by moss-draped oaks. To the side of the building stood a fifteen-foot-tall monument featuring a Confederate soldier standing atop a shaft of granite decorated with a Confederate flag. The statue, like others across the nation, had been erected by the UDC in a show of undying fealty to the Lost Cause in 1914. LET FUTURE GENERATIONS REMEMBER / THAT THESE WERE MEN / WHOM DEATH COULD NOT TERRIFY / WHOM DEFEAT COULD NOT DISHONOR. Wayne Moore remembered arriving each day and feeling as though he were passing through "a gateway to hell."

Judge Joshua James, a white judge with a reputation for fairness, presided over the trial. The majority of potential jurors were Black when voir dire began. Jay Stroud, a white thirty-three-year-old assistant district attorney, used his peremptory challenges to exclude a number of Black candidates, but at the end of selection, the panel comprised nine Black citizens and three white ones. As the trial's first week wound down, the defendants, all pleading not guilty, had good reason to expect that their case would be assessed by a group of people unlikely to convict them purely out of racial prejudice.

Stroud behaved strangely from the outset, making beginner's errors and calling people by the wrong names. After the lunch recess on Friday, he failed to reappear. His boss explained to the court that he had taken ill with gastrointestinal problems. On Monday, the state solicitor said it was unclear how long Stroud would be out of commission. Citing a lack of personnel, the solicitor motioned for a mistrial, which Judge James granted. The Wilmington Eleven's first trial was over before it had even begun.

A second trial opened in September under conditions far less favorable to the defendants. They were now the Wilmington Ten—between trials, one of the defendants had skipped bail. It was not a stretch to think this had been exactly the prosecution's intention in causing the delay. Judge James was replaced by Judge Robert Martin, a patronage appointee with segregationist sympathies. Unbelievably, he had presided over the controversial 1970 trial of Robert and Larry Teel for the murder of Henry Marrow, Ben Chavis's close family friend.

Back from his sickbed, Stroud used forty-one out of forty-two preemptive challenges to eliminate potential Black jurors. Ultimately, the new panel included only two Black people. During questioning, one juror, a white man, stated outright that he believed the defendants were guilty, while eleven jurors admitted that they considered an indictment to be evidence of guilt.

The opening of the trial was even more ominous. Bill Bailey, Burgaw's police chief, patrolled the courthouse square toting a machine gun, borrowed from the Marines. Rumors circulated that white supremacists had infiltrated the State Bureau of Investigation, and that "a plane had landed in Wilmington and a group of Black Panthers had gotten off it, and they were gonna come up here and cause trouble," a former judge from the county recalled. "And the second anybody did, Bill Bailey would have used it."

The Templetons were the only two adults who could speak credibly to the defendants' whereabouts on February 6, 1971, the night Mike's Grocery burned. They no longer lived in Wilmington, having fled town after a gunman opened fire on the parsonage. They had agreed to come back for the trial, and they intended to testify to the defendants' innocence. But when they landed at the Fayetteville, North Carolina, airport, they heard a message over the intercom:

"Will Mr. Eugene Templeton please come to the Piedmont counter."

Templeton reported to the counter, where someone handed him a telephone receiver. The voice on the other end spoke without hesitation:

"If you come to Wilmington, you'll be killed."

The Templetons had stood strong in the face of everything from social ostracism to urban warfare, but this specific threat to their lives was more than they could withstand. With the fates of ten friends riding on their testimony, they made the agonized choice to turn around and board the first flight back to New Jersey. Templeton recalled, "I guess I'm a slow learner, but something connected, finally, and I just thought, *We're going to get killed if we stay here*." The episode confirmed that Wilmington was still a fortress town, with self-appointed gatekeepers deciding who could come in and who would be kept out.

With the main defense witnesses intimidated into retreat, the prosecution introduced three star witnesses. They were all teenagers with compelling reasons to cooperate, and they all faced severe personal consequences if they did not. One, a thirteen-year-old middle school dropout, had recently been shipped off to reform school for robbery. Another had been convicted of killing a shopkeeper in 1971 and was awaiting sentencing when he implicated Chavis. A third witness, Allen Hall, had significant mental disabilities and a raft of legal issues.

The trial was marred by irregularities. Key elements of the witnesses' testimony didn't match their sworn statements; at other moments, their impossibly detailed recollections gave the distinct impression that they had been coached by police. During one cross-examination, Hall attacked the defendants and their counsel, lunging at them across a table.

In his closing statement, the defense attorney, James Ferguson, invoked Wilmington's long history of racial injustice. "I am willing to say to you that Wilmington had a problem before February 5 and 6, 1971," he said. "Wilmington is going to have a problem after February 5 and 6, 1971, because it's going to be a long time before people learn to live together." The students, he pointed out to the jury, had not created the discord in Wilmington, but they had attempted to change it, taking on a civic responsibility that elder generations had abdicated. They didn't deserve to be punished for trying.

After weeks of testimony, it took the jury only three hours to return their verdict. Ben Chavis, guilty. Jerry Jacobs, guilty. Reginald Epps, guilty. James McKoy, guilty. Wayne Moore, guilty. Marvin "Chili" Patrick, guilty. Connie Tindall, guilty. Willie Earl Vereen, guilty. Joe Wright, guilty. Ann Shepard, guilty. Collectively, the group's sentences, which would begin immediately, amounted to 282 years. The only white defendant and the only woman, Shepard was given the shortest sentence, of seven to ten years. Chavis, at twenty-four, received the longest, of twenty-nine to thirty-four years. A crowd of supporters outside the courthouse started singing spirituals as the young men, shackled and still in street clothes, were loaded onto a bus bound for the state penitentiary in Raleigh. "Isn't this beautiful?" Ben Chavis's mother yelled. "They're taking our boys away to prison."

On the bus, Wayne Moore pressed his nose to the window and watched "the autumn tans, golds, and coppers of the trees and surrounding fields" flicker by through a scrim of chicken wire. As the bus headed north, his thoughts drifted back in time. He wrote later, "The real message of our trial was that nothing had really changed in and around Wilmington: black oppression would go on, as it had from the Johnny Rebel-rousing of Hugh MacRae and the Secret Nine that gave us the Massacre of 1898 to the Rights of White People that hounded and hunted us almost a century later."

Chapter 39

THEY BLASTED MY SHOP

The explosion, one overcast evening in May 1973, was so loud that people heard it seven miles in each direction, all the way up to the Kings Grant subdivision to the north and Pirate's Cove to the south. T. C. Jervay, the publisher of *The Wilmington Journal*, heard it, too, mistaking the booming sound, at first, for a coming storm.

Minutes later, Jervay was at the paper's headquarters, helping detectives pick through the rubble in a tailored suit and hat. The explosion had demolished the paper's offices, on the first floor of the building, a two-story wooden structure with a clutch of palm trees out front. A couple who lived upstairs had managed to escape without injury. So had several neighbors, but their houses had been damaged badly enough that they would have to move out. The pattern of the wreckage—a scorched pit on the lawn, dented brickwork—pointed strongly to the use of an explosive device.

White authorities, skittish about the city's image after the violence at Gregory and the dubious convictions of the Wilmington Ten, tried to play down the attack's significance. "There is nothing to indicate that it was racial," Police Chief Fats Williamson assured the press. In reality, there was much to suggest a racial motivation in the attempt to blow up the *Journal*, the oldest and largest Black paper in the state. "It is part of the game," Jervay said, the day after the blast, vowing that the paper wouldn't miss a single issue. "The carpenters are ready to go. We got a city work permit today." He promised to start rebuilding as soon as the demolition squad was done.

Jervay knew Wilmington's history of racial terrorism intimately. He had grown up in its wreckage: In 1898, his mother's family had lived next door to the *Daily Record*. His father, meanwhile, had moved from South Carolina to Wilmington in 1901 to open a printing shop in the same neighborhood, on Seventh between Church and Nun. In the 1920s, the Jervay family acquired a linotype machine and started publishing the *Journal*, carrying on Alexander Manly's work of serving Wilmington's Black citizens "without fear or favor." The paper was both a regeneration and a repudiation, a means of saying to white supremacy: the hotter your fire, the harder our steel.

The attempt to destroy the *Journal* was also an attempt to destroy an idea. Whoever had bundled the dynamite and lit the fuse had exploded one of the city's most important Black-owned, Black-centered institutions alongside the building's bricks and planks. In addition to targeting the voice of the Black community, the attack struck at the history of Black Wilmington. The blast consumed decades' worth of archives, resulting in a loss "devastating to historians and others who seek to chronicle the twentieth-century African-American community in Wilmington," a local historian later declared.

Jervay's knowledge of history influenced his reaction to this destruction of physical, intellectual, and historical patrimony. "They blasted my shop, but I never missed an issue," he later bragged. His daughter recalled, "My daddy was very, very plain: 'You're not going to run me out of town. I was born here and I'm not going anywhere.' And what he was referring to was the fact that Mr. Manly had been run out of town in 1898."

AS IN 1898, WILMINGTON SERVED AS AN EXTREME CASE OF THE AMERICAN phenomenon of violent white resistance to Black success. A nationally syndicated article identified the city as a "racial hotbed." In addition to the bombings, it noted, the N-word was creeping back into public vocabulary around the city and housing discrimination was "being practiced in open defiance." White officials minimized the city's problems, rejecting any continuity between the recent attacks and those of seventy-five years earlier. "This isn't 1898, it's 1973," a spokesman for the Human Relations

Commission declared. "I think most whites today abhor this kind of thing." Yet when the Klan-coddling Sheriff Marion Millis resigned due to ill health, the county commissioners replaced him with H. R. Grohman, the segregationist deputy who had helped to organize Save Our Schools.

Three weeks after the *Journal* bombing, a blast ripped through a downtown apartment building. Days later, an explosion went off at the B'nai Israel Synagogue, followed by an attack on a Jewish-owned hardware store. Miraculously, no one was killed. Several weeks later, the police arrested an eighteen-year-old white man named Lawrence Little in connection with the first three bombings. Little had briefly served in the Marines before being honorably discharged for organizing a Ku Klux Klan klavern. He had joined ROWP and was now, he said, the group's minister of propaganda. On the night of one of the bombings, he had attended a ROWP rally at Hugh MacRae Park.

Little admitted that he had chosen to bomb the *Journal* for reasons of racial hatred, which he expressed in vile terms to white papers, who gladly printed them, fulfilling his stated goal of disseminating propaganda. At his trial, several fellow white supremacists testified against him, and an all-white jury convicted him in twenty-five minutes. The remaining members of ROWP, weakened by a raft of conspiracy charges, took to calling Little "the Wilmington One."

EVEN THE FANCIER BELLAMYS FELT THE HEAT THAT WAS ENGULFING THE city. Since 1948, when Ellen Bellamy's long-suffering housekeeper finally moved out, the Bellamy Mansion had sat empty. With Ellen's debts finally resolved, her heirs struggled to reach a consensus about what to do with the property, which "had become a cross between a white elephant and an albatross." Some descendants had wanted to turn it into the state headquarters of the United Daughters of the Confederacy, but the idea fizzled out due to the expense of repairs and maintenance. Eventually, the heirs put the house up for public auction, but it attracted such feeble bids that none were accepted.

In 1951, two of John Dillard Bellamy Jr.'s children had banded together to save the family seat, buying the house for twenty thousand dollars. The place was uninhabitable as a primary residence, and largely undesirable to white Wilmingtonians, who were abandoning downtown for the burgeoning suburbs. To defray costs, the Bellamy heirs brought on commercial tenants, ceding to a smattering of small businesses the basement rooms where enslaved people and then servants had once prepared the family's sumptuous meals. One can only imagine what John Dillard Bellamy would have made of the transformation of his secesh palace into a mini-mall. "We're a new shop in Wilmington," the proprietors of Deedie's Fabric Shop advertised, as the mansion approached its hundred-year anniversary. "Won't you drop in, let us say hello to you, and show you our selection of fine fabrics."

In early 1972, Hugh MacRae II and two cousins donated their interests in the house to a newly created nonprofit corporation, the Bellamy Mansion Inc. Hugh II had pushed hard for the gift, arguing that it would ensure the preservation of the run-down yet still-imposing and historically significant mansion. Less than a month later, he got a call: In the middle of the night, the house had almost burned to the ground in the latest of the wave of arsons plaguing the city. The damage was extensive: heat and smoke damage on the upper stories, water damage down below. Officials determined that arsonists had thrown milk bottles filled with gasoline through several lower-floor windows. In one room, the fire burned so hot that it melted a brass gasolier.

Like the Hemenway Hall fire, the crime remained unsolved, but observers speculated that the two cases were linked by a common factor: the Bellamy name. Some believed that the fires had to have been the work of white supremacists—that it amounted to a sort of monumental cross burning, intended to warn Heyward Bellamy that in administering the desegregation of Wilmington schools, he was betraying the values of his forebears. (Even though the Bellamy Mansion Bellamys weren't Heyward's close relations, it was widely presumed that they were.) Other people interpreted the blaze in exactly the opposite manner, as a strike at the city's good-old-boy network. They figured it had been set by Black activists, still smarting from the Williston fiasco, or by supporters of the group that came to be known as the Wilmington Ten. Even as they blamed opposing factions,

Wilmingtonians agreed on one thing: The Bellamy Mansion was a symbol of the Old South, and someone had wanted it gone, for reasons that stretched as far back into history as the charred wood laths that were now visible in one of the parlors, where 113 years' worth of paint and plaster had sizzled away.

Anyone who doubted that the Bellamy name—and all it connoted, from the eras of slavery and secession to Reconstruction, 1898, Jim Crow, and now desegregation—struck a deep nerve would have had a hard time explaining what happened next. Just months later, in August 1972, another mysterious blaze gutted another local landmark. This time, the target was the German Helmet—the sprawling Queen Anne residence that John Dillard Jr. had topped with a pickelhaube-shaped cupola at the turn of the century.* The twin arsons left both Bellamy Mansions scorched and humbled, the architectural scapegoats of a city that, depending on one's perspective, was either moving too quickly or refusing to change.

---

*The salvaged front door eventually went to Hugh MacRae II, who donated it to J. Michael's Philly Deli, a cheesesteak restaurant and a tenant at one of his shopping centers. It remains there to this day.

Chapter 40

PRISONERS OF CONSCIENCE

Far away from the Cape Fear River and the moss-draped oaks of Market Street, a diverse coalition of activists mobilized to challenge the convictions of the Wilmington Ten. Prominent among them was the activist and professor Angela Davis, whom racial justice organizations invited to Wilmington in June 1973. "As a concerned citizen, I do not think Angela Davis should be allowed to come into our town without the citizens having a voice in the decision," one local complained in a letter to the *Wilmington Morning Star*'s editor.

This time, the city's self-appointed sentries failed to hold the perimeter. Davis appeared on a hot, drizzly Sunday evening at Robert Strange Park, near the old Williston campus, for a three-hour rally attended by four thousand people. A soul band warmed up the crowd as vendors circulated with cold sodas. "Welcome to historic, evil, and oppressive Wilmington," a Black member of the board of elections said, welcoming Davis to the stage.

Flanked by Black liberationist figures such as Amiri Baraka, along with mothers of the jailed student leaders, Davis likened the Wilmington Ten trial to "another Watergate, revealing the corruption of justice in America." The city's white oligarchy, she argued, had instrumentalized the law to suppress a challenge to their power. "They saw in Ben Chavis a movement developing that could have threatened racism in this state and city," she observed. In the past, the city's Black people had lacked for outside allies in times of need, but Davis promised that help would be forthcoming for the Wilmington Ten. "They will not face this test alone," she vowed. "We are all fighting for our lives and we must ensure that they are set free."

Davis kept her word, publicizing the group's plight around the world. "*Qui connaît Ben Chavis?*" a headline in *Le Monde* asked after she talked up the case to human rights groups in France. Three years later, in 1976, the Wilmington Ten achieved an important break. Amnesty International, which had just won the Nobel Prize for its work on human rights, declared the Wilmington Ten "prisoners of conscience" and agreed to take on their case. Shortly thereafter, 350 concerned citizens—Harry Belafonte, Norman Mailer, and Dr. Benjamin Spock among them—sent a letter to President Carter, urging him to "speak out for the human rights of the Wilmington Ten as you have for those you felt were persecuted in other lands." The TV newsmagazine *60 Minutes* got involved, too, airing a report that cast doubt on the fairness of the trial. "It's the story that just won't go away," Morley Safer declared.

Then, Allen Hall, the prosecution's troubled star witness, recanted his testimony. Prosecutors, he said, had coerced him into testifying with promises and money, and coached him to lie on the witness stand, telling him he would spend the rest of his life in prison if he didn't cooperate. Another witness came forth to say that he had perjured himself, while a third admitted that the police had given him a minibike in exchange for his testimony. During the trial, it emerged, the prosecution had housed him and Hall in an oceanfront cottage, where they "gambled, drank, and smoked cigarettes," entertaining female visitors as they wished. The cottage's landlord was none other than the head of the local Ku Klux Klan, who admitted to paying "service calls" to the property. A letter from Hall to prosecutors emerged: "Just a few lines to tell you that I need a woman," Hall wrote, signing off with a promise to "be a good n——."

With the integrity of the trial in question, the court granted a hearing. The proceedings were again a mess, replete with purported blackmail attempts and secretly taped phone calls. Hall was scarcely coherent, seeming to recant his recantation. At one point, he even claimed he'd burned Mike's Grocery himself. In any case, it was incontrovertible that he was not a credible witness: He had either lied during the original trial, or he was lying now. Hall's backtracking alone provided a compelling reason to grant a new trial. So did the evidence of prosecutorial misconduct, along with exonerating testimony from the Templetons, who finally felt safe enough to tell their story in court. Still, the judge declined to grant a new trial.

Activists kept pushing, drawing global attention to the hypocrisy of racial injustice in a country that claimed to be a force of freedom in the world. If Washington was historically inclined to ignore the grassroots pleas of regular citizens from Wilmington, it proved far more difficult to tune out the taunts of America's geopolitical rivals. Soviet news agencies covered the case exhaustively and the Soviet chairman Leonid Brezhnev raised the Wilmington Ten's plight with America's ambassador. When Barbara Walters interviewed Fidel Castro in 1978, asking whether Cuba planned to free its political prisoners, Castro retorted, "The United States certainly hasn't set an example in that respect. You have the Wilmington Ten there. World opinion is demanding the release of those prisoners, but you haven't released them."

As courts continued to reject the Wilmington Ten's appeals, public pressure mounted on politicians to do something about their case. In North Carolina, motorists blacked out the "First in Freedom" motto on their li-

The Wilmington Ten attend a press conference, 1976.

cense plates with tape. Protesters chanted at Jim Hunt, the state's governor: "Hunt, Hunt, you racist dunce! Free the Wilmington Ten at once!"

The prisoners had always maintained their innocence. Chavis, for this reason, insisted that he would only accept a pardon, not parole. In January 1978, Hunt announced in a televised prime-time address that he would reduce the group's sentences. Yet he refused to pardon them. The sentence reduction meant that nine of the prisoners would be eligible for release within six months, but Ben Chavis still had two years to serve. In a memo, a cynical presidential adviser praised Hunt's political savvy: "You satisfy your racist constituency, and you don't openly inflame the blacks."

In Washington, sixty congressmen urged the attorney general to intervene. At the White House, journalists pressed Jimmy Carter to clarify his stance on the case. Carter evaded the issue, saying it wasn't his place to comment, but civil servants let their dissatisfaction be known in rogue comments to the press. In November 1978, the Department of Justice filed an amicus brief on behalf of the Wilmington Ten, asserting that "the trial was imbued with a fundamental unfairness and was in violation of the due process clause of the Fifth Amendment of the Constitution."

Still, Ben Chavis languished in prison. He was not released until December 1979, having served eight years. "The quest for freedom is a long struggle," he said, boarding a flight straight out of North Carolina. In time, Wilmingtonians would continue the fight, digging up family secrets, burying lies, and pushing the city toward a reckoning with history.

PART 4

THE TRUTH IS COMING ON THE SCENE

1990–2026

Chapter 41

LEGACIES OF PERSEVERANCE

With the legal phase of desegregation over and the physical violence that accompanied it trailing off, the 1980s marked a period of complacency. Public education had survived intact, and outright conflict abated, even if Black and white students remained distant. "I'm not sure they're integrated, but they're desegregated," one official said. By 1980, 24 percent of teachers and 34 percent of principals in county schools were Black, roughly in keeping with the area's demographics. In a look at how "race relations" had evolved during the seventies, the *Wilmington Morning Star* acknowledged certain problems—the disproportionate suspension of Black students, job discrimination, substandard housing—but assured readers that considerable progress had been made. Wilmington's longtime police chief, for example, had finally retired in 1975, and, in a push to disrupt the old-boy way of doing things, the city conducted a nationwide search for a replacement. The paper noted that "one applicant was a black from a large midwestern department, and, though he didn't get the job, he made it into the final 10." This result represented "by itself an indication of a shift in attitudes."

Wilmingtonians stowed away memories of the Williston closure and the Wilmington Ten as the city reinvented itself as an outward-facing, forward-looking destination, leaving behind its small-town identity in a period of unprecedented growth. In 1990, officials inaugurated an extension to Interstate 40, connecting Wilmington to the state capital in Raleigh (and if you kept driving, all the way to Barstow, California). After the Italian producer Dino De Laurentiis chose Wilmington for his film production company, "Wilmywood" began attracting an influx of liberal-minded newcomers. (Later, the area served as the picturesque backdrop to television dramas such as *Dawson's Creek* and *One Tree Hill*.)

But as much as boosters may have imagined that the city's problems of racial injustice had been resolved, they were merely in a dormant phase, and white people were much more likely than Black people to buy into the notion that racial healing had been achieved. The 1992 riots in Los Angeles following the acquittal of police officers who'd savagely beaten Rodney King demonstrated the fallacy of that belief, and the threat of racial violence, never dead, leapt back into public consciousness. In a survey the following year, 76 percent of Black North Carolinians, versus 52 percent of white ones, said that they thought racial prejudice and discrimination had stayed the same or gotten worse since 1980. About a third of members of both races agreed that "violent racial disturbances" like those that had recently taken place in Los Angeles were likely to happen soon in North Carolina.

CYNTHIA AND PHILLIP BROWN AND THEIR THREE CHILDREN MOVED TO North Carolina from Chicago in 1993, settling into a comfortable ranch house that Cynthia had inherited from her mother and stepfather. It was on Gordon Road, near Murrayville, a semirural residential area in the north of New Hanover County. Cynthia's grandparents' home at 802 Bladen Street was long gone. "After my grandparents died in the sixties, the family sold it, and then they tore it down—one of those 'urban renewal' things," Brown recalled. The program was supposed to bring new businesses and housing to the Northside, but the promised development did not materialize, leaving the community gutted and Black residents displaced. Meanwhile, many of the city's suburbs, developed using restrictive covenants, remained segregated.

Middle-class Black families like the Browns gravitated toward unincorporated areas such as Murrayville, which was conveniently close to the Corning optical fiber plant, one of the county's biggest employers of Black people. By the time the Browns moved in, on Gordon Road, the neighborhood had been drawing star seekers for a while. Their down-the-street neighbors were Deloris and James Jordan Sr.—the parents of Michael Jordan, the world-famous basketball player. As a teenager, Cynthia had babysat Michael Jordan several times. Her sons, Chicago Bulls fans, were crazy about Jordan. She'd tell them about her babysitting gig, but they never quite believed her. A year or so after the family's arrival in Wilmington, Deloris presented an athletic award at the high school where the Browns' older son was a student. Afterward, Cynthia approached her in the parking lot.

"Remember me?" Cynthia asked.

"Skinny Cynthia! Is that you?" Deloris replied, reaching out for a hug.

Cynthia's sons looked through the car window agape.

For a long time, Brown had put her curiosity about 1898 to the side. The thwarted visit to the library in high school had been discouraging. Then she'd been busy getting married, having kids, making her way in corporate America. But the luncheon, where the older women had bequeathed the answers to some of the mysteries of her family story, reawakened the historical detective in her. "As time went on, I got to thinking," she said. "When I was thinking, I went to D.C. to visit my father." He told her about how the contents of the old Howe settlement had been emptied out in a fire sale in the 1980s, after one of the family elders had died.

They decided to go to Baltimore, to call on a distant Howe relative. The relative was her father's cousin, getting up in age. After an awkward lunch, she led Cynthia and her father down to the basement to show them a family treasure: an oil painting of their common forebear, Fred Howe, framed in gilt and looking quietly distinguished in a three-piece suit. The portrait was a handsome one, but its condition pained Cynthia. "Why would you put this in the basement?" she wondered. She got out her camera and started snapping pictures of the portrait. "At a certain point, I said, 'This is the best I'm going to get,'" she recalled. "But you could see that the canvas was peeling on the edges, the paint was flaking off."

Just down the road, the Jordans were grappling with Wilmington's weight in their own way. Growing up in the seventies, Michael attended a public school "with minor racial tension." In ninth grade, he recalled, a white girl called him the N-word. In retaliation, he threw ice in her face, leading to his suspension. "I felt like it was us against the world," he later said. Jordan wanted to leave Wilmington, in part because of the racism, and he did, but his parents remained on Gordon Road. In the summer of 1993, months after Cynthia moved back, two teenagers—one Black, one Native American—murdered James Jordan, who had been napping in his car on the side of a North Carolina highway after attending a funeral. Two years after the murder, Deloris moved to Chicago, and, for a long time, Michael kept his distance from Wilmington. "When it comes to the relationship between basketball legend Michael Jordan and his hometown of Wilmington, it wouldn't be a stretch to say it's complicated," the *Star* admitted.

Yet in 2021, Jordan donated $10 million to fund two medical clinics for underserved communities in the region. "This is home," he said. In 2025, he gave another $10 million for a neuroscience institute. Jordan's great-grandfather Dawson Jordan, a lumberman and hunt club cook, was six years old in 1898, residing in the countryside near Wilmington; he lived until 1977, likely bestowing knowledge, explicit or implicit, of the terror to Michael alongside his famous habit of sticking out his tongue while concentrating. The scholar Imani Perry has suggested that Jordan's famous reluctance, for much of his career, to speak about race, "avoiding every action that was overtly political, might have been a strategic effort shaped by the repressiveness of Wilmington."

Cynthia Brown, for one, was determined to challenge the taboos that kept many of her friends and neighbors quiet. After the trip to D.C., she redoubled her efforts to speak out about 1898. Even though she was a city employee, she started joining committees and giving interviews, putting information that had so long been suppressed and hoarded into the public domain. In 1996, she told the story of what had happened to her at the library in the local newspaper. Two years later, she published an essay, gently taking "local gatekeepers of information" to task and urging them to correct this "legacy of deceit." In her family and others, she added, knowing what had happened in 1898 had "spawned legacies of perseverance, progress through education, and commitment to the success of our family and community." Athalia had handed Cynthia the flame of knowledge, and now she was stoking it, urging her fellow citizens to "gird ourselves with an awareness of the causes, and not just the effects."

AFTER A HUNDRED YEARS OF SECRECY, SILENCE, AND DISINFORMATION, the truth was starting to shake loose. As Brown understood, 1898 was a long-term event, touching great swaths of American history and entangling generation after generation—a sequence, not a singularity; a process, not a date. It was causes *and* effects: enslavement, war, Reconstruction, Jim Crow, the closure of Williston, the misprosecution of the Wilmington Ten. It was past and future, ancestors and descendants, grandparents and grandchildren, and that was why it was so important to talk about it now. Brown believed that the truth would set us free, as the Bible promises. But someone had to set the truth free first.

Brown had hope that this could happen. Yes, America was still America, and Wilmington was still Wilmington. But there were signs that the white elites' grip on the city and state was slackening, and with it, the silence around 1898. Just a few years earlier, in 1992, the congressional district covering a large swath of northeastern North Carolina had elected Eva Clayton to Congress—the first Black person to represent the state since George Henry White left more than ninety years earlier, lamenting that he couldn't live in North Carolina and be treated like a man. Clayton's election and subsequent reelections finally defied Alfred Moore Waddell's injunction "to make it impossible for a negro ever to hold office in this state." And with the goal of "healing the wounds" by "telling the story" of the massacre and coup, a committee of citizens, including Black and white descendants, began to plan commemorations for 1998.

With the centennial approaching, people started to talk. Loosened tongues revived memories and unlocked boxes. Those first tentative whispers encouraged more substantive conversations, which led to public observations, with the simplifications and pushback that such initial attempts at reckoning always bring forth. In time, these efforts would reach the

Halseys, living in New York, unaware, for the moment, of the long-ago tragedy that had sent their family north. Even those who knew plenty about 1898 and simply preferred to stay mum would soon be forced to grapple with the past, in part because of the publication of a novel that named names.

EUNICE "BAMBI" TAYLOR MACRAE GREW UP IN A MIDDLE-CLASS HOUSEhold in the suburbs of Columbus, Ohio. Flipping through the newspaper one day as a young woman, she came across an article saying that Pan Am was interviewing, so she drove downtown and was hired on the spot. When she met Hugh MacRae II, she was a flight attendant based in Miami. "I had seen the world and I was having a good time," she recalled.

Bambi had been planning to transfer to Honolulu. Hugh was married, going through a difficult time in the throes of a divorce. "He was worried about his children and didn't know what to do," Bambi recalled. "He had suffered so much about it and gone to a psychiatrist. I said, 'Well, why don't you just go back to North Carolina and think about it some more?'" Bambi didn't hear from him for six weeks. Then, she got a call. "I tried to do what you said," he told her. "It didn't work." They married in 1967.

Arriving in Wilmington as Hugh II's new wife, Bambi was entering a culture as foreign to her as anywhere she'd traveled with Pan Am. Weeks after her arrival, the couple attended an annual white-tie ball thrown by the L'Arioso German Club, an exclusive social club for blue-blooded white men. According to a history of the club, its founding in 1871, as federal troops occupied the South, constituted an act of white fortitude, offering "brisk and lively gayety" amid nights "haunted by fears generated in the evils of Reconstruction."

At the club's 1896 Christmas dinner dance, each woman was given a silk pouch in the form of a strawberry, with a silver calyx and red tassel. Now the white women of Wilmington wasted no time initiating Bambi into their customs and expectations. One woman pulled her into the country club powder room to warn her against uttering so much as a word of gossip or criticism aloud. "Everybody in this town is related to everybody else," she said, as debutantes swirled around the ballroom in white gowns. "So, if you have anything ugly to say about anybody, you go in the closet, you close the door, and you don't even say it out loud to yourself, because it'll be all over town the next day."

Another evening, one of Hugh II's cousins, an imposing woman on her second or third Scotch and water, offered even more pointed instructions.

"You have to register as a Democrat," she said.

"I'm an Ohio Republican," Bambi replied. "I am not registering as a Democrat."

"Well, you *will* register as a Democrat, or you will not get to vote."

Bambi told the cousin she was being ridiculous. But the cousin persisted.

"Listen, let me tell you something," she said. "Your name is not Taylor anymore. You are a MacRae, and you are a Wilmington MacRae. And you are a Democrat. Now you go down there, and you register as a Democrat."

OVER THE COURSE OF HER MARRIAGE, BAMBI ACCLIMATED TO WILMINGTON, embracing her husband's world. She became a pillar of the white establishment, which was extraordinarily effective at transforming newcomers rather than being transformed by them. She won golf and tennis trophies. She put on a billowing blouse and a tartan skirt and sat for a portrait. In the end, it was Hugh II who would change his party affiliation, but only because by the 1970s, the Republicans and the Democrats had basically traded platforms.

One day late in 1993, Bambi was at home when the phone rang. James Leutze, the chancellor of the University of North Carolina Wilmington, was on the line. Bambi knew the chancellor well. She and Hugh II were longtime supporters of the university, sponsoring events such as performances by Scottish military bands. At the moment, Bambi was chairing the university's board of trustees.

"I've got to tell you something," the chancellor began, explaining that the subject of his call was an upcoming book by Philip Gerard, a professor of creative writing at the university.

A Delaware native, Gerard had arrived in Wilmington from Chicago five years earlier. He was thirty-eight, garrulous, with a brushy mustache and crow's feet coming in around twinkly eyes. Gerard was an amateur musician (harmonica, pedal steel guitar, hammered dulcimer) and a passionate sailor (he named his Beneteau sloop *Savoir-Faire*). But his real gift was for collecting stories, for *hearing* them—the more unanticipated, the better—and delivering them to the public in a captivating style. "I don't really believe in 'write what you know,'" he once explained. "I believe in writing what you really want to find out about." His first few books had been innocuous enough, including a "schooning memoir" about sailing from Nova Scotia to Mystic Seaport, and a novel about lighthouse keepers on Cape Hatteras. His latest book, however, was about Wilmington. And it was set in 1898.

Leutze thought that he'd better warn the MacRaes. The book was a novel, yes, but it hewed uncomfortably close to some sensitive facts. "Based on actual events, *Cape Fear Rising* tells a story of one city's racial nightmare—a nightmare that was repeated throughout the South at the turn of the century," the jacket copy of its paperback edition read. "Although told as fiction, the core of this novel strikes at the heart of racial strife in America."

The book used the real names of many of the white ringleaders: Hugh MacRae, George Rountree (whose grandson, George Rountree III, had until recently served as a university trustee), and Colonel Walker Taylor (whose grandson, Walker Taylor III, ran the insurance agency that his grandfather had founded and sat on a plethora of boards). Creative choices aside, the simple fact that Gerard had written a book about 1898 would have been enough to rattle the university administration. After nearly a century of omertà, he was talking about the thing that no one in Wilmington talked about. He was talking about something that might sully reputations and blow the dirt off hastily hidden graves. Hugh MacRae, in fact, appeared on the very first page of the very first chapter.

INITIALLY, GERARD HADN'T KNOWN WHAT HE WAS GETTING INTO. FROM the moment he arrived, Wilmington had struck him as a strange place. A spikiness emanated from somewhere that he couldn't quite identify. He'd never seen a city so insistently segregated. He was white. His neighborhood was white. His church was white. He encountered "only white faces at restaurants, concerts, grocery stores—even on the university campus." His insurance agent was Black, but, Gerard learned, he was the only Black insurance agent in the entire county.

Finally, Gerard asked one of his few Black colleagues what the deal was in Wilmington. The colleague gave a vague response, saying that it had something to do with "the riots." With white people, the story was no clearer. "I would bring it up at every cocktail party, and people would go, 'Oh yeah, that's when the Black people came in and rioted in 1900,'" Gerard recalled. Later, he would say that his ignorance was the main thing that kept him curious: "As a relatively naïve, untenured assistant professor new to the city, I wrongly imagined that the events were *historical*—that is, that they were far in the past, removed from present passions and agendas."

In his second year at UNCW, Gerard went to the library and read everything he could find on 1898, which wasn't all that much—a valedictory account written in 1936 by a journalist with white supremacist leanings, and Helen Edmonds's pioneering but dry 1951 analysis of "Negro and Fusion politics" in North Carolina. The Black writers Charles W. Chesnutt and David Bryant Fulton had both wrestled with 1898 in novel form, but their books were almost a hundred years old. Gerard wasn't aware that, in 1984, H. Leon Prather Sr., a historian at Tennessee State University, had published an excellent book called *We Have Taken a City*, calling 1898 a racial massacre. One Black 1898 descendant so valued the book that he xeroxed it and passed it around, samizdat style. Prather had given a lecture in Wilmington, but the white establishment remained largely unruffled—perhaps because Prather was writing primarily for an academic audience, perhaps because he was a Black man from out of town.

In 1988, the Bellamy Mansion Inc. had commissioned a comprehensive report on the history of the house and the family who had built it. Two years later, the local historian Diane Cobb Cashman submitted a manuscript of more than a hundred pages to the Mansion's board of directors, whose members include, in perpetuity, representatives of the Bellamy and MacRae families. A single paragraph of the report concerned "the 1898 'Revolution.'" It read, in part:

> Back in Wilmington, emotions ran high and were exacerbated by an offensive editorial in the local black paper edited by Alexander Manly and leaflets distributed by the Red Shirts. . . . It was inevitable that opposing forces would clash and they did in a violent confrontation, that took place three days after John D. Bellamy was elected to Congress. When it was over the Republicans and many militant blacks were sent packing—ridden out of town—literally on a rail. The Hon. Alfred Moore Waddell was elected mayor of Wilmington. According to Ellen Bellamy, "a reign of peace and justice began."

The narrative then skipped directly to the "extensive remodeling" of the John Dillard Jr. home at 602 Market Street, without so much as a mention that dozens of people were murdered. (Buried in the footnotes was an acknowledgment that some historians have described the events as a massacre or a coup d'état.)

By this point, Gerard understood that he was poking around an explosive subject. He kept his research a secret, working only with primary documents. He didn't want anyone's "secondhand family tales" clouding his view of the story, and he wanted to avoid the social pressure that would inevitably accompany their telling. As Gerard started to grasp the magnitude of 1898, he decided that a novel was the best vessel for the story. "I was really interested in the protagonists' motivations, because these weren't your typical bad guys, they were deacons and fathers," he recalled. "I wanted the imaginative leeway."

He set some ground rules for himself: His characters would speak in the language of the time, even when it offended modern ears; anytime he wrote about a public event he would hew to the historical record. He could invent thoughts and feelings for his characters, but he would use their real names, on the grounds that doing so would prevent readers from getting caught up in "a guessing game of pseudonyms." A historical novelist writing about the Battle of Gettysburg, he figured, wouldn't turn Pickett's Charge into Smith's Charge. "Nothing I'm doing to them by putting a little bit of dialogue in their mouth is as bad as what they did in 1898," he reasoned.

Gerard submitted a proposal to an editor at an independent publishing house in Winston-Salem, North Carolina. The editor asked if he could give Gerard a call to discuss some urgent concerns.

"We're very interested in this, but our lawyer has a question," the editor said. "He wants to know if everyone you're writing about is dead."

"I think they are," Gerard replied.

"Make sure."

BAMBI LISTENED INCREDULOUSLY TO CHANCELLOR LEUTZE. HE DEFENDED Gerard's right to publish *Cape Fear Rising* but distanced himself from its content, saying it was "unduly provocative" and didn't represent the university's position on 1898. "You can't go back into history and change it," she thought.

On the weekend of the book's release, the *Star* ran a front-page story that focused on the book's portrayal of "prominent local families," accompanied by a review criticizing Gerard for "asking to have it both ways" by mixing fact and fiction. "My own view is that we have enough challenges in 1994, and we should concentrate on those," Walker Taylor III told the paper. Hugh II dismissed the book as "a highly exaggerated work of fiction" that had made "an almost unrecognizable character" of his grandfather, who was "absolutely colorblind and was in favor of good relations between people of all races." Bambi recalled, "Hugh was horrified that his grandfather's name would be associated with a racist, because he just *wasn't*. He didn't even have—well, he had Black people working in his home—but he didn't have any slaves or anything like that."*

In a letter to the editor, one newspaper reader complained that Gerard had basically "[thought] up stuff" for his characters to say. "This is not a

*Hugh MacRae was born in 1865, the year the Thirteenth Amendment outlawed slavery in the United States.

very nice thing to do!" she wrote. When Gerard appeared on a local radio show, the phone rang and rang. Gerard recalled, "People would say, 'He's making that stuff up. I lived here all my life, I went to school here, that never happened.'"

The response from a minority of residents—mostly Black—was warmer, if still wary. On the morning of the article's publication, Rachel Freeman, the only Black member of the school board, rang Gerard at home. "I just called to start your day with a happy phone call," she told him. "Because you are going to get a lot of awful phone calls today." A few Black politicians turned out for his book launch. Ironically, it was the most integrated event Gerard had ever attended in Wilmington.

Behind the scenes, the city's white power brokers moved to rein in Gerard. The local chapter of the Kiwanis Club rescinded an invitation for a speaking engagement after a white descendant threatened to pull funding from a charitable organization that the club and his family had supported for a century. At UNCW, the board of trustees launched a motion to deny Gerard tenure. (He learned later that a descendant of William Rand Kenan, the 1898 machine gunner, had defeated it, arguing that penalizing Gerard would "go against the core value of academic freedom.") Another board member had summoned Gerard to a diner breakfast and castigated him for ruining a fundraising drive. A local bank, he said, had withdrawn a ten-thousand-dollar gift as talk of the yet-unpublished novel circulated.

Gerard's omelet went cold as the man berated him.

"What do you want?" Gerard, exasperated, finally said.

The trustee replied, "I want you to change the names."

Gerard's phone rang at night with drunken rants and prank calls, but he refused to alter the book. Somebody told him a descendant of one perpetrator took *Cape Fear Rising* off the shelf at a local bookstore, crossed out all the mentions of his forebear's name, and put the book back on the shelf.

Gerard mostly shrugged off the blowback, but a few incidents truly unsettled him. To get to his best friend's house in the neighborhood where they both lived, he often cut through another neighbor's property. One morning, the neighbor came out of his house, distraught. Someone had stuck a pole topped by a bloody deer's head in the middle of his front yard.

"I can't figure out who would have done that," the neighbor said. Gerard realized that someone watching him come and go could easily have mistaken the neighbor's house for his.

As part of his research, Gerard had visited the old Wilmington Light Infantry Armory. At the bottom of a back staircase, his guide showed him a big metal door that led to an underground tunnel—part of an old network that connected important residences, business, and churches downtown. The tunnels were likely originally built for drainage and sewage, but, in the nineteenth century, they were bricked over. Rumors have long persisted that they were a secret route for smugglers, or that criminals used them to escape from the county jail. Gerard saw them as the perfect metaphor for white Wilmington's secret, interlaced, and durable networks of power.

Chapter 42

DANGEROUS MEMORIES

Had Philip Gerard not written *Cape Fear Rising*, the hundredth anniversary of 1898 might well have passed without major public commemoration. But the book got people talking, whether they appreciated its contents or were outraged by them. By 1996, several community groups had begun planning activities. They eventually coalesced to form the 1898 Centennial Foundation, a nonprofit organization that aimed "to develop and coordinate a broad-based community effort in appropriate remembrance of the Wilmington coup and violence of 1898."

The Centennial Foundation was an explicitly biracial enterprise—its executive council membership was almost evenly split between Black and white people, with men and women accounted for almost equally, and every committee had a Black and a white cochair, as a way of encouraging shared decision-making. Its leadership leaned on the traditional pillars of the community: ministers, educators, businesspeople, city officials, philanthropists, civil rights activists, an artsy person or two. Even if the working classes of both races were largely absent from the group, and Black women were underrepresented, the foundation amounted to the city's most ambitious experiment in cross-racial cooperation since Fusion itself.

Verboten in the public sphere, the memory of 1898 had long flourished in the realm of gossip, conjecture, and folklore. The lack of conclusive evidence, compounded by deliberate attempts to conceal it, lent itself to febrile speculation. In the absence of reliable tolls of death and other losses, both Black and white oral traditions used the river as a unit of measure. Some Black residents remembered their grandparents telling them that blood had turned the river red. One Black foundation member had heard that there were enough bodies to build a bridge from one side of the river to the other. The woman recalled, "I was at a luncheon and told this to a white wealthy Old Wilmington friend of mine who said, 'Why, Mildred, that's what we were told all my life!'" (To this day, Kent Chatfield, a roofer and local historian, swears that he once saw the white supremacists' mounted machine gun sitting in a trophy case in the living room of a retired sheriff's deputy.)

As the Centennial Foundation was getting off the ground, no one knew what to expect. Rumors circulated that Louis Farrakhan was coming to town and that, as in 1898, white people were stockpiling guns. Some prominent white residents fretted privately that a commemoration could "worsen race relations," while some Black residents worried that it would cause violence and "stir up animosities." The news that the city's corporate movers and shakers, many of them white, were planning something for the 1898 centennial led some Black Wilmingtonians to assume that the event would be a *celebration* of 1898, rather than a sober memorial.

Support from UNCW and private foundations, and, eventually, the blessing of the city, which contributed fifteen thousand dollars, gave the foundation ballast. The group hired staff and adopted a conciliatory mission statement: "Tell the Story; Heal the Wounds; Honor the Memory; and Restore the Hope." Certain participants thought the foundation should throw its weight behind the pursuit of reparations, but the idea was quickly squelched—one white member recalled them as "unquestionably the most potentially divisive issue the foundation faced."

Inez Campbell-Eason, a descendant of Isham Quick, a member of the Committee of Colored Citizens summoned by the white supremacists in 1898, would later observe, "They wanted to make it a celebratory event—like 'We are the World,' everybody's in harmony—when they know that's far from the truth." Like white Northerners of the 1890s, the foundation's leaders privileged reconciliation over justice. "No one living in Wilmington today was a participant in the events of 1898," the group stressed, absolving potentially defensive white people of "any personal responsibility for what happened."

The perpetrators of 1898 had largely escaped public accountability for a century. Their families enjoyed excellent reputations uncomplicated by historical wrongs. "MacRae Finds Long Family Tradition to Be No Burden," read the headline to a glowing 1985 newspaper profile of Hugh II, which covered the contributions of "his landed clan" to recreation, farming, and real estate, but failed to mention 1898 at all. If the subject of 1898 did come up, Hugh II and his cohort had long been able to swat it away like a stray fly. As community groups began planning for the centennial, Hugh II declared his preference for a "constructive" commemoration. Meanwhile, George Rountree III decreed that only a "positive" initiative would elicit his support. "If the effort is designed to—or actually does—polarize the constituent elements of this community," Rountree vowed, "then I would oppose that with all the vigor I can muster."

The organizers had a difficult task in trying to program events that would unify the city while remaining meaningful to its diverse constituencies. Sometimes, they erred on the side of soft-pedaling. An "official history," for instance, referenced property damage and lives "forever altered" but bizarrely avoided any mention of murder. Yet their energy and imagination galvanized discussion. The Centennial Foundation arranged a visit by the mayor of Tulsa, which had recently memorialized its own racial massacre, in which a white mob murdered Black residents and incinerated the Greenwood business district, known as the "Negro Wall Street of America" in 1921. A series of "dialogue sessions," bringing Black and white residents together to talk about race in small groups, was a huge success, attracting 450 participants, with another 150 on the waiting list. One group appreciated the experience so much that they created Wilmington's "first interracial community garden," growing corn, okra, peppers, and tomatoes.

One major holdout was *The Wilmington Journal*, the city's Black-owned newspaper. The Jervays felt that the foundation was more focused on appeasing white people than on getting to the bottom of the 1898 conspiracy. "We believe that only part of the story has been told," the editors would write, adding that "the first step of atonement cannot take place" until a credible effort has been made to determine the death toll and damages, as well as to account for those who lost their businesses and property. Another column called out the organizers' illusory notion of progress, pointing to the ongoing marginalization of Black politicians and civil servants, the awarding of municipal contracts to white businesses, and the gentrification of the Brooklyn neighborhood. "It doesn't take a rocket scientist to know that equality can only be obtained through opportunities in employment and contracts," the column read. "Show me the money!"

NATIONALLY, THE MOOD WAS SHIFTING FROM DENIAL TOWARD ACKNOWLedgment. In 1994, the Florida legislature passed a bill awarding compensation to survivors and direct descendants of the 1923 Rosewood massacre, in which a white mob destroyed a Black town in Florida, killing at least thirty residents. In 1995, the Southern Baptist Convention apologized for its defense of slavery, and 1996 brought the first public observances of the Tulsa massacre.

Many of the city's white residents supported the effort. Even if they might have preferred to let the anniversary pass without comment, they appreciated the foundation's non-accusatory, apolitical tone, and preferred the group's emphasis on "healing the wound" rather than seeking redress from those who inflicted it. ("The issue is a very sensitive one and must be handled with care," one tactful letter to potential donors read. YOUR PRAYERS ARE DEFINITELY NEEDED!!!!)

Hugh MacRae II wanted to "settle the matter" of 1898 once and for all, and sent the group a check for ten thousand dollars. George Rountree III initially rebuffed the foundation's invitations, but ultimately agreed to take part in a lecture. The hotly anticipated event paired Rountree with John Haley, a Black professor of history at UNCW. Titled "Different Perspectives on the Causes of 1898," it bravely attempted to fulfill a goal that Isaiah Madison, a Black lawyer and consultant, had set out in a report for the foundation. Madison cited the sociologist Robert Bellah: "If the community is completely honest, it will remember stories not only of suffering received but of suffering inflicted—*dangerous memories*, for they call the community to alter ancient evils." Madison concluded that this sort of unflinching confrontation "is the price of the community re-energizing deeply desired by many Wilmingtonians."

The venue for the event was St. Stephen AME Church. In 1898, Reverend Lee had stood on the church's steps, facing off against white gunmen as Athalia Howe and her family looked on in horror. Now, as word of the event spread, organizers decided to move it from the church's educational hall to the larger sanctuary, where a racially mixed, "near capacity crowd" packed the "hushed, tension-filled" room.

Haley opened the program with a short, factual summary of the 1898 violence. Then, Rountree stood. As one attendee recalled, "He began with a declaration of support for equality by evoking his appreciation of a childhood mammy." Audience members shifted uncomfortably in the pews, but Rountree kept on, defending his grandfather's actions by saying that he was "the product of his times." In a question-and-answer session after the speech, one audience member demanded "reparations to the Black community for what it had suffered and lost," to shouts of support, but Rountree doubled down, insisting that he bore no responsibility for events that took place long before he was born. The evening closed on a civil note, with Black dignitaries thanking Rountree for coming. But his performance proved, for some in the audience, that dangerous memories were still being made in the very moments designed to defuse their power.

Today, one might argue that Rountree didn't deserve a platform. The organizers, however, considered the event "the high point of the series," bringing into the open perspectives that Wilmingtonians had been cultivating for years behind closed doors. The experience of coming face-to-face with people whose grandparents his grandfather had helped to murder, banish, and disenfranchise seemed to make little impression on Rountree. Interviewed by the *News & Observer* later that year, he dug in his heels. His grandfather, he explained, had simply provided legal advice on how "in an orderly, nonviolent fashion to cause the blacks and whites who had been put in office" (i.e., elected) "to resign and leave the county" (i.e., give up their jobs at gunpoint and flee or die). Asked to sum up the legacy of 1898, Rountree replied, "Number one: You cannot foist change upon a society that has for hundreds of years operated on a given standard without expecting a violent reaction."

Rountree was pleased to have taken part in the conversation at the church. Years later, when the foundation was raising money to build a memorial to commemorate 1898, he donated five thousand dollars. "Sylvia and I appreciate your thinking of us in connection with the campaign whose philosophy focuses on 'a community . . . in which racial justice and harmony flourish,' rather than imposing responsibility for the 1898 conditions," he wrote. "Wilmington has been kind to me and my family, and I try to reciprocate."

THE CENTENNIAL FOUNDATION'S EFFORTS CULMINATED IN NOVEMBER 1998. The choir of Saint Luke AME Zion, from whose steps parishioners had watched white rioters torch the Manly press, held a joint concert with the choir of First Presbyterian, whose minister had joined the mob and famously bragged about taking the city. At Thalian Hall, more than a thousand spectators watched an original drama that imagined 1898 from the perspective of Carrie and Alexander Manly. After the performance, they signed "The People's Declaration of Racial Interdependence," offering an alternative to the White Declaration of Independence that white supremacists had ratified a hundred years earlier. Interest was such that one independent ministry organized a spin-off event, appealing to mystics to provide answers to questions that humans could or would not. SECRETS OF 1898 REVEALED & DECLARED FROM THE MOUTH OF THE PROPHETS, the handbill read. The organizers promised that a pair of seers would reveal "God's restoration plan for the city."

The historian John Hope Franklin—the same historian whom Mrs. Isaac Bates Grainger of Park Avenue had chided, in 1964, for giving a more realistic estimate of the number of Black people murdered—headlined the marquee event, a two-day symposium at UNCW. In addition to being a preeminent expert on American history, particularly Black history, Franklin had a personal connection to the subject at hand. In 1921, his father, B. C. Franklin, had witnessed the white mob's rampage from his Tulsa law office. "I could see planes circling in mid-air," he wrote. "They grew in number and hummed, darted and dipped low. I could hear something like hail falling upon the top of my office building." (His account later inspired the depiction of the Tulsa massacre in HBO's 2019 *Watchmen* series.)

"We need to confront our history," Franklin urged the audience. "If Wilmington brought the nineteenth century to an inglorious end, violence in other cities would soon help usher in the twentieth," he continued, linking 1898 to similar events in Louisiana, Georgia, Illinois, and, of course, the Tulsa violence, which his father described as "the great holocaust." When he finished, the crowd gave him a standing ovation. "After the committee and the colloquium and all the publicity surrounding them, it was impossible for anyone to say any longer that they didn't know what had gone on," James Leutze, the former chancellor, recalled. "The white community could no longer turn a blind eye." The dangerous memories were out of the box, calling for action.

Chapter 43

GROUNDBREAKING

Eight shovels hit the ground in unison, scraping hard-packed earth and rising again, sending dusty topsoil flying. The groundbreakers stood in the middle of a bare lot on a desolate corner near the northwest entrance to the city, dressed in suits and sunglasses, lapel pins and ties. One woman wore a candy-red pantsuit and a black straw hat with a matching band, shading her face from the stark November sun. They were dressed to make a statement of public respect, but save for the passengers of a few cars whizzing into town from the Martin Luther King Jr. Parkway, their efforts were largely hidden to passersby.

In 1998, once the flurry of events had died down, the Centennial Foundation had decided that one major objective remained—to "honor the memory" of 1898 by erecting a permanent monument. Not a memorial to the victims of 1898, per se, but a tribute to "tolerance and understanding." Even this gentle mission threatened to be too much for one prominent white Wilmingtonian, the descendant of a perpetrator, who swore that he would tear down any structure that was built. It had taken nearly ten years just to get to the point of shovels hitting the dirt.

The initial cochairs of the 1898 Memorial Park Campaign were Hugh MacRae II, Katherine Taylor (Walker Taylor's great-granddaughter), Frankye Manly Jones (a niece of Alexander Manly), and Luther Jordan (an undertaker and state senator). The quartet was meant to evoke equality: a white man, a white woman, a Black woman, and a Black man working together to create a memorial that would "gracefully and without rancor . . . salute the sacrifices and contributions of the black and white citizens of southeastern North Carolina." But the committee's composition also suggested equivalence, as if white, Black, perpetrator, and victim all evened out in some sort of soothing racial math. "We forgive ourselves and each other; we begin in love again," participants at a candlelight vigil, held on the banks of the Cape Fear River, were instructed to chant. The foundation was understandably eager to demonstrate unity in a community that had sorely lacked it historically. But in doing so, it sometimes collapsed the very distinctions that made commemoration meaningful, offering healing without hurt, absolution without sin.

The committee chose a location for the memorial on the corner of North Third and Davis, in Brooklyn, close to where the violence began. The state agreed to donate the land and the city agreed to maintain the site and monument in perpetuity. Fundraising began in 2000, and by the end of the year, donors had pledged all but thirty-seven thousand dollars of the estimated two-hundred-thousand-dollar goal. Both white and Black descendants underwrote the project. Despite his wariness of Wilmington, Cynthia Brown's father, Dr. James Brown, believed so strongly in the need for a marker that he gave ten thousand dollars toward its construction. To his family's lasting pride, this put him in a rank of donors alongside Hugh MacRae II, Bellamy descendants, and a gift in memory of Alice Moore Sisson, one of the Colonel's granddaughters.

To realize the monument, the committee chose Ayokunle Odeleye, a Black sculptor from Atlanta. His design was simple and mostly abstract: six sixteen-foot bronze-cast paddles, arranged in an arc around two low walls featuring explanatory text. The paddles were to be engraved with images of Wilmingtonians, Black and white, who "have played a role in improving the city's race relations." (Ultimately, they were left blank.) Odeleye explained, "We wanted a memorial that did not blame anyone—that did not make anyone feel guilty."

Plans for the memorial whizzed along until 2002, when, at the end of a community meeting, Thomas Wright, a Black Democrat representing New Hanover County in the state legislature, rose and, as the *Wilmington*

Morning Star reported, "dropped something of a bombshell." Wright was a Wilmington native and a certified paramedic. His late brother, William "Joe" Wright, had served more than four years in prison as a member of the Wilmington Ten, dying three months after his conviction was voided on appeal. Thomas wasn't afraid to needle the establishment, particularly when its fetish for civility eclipsed the prerogative of racial justice. He felt that the land designated for the memorial would be better used for a grocery store, which the neighborhood had been lacking for years. "The park just becomes another monument that tens of thousands of cars pass by," he said. "It won't provide one job, it won't feed one family, and it won't educate one person the way it's planned now."

Committee members brushed off Wright's "alienating" and "negative" objections, pointing out that an earlier effort to lure a supermarket to the area had failed. Wright persisted, claiming he'd found a better site for the monument. The committee agreed to entertain his proposal, but he refused to say where the land was, and, plagued by setbacks, a deal never materialized. As the project languished, fundraising dropped off. By 2005, the committee was struggling to cobble together enough money to meet Odeleye's payment deadlines.

Meanwhile, Wright kept pushing for a more honest accounting of 1898 and for concrete redress for descendants. In the state legislature, he co-founded the Wilmington Race Riot Commission, which, in 2006, published a seminal, five-hundred-page report that led the state Democratic Party to issue a formal apology. As centennial-era initiatives that had promised to improve Black economic inclusion fizzled out, Wright introduced a slew of 1898-related bills, including one that would allow descendants of those killed or injured in 1898 to sue for damages.

In 2007, Wright was indicted on charges of fraud and obstruction of justice, one of them pertaining to his efforts to secure funds for a Black history museum near the memorial site. He was stripped of his office, the first member of the State House to be expelled in more than a century. By the time committee members broke ground on the memorial, he was serving a six-year prison sentence. Few people denied that he had erred, but the timing of his downfall struck some observers as suspicious. "I'm not going to sit here and say Tommy didn't do anything wrong," Wayne Moore, the former student organizer and Wilmington Ten member, said. "But I don't think he would have been prosecuted to the extent that he was prosecuted. See, people don't like old wounds opened, and that's the bottom line."

The memorial, completed in 2008, drew criticism from some residents. "When I drive by at night, I just get so upset," Wayne Lofton, a member of a Black family with deep roots in Wilmington, said. "Every time I see it, I don't know whether I'm looking at African paddles, or Campbell's soup spoons. Nobody really understands what it is when they see it. What we should have done in this community to commemorate the people who went down in this massacre is to bring back what they took. They took businesses, they took economic opportunities, they took political power. Those are the things we should have been asking for, to restore once you pillage and took it all. If I saw a library or a grocery store or a pharmacy, then I could say, 'Wow, they really understood, those people didn't play.'" But despite its inadequacies, the 1898 Memorial represented a major step for Wilmington: a solid, immovable, six-and-a-half-ton acknowledgment of a painful history that had finally come to the fore.

1898 Memorial, 2008.

Chapter 44

RETURN TO LIVE OAKS

Cynthia Brown was glad she'd moved home, but professionally, she'd had a tough run in Wilmington. The job as the city's director of human resources had been a political nightmare. After four years, she quit to found *Southern Hues*, a magazine she'd dreamed up to fill the space between *Southern Living*, which covered the South but largely ignored Black culture, and titles like *Ebony* and *Black Enterprise*, which covered Black culture but didn't emphasize the South. Cynthia invested twenty thousand dollars and stores of hope in the venture. "We decided we don't have that kind of money, but we also decided it's only impossible if you believe it's impossible," she said. For once, instead of worrying about the weeds, she was focusing on the blossoms.

As the staff was putting together the second issue, Cynthia arrived at the office one morning to find a clutch of police officers standing around a shattered front door. Someone had broken in, stealing more than eight thousand dollars' worth of computer equipment and vandalizing the office. Cynthia's desk had been overturned and hacked in two. She had no clue who was behind the robbery, or why. A deep sense of fatigue enveloped her, but she put on a brave face for the public, saying that insurance would cover the stolen equipment and that she expected to put out an issue on time the next month. "My father called me from the Washington area," she told a reporter. "He said, 'Cynthia, people fall all the time in life, but the real test is how well you get up.'"

The following year, she took a position as the executive director of an agency that ran Head Start early childhood development programs in Wilmington. The previous director had resigned amid controversy, and the agency had been warned that it stood to lose federal funding. Cynthia knew that reform would be difficult, but she believed she was savvy enough to avoid the traps and snares that, according to her father, were sure to take down a Black professional in Wilmington. She lasted fifteen years, but ultimately, the federal government withdrew support and the agency closed down.

Despite these professional frustrations, Cynthia thrived as a volunteer. She built community the way her forebears had built houses—tirelessly and elegantly over the course of years, tending to graves at Pine Forest Cemetery and organizing luncheons to draw attention to heart disease. (Her mother, grandmother, and great-grandmother had all died from heart disease or sudden heart attacks.) "I had to confess I'm a Kellogg's person," she joked, accepting a five-thousand-dollar check from the maker of Cheerios for her work in raising awareness. The cause dearest to her, however, was historical education: the work that her great-grandmother Athalia had urged her to continue, of giving back by telling truth.

In 2011, Cynthia was serving on the board of the Historic Wilmington Foundation, an old-line preservation organization. As the only Black board member, she tried to promote a more capacious view of local history and to remind her peers of the rich patrimony of Black communities that they often overlooked. To fund its projects, the organization held an annual black-tie fundraiser. When the venue for that year was announced, Cynthia gasped. The gala was to be held at Live Oaks, the Parsleys' octagonal, coquina-encrusted mansion on Masonboro Sound, where Grandma Thalia had worked as head cook.

Cynthia bought her expensive ticket and laid out her fanciest dress. But when the day arrived, she was consumed by ambivalence. It was unusually cold for an autumn day, and her husband had come down with a fever. She didn't really want to go to Live Oaks alone. She didn't really want to go to Live Oaks *at all*, except maybe to reclaim Grandma Thalia's territory as an honored guest. She called her father and told him she was going to sit the party out, that the thought of going gave her an uneasy feeling in her soul. But he insisted that she attend and call him back the next morning to hash over every detail. Ever the dutiful daughter, Cynthia enlisted her son PJ to accompany her. Fortunately, his father's tuxedo fit him perfectly.

As they drove to the party, Cynthia talked to PJ about Grandma Thalia, the Parsleys, and 1898. The car ride was to her as the pound cake luncheon had been to her elders—the moment to impress on the next generation the consequences of this history, to bestow it upon PJ intentionally as a gift, albeit a heavy one, rather than just leaving it moldering in the attic, hoping that somebody someday would open it. They pulled up the long, oak-lined drive. A valet parked the car, and they stepped out into the crisp air. Brown was glad she'd lived in Chicago. PJ took his mother's arm and led her up a pathway and through the columned portico into the party.

Inside, Sarah Parsley greeted partygoers. Her husband, Walter Parsley II, had died a decade earlier. The matriarch of the family at almost ninety, Sarah presided over the party from a wheelchair, assisted by a Black nurse. Brown and PJ said hello and thanked Sarah for her hospitality. A few minutes later, the nurse approached Brown.

"She thinks she knows you," the nurse said of her employer.

"Well, she might," Brown replied. "My great-grandmother was down here when she was a young woman."

Brown didn't know what to make of the encounter. Had Sarah Parsley known Thalia and recalled her features or even just her aura so distinctly that she was able to identify Thalia's great-granddaughter, more than half a century later, at first sight? Was the comment just a freak coincidence? Or could it have emanated, as fact fuzzed into folklore, from some subconscious halfway between memory and happenstance? Could a place remember? Live Oaks seemed to know that the Parsley and Howe families were linked by violence, work, mutual dependence, and the partial yet lasting intimacy that decades of these shared experiences produced.

Brown and PJ slipped away from the tent that had been set up on the estate's grounds for the gala. It was so cold outside that it was just them and their smokelike breath, under a heavy moon encircled by a halo. They strolled to the water, talking about the past and how it shapes the present.

Then, they went inside, ate dinner, posed for photographs, and checked out the silent auction.

For Brown, the evening, though tinged with melancholy, amounted to a small triumph of transmission. "My parents always taught me that you must know your history to understand where you're going (or possibly where you don't want to go back to)," she later wrote. "On this occasion, I was able to help [PJ] see the relevance of his past to the present and to look beyond the present to the unlimited potential of the future. My soul was lifted, and I had a divine assurance that the legacy of documenting, preserving, and telling our family's history would not be lost to the winds of time." Pleased as she was to have walked through the Parsleys' door as a dignitary, she was even prouder to have translated her great-grandmother's story into a form that meant something to her son.

Chapter 45

PARDONS OF INNOCENCE

Beverly Perdue, North Carolina's Democratic governor, was set to leave office in a week, turning the Governor's Mansion over to a Republican successor. On December 30, 2013, with less than twenty-four hours until the deadline for issuing pardons, she still hadn't made up her mind about the Wilmington Ten.

Ben Chavis had become a nationally prominent civil rights leader, even heading the NAACP in the 1990s, before his dismissal in a sexual harassment scandal. But since receiving parole in the late seventies, and despite their convictions being overturned on appeal in 1980, most of the Wilmington Ten had struggled to regain their momentum. Jerry Jacobs had been a tennis prodigy, Hoggard's top-ranked player. By the time he was released from prison, wrecked by the chain gang, it was too late to pursue a career in sports. The late Connie Tindall had tried to make a go of it as a longshoreman, starting at a ten-year disadvantage to his peers. Some members earned college degrees; others were treated as pariahs, couldn't get jobs, and struggled with alcohol and drugs. Joe Wright said that he didn't regret going to prison, he regretted going to prison for something he hadn't done. "We were kids," he told a reporter before his death. "We paid a price. They took us through hell. They did this to us out of hatred, and out of racism, and I'll never, ever forget that."

Surrounded by stacks of transcripts and petitions, Perdue tried to tune out the "rumor and innuendo" that swirled around every discussion of the case, the know-it-all legal grandees who warned that one should never disrespect the outcome of a jury trial. Finally, with hours left, she came to a decision. She was doing it. On the afternoon of the 31st, she issued a pardon of innocence to each member of the Wilmington Ten. Perdue wrote that the their convictions "represented an ugly stain on North Carolina's criminal justice system" and "were tainted by naked racism."

The pardons of innocence exonerated the Wilmington Ten of all wrongdoing. Unlike regular pardons, which operated on the principle of clemency, they acknowledged that the state had erred. They gave the group members back their names and reputations, even if they could never restore the time, relationships, educations, jobs, health, hope, and morale that their wrongful prosecution had destroyed. Four members of the group had died without redress. (A court later awarded roughly fifty thousand dollars for each year of imprisonment to the group's surviving members but denied the dead victims' families compensation.) "I'm old, half blind, and crippled," Marvin "Chili" Patrick said, at a news conference in Wilmington. "I just want to go forward and make the best of the piece of life I have."

Perdue said that she had been moved by the advocacy of the NAACP and the National Newspaper Publishers Association, the Black press's most powerful professional organization. The Jervays, of *The Wilmington Journal*, had persuaded the NNPA to launch a national campaign on the Wilmington Ten's behalf. For more than a year, articles and editorials in the local and national media had been alerting Perdue to an important trove of papers. They had been released by the NAACP, who had gotten them from the historian Tim Tyson, who had gotten them from the New Hanover County district attorney, who said that he found them gathering dust in a box in the back of an office closet.

The documents were shocking. They offered tangible proof, so often elusive, of the prosecution's racist conduct in the Wilmington Ten trial, yet they simply confirmed what the Ten and their supporters had been saying all along. In one list, Jay Stroud—the prosecutor who was purportedly battling gastrointestinal illness—considered the comparative disadvantages and advantages of a mistrial. "Different judge," Stroud wrote, in the positive column. "Fresh start with new jury from another county."

Stroud's jury selection notes, neatly written on a sheet of yellow legal paper, confirmed that he had explicitly excluded Black people from the jury. "Stay away from black men," he'd jotted at the top of the page. (He wrote, of one of the few Black candidates he didn't plan to strike: "sensible: Uncle Tom type.") As for white people, he actively sought those whom he perceived as more likely to be racist. His notes were a horror show of both individual racist thought and systemic discrimination:

1) Pridgen (KKK?) (good)
6) Heath (O.K.) KKK?)
26) Turner (little white woman, fine)
51) No! Black from Maple Hill
52) Bryant (KKK) good

"The case of the Wilmington Ten amounts to one of the most egregious instances of injustice and political repression from the post–World War II black freedom struggle," the scholar Kenneth Janken has written. The Justice Department's amicus brief had acknowledged the FBI's role in the persecution and prosecution of the Wilmington Ten. As Janken noted, "Federal action helped to create the problem and the government should be accountable to remedy it." The brief failed to account, however, for the federal *inaction* that, for generations, allowed racial inequality to exist and fester and white supremacy to reign unchecked; the federal inaction that had created or perpetuated the conditions—slavery, war, the broken promises of emancipation and the abandoned projects of Reconstruction, Jim Crow, unequal education and its inequitable dismantlement—out of which injustices like the Wilmington Ten arose. It made sense that Willie Earl Vereen, receiving his pardon, reached deep back into that history to express his sense that his ordeal was part of a continuum. "I felt free, but not the real freedom," he said. "I want my forty acres and a mule."

Chapter 46

A MATTER WHICH HAS BEEN SETTLED

It was with a sense of disorientation that, in 2015, Hugh II opened the newspaper to a new broadside from Philip Gerard, arguing that the city ought to rename Hugh MacRae Park. In Gerard's view, a rebrand would cleanse the park of its association with "a calculating and ruthless leader" who drove Black citizens out of the city "at bayonet point" in 1898 and "never stood trial for [his] crimes." The push to strip the park of the MacRae name, as much as it pained Hugh II, ought not to have been totally unexpected. In Charleston, Dylann Roof, a white supremacist, had recently murdered nine Black churchgoers, leading the South Carolina legislature, at long last, to remove the Confederate flag from the statehouse dome and lending momentum to movements for racial justice.

The park was one of Wilmington's most popular, and certainly one of its best equipped. Among other amenities, it offered an equestrian ring, a duck pond, an off-leash dog park, a baseball field, walking trails, and four lighted tennis courts. It wasn't beautiful, exactly, with its sandy soil and patchy grass carpeted in pine needles. Located in the middle of the city, it sweltered in the summer, profiting from neither the ocean air nor the river breeze. But the park was a local standby, with picnic shelters where Wilmingtonians enjoyed family reunions and birthday parties, dumping the sticky remains of grocery-store sheet cakes into trash barrels swarming with bees.

Hugh MacRae had donated the land for the park to the city in 1925. The original deed included a restrictive covenant specifying that the gift was to be used for the benefit of "white citizens" alone. For decades, the park's users remained predominantly white. In 1980, Hugh MacRae II and his cousin Hugh Morton formally voided the restrictive covenant. Thirty-five years later, the park was open to all, and its constituency had diversified, but some Black people continued to feel unwelcome.

Despite the controversy over *Cape Fear Rising*, Gerard had prospered at UNCW, founding the university's MFA creative writing program and writing a dozen more books. Still, he was aware that he would never be able to measure the true effect that the novel had had on his career and life in Wilmington. "It's the South—so much happens that's unstated and secret that you never know when somebody's got you," he said. "I'll never know what could have come my way and what didn't." He didn't particularly care. Now a respected figure in progressive quarters of the community, he was lending his clout to the campaign to rename the park. He argued that it ought "to honor someone or something that all citizens can value, not serve as an eternal reminder that, all too often, the bad guys win."

Hugh II didn't understand why the park thing was coming up again. He thought he had put the whole issue of 1898 to rest back in 1998, by contributing generously to the Centennial Foundation, and then by helping to get the monument built. Responding to Gerard's campaign, he tried to sound a note of conciliation, but feelings of identification with his grandfather seeped in. "Being in the Secret Nine, as near as I can understand, is doing often what groups of businessmen do today, they get together and figure out how they can get more of their representatives into political position," he'd said in a 2001 radio interview, as though orchestrating a massacre and coup were akin to contributing to a PAC. Hugh II's willingness to pronounce on these issues suggested that he was at ease with his family's legacy. Instead of riding out the debate over renaming the park in discreet silence, he wrote to the newspaper to defend his ancestor, declaring, "We know that Mr. MacRae was a kindly gentleman, friendly to everyone around him."

Hugh II contended that his grandfather's motive in life, as in donating the park tract, was "to improve the lot of all people in Wilmington, New Hanover County, North Carolina, and our country." The restrictive clause reserving the park for white users had been a formality, "normally included in most deeds of the time." Anyway, he claimed, no one had enforced it. Hugh reminded readers that he and Hugh Morton had voided the restriction decades earlier. He concluded, "Everyone concerned thought that this settled the matter forever, which it did. It is not helpful, appropriate, or constructive to reopen a matter which has been settled."

Hugh II's language was a sort of restrictive clause itself, reserving access to the meaning of 1898 for those who happened to share his viewpoint. Who constituted the "we" who "knew" that Hugh I was a kindly gentleman, and what gave them the authority to make that claim? How did one qualify for "everyone concerned" (and, if you still wanted to talk about the park and 1898, did that make you a nobody)? Hugh II was writing history like his grandfather had written the park deed—like he owned it, like he could fence it off from intrusion in perpetuity.

The concentric circles of Hugh II's understanding went even tighter than his country, his state, his county, and his town, narrowing all the way to his race, his social class, and his family. His defensiveness went deeper than a fear of staining the family name. One reason that white descendants of Hugh II's generation had such a difficult time acknowledging the crimes of their ancestors was because the stories they heard about them had transformed radically within their own lifetimes. Hugh II had always admired his grandfather, from whom he inherited a flinty business sense along with a name. His own parents had told him that his namesake was a good person who had done wonderful things. That wasn't what he was hearing now, but to accept a more complicated truth would be to impeach the personal integrity of people he had known and loved. It would be to defile his childhood, and you only get one.

Grand white families tended to the transmission of their histories with such care that it didn't always occur to them that parts of their patrimony spilled into other lives, slipped out of their control: Other people had stories, too. Little did the Bellamys suspect, in 1860, as they toasted the Confederacy with salmon-edged china cups, that an enslaved artisan had carved his initials into their dream home. "WBG," the monogram read, scratched

A message from William B. Gould.

in a swooping cursive onto the back side of a section of ornamental plaster moldings in one of the Bellamy Mansion's front parlors.

Restorers discovered the inscription in 1995. Eventually, researchers matched the initials with those of a man named William B. Gould, who freed himself from slavery in Wilmington in 1862 and joined the United States Navy, leaving behind a diary that offers a very rare account of the life of a Black sailor during the Civil War. His signature at the Bellamy Mansion might be thought of as a sort of early draft of his extraordinary life story. "I wrote this," it proclaimed, inscribing Black authorship into white plaster.

Nor was Hugh II likely to have known that, across town, a Black man slept in Hugh MacRae's mahogany bed, his mind filled with different dreams, meanings, and interpretations. The man, Wayne Lofton, had inherited the bed from his grandmother, Mary Lofton, who, he said, had received it as a gift from Hugh's widow sometime in the 1950s. "My grandmother was the housekeeper for the MacRae family, and she raised all those children," Lofton recalled. The Loftons had hung on to the bed because it was valuable, not only monetarily. It stood as hefty, massive proof of their place in Wilmington's history, and of the "very intense connection" between the two families. Lofton regarded it wryly, as a wooden irony, a piece of the past that you could climb into and toss around in. "I love to brag on this fact!" he said. "Hugh MacRae, who initiated the riot—I have his bed in my house."

Just as the Lofton matriarch surely popped up in a MacRae family photo or two, the MacRae patriarch was also part of the Loftons' lore. Seen from their vantage point, he was not a heroic protagonist. He may have been rich, run companies, and owned a lot of property, but there was torment in his soul. "My grandmother used to tell me that Ole Man Hugh MacRae was certainly burning in hell, because the last years of his life, he would just sit in front of a fireplace. Even in summer, he would burn a fire—he would wrap himself in a quilted blanket and just sit there and look at the fire all day long," Lofton recalled. "He knew where he was headed for what he had done." The bed that Hugh slept in was the bed that Mary laundered, ironed, and polished for decades. In the end, she was also making it for her grandson.

Chapter 47

MOM-OSAS

In the first ten years of the twenty-first century, Wilmington's population increased by 40 percent. With staggering growth came demographic upheaval, turning the area older, whiter, and richer with every moving truck. In 2008, New Hanover County went to John McCain by the slimmest of margins, and in 2012, Mitt Romney defeated Barack Obama by a slightly wider one. Four years later, as the 2016 presidential election swerved into its final demented stretch, Donald Trump announced that he was coming to town.

Lara Yunaska married Trump's son Eric in 2014. She grew up in Wilmington and attended Emsley A. Laney High School, Michael Jordan's alma mater. Her parents, who built yachts, still lived in the area, and her father was a chronic writer of letters to the paper; his interests, over the years, had evolved from preventing teen smoking and cheering the war on terror to touting Donald Trump's accomplishments. Lara returned home often. In 2017, she celebrated her first baby with a shower at a downtown bar, where guests enjoyed a "mom-osa" buffet, leaving with succulent plants as party favors.

After her father-in-law became the Republican nominee in 2016, Lara volunteered to join him on the stump in North Carolina. "I said to him, 'Look, this is my home,'" she said. "'I know the people in North Carolina and I want to go down there.'" She made the rounds of the regional media, playing up her local ties and vouching for Trump's concern for the area. She assured a reporter, "There is Southern blood in the Trump family now."

On August 9, 2016, a cheering crowd of six thousand supporters greeted Trump at UNCW's Trask Coliseum. Despite a ninety-degree haze, another three thousand people waited outside. It was Trump's first campaign visit to southeastern North Carolina, and something about the setting seemed to make him even more viciously berserk than usual. Among his targets were the federal courts, one of which had recently overturned a bill by which the Republican-dominated state legislature had sought to exclude voters at the polls. "Voter I.D., why aren't we having voter I.D.?" Trump complained. "You won't vote fifteen times. But people will."

Trump didn't have to say which people he was referring to, because it was perfectly clear. The overturned law, crafted using data that tracked voting preferences by race, required voters to furnish exactly the types of identification that Black voters were least likely to have. It did little to prevent voter fraud, while "target[ing] African Americans with almost surgical precision," a federal appeals court had written, concluding that it amounted to "the most restrictive voting law North Carolina has seen since the era of Jim Crow."

The law was only the latest gambit in an audacious voter suppression effort that North Carolina Republicans had been pursuing since gaining a supermajority in the state legislature in 2012. Their victory was heavily aided by gerrymandering: In congressional races that year, for example, more than half of the state's voters chose a Democrat, but Republicans walked away with nine of thirteen seats. Sweeping into power for the first time in more than a century, Republican lawmakers gutted unemployment benefits, slashed corporate taxes, rescinded environmental protection laws, protected Confederate monuments, restricted abortion, and passed the nation's first "bathroom bill," preventing transgender people from using the facilities of their choice. "North Carolina is proving itself to be the poster child for all that is wrong with modern American democracy," the legal correspondent Dahlia Lithwick wrote, describing the new voter ID rules as "probably the most draconian in the nation" and decrying "a vote suppression regime that can only really be described as political performance art."

The project was, in other words, the latest iteration of the North Carolina Way.

The Supreme Court had enabled the initiative, dismantling key provisions of the Voting Rights Act of 1965 with its infamous 2013 *Shelby County v. Holder* ruling. But in the summer of 2016, a federal appeals court had intervened, blocking the attempt to disenfranchise Black voters just months before the coming elections. Should Hillary Clinton win, Trump warned, gun rights would be the next thing to go. "If she gets to pick her judges, nothing you can do, folks," he said, shrugging, as the crowd booed and jeered. "Although, the Second Amendment people—maybe there is, I don't know."

Here Trump was, standing on the site of an American coup, practically soliciting a hit man to take out Clinton in the event that she was elected and started appointing Supreme Court justices he didn't like. It was tempting to read into the location, to think that Lara, while pumping Southern blood into Trump veins, might have put a bug in her father-in-law's ear, just as John Dillard Bellamy Jr. could have done with Woodrow Wilson, regaling him with tales of Winchester justice, of Wilmington's status as a sacred site of white rule. But this is unlikely, for reasons beyond Trump's congenital disinterest in history. During her time in New Hanover County public schools, Lara would not have encountered the murderous government takeover of 1898 as part of the required curriculum.

In any case, Trump read the room correctly. On Election Day, he bested Clinton by four points among the county's voters. Locals praised the glamour of the Trump brood: the grinning, spit-combed sons; the daughters and daughters-in-law in blowouts and sheath dresses, descending from SUVs on teetering heels—a 2016 version of beautiful young ladies dressed in white, descending from a horse-drawn float. In Wilmington and across the country, the 1898 mentality was back, and a revanchist movement was spoiling to shrink the definition of a real American, to wrest away hard-earned rights, and to bypass the democratic process with brute force.

Chapter 48

UNRAVELING

Fifty years after its abrupt closure, Williston Senior High School was not forgotten. Well into their sixties and seventies, its final graduates still organized reunions. The glee club carried on as the Williston Alumni Community Choir, performing a repertoire that ranged from Handel's *Messiah* to the spiritual "I've Been 'Buked" in tuxes and long crimson taffeta skirts with black velvet bodices and boutonnieres that resembled gold-colored chrysanthemums. When an alumnus died, whichever relative wrote the obituary knew to shout out "the greatest school under the sun."

For all that Wilmington's Black community had lost with the end of Williston, little permanent progress had been made in terms of integration. For several decades, New Hanover County Schools had maintained racial balances that reflected the makeup of the area's population, but in 2006, a Republican-led school board implemented a "neighborhood schools policy." Board members said that it would promote "buy-in" and "kinship" among the families that attended the schools. In practical terms, given that Wilmington's neighborhoods tended to be both economically and racially segregated, many schools became essentially all Black or all white. Opponents of the plan denounced it as a de facto return to segregation and predicted that white-majority schools would hoard a disproportionate share of resources, just as they had in the pre-*Brown* days. The vice president of the local chapter of the NAACP told a reporter, "We feel it will be just about educational genocide."

It did not take long for it to become clear that their fears were well-founded. Without busing, educational resegregation followed inevitably from rigid residential segregation in the county, where white people who had once sequestered themselves behind red lines and restrictive covenants now clustered in neighborhoods with street names like Jeb Stuart Drive and Bedford Forest Drive, lined with single-family houses that were nearly impossible to afford without generational wealth.* Assessing the legacy of the *Brown* decision in the *Chicago Defender*, Marian Wright Edelman, then president of the Children's Defense Fund, called out the New Hanover County school board's decision as among the "local signs of a troubling national trend toward resegregation" and observed that Dr. King's dream "is unraveling before our eyes." Several years later, the city's Democratic mayor acknowledged that Edelman's prediction had been fulfilled. He told a reporter, "We're basically back to the same place we were in 1966."

Across the state, schools had become more unequal. A 2018 report identified New Hanover County as having one of the largest increases in income-based segregation in North Carolina over the past decade, while a 2022 *StarNews* investigation confirmed that the neighborhood schools policy, fifteen years in, had "opened up massive equity and achievement gaps," resulting in a return to a Jim Crow–era binary in which white students enjoyed more resources, more experienced teachers, and better-equipped buildings at the expense of their Black and Hispanic peers. New Hanover County Schools effectively comprised two systems: one in which white, suburban students achieved at reasonably high levels, and another in which Black students in the downtown area fell behind. At one elementary school, for example, the percentage of white students dipped from around half in 2005 to less than 9 percent in 2016. At the same time, the school's performance ranking plunged from 180th in the state to 1,396th. By 2019,

---

*Bedford Forest Drive, while misspelled, is indeed named for the Confederate general Nathaniel Bedford Forrest, who served as the first Grand Wizard of the Ku Klux Klan.

Dr. Hubert Eaton Sr. Elementary, named after the tennis-playing physician who had sued the school board for neglecting *Brown*, had become one of the most segregated schools in the county.

THE 1898 WILMINGTON RACE RIOT COMMISSION REPORT OF 2006 NAMED education as one of its chief objectives. Its authors recommended that the North Carolina Department of Public Instruction incorporate 1898 into the statewide public-school curriculum, developing course materials and training teachers, but, three years in, state legislators had refused to allocate the two hundred thousand dollars needed. At that point, even in New Hanover County, a child could start public school in kindergarten and graduate thirteen years later without ever hearing mention of 1898.

Since 2009, third graders have visited the 1898 Memorial as part of a downtown walking tour developed by the Historic Wilmington Foundation. Led by volunteers, the tour is age-appropriate, accurate, and interesting. It starts at a marker honoring Robert R. Taylor, the Tuskegee architect, and passes by the Bellamy Mansion and a pair of churches before pausing in front of the former Wilmington Light Infantry building. As the children behold the marble mansion, the guide reads from a script: "A little over 120 years ago in 1898, something bad happened in this city. Many of the city's leaders and other African Americans were killed or run out of town because of their race or political beliefs. The illegal military force that helped lead this bad event started from this building." The group continued to other landmarks—another church, Thalian Hall, the public library, the post office, an obelisk. If time remains, the group leader can tack a visit to the 1898 Memorial onto the end of the field trip.

Around the same time, New Hanover County Schools introduced an eighth-grade American history lab unit in which students were encouraged to "act like historians," combing through primary and secondary sources about 1898. "When we talk about 1898 and how it was here in their backyard and not just out somewhere in the United States, there is a lot of anger, shame, and genuine intrigue from them," one teacher said. "They want to know more about it." Per the school district's standards, students study slavery, "the dysfunctional relationship North Carolina had with the Confederacy," and Reconstruction, paying close attention to "the tragic violence and racism of the Wilmington events of 1898." At one point, they were asked to weigh in on a question: "Should the current governor issue a formal apology for the events of Wilmington 1898 on behalf of the state of North Carolina?"

In 2021, the North Carolina Department of Public Education updated its statewide social studies standards. The "Wilmington Race Riot" and the Wilmington Ten are now listed as suggested topics for a unit in which fourth graders explore "the ways in which revolution, reform and resistance have shaped North Carolina." Cara Ward, who researches elementary education at UNCW, observed, "I'm so glad it was finally included, but of course the terminology is outdated and a false portrayal of the event." In Wilmington, many fourth graders also participate in field trips to the Cape Fear Museum's exhibit on the 1898 coup and massacre. Local teachers use a *Britannica Kids* entry to plan their lessons, but even those who consider the subject worthwhile sometimes lack the resources to handle it confidently. One high school teacher said, "Even though I've been doing it for over a decade, my lesson on 1898 is still in like a rough, rough draft version."

Despite the hunger for education about 1898, the North Carolina Department of Public Instruction does not mandate any follow-up at the high school level; while New Hanover County Schools strongly recommends the inclusion of 1898 in American history courses, it is not mandatory. In 2020, state authorities proposed cutting American history instruction in half, to a single semester, in order to make time for a class on personal finance literacy and economics. Now required to squeeze the nation's entire four-hundred-year history into eighty days, even well-intentioned educators have been hard-pressed to find sufficient time for the Wilmington massacre and coup. The high school teacher who had taken it upon herself to build up an 1898 lesson plan pointed out that many teachers ended up racing through the "presidents, wars, and inventors, all of which tend to be older white men" that were likely to feature on standardized tests. She explained, "I have found it to be a real challenge in feeling like I can do it justice because it needs days to teach and we just don't have that time."

Chapter 49

ALEXANDER MANLY PARK

In the pandemic spring of 2020, the police murder of George Floyd compelled tens of millions of Americans to join the most dynamic racial justice movement in more than fifty years. Already, progressive activists in North Carolina had begun to challenge the Republican-controlled legislature. The Reverend Dr. William J. Barber II, calling for a "Third Reconstruction," had created a multiracial, cross-class coalition that consciously drew inspiration from Fusionists in seeking to overcome "the elites who had inherited the spoils of white power and had run North Carolina by proxy for generations." With the publication of David Zucchino's *Wilmington's Lie*, the *StarNews* reported, "Wilmington's dark past was cast into the national spotlight."

Locally, a thirty-six-year-old Black software developer running on a left-wing platform had nearly unseated Wilmington's six-term white Democrat mayor, losing by six hundred votes. Donny Williams, a Black Wilmington native who had grown up in public housing, was serving as the interim chief of police. Wilmingtonians marched in the streets, a new generation of Black leaders at the megaphone, facing off against Trump supporters waving little American flags.

On June 24, 2020, a few weeks after the George Floyd protests began, Donny Williams called a press conference. His nomination had just been confirmed by the city council, and it was his first day on the job as the city's first Black police chief. Williams stepped up to the podium and began without preamble. "Today is a challenging day for me, because, as your new police chief, one of my first major tasks is to announce the termination of three veteran police officers," he said.

The officers—James B. Gilmore, Michael Kevin Piner, and Jesse E. Moore II—had all been with the department for decades. None had overlapped with Millis, the Klan-connected sheriff, but one was hired in 1998, and the other two started in 1997, two years after Jerry Spivey, Wilmington's district attorney, had been removed from office for calling a Black man the N-word in a bar. Like Spivey, the officers were being terminated for misconduct. Williams explained that a supervisor conducting a routine audit had stumbled across conversations—accidentally recorded by a dashboard camera—in which the officers, all white, had used racial slurs and hate speech.

The officers were upset by the Black Lives Matter movement: In their estimation, it was dedicated to "worshipping Blacks" and "kneeling down with the Black folks." Like the white supremacists of 1898, they feared interracial cooperation and Black success, and, like the white supremacists of 1898, they transposed their political anxieties into the realm of sex. Gilmore complained that he'd seen a video on social media of "a fine looking white girl and this punk little pretty boy" consorting with Black activists, "bowing down and kissing their toes." In another conversation that day, Moore described a Black official as "a fucking negro magistrate."

The officers verbally abused the targets of their ire—Black protesters, Black officials, white women who got too close to Black men, white men emasculated by proximity to such encounters—while fantasizing about the violence they could wreak in the streets. A Black woman he had arrested, one officer said, was asking for "a bullet in her head." The officers allowed themselves to believe that they were protectors, not antagonists. Paladins of God, family, and country, they had been goaded into war. This was the primordial white supremacist fantasy that begat so many other fictions, making liars out of beloved Grammies and Paw Paws and Mamas and Daddies who didn't otherwise shirk or cheat or dissemble, so what they said must be true. White supremacy was a form of embarrassment masquerading as aggression. The truth was too ridiculous, too weak, so people like the officers couldn't just say it—that they didn't like it when Black people asserted themselves politically, because they understood democracy as a racialized, zero-sum contest.

Piner was persuaded that a "civil war" was coming. He was "ready" and planning to buy a new assault rifle in the next couple of weeks.

"We are just gonna go out and start slaughtering them fucking n——s," he crowed. "God, I can't wait."

He continued, declaring that society needed another civil war to "wipe 'em off the fucking map. That'll put 'em back about four or five generations."

Piner's tossed-off math was less a calculation than a reflex, suggesting the subconscious fluency of someone who'd been drilled in white supremacy from a young age. If a generation spans three decades, four generations makes a hundred and twenty years. The officer, then, wanted to set the clock back to the turn of the century, when white men could murder Black ones with impunity, when the era of the grandfather clause cordoned off the ballot box, and Jim Crow sundered every American space that held the possibility of becoming whole. The epoch that he longed for was not the loss of 1865, but the victory of 1898.

WITH THE BLACK LIVES MATTER MOVEMENT GAINING PURCHASE ACROSS the country, the campaign to rename Hugh MacRae Park, dormant since 2015, found new vigor. In June, someone spray-painted "BLM" on a pair of signs at the park's entrances. Downtown, the Kenan Memorial Fountain—honoring William Rand Kenan Sr., the 1898 machine-gunner—was also tagged, suggesting that whoever wrote the messages wanted to emphasize the link between the police murder of George Floyd in 2020 and the murders of Black men in 1898. Several hundred protesters staged a sit-in at Hugh MacRae Park, gathering near the picnic huts where ROWP had called for "race war" in the 1970s. "This park is named after someone who conspired to murder Black people in 1898 on November 10," Lettie Gore, a historian, professor, and racial equity consultant, reminded the crowd. The sound of bongo drums ricocheted under towering pine trees that ringed the newly renovated playground, which three years before had been named one of America's ten best.

A Change.org petition to rename the park garnered some eighteen thousand signatures in a matter of days. "That man was a racist pig," one of the signers declared. Another wrote that she had lived next to the park all her life, only to learn recently about its history. "It appalls me that this public park has the name of a stone-cold murderer," she wrote. "I could care less about his stature in the community or his family's even now; to keep his name on this park is like Germany naming one of their parks Aushwitz [*sic*] Park."

In 2015, the campaign to strip MacRae's name from the park had hit a wall of apathy and accommodation. Many of the citizens who bothered to speak up about the issue argued in the "heritage not hate" mode that MacRae had been a man of his time and that you couldn't change history, whether it was good or bad. At one panel discussion dedicated to "The Impact of the Confederacy," in 2019, a white woman stood up and said that her family had been in the area for three hundred years. "We were involved in slavery and segregation," she said, explaining that her ancestors "weren't bad people, they thought they were doing the right thing." Still, she thought differently and agreed that the city's Confederate memorial had to go. "So I have a suggestion," she continued. "I would like to see a monument to members of our Black community who are outstanding, who historically took care of white children. Yes, ma'am—nannies."

"You mean *mammies*?" a flabbergasted voice yelled from the back of the room.

Now a new generation of activists were leading the debate with urgent clarity. All over the country, icons of white supremacy began to fall, hoisted off their pedestals as crowds cheered, or scuttled away by sheepish authorities in the middle of the night. The eight-foot-tall George Davis statue that reigned over downtown came down, shunted off to an undisclosed location along with a memorial to the Confederate dead. In Raleigh, Josephus Daniels's descendants removed a statue of their ancestor from a public square near the old *News & Observer* offices and put it into storage, saying, "The time is right."

ONE MORNING NEAR THE END OF JUNE, WILMINGTONIANS WOKE UP TO A surprise: Someone had covered the sign at the main entrance to the park with an enormous, professionally printed vinyl replacement. Its black letters were large enough to be seen from the road: ALEXANDER MANLY PARK. A day or so later, Marguerite ("Meg") Bellamy MacRae checked her Facebook account and saw a message from John Staton, an old friend. They'd both grown up in Wilmington and run around with a wild crowd as twentysomethings. Staton was now a reporter, covering "the arts, entertainment, film, local history, and whole lot more" for the *StarNews*. He was working on a story about the push to rename Hugh MacRae Park.

Did Meg want to comment?

Meg was the only child of Bambi and Hugh MacRae II, who died in 2018. Staton had reached out to her because of the MacRae connection, unaware that, as a great-granddaughter of Hugh MacRae *and* John Dillard Bellamy Jr., Meg actually descended twice over from 1898 perpetrators. Her name honored the latter's daughter Marguerite, who'd married the former's son Nelson. Like the Bellamy Mansion, her name "evoke[d] the grandeur of the Old South despite the lack of a fresh coat of paint," as *The New York Times* wrote of the house when Meg was a teenager.

From a young age, Meg had resisted the strictures of her upbringing. At ten, she ran away—far, miles down the road from the big neo-Georgian house where she lived with her parents amid hand-painted wallpaper and heirloom portraits. The sun was going down. Walking along the shoulder of the highway, she noticed a man following her, the cherry of his cigarette getting closer and closer in the gloaming. She ran, but the man gave chase. Finally, she reached an arcade where she saw Mike, an older kid she knew from the skating rink, standing outside. She went running up to him and told him she was terrified. Mike approached the strange man, and they got into a shouting match. The police arrived just then, and shoved Mike, who was Black, into the cruiser. Meg recalled, "They're just talking to the guy who was chasing me, and then my parents come, and I get sort of reamed out, like, 'What are you doing down here with a Black man?'"

The racial rules of the world that Meg was born into were well understood even if they were not explicitly articulated. Her elders never told her that they did not think of Black people as equals. But she could see that they were present only as custodians or waiters, serving French dip sandwiches and Shirley Temples at the Cape Fear Country Club, which her MacRae great-grandfather and his brother helped to found in 1896, laying out its fairways in tandem with their plans for white dominion.

"Why aren't there any Black people at the country club?" Meg asked, when she was in grade school.

"They don't want to be members," she was told.

Like her father and grandfather, Meg was sent to St. Paul's, the elite New Hampshire boarding school. As a teenager, she pulled away from her family even more. Feeling like an "odd bird" in Wilmington, she went to Sarah Lawrence for college and moved to New York City after graduation. She buzzed her hair, got tattoos, joined a Roller Derby team, and listened to punk rock. "I'm not saying my name means all that, but I'm saying being in Wilmington and being a MacRae, there is a certain judgment," she recalled. "It just felt really nice to go somewhere where nobody gave a rat's ass about my name and neither did I."

Now, at fifty, Meg lived near Nashville with a black cat and a tiger tabby. A former road manager for Shania Twain and the Eagles, she worked freelance as a production coordinator for major bands. In her off time, she made her own music and traveled to such places as Malawi, Costa Rica, and India, where she'd recently spent a month at a sri vidya tantra immersion ashram led by a Los Angeles sexologist. She had been sober and clean for twenty-one years after struggling with addiction to heroin. She found pleasure now in crystals, potbellied pigs, stargazer lilies, and hot chocolate with sprinkles. In her forties, she'd gone back to school for a master's in spiritual psychology. One of her favorite affirmations read "The depth of your ability to love will always be mirrored by your ability to be honest."

For years, Meg had kept her distance from Wilmington, even avoiding holiday visits, but, recently, she'd been spending time there again, to care for her parents as they aged. She happened to be in town when Staton messaged. She had been following the debate over the park and got back to him quickly. She told him that she wanted to come out in support of the name change.

Then she went to her mother, with whom she is close, and told her about her plans. Bambi was not in favor of removing Hugh MacRae's name from the park. "That man gave three hundred and fifty acres to this city in good faith," she explained later. "And he had nothing to do with that little clause in there for white people. The Black people think taking the name off the park is going to help, but it's not going to help at all."

Despite their differing views, Bambi encouraged Meg to do what she felt she had to do. Even as Meg made up her mind, she braced for the backlash of dissent from a community that made conformity its highest value. The writer Edward Ball, a descendant of Charleston enslavers, has observed, "In some places in the South, the descendants of slaveholders comprise a distinct society with its own folkways, memories, and pride. Families such as mine know who they are, in part because if your people once owned vast tracts of land, gorged themselves on exquisite things, and were followed through life by clouds of workers and servants, many of whom called you 'master,' the memory of these experiences is not allowed to fade. Instead, it is preserved and honored." The members of this society recognize each other through subtle cues: the portraits they hang in their homes, the way they pronounce certain words, the distinctive family names they bestow upon their children.

Even today, their sense of belonging and cohesion casts a powerful spell. There is a potent there there in the unchanging aesthetics and rituals, in the tobacco leaf dishes and smocked layettes, the oyster roasts and chess pies, the sprig of rosemary in a wedding bouquet, the bronzed children jumping from the commodore's tower into the water holding hands and yelping with glee, returning years later to watch their own children do the same. It's said that it takes a village to raise a child, but it also takes a village to make one obey. Meg thought about what her parents' friends at the country club might say. She recalled, "What I inherently hear in my head is, How *dare* that child!"

Meg told the paper that she supported the name change but explained that she didn't want the piece to center her, as if permission was hers to grant. She asked Staton if he could connect her with Black activists campaigning on the issue. She was acting, she noted delicately, out of personal conscience: "I don't speak for anybody else, but I think it's really important. . . . I don't want to feel like I'm speaking out against my family. I'm not against [them], but I am for equality and justice and reform."

That week, Meg had met with Sonya Bennetone-Patrick, a leader of the Black Lives Matter chapter in Wilmington and one of the activists who were lobbying to change the park's name. Meg's half brother Hugh MacRae III had invited Bennetone-Patrick to his office for a chat a few days earlier but hadn't committed to a position. Another of her half-siblings, Nelson MacRae, opposed the renaming entirely. "I feel like the pendulum has swung too far in this environment, where the white people have done everything wrong," he said later. The talk about 1898, he felt, amounted to "trying to pound my family more," when he and his children "had nothing to do with any of this."

It is a telling quirk of the way repair is negotiated in America that the descendants of perpetrators of racial violence are considered primary stakeholders, permission-givers who must be consulted. Yet the conversation was meaningful to both women. Meg had been helping her mother negotiate

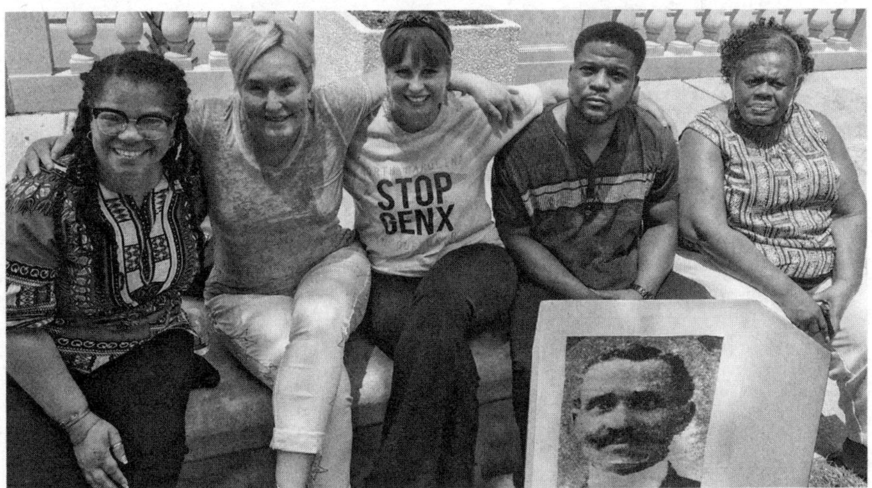

Sonya Bennetone-Patrick (*far left*), Meg MacRae (*second from left*), and other activists with a photograph of Rev. Dr. J. Allen Kirk, pastor of the Central Baptist Church, in 1898.

an inheritance lawsuit that pitted her against Hugh II's sons and other financial trustees. The experience of tangling in court with her brothers had deepened Meg's sense that the old boys' club still wielded undue power. "I know this is a woman issue, not a racial issue," she said, "but it's like if you speak up and say, 'I have a right,' they're gonna figure out a way to tell you that you don't." She continued, "You question it, and there's a wrath that comes down." (The case has since been settled and relationships repaired.)

Bennetone-Patrick traced her lineage back to Black Union soldiers who liberated the city from Confederate rule. For her, the MacRae name connoted pain, not prestige. "Seeing the horrible parts of our past being glorified, it's an emotional weight," she explained. "The name change would be a step in the direction to take that weight off the community." And whatever the outcome of the campaign, she appreciated the fact that Meg was putting herself out there and that Hugh III had agreed to meet. Being able to talk to the MacRae siblings about renaming the park was, Bennetone-Patrick said, "kind of like a release."

Media buzz around the women's encounter helped to make the name change an immediate political priority. Barely a week later, much faster than anyone could have expected, the New Hanover County board of commissioners announced that they had decided to move on the proposal. By a vote of 3 to 2, the board approved the name change. Effective immediately, Hugh MacRae Park would be known as Long Leaf Park. (Not everyone was thrilled: "If I wanted to get a petition to change the name back, I bet I could get tens of thousands of signatures in pretty short order," Nelson MacRae said later.) The day after the commissioners' decision, a man in a cherry picker hovered in front of the iron arch that marked the entrance to the park, removing the letters of Hugh MacRae's name one by one.

Walter L. Parsley Elementary was next. Within a few months of the Hugh MacRae vote, the school board decided to change the school's name to Masonboro Elementary. Why not Alexander Manly Park, as activists had proposed? Why not the Alfred Howe School or Joshua Halsey Elementary? Apparently, county officials had instituted an informal rule stipulating that name changes could only pay tribute to uncontroversial, inanimate objects, like conifers and bodies of water. Even while attempting to redress a historical wrong, they still treated 1898, as the librarian had years earlier, as an issue that might "make a stink." But now many of their constituents knew better. Two members of a local reading group who had been studying 1898 paid to have a billboard erected near one of the city's busiest intersections. 1898. 2020. VOTE, it read. When Election Day came, Joe Biden won New Hanover County by a paper-thin margin.

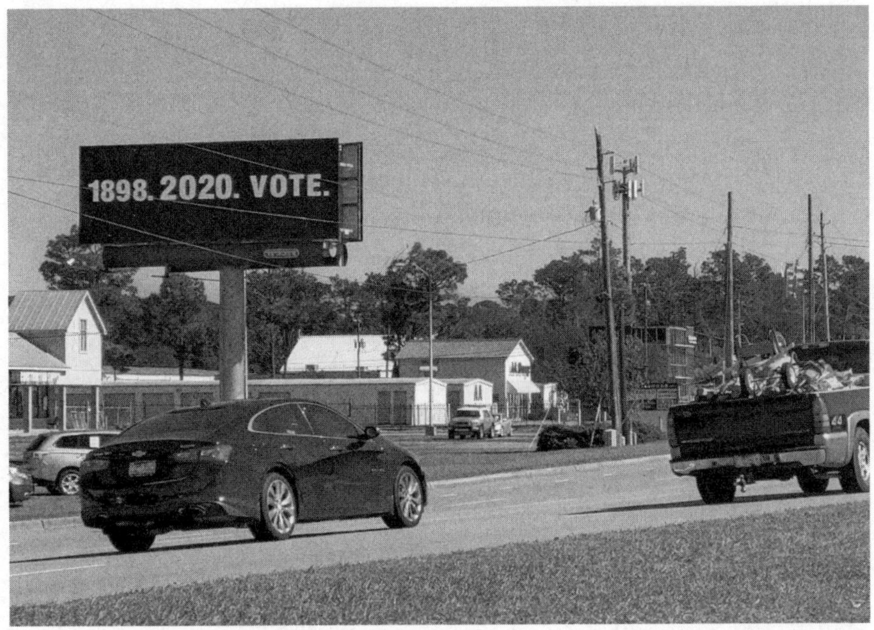

Eastwood Road, Wilmington, November 2020.

Chapter 50

WOOOOOOO!

A seedy, vainglorious politician takes the stage in front of a big white building and looks out upon a big white crowd. They are already angry, and for weeks, their media have fed their rage, telling them that voter fraud is rampant, that the people in charge are both lesser and omnipotent, that they are living under the thumb of wimps, radicals, and degenerates. They must act now, and they must show strength because the real people who built the country will never take it back with weakness.

On January 6, 2021, President Donald Trump incited what would have been the ultimate coup d'état on American soil, had it succeeded. He did not explicitly mention race, but he drew from the same deep well of racial animosity that Alfred Moore Waddell did when he took the stage at City Hall in 1898 and called on white men to seek "righteous vengeance" for "the salvation of society." Both had lost elections in which Black voters overwhelmingly supported the other candidate. Both believed that strong interracial coalitions spelled their political death. "If you don't fight like hell, you're not going to have a country anymore," Trump said to the crowd. He wasn't far off from urging them to choke the Potomac with carcasses.

The 1898 and 2021 mobs came together in different contexts—one local, one national; one high on victory, the other stewed in defeat—but they fed on common entitlements and animus. Like their November 10 predecessors, the January 6 attackers saw themselves as patriots. They were redeemers, drainers of the swamp, righteous purifiers of a world gone to shit. (The latter were joined by some women and people of color. AMERICAN SUPREMACIST, read a T-shirt that the Cuban American leader of the Proud Boys wore at an event.) Just as white Democrats complained in 1898 that Black voters were dominating elections, the conservative media featured Republican politicians who warned constantly of the "great replacement." Immigrants, they warned, would "take over our country without firing a shot," overpowering "legacy Americans."

In the post-Obama era, just as in the post-Reconstruction years, racial progress awakened racial backlash. A window of possibility opened, and white conservatives slammed it shut, worried they'd let in too much democracy. The continuities between the Lost Cause and the Big Lie were not just subtext. Alongside memelike, plausibly deniable emblems of hate, members of the January 6 mob flaunted the traditional tools of vigilante terrorism. "Hang Mike Pence!" the mob chanted, threatening to execute the vice president, a white man who'd let down the cause.

Trump's audience perfectly understood his codes and meanings. White nationalist paramilitaries such as the Proud Boys, Three Percenters, and Oath Keepers turned out to "Stop the Steal" with tactical armor, zip-tie handcuffs, hockey sticks, bear spray, sharpened poles, and stun guns such as the ZAP Hike 'n Strike 950,000 Volt Stun Gun Walking Stick. They flashed the "OK" symbol, connoting white power, because the fingers and thumb form a *W* and a *P*, and waved the VDARE flag, honoring Virginia Dare, said to be the first white child born in Britain's American colonies. Instead of red shirts, they wore red hats.

Following Trump's instructions, the crowd paraded down Pennsylvania Avenue to the Capitol, and then it attacked, surging through barricades, shoving past and attacking police officers, and finally, breaching the Capitol building. The nation watched on television as security guards held their guns to the door of the House chamber, trying to hold back the mob.

The call went out over the police radio:

"This is now effectively a riot!"

As a shirtless, spear-carrying man in a fur headdress occupied the vice president's chair in the Senate and rioters ransacked Nancy Pelosi's office, a Black officer tried to secure an area near the House rotunda. "*Wooooooo!*" one man screamed, climbing through a bashed-out window.

"No, man, this is our house," one of the intruders said. "President Trump invited us here."

"We're here to stop the steal," another added. "Joe Biden is not the president. Nobody voted for Joe Biden."

"Well, I voted for Joe Biden," the officer replied. "Does my vote not count? Am I nobody?"

A woman in a pink MAGA shirt turned to the mob. "You hear that guys? This n—— voted for Joe Biden!"

"Boo, fucking n——!" the crowd screamed.

WHEN THE DAY WAS OVER, FOUR PEOPLE WERE DEAD. ONE MEMBER OF THE mob had a heart attack, a second had a stroke, a third was crushed to death, and a fourth was shot by a police officer as she tried to break through a barricaded door. On January 7, a police officer died after suffering strokes hours after his confrontation with the mob. Four more officers died by suicide before the end of the summer. The Black officer who confronted the mob told a congressional committee that he and his Black colleagues had been forced to fight two battles that day: one against invaders and the other against racists. One colleague had told him that "never, in his entire 40 years of life, had [he] been called a n—— to his face, and that streak ended on January 6th." The day also marked the first time in the history of the American republic that a Confederate flag was paraded inside the Capitol building.

Trump showered the insurrectionists with praise, and they were treated with astonishing leniency as they laid siege to the Capitol. As in 1898, the high-level instigators of the attacks faced few consequences. The prosecution of the January 6 rank and file did little to make the country less vulnerable to undemocratic seizure by means such as gerrymandering and election subversion, but for a time it seemed, at least, that the rioters wouldn't get away scot-free. By early 2025, more than fifteen hundred had been charged, and over seven hundred went to jail for some period of time.

Alfred Moore Waddell incited a coup and became mayor. Donald Trump incited a coup attempt and, in 2024, was elected president again. (He won North Carolina but lost New Hanover County by a hair.) In the aftermath of January 6, many Americans wanted to believe that "this is not who we are," but in fact, white supremacist violence is a through line of our country's history, not a flashback or a regression. White supremacists will continue to try to take what they think is theirs until the consequences of such acts outweigh the spoils. According to a 2022 Senate report, both the FBI and the Department of Homeland Security have repeatedly identified domestic terrorism, and, in particular, white supremacy as America's "most persistent and lethal terrorist threat." Under both Democratic and Republican administrations, the federal government, the report warned, has failed to conceive of and fund a response commensurate with the extent of the danger.

Trump is often associated with 1950s-style white conformity, but he reserves his greatest nostalgia and admiration for the protectionism, imperialism, and ruthless capitalism of the 1890s. One of the first acts of his second term was to restore the name of William McKinley—one of his favorite presidents—to Denali, North America's highest mountain peak. He will be remembered, per presidential order, for having "heroically led our Nation to victory in the Spanish-American War" and for "his steadfast commitment to American greatness," rather than for his decision to let the Black residents of Wilmington "die like rats in a trap," as the terrified correspondent who vainly sought his help in 1898 feared.

Upon assuming office, Trump immediately pardoned some sixteen hundred people who had been charged or convicted in the January 6 riots. Then he initiated a purge of the Justice Department, where more than two dozen prosecutors who worked on January 6 cases have been fired or demoted. His supporters likened the act to Andrew Johnson's forgiveness of Confederate partisans after the Civil War—a decision that, as Ibram X. Kendi observed, allowed them to reclaim power, distorting history, banning books, and building Jim Crow on lynching and lies. The decision, Trump claimed, was the opening salvo of "a process of national reconciliation": our country's time-worn code for historical erasure, a get-out-of-jail-free card for those who murder, rampage, and maim—and know they'll probably get away with it.

Chapter 51

THE GUN

On a late winter afternoon in 2021, sunlight was pouring into the ground-floor home office of Dr. William (Bill) Eliason Sisson Jr. A breeze from Motts Channel, a quiet offshoot of the Intracoastal Waterway, crept in through a cracked-open sliding door. The walls were covered with split bamboo poles. Boating guides and binders of old tax returns filled the bookshelves. Sisson stood up, left the room, and returned several minutes later, carrying a gun. It was still in its holster, a battered brown leather number with a brass clasp and the attenuated shape of an elephant's trunk. He placed the gun on his desk, where it sat in unsettling counterpoint to the surf-shack vibe.

Sisson put on white cotton gloves and took out the gun, a Colt .44 cap-and-ball single-action revolver. A chiropractor by trade, he handled the weapon with the steady gestures of someone accustomed to manipulating things that other people might be hesitant to touch. The gun wasn't fragile, really; just old. Sisson usually kept it in a locked cabinet. He had inherited it from his maternal grandfather, (Henry) Roger Moore, who had inherited it from his father, Colonel Roger Moore.

Sisson, age seventy-three, had first encountered the Colonel's weapon as a boy. On Sundays, the Moore family would gather for lunch at his grandfather's house at Masonboro Sound. (The bamboo lining Sisson's home office came from a grove that once grew around an oyster house on another family estate.) While the adults lingered over their meal, Sisson would set off exploring. "My grandfather had a little workroom off the back porch, and I would take the gun back there and futz around," he recalled. "One time, I almost tapped the pin out, and I got freaked out and had to tap it back in. I never fully dismantled it, but I got real familiar with it. And so, when he died, he left it to me."

According to family lore, the Colonel had acquired the gun during the Civil War. At some point, he likely crossed paths with D. D. Rosencrans, a Union soldier—his name is stamped on the holster in stylish black letters. The Colonel might have killed the man and taken his gun, or the man might have been dead already, or a prisoner of war. In any case, the Colonel ended up with Rosencrans's revolver and held on to it for the rest of his life, passing it to his heirs. A lean man with a gray corona and a deliberate manner, Sisson turned the gun slowly, pointing out a naval battle scene etched onto the cylinder. He rotated it another few degrees to reveal that the Colonel had added his own initials, "R.M.," engraved in cursive letters on the brass-plated underside of the gun's walnut grip.

The gun was coveted by some collectors, including, Sisson said, his

Colonel Roger Moore's Colt .44 cap-and-ball single-action revolver, March 13, 2021.

second cousin, Louis Moore Bacon. "He was falling all over himself to try to get me to give it to him," Sisson said at one point. Would he ever consider it? "Hell no!" he said, laughing. "First of all, I think that Louis has more than enough of just about everything and, secondly, if I'm going to give it to any entity, I want it to go someplace where the public can have access to it."

Bacon is a great-grandson of Colonel Roger Moore, like Sisson, and a grandson of the local historian Louis Toomer Moore. He grew up in Raleigh, moved to New York, and made a fortune running his own hedge fund, Moore Capital Management. According to *Forbes*, Bacon was in 2016 the 374th richest person in the world. In 2010, he paid the Sprunt family $45 million to buy Orton, "King" Roger Moore's eight-thousand-acre plantation on the Cape Fear River, with its fragrant gardens and columned mansion. The purchase brought the estate back into the Moore family's possession for the first time since 1826. "There was a sense of taking back into the family something that was lost over time," Bacon said. "So it was kind of, maybe, a childhood dream."

Orton had been open to the public since the 1930s, but Bacon, a renowned conservationist, closed its doors. He did not share many details about his plans at first, but, in 2012, he declared that he was trying to bring the plantation "back to its original landscape." He has seemingly spared no cost in pursuing this goal of revivifying the environs of the eighteenth century. His foundation has supported efforts to preserve the habitats of coastal birds such as the American oystercatcher and the white ibis, and at the plantation his team has been restoring the massive longleaf pine forest through controlled burns. His most ambitious project involves the renewal of the plantation's antebellum rice fields, which operated on an intricate dike system built and worked by people the Moores enslaved. Bacon sees this work as a tribute to the labor of the people his ancestors enslaved and hopes to install a monument in their honor. "Restoring the historic rice fields recognizes centuries-old rice farming practices of enslaved Africans," he said in a statement to the *News & Observer*. "I am awed and inspired by the resilience that helped create these fields, and by saving them, I have an opportunity to commemorate the lives of those who were critical to the development of this land, rather than have their prodigious work swept under by the Cape Fear River." He explained recently, "It's too much of a part of Orton Plantation not to address it and not to have it front and center."

Sisson had never met his cousin until a few Thanksgivings ago, when Bacon invited family members to a gathering at Orton. "He took us up to the third floor where he has this sort of mini-museum," Sisson recalled. "He's preserved the room that was used as a hospital for Confederate soldiers and so forth." Bacon showed Sisson a picture of their mutual great-grandfather. Sisson recalled, "He said, 'I have a picture of Colonel Moore,' and it was a picture that appeared to have been taken during the war. But the person in the picture didn't look at all like any of the later photographs of my great-grandfather that I've seen." In the images Sisson had seen, the Colonel was always posing—in a room, in a studio. This one, taken from a distance, showed him standing out in the fields, surveying the land he loved.

A THROUGH LINE OF WHITE SUPREMACY CONNECTED THE COLONEL'S CONfederate career with his Ku Klux Klan and vigilance committee leadership, but Sisson grew up believing that his great-grandfather was a hero. His Klan activity, Sisson recalled, rated only "a passing mention" in conversations with family members, who downplayed the group's raison d'être of upholding white supremacy through racial violence, claiming that the Klan "had to do with fighting the influence of the carpetbaggers more than anything else." The way he learned the story, Sisson recalled, any "white-black issue" was strictly incidental.

Sisson's mother, Alice Borden Moore Sisson, was a family therapist and clinical social worker, respected by many for her volunteer work with food banks, domestic violence shelters, and mental health clinics. She was a "champion of the underdog" and "absolutely loathed and abhorred bullying," he recalled; yet she, like many of his relatives, was proud of what she'd heard about the Colonel's conduct in 1898. The stories she'd inherited emphasized his role in protecting a group of Black employees at Sprunt's cotton compress and in preventing the mob from lynching six Black men who were being held at the city jail. The family interpreted these incidents as evidence of the Colonel's innate sense of justice, and as a sign of his superiority *within* the white race. In their telling, racial terrorism was the unfortunate excess of the "poor white trash" element of Wilmingtonians, who had lacked discipline in executing the righteous political takeover that their social betters had designed.

This cherished image of the Colonel bravely facing down a lawless rabble conveniently excluded the fact that he was one of the people who—in the hours, days, years, and decades preceding that moment—had worked to create it. Sisson struggled to reconcile the omissions that marked his family's stories with the fuller tellings that he encountered later. "This may sound very strange, because the story I heard depicted him as a man who believed in the rule of law," Sisson said. "And I'm not necessarily talking about it in a legal context here, but in a moral sense. It might have been necessary to raise a revolt, but it was not necessary to do it in an immoral fashion."

When Sisson graduated from New Hanover in 1965, he recalled, he "couldn't get out of Wilmington fast enough." Despite the privileges of race and class that he enjoyed, he, too, felt stifled by the city's rigid hierarchies, "sick of the racism, sick of the segregation, sick of the chokehold I thought the old guard had on this place." He understood these problems, however, as impersonal forces, rather than intentional systems that his ancestors had created and maintained. After college in Ohio, amid the chaos of the Vietnam War, he sought to find himself. Eventually, he moved to Los Angeles, earning master's degrees in Latin American studies and urban planning at UCLA. Then he took a job with the City Planning Department. It's eerie to imagine him hunched over a map of Hollywood, summoning the Colonel's talent for breaking down a city block by block.

A political slight relegated Sisson to "the Outer Mongolia of the Planning Department," and he decided to switch careers. He had already gotten a massage license, to help pay for his studies, so he enrolled in chiropractic school, graduating in 1985. At thirty-seven, Sisson considered himself "too old and too ornery to work for anyone else." He and his wife, Joy, were trying to assert their independence. They had just had their first child—they named him Misha, not Roger or Bill. They started looking for a place to open a practice, stopping by Wilmington to visit family on a tour of the East Coast. When they got back to California, they received a phone call from Sisson's father, a Virginian who'd come to Wilmington to work at the shipyard during the Second World War and then made a small fortune in oil and gas. "I've made a down payment on a house," he said. And so it was that Sisson, as he recalled to me, "moved back to the last place to which I imagined I would ever return, my hometown."

Sisson worked with chi, not bricks. He had only seen his Moore grandfather in shirtsleeves a few times in his entire life, at the breakfast table, but he turned up for the unveiling of a plaque at one of the family's historic houses wearing a silky black Hawaiian shirt with a hibiscus print. Although Sisson was less conservative than his ancestors in both politics and style, he shared their attraction to local government. In 1992, he successfully sought a seat on the New Hanover County board of county commissioners, following in the footsteps of the Colonel, who was elected to the same board in the summer of 1898.

The only Democrat on a five-member panel, Sisson opposed overdevelopment, sought funding for public schools, and, at one point, defended a controversial local museum program that was designed to educate the public about the region's cultural diversity. When a Republican colleague called the cultural diversity provision racist, because "people should focus on being American," Sisson accused her of "trying to be the Newt Gingrich of New Hanover County." Many people in Wilmington, he observed, "have no idea how the region developed, and talking about it shouldn't divide the population."

AFTER EXAMINING THE GUN, SISSON WALKED OUT TO HIS DOCK, WHERE the late-afternoon sun was glinting off the water. In the distance, across the marsh grass of the channel, you could make out seafood restaurants and a marina where the Confederate flag could be seen flying a few years ago. He had inherited the house from his parents. In the 1920s, his grandfather and his grandfather's brother-in-law had developed Shore Acres, the neighborhood in which he lives, transforming an uninhabited marshland into choice real estate. Stopping at the edge of the water, Sisson indicated a ramp that had once led to "a little boathouse" that his father had built. "He had an electric winch at the end, with a telephone anchor guy-wired back into the ground," he remembered.

It was getting chilly. Sisson went back into the office. A russet-colored wooden plaque sat on the floor, propped against the bamboo wall. The Historic Wilmington Foundation—the same preservation society that Cynthia Brown volunteered for—had issued it in appreciation of Shore Acres House, the neighborhood's first home. Sisson had owned that house, too, having inherited it from an uncle's caretaker, and had sold it in 2019. The plaque, which had hung near the door, traced the property's pedigree and the contributions of its owners to the community's civic and business affairs. It concluded, almost triumphantly, THE HOUSE REMAINS IN THE FAMILY.

Despite his impatience with his colleagues' resistance to acknowledging the many strands of local history, Sisson hadn't always been clear-eyed when it came to his own family's past. In 1992, he had launched his campaign for a seat on the county commission on the steps of the county courthouse, standing in front of a cornerstone that bore the Colonel's name. The scene created a sense of inevitability, implying the natural transmission of power from one safe pair of hands to his progeny. Not only did the courthouse scene imply hereditary entitlement, but it was also the very place where, ninety-four years earlier, his great-grandfather had helped to lead the meeting in which Wilmington's white Democrat men plotted their postelection rampage, signing his name to their White Declaration of Independence.

Thirty years later, Sisson said that he regretted the courthouse photo op. The image of the Colonel had changed, he explained, "from the one that was prevalent when I grew up, which was a revered and respected community leader" to that of a participant "in a villainous conspiracy that resulted in the massacre of many and to the driving of others completely out of town." Asked how that made him feel, Sisson thought for a minute and answered, "Like I want to keep my head down."

Sisson didn't want to see what his ancestors saw, it seemed; he wanted to unsee it. He found it difficult to reconcile the precepts that had been drilled into him as a kid—the perfidy of carpetbaggers, the folly of congressional Reconstruction, the inconsequential relationship of race to it all—with newer input that told a different story. Right was becoming wrong and guilty was becoming innocent. One way to deal with this was to qualify that input. It was an error, Sisson argued, "to look at what happened only through the lens of current values and current history." That said, he acknowledged that "a wrongful act, whenever it might have been committed, is always a wrongful act. The historical context does not make it any less wrong." He continued, "I feel shame and a sense of shared guilt, even though it wasn't me who did those awful things."

He examined the gun one last time before placing it carefully back into the holster. It was an intimate object, something the Colonel had kept close to his body, held in his hands, and possibly killed with. Now, more than a century later, his great-grandson was cradling it in his palms. No one had donated the gun to a museum or decided it was more encumbrance than treasure. It meant something more than a painting, a pocket watch, a wedding ring—all the other things that might, but in Sisson's case hadn't, come down the family line.

The artifacts of 1898 are repositories of unarticulated history. Yet they speak eloquently about the people they represented and the legacies they were able to leave behind, the choices they made or were denied. Bill Sisson got his great-grandfather's Colt .44 cap-and-ball single-action revolver, and it seemed more dangerous with every year that went by.

CHAPTER 52

NEVER FORGOTTEN

Hesketh Nathaniel (Nate) Brown Jr. did not inherit any precious antiques or priceless heirlooms. He could tell you that people in his family tend to be good at puzzles, incline toward sobriety, and apply a certain single-mindedness to whatever it is they're doing, be it walking four miles to save a dollar bus fare or chopping onions for lima-bean soup. Other than that, he didn't know much else about his background and had never really cared to, until 2017. The year before, his seventy-four-year-old mother, Joan Starks Henry, had lost all three of her siblings. Brown was cruising the internet for a Christmas gift for her when an ad for Ancestry.com popped up. He figured that genealogy might be a comforting hobby for Henry, giving her an opportunity to "reminisce and refresh" as she grieved. By learning more about her family, he thought, she might find some closure to her bereavement. He bought her a subscription and left the kit under the tree.

Brown and his wife, Linda, lived in Queens with their teenage son, nicknamed Little Nate. They bought their house, which sits a few blocks north of Idlewild Park, in 2012, but they were Brooklyn through and through. Brown was reared in Prospect Heights and East Flatbush. He still drove back to his old neighborhood to see his favorite barber, who knew exactly how to cut his hair so that his one little bald spot didn't show. Queens felt like the countryside to him. The sky was full of birds and planes, gliding low over the house to land at JFK, their bellies practically grazing the roof.

Brown graduated from Boys and Girls High School in Bedford-Stuyvesant in 1980. Then he enrolled in trade school, earning a certificate in digital electronics and computer technology. For a while he repaired electrolysis machines. "I walk into Bergdorf or Bloomingdale's, and I'm wearing a weird tie, making minimum wage," he recalled. But Japanese technology was ascendant, and it was hard to find work, so he decided to take the civil service exam. In 1985, he got a job with Metro-North, commuting four hours a day "past Sleepy Hollow and all these mansions" to fix trains. He joined New York City Transit a few years later and retired in 2018, having worked his way up from electrician (a job he loved) to maintenance manager (a job he hated, because of the managing, not the maintenance). "Back in the eighties, getting a transit job was like being listed on the top 100 bachelors in New York City," he recalled.

Brown is a shy yet gregarious man with a gap-toothed smile. His transit colleagues called him "Dr. Brown" because of his talent for solving complex problems. Sometimes he described himself as "autistic," which was a way of acknowledging, without bragging, the intense intelligence that accompanied his occasional social awkwardness. He could fix a malfunctioning air-conditioning system or repair a loose brake. He was good at assimilating new technology and accustomed to painstaking work that required insane amounts of patience. Now that he had leisure time, he quickly mastered Ancestry's public records search functions and started building his mother's family tree. Before long, he decided to have his DNA analyzed, in hopes that it would connect him to more relatives. He encouraged his mother, Joan, to do the same.

On her paternal side, Joan had roots in rural Alabama. Her father, Grady Starks, had migrated to Pennsylvania as a child sometime around 1910, making his way to New Jersey and then to Brooklyn, where, as *Look* reported, he worked as a doorman. Brown thought he knew these family stories well, but Joan's DNA test yielded a major surprise: It didn't match that of other members of the Starks family. Instead, it linked her, through her father, to a bunch of strangers with the last name Clark. Acting as his mother's emissary, Brown contacted Clark family members through Ancestry. "They're like, 'Who's this lady? Who are these people?'" he recalled. Eventually, however, they agreed to share their information, and it became clear that Grady Starks's father had likely been a Clark, rather than a Starks.

Brown had researched his way into one of those classic bioethical bombshells that can blow a family apart, but his mother and the rest of his relatives took the news in a philosophical manner. They were players of spades, tonk, bid whist, poker, and dominoes, lovers of word searches and sudoku. The quest to identify their ancestors was a kind of next-level decoding game. "We got stuck into it," Brown said. Besides, he figured, he'd already found the most shocking family secret there was to find. He decided to keep going.

In the 1940 census, he found his grandparents Grady and Juanita Cato Starks living at 77 Summit Avenue in Summit, New Jersey, with their son and various relatives. Brown had known all these people well. But the census showed a sixth household member, "Sally Hosley," with whom he was not familiar. Brown was able to deduce that her name was actually Sallie Halsey, and that she was his maternal great-great-grandmother.

Before Sallie came into the picture, Brown hadn't known much about the Halseys, Wilmington, or 1898. Now he learned that the city had been his mother's family's Southern homeplace, and that Sallie had lived there with her husband, Joshua, and their children in a mostly Black neighborhood called Brooklyn. "Fake Brooklyn!" Brown joked.

"My mother kept telling me something about someone who was killed in a race riot," Brown recalled. "So, I said let me just look for 'race riots in Wilmington.'" Using Google, he quickly discovered the city's history of racial terrorism. Next, he went to Newspapers.com and searched for a mention of the Halsey name in 1898. One of the hits was an article dated November 13, 1898, from the *Wilmington Morning Star.*

Brown clicked on the article and the scanned image of a faded broadsheet filled his screen. He read quickly, absorbing the paper's boosterish assurances that businesses were open in all parts of the city and that order had been restored by the newly installed city government. Brown found Joshua Halsey's name in the tenth paragraph of the story. It reported that he and six other Black men had died by gunshot wound in the "fight between the whites and the blacks." Sworn testimony from white witnesses, the article declared, "will prove conclusively that the negroes were the aggressors."

Brown was stunned by what he'd found: Not only did the articles corroborate a family story that he'd assumed was folklore, but they established the intentional and gruesome nature of his great-great-grandfather's death. Later, he read other primary sources, including a detailed account of Halsey's being shot in the back as he fled the white mob. "The murder was horrific," Brown recalled. "The lies told about it were upsetting. But when I told my family, we kind of celebrated it. We'd just found out that someone had brutally murdered my great-great-grandfather, his wife was forced to suffer, and we were relieved in some way because it was a kind of closure."

Brown eventually concluded that he and his relatives felt assuaged by knowing the truth about their past. The partial restitution of their story, even in its excruciating particulars, filled a void, redressing the sense that they were missing something. They needed to know Joshua and Sallie Halsey and to understand what had happened to them to be able to complete the puzzle of who they were.

Continuing his research, Brown was able to ascertain that by 1898, Joshua and Sallie had been married for almost twenty-two years, and that they were the parents of four daughters, one of whom had died as a child. That Joshua was forty-six when he was murdered. That he died a block from his family's home. But the work of reconstructing his life required creativity as much as it did technical skill. No pictures survived of Joshua or Sallie, so Brown needed to conjure them in his mind's eye. Summoning Joshua, he said, "I'm getting a dark-skinned man, probably in the area of five-eight to five-ten, well-dressed and popular with the ladies, or with the community, is what I'm getting from the vibe."

As he scanned the papers, Brown came across the "woman sneak thief" story detailing Sallie's arrest for stealing napkins and a butter jar. He tried to imagine what kinds of strains she was under, not quite two years after her husband's murder. "You're looking for heroes, and you found some heroes in the story, but you found realism in the story, too," Brown said. Joshua was thought to be buried in an unmarked grave in a Black cemetery in Wilmington. Brown imagined walking through the pine forests, talking to him. "My family was decimated and spent decade after decade trying to recover from this tragedy while living through the lies, horrors, and evil intent of the aggressors," he wrote, announcing his discovery on Facebook.

Learning about the trauma that his grandmother Juanita Cato Starks had inherited from Sallie Halsey helped Brown to make sense of some aspects of his family that had always troubled him. It shed light on the poverty they had experienced at various times, and on physical and psychological symptoms that continued to affect him and his relatives. "The most telling aspect of it is resolve," he said, recalling how Juanita walked everywhere well into her eighties. "My grandmother was the sweetest thing on two legs, and she used to watch sports on TV," he recalled. "A basketball game would be on, and she'd say, 'Who's playing?' And I would say, 'Oh, Grandma, it's the Knicks and the Charlotte Hornets.' And she'd say, 'Well, who's got the most Blacks?' I'd say the Knicks, and that's the team she would go for." He explained, "She was just rooting for Blacks to be OK, and I understand that now."

One day, after his profile had been on Ancestry for a while, Nate noticed that he had a message on the site. It was from Tim Pinnick, a retired track coach and an accomplished amateur scholar, focusing on African American history and genealogy, who had moved to Wilmington from Illinois a few years earlier. Pinnick wrote:

> Good morning Hesketh!
>
> I am working with the New Hanover County (NC) Community Remembrance Project whose current goal is to add racial terror victims from here to the National Memorial for Peace and Justice in Montgomery, Alabama. We are attempting to find descendants of the victims of the 1898 massacre in Wilmington, NC, to include

them in an upcoming ceremony in November. . . . We would like to speak with you at your earliest convenience.

Sincerely, Tim Pinnick

A LITTLE MORE THAN A YEAR LATER, IN NOVEMBER 2021, BROWN AND some two dozen family members rode through the streets of Wilmington in a fleet of gleaming black cars. A police escort cleared the way as the cortege wended its way from the corner of Sixth and Bladen to Red Cross Street, proceeding east to Pine Forest Cemetery. At the head of the procession, a white horse pulled a white hearse, which carried a handsome dove-gray casket with silver scallop-shaped hinges. A large arrangement of red roses and calla lilies lay across the top. Inside, the casket was empty, except for a jar of soil, gathered from the site where Joshua Halsey was murdered.

Brown had responded immediately to Pinnick's message. Pinnick explained that he was working with community groups to honor the victims of the 1898 massacre. "Wow!" Brown wrote on Facebook. "Thanks to Ancestry.com, my great great granddad and family may finally receive a little closure for the injustices they suffered because of their race."

Now he and Joshua's descendants had traveled from all over the country to attend the commemorations. Brown flew from New York with his teenage son and his seventy-eight-year-old mother, Joan Starks Henry. His sister Elaine Brown, a spoken-word poet, met them there. The Browns' cousin Gwendolyn Alexis came in from California, where she teaches in the African American Studies program at California State University, Fullerton. A great-granddaughter of Joshua Halsey, Alexis had learned about her ancestor's murder only after connecting with Brown, who had posted the results of a DNA test on Ancestry.com. "We're honoring the people who hid in the swamps, we're honoring the people who never came back to their homes, we're honoring so many ancestors along with our family, our blood," Alexis said. "History is on that horse-drawn carriage."

Earlier in the day, the family had loaded into rental cars and ridden from their hotel to 1898 Memorial Park to participate in a ceremony that community groups had organized in collaboration with the Equal Justice Initiative's Community Remembrance Project. The EJI has found that the work of remembering racial terror is "most impactful" when undertaken at the local level. Under the program's auspices, communities have collected soil from more than seven hundred lynching sites across the country, using it to fill jars, which are displayed at the Legacy Museum in Montgomery. The jars serve as a tangible way to represent the unresolved trauma of racial violence, situating it in the ground that we tread every day. "In this soil, there is the sweat of the enslaved," Bryan Stevenson, the executive director of the EJI, has said. "In the soil there is the blood of victims of racial violence and lynching. There are tears in the soil from all those who labored under the indignation and humiliation of segregation. But in the soil there is also the opportunity for new life, a chance to grow something hopeful and healing for the future."

The historian and racial equity consultant Lettie Gore opened the ceremony for Halsey and seven other known 1898 victims under a canvas shelter rippling in a blustery wind. "We must look at *transformative* justice, not just restorative justice," she said. "I'm not trying to restore anything to what it was years ago. No!"

Elaine Brown performed a poem she had written for the occasion, called "Joshua's Tree." Her voice was stronger than the rushing wind as she took the audience through the eras of slavery, war, Reconstruction, and Fusion, when "words like *diversity* and *inclusion* suddenly had a meaning." Having established the story's framework, Elaine zoomed in close. Her voice was still steady, but suddenly, her perspective switched, and she wasn't talking to the crowd about her ancestors anymore. She was talking to them directly, or maybe they were talking to her.

It was there that I heard my calling, like music through
The trumpet of conch shells
I heard my Grandpa Joshua!
I heard my Grandma Sallie!

Joshua Halsey's funeral procession, November 6, 2021.

[. . .] And I hear them yell
Tell our stories, tell our stories

When Elaine had finished, Gwendolyn Alexis walked to the front of the tent and performed a libations ceremony, instructing a helper to pour water from a pitcher into a glass as she read the names of the known victims of the 1898 massacre. Then, she invited the audience to shout the names of their own forebears.

"Keep it coming!" Alexis urged the crowd. "They're here with us today!"

The cortege rolled into Pine Forest Cemetery, jostling gravel. The day was gray and getting grayer, and somber emotions had begun to settle in. Joshua's descendants filed out of the shiny cars and took their seats under a blue tent, huddling under blankets as they waited for his funeral to start. In previous months, researchers with the Third Person Project, a community-driven research initiative led by the writers John Jeremiah Sullivan and Joel Finsel, had combed through the cemetery's archives and managed to pinpoint the exact spot where, in 1898, Joshua had been hastily buried in an unmarked grave. They had raised money for the casket and arranged for an impressive lineup of dignitaries to lay him properly to rest.

The event was being broadcast live on local television. Several hundred mourners jolted to attention as a female singer, accompanied only by wind rustling through pine branches, sounded the powerful first notes of "Freedom Is a Constant Struggle." A duo of pallbearers in white gloves and red fezzes escorted the jar with Joshua's name on it through the crowd and placed it next to his grave site as an honor guard stood at attention, sabers gleaming. A new granite headstone read:

JOSHUA HALSEY

BORN 1852

DIED NOV. 10, 1898

HUSBAND TO SALLIE

FATHER TO MARY, SUSAN, SATIRA, AND BESSIE

NEVER FORGOTTEN

The Reverend William Barber II had made the trip from Goldsboro to deliver the eulogy. The rain was starting to come down, and a few speakers were struck from the program in concession to the worsening weather, but Barber was in no mood to rush through a tribute so long delayed. The reason it was raining, he said, citing Genesis 4, was that when a person dies through injustice his blood cries out from the ground. "The blood of Joshua Halsey still cries, and the question is, can we hear it?" Barber asked.

He presented Joshua's murder as a sort of political whodunit. "Joshua was murdered by a system," Barber said, reminding the crowd that it was "not some insane folk" who were responsible for the crime, but rather the leading lights of a political party, the government, the church, the military, and the press. "We cannot have a normal funeral, as though he and others died a normal death, ordained by God," he proclaimed. "I'm telling you this history 'cause we need to know who was killed, say his name . . ."

Joshua Halsey!

Barber's voice grew hoarse as he worked to a crescendo. "All the people invested in greed killed him," he said. "All the people invested in lies killed him. All the people invested in racism killed him." This was not an abstract indictment, Barber noted. Unless people called out their elected officials on voter suppression, on the resegregation of schools, on police violence, on environmental injustice, on mass incarceration, they would continue to send the lowest citizens on the ladder of race and class to early graves. Barber thundered, "I'm here to tell you that what killed Joshua is still alive today!"

It had taken 123 years, but an unearthing was happening. The soil was churning, the truth coming out in the site where Joshua's body had been laid in the ground. Barber urged the crowd to "do something more than just stand out in the rain and hold hands." A ceremony wasn't enough. "The only way to honor Joshua and all of those who were murdered like him is to understand we don't heal because we have a funeral," he said. "We heal because we listen to their voices. We heal when we hear the blood still crying." He was listening to the blood, he declared, and he knew exactly what it was saying: "*Don't y'all do this again.*"

IT HAD BEEN AN INTENSE DAY FOR NATE BROWN, FULL OF OBLIGATIONS, introductions, and the logistics of herding a large family to back-to-back events. It had been complicated emotionally, too, attempting to come to terms with the murder of a relative he'd never known while shouldering the collective needs of a city where he'd never lived. After the funeral, camera crews and community stakeholders had followed Nate and his family to the place where Joshua was killed and to the site of the Halseys' former home. "We took pictures in there, but it was just starting to seep into me what was going on in 1898," Nate recalled.

He needed a breather now. Something was pulling him away from the crowd, so he drove from Pine Forest to the Cape Fear River, the other natural boundary of the 1898 violence. He parked his car, Wilmington at his back, and stared out at the horizon. "I watched that deep, raging river," he said. "Black water raging that way, and I just imagined that night in November 1898, what that community was going through, that unimaginable terror. In some ways, Joshua might have suffered the least—out in the cold, racists is chasing you, you've got to choose between the cemetery and that horrible river. It was the spookiest thing I've ever seen, first going to the funeral and then watching that water rage like that. There was no peace. It just seemed like the spirits were talking. And I was listening."

What he heard was that the fear was unforgettable. He heard pain, but he didn't hear shame. He heard the banged-up, enduring pride of people who didn't have any hope and found some nonetheless.

"If you asked me if I wanted to be a descendant of Joshua, or a descendant of one of these famous people who did this?" he said. "It's Joshua by a million years."

Chapter 53

THE INVOICE

Twenty years ago, in 2006, *The 1898 Wilmington Race Riot Report* called on the North Carolina legislature to fund reparations for "the long-term economic disadvantages created by banishment, loss of civil service positions, and intimidation." Specifically, the report recommended that the state support legal efforts to compensate the documented heirs of 1898 victims—people like Nate Brown and his family. The report also called on the legislature to provide tax incentives to attract minority-owned businesses to the neighborhoods where the massacre took place and to encourage Black homeownership in the same areas by acquiring abandoned properties and selling them to low-income residents on guaranteed mortgages. Nearly two decades later, these forms of redress have not come to fruition, and 1898 remains one of the most flagrant cases of unrepaired racial injustice in American history.

The Duke University economist William A. Darity Jr. and the folklorist A. Kirsten Mullen have identified three instances, between 1993 and 2005, in which compensation for injustice against Black Americans "was pursued through different governing bodies to some level of success." In Florida in 1994, the state legislature awarded payments of $150,000 apiece to nine survivors of the 1923 Rosewood massacre and set up a separate fund that offered small payments and scholarships to direct descendants. In 1999, a court ordered the US Department of Agriculture to settle a racial discrimination lawsuit brought by Black farmers: the total payout to around sixteen thousand claimants eventually amounted to about a billion dollars. In 2005, the state of Virginia offered scholarships to around sixty of the two thousand Black adults who were denied an opportunity to pursue their educations when Prince Edward County chose to close its school system for five years rather than to comply with *Brown*.

Darity and Mullen include Wilmington and Tulsa in a "bill of particulars" for reparations, enumerating such crimes as slavery, Jim Crow, the exclusion of Black veterans from GI Bill benefits and many Black workers from New Deal programs, redlining, and continuing discrimination. They contend that local efforts will not suffice to untangle "the complex web of harms imposed on black Americans," whose median household net worth, in 2016, amounted to only one tenth of that of their white counterparts. (Black people working full-time had *lower* median net worth than unemployed white people.) In searching for an appropriate form of reparations, Darity and Mullen emphasize restitution over atonement. Specifically, they propose a fourteen-trillion-dollar, congressionally mandated program of direct payments to citizens who have identified as Black for at least twelve years and can show that at least one of their ancestors was enslaved in the United States. "Laissez-faire or piecemeal reparations may assuage individual guilt but cannot meet the collective national obligation," they write. "The invoice for reparations must go to the nation's government."

Ta-Nehisi Coates argued persuasively more than a decade ago, "Reparations—by which I mean the full acceptance of our collective biography and its consequences—is the price we must pay to see ourselves squarely." Two survivors of the Tulsa massacre were still living well into 2025. One of them, Viola Fletcher, had spent her 109th birthday in a courtroom, seeking to hold the city and the state responsible for the terror that she had survived as a seven-year-old, passing heaps of dead bodies and watching a white man blow a Black man's head off as family fled in a horse-and-buggy. "I live through the massacre every day," she told a congressional committee.

She remembered Greenwood, as it had been and as it might have been, with undiminished pride:

> On May 31, 1921, I went to bed in my family's home in the Greenwood neighborhood of Tulsa. The neighborhood I fell asleep in that night was rich—not just in terms of wealth, but in culture, community, and heritage. My family had a beautiful home. We had great neighbors and I had friends to play with. I felt safe. I had everything a child could need. I had a bright future ahead of me. Greenwood could have given me the chance to truly make it in this country.

Her testimony underscored the urgency of redress and has helped to make the stakes of an abstract-seeming conversation undeniably concrete, but she died in November 2025 without seeing justice done.

According to a 2022 poll, only 30 percent of Americans agree that the descendants of American slavery should be compensated in cash or land. Support for reparations varies dramatically along racial lines, with more than 77 percent of Black Americans approving of them, versus only 18 percent of white Americans. Every year from 1989 until his resignation in 2017, Representative John Conyers Jr. of Michigan introduced a bill, HR 40, to establish a commission to study reparations and recommend "appropriate remedies." Every year, the bill died without a vote. President Barack Obama kept his distance from the issue. A few years ago, he described it as "a nonstarter" and "potentially counterproductive," citing "the politics of white resistance and resentment" during his presidency. In 2021, following the Black Lives Matter protests, the House Judiciary Committee finally voted to advance Conyers's bill for consideration, but it was not brought to the floor for a vote. (The legislation was reintroduced in 2025, but no real progress has been made.)

In the absence of sweeping national legislation, activists pursued local redress in about a hundred efforts around the country. In 2021, the city of Evanston, Illinois, for example, established a Restorative Housing Program offering twenty-five thousand dollars to Black residents who can show that they or their direct ancestors lived there between 1919 and 1969. (In 2024, a group of non-Black residents filed a class-action lawsuit alleging racial discrimination.) California's reparations task force issued a hefty report proposing more than a hundred different policies, while universities such as Georgetown and Harvard have dedicated funds to reckon with their involvement in enslavement and exploitation. Yet for every patchwork repair, another tear in the fabric of racial justice appears. In North Carolina, after the city of Asheville empowered a reparations committee to make "short-, medium-, and long-term recommendations that will make significant progress toward repairing the damage caused by public and private systemic racism," the Republican-controlled state legislature passed a bill banning public school teachers from suggesting that "an individual, solely by virtue of his or her race or sex, bears responsibility for actions committed in the past." In other words, by discussing reparations in the classroom, a North Carolina teacher could risk his job.

Even though experts see Wilmington as one of the nation's most obvious candidates for local reparations, activists have had a hard time making headway. After winning a billion dollars' redress for Black farmers, the defense attorney Johnnie Cochran Jr. and other prominent Black lawyers and academics planned to bring a class-action lawsuit, seeking compensation for slavery, against the United States government. A delegation from Wilmington met with him in Washington, D.C., on September 10, 2001, to discuss the possibility of incorporating the claims of 1898 descendants. The next day, the Twin Towers fell, and in the ensuing jingoistic atmosphere, the lawsuit fell by the wayside.

In 2020, the Wilmington chapter of Coming to the Table, a national organization working for racial reconciliation, created a Change.org petition seeking reparation for "historical violence" against Black people in New Hanover County. "My 2nd great grandpa paid the ultimate price," Elaine Brown wrote. "Put some respect on his name." Two months earlier, the petition to change the name of Hugh MacRae Park had proved highly effective, garnering eighteen thousand signatures, but this one languished with less than fifteen hundred. The city council of Wilmington, Delaware, launched a reparations task force in 2022, but no such effort exists in Wilmington, North Carolina.

Funding possibilities are clearly there, if the political will could be summoned. In 2020, the New Hanover County board of commissioners made the controversial decision to sell the county's publicly owned hospital to Novant, a "super-regional" care system, resulting in the creation of the New Hanover Community Endowment, which now controls more than a billion dollars intended to benefit the community in four areas, including health and social equity. The deal was unpopular in the Black community. One racial justice advocate even surmised that the county had only announced the surprise renaming of Hugh MacRae Park in order to draw attention away from the hospital vote. The endowment, which had disbursed over a hundred million dollars by the end of 2024, is controlled by a board of thirteen appointees. Only two are Black, while several white members have family ties to 1898 participants. The endowment has promised "transformative systemic change"—so far, reparations for 1898 have not figured into its plans, but there's no reason they couldn't.

Even as formal campaigns for reparations in Wilmington have sputtered, individuals have tried to compensate. One white Wilmington woman finally got rid of a framed document that her husband had inherited, detailing the sale of a little boy. "I took it and I broke it into pieces and said, 'Now you're free,'" she recalled. This was a nice fantasy, but it entailed no actual repair. Other efforts, if equally small-scale, have been more substantive. Working with Cynthia Brown, Lucy McCauley, a Texas-based great-granddaughter of William Berry McKoy, a White Government Union leader, used inheritance money she received from the sale of her family home to set up the Howe Scholarship Endowment. The fund honors Alfred "Fred" Howe, who built the house, and provides an annual award of fifteen hundred dollars to a Black student in the building arts and sciences. "I'm committed to ensuring that the lying stops in my generation," McCauley wrote.

"I have a hard time accepting diversity as a synonym for justice," Angela Davis once said. Similarly, individual acts of atonement, repayment, or generosity, however worthwhile, can never settle America's debt to its Black citizens. A million-dollar check that a marketing entrepreneur wrote to Viola Fletcher and her fellow Tulsa survivors allowed her to move out of a one-bedroom apartment and into a comfortable nursing home, but it was a capitalist response to an existential dilemma of American democracy. Checkbooks and scholarships are salves, not long-term solutions, and philanthropy cannot offset the fiduciary and moral abdication of the federal government. Only the state's acknowledgment and action can begin to meaningfully resolve racial injustice at scale, because the state created it.

CHAPTER 54

YOU KNOW THE WAY

The handmade signs keep appearing. They go up as if by magic, nailed to a telephone pole or a tree trunk in the middle of a field. They are simple in aesthetic and message, color-blocked boards bearing primordial truths. They speak with the confidence of the Greek chorus, commenting on the moral implications of long-running American dramas of dispossession, discrimination, and denial. "1898 WAR CRIME." "ANCIENT CAPE FEAR." "FIRST PEOPLE." "SOMETHING HAPPENED."

The man who puts them up is named Marvin Graham, a general contractor and organic farmer. Graham fertilizes the old-fashioned way, using rotting fish heads. He goes by the nickname Chief Watcoosa, honoring a leader of the Cape Fear Indians, who were driven from their land by Colonel Maurice Moore in 1715 and from whom he descends. His African ancestors were brought from Barbados and enslaved on area plantations: Old Town, Pleasant Oaks, Clarendon. Graham grew up on the outskirts of Old Town Plantation, one of the old land grant estates, on a secluded part of an eight-hundred-acre tract that is owned by the MacRae family's Oleander Company. "It don't take no rocket scientist to figure out if the people still living in the land where the land was conquered, they the ancient people," he said. "See, we've been here for millennia."

One chilly, damp day, Graham was out in the woods checking up on Moore's Chapel AME Zion Church, where Black people living in the Old Town community gathered to worship from 1874 to the 1980s. Preservation groups have called attention to the church's historical significance, but today the building is weathered and dilapidated, with broken boards collapsing into the void where a church bell used to ring. Graham thinks a TV crew made off with it when they shot a pilot there in 1998. Dressed in jeans, an ocher work jacket, and a red bandanna, he picked his way through trash and weeds and stepped gingerly into the sanctuary. "I was told it was going to be a pot of gold, but that's not what it was, because they put a hole in the floor," he said.

Farther back on the property lies a burial ground that holds the remains of generations of his ancestors. Graham led the way to an iron gate flanked by a pair of brick pillars topped with eagles carved in stone. OLD TOWN, 1664, the inscription read. He said that his family had enjoyed free access to the cemetery until sometime in the 1980s. "We had a key, but then the elders died and things went downhill," he recalled. In 2010, members of several local families banded together and petitioned the Oleander Company for access. "Let us go back and reclaim our love[d] ones," read a letter that one of Graham's cousins wrote. Fourteen years later, Graham said, the family has not received a response from the MacRaes. (Nelson MacRae said that he recently donated fifty thousand dollars to Bethlehem Missionary Baptist, a Black church near the plantation, and that he has always granted access to Old Town graveyard, unless the person asking has "anterior motives, wants to cause destruction, or wants to see something other than the graveyard." The property, he noted, has a conservation easement that limits any future development. He added, "If one letter slipped through the cracks, there are dozens who have been given access to that property. Whoever wants to schedule a visit to the graveyard, they will be admitted—all they need to do is ask permission.")

The distinction between history and current events, then and now, seemed to Graham so superfluous as to defy demarcation. "When you talk about '1898 war crime,' that's not only 1898, you've got to back that thing up now," he said. "Anytime you tamper with history, that's a war crime, OK?" The city had recently ordered him to stop his guerrilla sign campaign or face a fine. "When truth comes on the scene, everybody gets scared," he said. He was undeterred. "These are the signs of the times! We had to jump out of the history books right into the future."

COMMEMORATIONS OF THE 125TH ANNIVERSARY OF 1898 STRETCHED OVER the better part of a month. Downtown, outside the old Wilmington Light Infantry building, a marker finally went up, acknowledging it as the meeting point of the white mob. A calendar published by the New Hanover County Office of Diversity and Equity listed film screenings, panel discussions, a pastoral luncheon, a racial equity and trauma training, an art exhibition, a symphony concert, a tree planting, and an urban hike. At a "Movie and a Mixer" event, residents could preview clips from *Wilmington on Fire: Chapter II*, Chris Everett's new documentary, and dance until midnight "to tunes from DJ Disc Pistol, aka Kieran Haile, a descendant of Alexander Manly."

Haile, who lives in Los Angeles, had first come to Wilmington at the invitation of organizers in 2021. "Part of me was afraid that there's just going to be someone with a shotgun at the airport ready for me, like the town is still on a high alert for that damn Manly, you know?" he said. But he'd been warmly welcomed, and he and other relatives now made the pilgrimage to Wilmington each November. "It's difficult to wrap your head around the fact that, yes, things that happened over a hundred years ago affect us today, right now," he said. "My family and others lost a lot of property and generational wealth just because of this event, and so there's a growing effort to try and see some of that return to those families."

Since the first major commemoration of 1898, twenty-five years earlier, the tenor of the conversation had become more heterogeneous and more human, in the sense that it acknowledged a gamut of meanings and emotions, rather than seeking anodyne consensus. Wilmingtonians were starting to connect the dots between the long run-up to 1898, the events themselves, and their prolific afterlife. In 2022, at ninety-three, Dr. Bertha Boykin Todd—a former Williston and Hoggard librarian and assistant principal who served as a crucial liaison between administrators and students during the Gregory church siege—published a memoir about her work with the 1898 Centennial Foundation. "We couldn't even say the word 'massacre' then," she recalled. At one of her book signings, local officials got to talking with former Williston students who had been abruptly transferred to New Hanover and Hoggard. The conversation inspired the city, the county, and the school district to organize a "legacy graduation" for the Williston High School classes of 1969 and 1970. More than 150 septuagenarians showed up, decked out in maroon robes and mortarboards and gold stoles, to finally claim their diplomas from "the Greatest School Under the Sun."

On the morning of November 9, 2023, for the 125th anniversary of the massacre and coup, city officials laid a wreath of white chrysanthemums, purple statice, and mauve roses at the foot of the 1898 Memorial. A purple sash bore a message written in gold glitter: IN LOVING MEMORY OF LIVES LOST IN THE 1898 MASSACRE. Two days later, *The Wilmington Journal*, in a precarious financial state but forging on, sponsored an 1898 symposium and essay contest at Williston Middle School. It was emceed by Cash Michaels, a *Journal* writer whose reporting was instrumental in securing pardons for the Wilmington Ten. A power cut dimmed the auditorium and silenced the microphones, but no one had trouble hearing the Reverend William Barber pray for the birth of another Fusion movement.

Meg MacRae was on tour with Pantera and unable to attend the commemoration, but, earlier that day, her half brother Hugh MacRae III—alongside descendants of William R. Kenan Sr. and Walker Taylor, as well as descendants of Black 1898 families—quietly ducked into a small-group conversation that community activists had organized to "facilitate racial healing" in Wilmington. "At first I wasn't going to go, but I told myself, 'It's just three hours on a Saturday morning and 1898 isn't going anywhere,'" Hugh III said. "Hopefully, over the last five to ten years, I've become more of a listener, rather than reacting to folks that have different political opinions."

Over at St. Mark's, Nate Brown presented "The Story of Joshua Halsey and His Descendants," a survey of his genealogy work in more than seventy slides. "The research is difficult, but it is also a labor of love," he said.

"My dream is that one day all of the 1898 descendants will have access to their story." At the end of the presentation, he invited his mother to join him in singing her favorite song, the Mello Harps' "Love Is a Vow." The song played as Brown delivered his conclusions. "The Halsey story is one of survival," the final slide declared, lingering on the screen. "We Halseys refuse to lay down and die. We RISE!"

CYNTHIA BROWN WAS ABSENT FROM THE COMMEMORATIONS. SHE WAS suffering from pancreatic cancer, and even as she'd maintained hope and a positive attitude and the tiring work of giving interviews and talking to schoolchildren and meeting with documentarians and attending webinars and getting on the phone with anyone who needed to know something about 1898, she just wasn't up to it. Her care at Novant had been chaotic, and she had been traveling back and forth to Durham for months for chemo appointments. "I will probably look like I'm from Wakanda, head wrap and all," she joked. "My hair is really coming out now, but I'm OK with it." She had milestones of all kinds on her mind. She texted a friend, "Who

Cynthia Brown at Pine Forest Cemetery, September 2020.

knows the ways of life . . . only that we won't be here forever. I had hoped for a longer stretch of good health, but a sixty-seventh birthday and a fortieth wedding anniversary last month may have been the portion the heavens allotted me. That said, I plan to fight. I want more out of life."

Cynthia died on Thanksgiving Day. Her family celebrated her life in front of a packed house at St. Stephen. Her husband, an aunt, and three of her longtime friends gave eulogies, remembering her service to the community and her passion for history. Her family also invited Lucy McCauley, the white descendant who founded the Howe Scholarship Endowment, to speak. "Over the last year of her life, Cynthia Brown planted many seeds for the future," McCauley said. She added that the "gift of her friendship changed me," and that "with her abiding wish to help heal ancestral wounds, she transformed my sense of what was possible." After the service, the family buried Cynthia at Pine Forest Cemetery, where she lies surrounded by her ancestors going all the way back to Anthony Walker and Tenah Howe.

One recent evening, her son PJ, a mail carrier and photographer, was driving home after a rough day at work. He felt something pulling him downtown, to the 1898 Memorial. When he got out of the car, the sun was going down and it was quiet. He wasn't sure, exactly, why he had come. But standing there, in front of the memorial that his grandfather had paid to help erect, to commemorate an event that his mother had dedicated herself to transmitting to another generation, just felt right. He explained, "It's like she's still here, if that makes sense."

PJ plans to continue his mother's work. Until she lost her strength, she was pulling out boxes, plying him with photographs and papers. "It's almost like she was trying to prepare me," he said. "I think she wanted to make sure that there were tangible things that I can read and kind of soak myself in. She told me, 'I don't want you to feel like you have to do exactly what I did, or do it the way that I did it. Because you have to do it in a way that's authentically you.'"

At Brown's funeral, the pastor read from the opening verses of John 14, the chapter in which Jesus beckons the disciples to his Father's house of many rooms. "And if I go and prepare a place for you, I will come again and receive you to myself: that where I am, there you may be also," Jesus promises, jogging among tenses. "And where I go, you know, and the way you know." The verse was perfect for Cynthia, proposing a sort of temporal trinity uniting past, present, and future—the coequal, coeternal, and consubstantial nature of history taken in its full measure.

TWO HUNDRED AND FIFTY YEARS OF NATIONHOOD CONFIRM AN ENDURing American paradox: The closer we come to perfecting the union, to realizing its foundational promise of equality, the fiercer the opposition from the part of society that prefers its democracy partial and exclusive. Pursue Reconstruction, get Jim Crow. Desegregate, be met with massive resistance. Elect a Black president, endure a white nationalist one who denies that his predecessor was born a citizen. On the other side of any era of the expansion of rights, someone is waiting to claw them back. In the historical context, it makes perfect sense that the George Floyd protests and the advances in policing, the workplace, and education that they initiated should be followed by Trump's reelection, bringing American revanchists back to power.

Wilmington presents a particularly flagrant case study in the thick American ledger of Black achievement and white backlash. Looking closely at its trajectory from incubator of Black business and political agency to hotbed of racial terror, segregationist stronghold to protest ground, putsch site to political bellwether can help us make sense of the cycles and shifts that characterize the history of the country at large. As New Hanover County undergoes demographic and political shifts, shading from reliable red into a poorly mixed purple, the city and its environs continue to serve as a critical revelator of the bigger American picture.

In 2022, the New Hanover County school district updated its curriculum, introducing a brief overview of 1898 for fourth graders: Students would "investigate the causes, the events, and the legacy of Wilmington 1898." A Republican school board member questioned the initiative, suggesting that history was "being changed and repackaged." Local conservatives railed against critical race theory, the pedagogical bugbear of the Trumpist movement, even as the school superintendent explained that CRT was not taught in the county's schools. In 2023, the school board passed a book ban, removing Jason Reynolds and Ibram X. Kendi's *Stamped: Racism, Antiracism, and You* from the classroom. The mother who brought the complaint, an adherent of the "parents' rights" movement, expressed her satisfaction: "The best solution that we have as parents, as We the People, is to opt our kids out of books en masse because that beats the activist teacher at their own game." Her complaint amounted to a contemporary White Declaration of Independence—this time, from inconvenient history.

In 2024, the Republican-led school board voted to oust Dr. Charles Foust, the district's first Black superintendent, who had been hired in the summer of 2020. A few months earlier, William Buster, the Black CEO of the New Hanover County Endowment, had abruptly resigned barely two years into his tenure. Protesting Foust's firing in an open letter, a group of Black residents acknowledged that their opponents were likely to accuse them of "playing the race card." So be it, they wrote—race was as much at play in these developments as it had been in every era of the city's history. One signatory asked, "When you see things happen, what is the reaction supposed to be when you lived through those experiences, when you lived through the Wilmington Ten, when you lived through Richard Nixon [sending] in federal troops because there are riots in the streets?"

In 2024, complying with a mandate from the right-leaning UNC board of governors, UNCW eliminated its Office of Institutional Diversity and Inclusion, which had used discretionary funds to support research into 1898 at the school. In 2025, the National Endowment for the Humanities did not renew a grant that had brought middle- and high-school educators to the university for a two-week-long seminar about teaching the coup and massacre, to glowing reviews. (None of the twenty projects chosen for next year mentioned "race" in their title; three were about Shakespeare.) Kimi Faxon Hemingway, a senior lecturer at UNCW who has worked on 1898-related projects, observed that enthusiasm about teaching 1898 had given way to caution and even subterfuge in grant applications and on syllabi. She explained, "I think people are still teaching 1898 in the safest way they can, which is to not say what it is."

The George Davis statue that watched over downtown Wilmington for more than a century resurfaced in Davidson County at Valor Memorial Park, a private venture devoted to resurrecting monuments that were pried off their pedestals during the 2020 racial justice movements. With Trump's reelection, the secretive firings and replacements have escalated into the unapologetic and outright gutting of programs designed to foster inclusion. As DOGE slashed the federal civil service and Trump called on the Secretary of the Interior to purge American cultural institutions of programs that "divide Americans based on race," local activists gathered at the 1898 Memorial with placards reading STOP THE COUP.

Savvy to the ways of white supremacy, Wilmingtonians have found ways to challenge the latest drive for suppression and erasure. In November 2024, just a week after Trump's victory, William Buster announced that he had taken a job as lead consultant to the Wilmington 1898 Museum for Healing, Education, and Democracy—a new museum "dedicated to preserving the history of the Wilmington massacre and coup, educating the public about its significance, and being a vehicle for community healing around this event and its subsequent impacts through history until the present." Founded and funded by Leigh Carter, a white Wilmington native and trauma therapist, the multimillion-dollar project aims to open in 2028. Carter has hired Zena Howard, the architect who managed the design of the Smithsonian's National Museum of African American History and Culture in Washington, D.C.—the "Blacksonian"—to design it on land at Third and Davis, across the street from 1898 Memorial Park, with the ambition of creating a "world-class" institution. "We want this history to be truly integrated into the fabric and consciousness of Wilmington so that we can really know and understand ourselves and have meaningful dialogue and problem solving discussions from a place of solid historical data," Carter said.

Wilmington provides crucial context for understanding what is happening in America—the audacious and brutal grab-back of a once-defeated regime. Just as Wilmington's white elite lost a war, seethed under Reconstruction, plotted Redemption, and exacted revenge in 1898 and far beyond, the white nationalists of 2026 are nurturing a narrative of victimhood to justify physical, political, economic, and environmental violence whose consequences will be felt for years to come. Armed with an accurate, expansive, and long-range understanding of what came before, and the ways it affects us still today, we can prepare for the battles coming down the line. Truth heals, but it can also fight.

Acknowledgments

To conceive, report, and write this book took nearly ten years, during which I've stretched in every sense to make its ambition commensurate to its subject. At times I wondered if I'd taken on more than I could manage. Colleagues, friends, family, and complete strangers pulled me through at each such moment, and it's these encounters that have immeasurably enriched my life over the past decade, as well as this work.

Where to begin? At the beginning, why not. Ann Godoff trusted me to take on a subject that couldn't have had less to do with my previous book. Scott Moyers gave of his time and wisdom. Ginny Smith saw the manuscript to completion with kindness and verve. Iris Chen was a superstar in all the areas that I am not, while Claire Leonard managed the legal front with calm aplomb. Thank you to Casey Denis, and to Juli Kiyan, Danielle Plafsky, and the Penguin Press design, marketing, and publicity teams for your fine work. Thank you to my agent, Elyse Cheney, and all of her colleagues at the Cheney Agency.

I stand in awe at the stores of knowledge that reside in the files and brains of the librarians and scholars who generously lent their expertise. The more arcane the question, the more exhaustive the answer. The gnarlier the deadline, the quicker the response. Thank you, Kate Collins (Duke University Libraries), Alison Dineen (Lower Cape Fear Historical Society), Lyric Grimes (Louis Round Wilson Special Collections Library, The University of North Carolina at Chapel Hill), Eliot Rambach (The American

Library of Paris), Holli Saperstein (The Wilmington Railroad Museum), Joseph Sheppard (NHCPL), Travis Souther (NHCPL), Rebecca Taylor (The Federal Point Historical Society), Alison Thurman (SANC), Matt Turi (LRWSCL), LeRae Umfleet (North Carolina Department of Natural and Cultural Resources), and Ashley Yandle (State Archives of North Carolina). Thank you, Gordon Bock, Brandon Byrd, David Cecelski, Esther Cyna, Marlene Daut, Kira Felsenfeld, Jacob Finegan, Sheila Flemming-Hunter, Glenda Gilmore, Mary Greene, John Haley Jr., Peter Hinks, Andy Horowitz, Olivia Hosken, Kenneth Janken, Vincent Lowery, William Seraille, Graham Swennes, Marcia Synott, Beverly Tetterton, Cara Ward, and Patrick Weill. Thank you to the writers of the books, the makers of the films, and the keepers of the archives, public and private, who nourished my understanding of 1898 and its long afterlife. Special thanks to Rebecca Baugnon (Center for Southeast North Carolina Archives and History Special Collections, University of North Carolina Wilmington), Samantha Crisp (CSNCAHSC), Jan Davidson (Cape Fear Museum), Gareth Evans (Bellamy Mansion Museum), Leslie Randle-Morton (BMM), and Jennifer Finley (NHCPL), who pulled one last seemingly irrecoverable citation out of a hat.

I am profoundly grateful to the participants and descendants who shared their stories with me. You are the reason this book exists, Lisa Adams, Louis Moore Bacon, Cliff Bellamy, Mary Louise Bellamy, Ira Braswell IV, the late Cynthia Brown, Nate Brown, PJ Brown, Inez Campbell-Eason, Barbara Bell Coleman, Vivian Colon, Amy Gerber-Stroh, Regina Gregory, Laurie Gunst, Kieran Haile, Luke Hankins, Joan Starks Henry, Frank H. Kenan II, Wayne Lofton, Bambi MacRae, Hugh MacRae III, Meg MacRae, Nelson MacRae, Lewin Manly Jr., Lucy McCauley, Wayne Moore, George Rountree III, Armond Scott III, Bill Sisson, Annie Gray Sprunt, David Sprunt, Lori Keith Robinson, Donna Templeton, Eugene Templeton, Willie Vereen, and Geoff Ward. Tom Keith, thank you, especially, for your humor and encouragement. Thank you all for being willing to engage, with such care and energy, when it can be easier not to. I'm honored by your confidence.

For all manner of intelligence, inspiration, and hospitality in Wilmington, thank you to Sonya Bennetone-Patrick, Anne Brennan, Oliver and Virginia Carter, Leigh Carter, Wiley Cash, Kent Chatfield, Kim Cook, Ben David, Joe Finley, Joel Finsel, Ray Funderburk, the late Philip Gerard, Lettie Gore, Marvin Graham, Cedric Harrison, Kimi Hemingway, Rachel Lewis Hilburn, Zena Howard, Joyce Jones, Irving Joyner, Betsy Kahn, James Leutze, Kevin Maurer, Deborah Dicks Maxwell, Melton McLaurin, Craig Newkirk, Dierdre Parker, Harper Peterson, Tim Pinnick, Gwenyfar Rohler, Anne Russell, Earl Sheridan, Reggie Shuford, Harriet and John Smith, John Staton, John Jeremiah Sullivan, the late Larry Thomas, Linda Thompson, the late Bertha Todd, Gary Trawick, Meade Van Pelt, Kate Woodbury, and Kellie Woodbury. Thank you, Christopher Everett, for your groundbreaking work. Thank you, Millicent Brown Fauntleroy, for helping me to see the necessity of connecting 1898 to 1971 and beyond.

At *The New Yorker*, my journalistic home of more than twenty years, I cherish working with David Remnick, Deirdre Foley-Mendelssohn, Susan Morrison, Daniel Zalewski, and Rachel Arons. I'm indebted to Daphne Brooks, Ed Caesar, Jelani Cobb, Thomas Dodman, Angela Flournoy and Ian Blair, Chris Furr, Thomas Gebremedhin, Guillaume Gendron, Patrick Keefe, Julian Lucas, Andrew Marantz, Penny Martin, Rebecca Mead, Siddhartha Mitter, Alexis Okeowo, Matt Ortile, Gary Pomerantz, Elaine Sciolino, Wright Thompson, and Lauren Williams for collegial advice and assistance. I'm grateful to Cedric Terrell for a much-needed photo update. I could never have gotten this book over the line without Helen Handelman, Katie King, and Thea Traff. It has profited especially from the exceptional talents of Sameen Gauhar and Carrie Frye.

Thank you to beloved friends Darius Aboue, Ajiri Aki, Christina Barba and Sean Mullen, Fanny Boucher, Lila Byock and Sam Shaw, Amy Campos, Sutanya Dacres, Monica de la Villardière, Poppy Harlow, Alexis and Liora Jakubowicz, Rhon Manigault-Bryant, Zoey Poll and Nicolas Maiarelli, Lindsey Tramuta, and Helen Williams Walsh.

Thank you to Violeta, Teddy, Jacques, Fabrice, Maïa, Noé, and Hugo. Thank you to Matt, Melissa, Henry, and Coco. (The library card was especially clutch!) Dad, I wish you were around to see this finally come to fruition. Mom, your unwavering support means everything. All of you have given so much so that I could see this project through. Olivier, Claudia, Louis—thank you for being by my side every day and for understanding why I needed to write this book. I hope it makes you proud.

NOTES

INTRODUCTION

xix **"Before Rosewood":** *Wilmington on Fire*, written and directed by Christopher Everett (2015; Speller Street Films).

xix **decided to write a short article:** Lauren Collins, "American Coup," *The New Yorker*, September 19, 2016.

xx **"poor man's Charleston":** William E. Schmidt, "Correspondent's Choice; A Highly Private Little Guesthouse," *New York Times*, April 28, 1985.

xx **"dreamiest places":** Lisa Cericola, "The 10 Dreamiest Places to Live in the Coastal South," *Southern Living*, May 18, 2025.

xx **snug town:** *1990 Census of Population: General Population Characteristics, North Carolina* (U.S. Government Printing Office, 1992), 7.

xx **aggressively segregated:** "Wilmington: Data for the City Area," *Diversity and Disparities Project*, American Communities Project at Brown University.

xx **forty-eight census tracts:** Census Tracts for New Hanover County, NC, Block Group 2, Tract 105.03, American Community Survey 2023, Census Reporter.

xx **live below the poverty line:** Patrick Brien et al., *Cape Fear Inclusive Economy Report* (Cape Fear Collective, 2020).

xxi **"pretty little city":** Colonel Alfred M. Waddell, "The Story of the Wilmington, North Carolina, Race Riots," *Farmer and Mechanic*, November 29, 1898.

xxi **"the heart of Black political power":** Walter Hölbling and Justine Tally, "The 1898 Wilmington Massacre in History and Literature: An Essay on the Discourse of Power," in *Black Liberation in the Americas*, ed. Fritz Gysin and Christopher Mulvey (LIT Verlag, 2001), 71–93.

xxi **explicitly chose to center:** Furnifold Simmons, "Chairman F. M. Simmons Issues a Patriotic and Able Address," *News & Observer*, November 3, 1898.

xxi **sensational articles:** Helen G. Edmonds, *The Negro and Fusion Politics in North Carolina, 1894–1901* (University of North Carolina Press, 1951), 141; "Stole Cheese: Negro Man Boldly Purloins a Cheese from in Front of the Establishment of Stevenson & Taylor," *Wilmington Messenger*, September 15, 1898.

xxi **"vampire that hovers":** Norman Ethre Jennett, "The Vampire That Hovers over North Carolina (Negro Rule)," *News & Observer*, September 27, 1898.

xxi **grotesque speech:** J. A. Holman, "Mrs. Felton Speaks," *Wilmington Morning Star*, August 12, 1898.

xxii **confronted the ultra-taboo subject:** Alexander L. Manly, "Editorial," *Daily Record*, August 18, 1898.

xxii **"Shall we surrender?":** "Sizzling Talk: The Most Remarkable Speech by the Hon. A. M. Waddell," *Wilmington Semi-Weekly Messenger*, October 28, 1898.

xxiii **"Men of large business interests":** *Wilmington Messenger*, November 11, 1898, quoted in H. Leon Prather Sr., "We Have Taken a City: A Centennial Essay," in *Democracy Betrayed: The Wilmington Race Riot of 1898 and Its Legacy*, ed. David S. Cecelski and Timothy B. Tyson (University of North Carolina Press, 1998), 31.

xxiv **restored and reinstalled:** C. J. Clemmons, "Confederate Memorial Will Rise Again Sunday," *StarNews*, August 11, 2000.

xxiv **"stunning event venue":** "Brooklyn Arts Center History," Brooklyn Arts Center & The Annex.

xxv **"bone-chillling, drizzling rain":** "Rev. Charles S. Morris Describes the Wilmington Massacre of 1898 [January 1899]," *BlackPast.org*, January 28, 2007.

xxv **lynching victims:** *Lynching in America: Confronting the Legacy of Racial Terror* (Equal Justice Initiative, 2017), 41.

xxvii **"implicated subject":** Michael Rothberg, *The Implicated Subject: Beyond Victims and Perpetrators* (Stanford University Press, 2019), 17.

xxviii **"mercy of late birth":** Rothberg, *The Implicated Subject*, 17.

xxviii **"structures, institutions, and webs of ideas":** Quoted in Rothberg, *The Implicated Subject*, 79.

xxx **"murder's best work is done after the fact":** Glenda Elizabeth Gilmore, *Gender and Jim Crow: Women and the Politics of White Supremacy in North Carolina, 1896–1920* (University of North Carolina Press, 1996), 92.

PROLOGUE

1 **not an ordinary weekday lunch:** Cynthia Brown, interview with author, August 19, 2020; C. J. Brown, *A Metamorphosis of the Soul: Lessons from My Journey on Faith, Hope, Love and Perseverance* (Westbow Press, 2014).

1 **high-flying corporate jobs:** Brown, *Metamorphosis*.

1 **Her mother's sudden death:** Cynthia Brown, interview with author, November 18, 2018.

4 **her favorite book:** Daniel J. Foley, *Christmas the World Over* (Chilton Books, 1967).

4 **"The Howes thrived":** "Mary Jane Langdon House," North Carolina Architects & Builders: A Biographical Dictionary.

5 ***"You have to know":*** Angela Mack, "Family Looks Back at Violence," *StarNews*, November 17, 2006; Phoebe Judge, host, *Criminal* podcast, episode 158, "If It Ever Happens, Run," *Vox*, February 12, 2021.

6 **"family historians":** C. J. Brown, *Metamorphosis*.

6 **thought might "make a stink":** Leslie H. Hossfeld, *Narrative, Political Unconscious, and Racial Violence in Wilmington, North Carolina* (Routledge, 2005), 95.

6 **Brown left empty-handed:** Mack, "Family Looks Back."

6 **"saved from being slaughtered":** Nada McDonald Cotton, "A Historical Incident," undated manuscript, McDonald–Howe Family Papers (SC-MS-034), box 1, folder 20, Center for Southeast North Carolina Archives and History, UNCW Library.

7 **"it's time now":** C. Brown, interview, November 18, 2018.

CHAPTER 1: THE HOWES ARISE

11 **hurricane season:** Nada R. McDonald Cotton, "Anthony Walker, an Ibo of Nigeria, Africa," The Walker–Howe Family of Wilmington, North Carolina in New Hanover County, undated, item 1, box 1, folder 22, McDonald–Howe Family Papers, SC-MS-034, Special Collections, Center for Southeast North Carolina Archives and History, UNCW Library.

12 **fifteen years old:** Peter P. Hinks, *To Awaken My Afflicted Brethren: David Walker and the Problem of Antebellum Slave Resistance* (Pennsylvania State University Press, 1996), 13.

12 **exported approximately 1.2 million:** Randy J. Sparks, *The Two Princes of Calabar: An Eighteenth-Century Atlantic Odyssey* (Harvard University Press, 2009), 39.

12 **134 human beings:** Stephen D. Behrendt and Eric J. Graham, "African Merchants, Notables and the Slave Trade at Old Calabar, 1720: Evidence from the National Archives of Scotland," *History in Africa* 30 (2003): 37–38.

12 **have been Oboto:** Cotton, "Anthony Walker"; Hinks, *To Awaken My Afflicted Brethren*, 13.

12 **"He and his playmates":** Cotton, "Anthony Walker."

12 **thousands of trees to a man:** Hinks, *To Awaken My Afflicted Brethren*, 2–3.

12 **"every crook and eddy":** James Sprunt, *Chronicles of the Cape Fear River, 1660–1916* (Edwards & Broughton Printing Co., 1916), 206, quoted in Hinks, *To Awaken My Afflicted Brethren*, 3–4.

13 **only a week after childbirth:** Jeffrey J. Crow et al., *A History of African Americans in North Carolina* (North Carolina Office of Archives and History, 1992), 17.

13 **their own time:** Jeffrey J. Crow, *The Black Experience in Revolutionary North Carolina* (North Carolina Office of Archives and History, 1977); Janet Schaw, *Journal of a Lady of Quality; Being the Narrative of a Journey from Scotland to the West Indies, North Carolina, and Portugal, in the Years 1774 to 1776*, ed. Evangeline Walker Andrews and Charles McLean Andrews (Yale University Press, 1923), 176–77.

13 **knew how to use the leftover:** Schaw, *Journal of a Lady.*

13 **remaining Native people:** David S. Cecelski, *The Waterman's Song: Slavery and Freedom in Maritime North Carolina* (University of North Carolina Press, 2001), 8.

13 **best tides:** Cecelski, *Waterman's Song*, 8.

13 **John Walker:** Cotton, "Anthony Walker"; Hinks, *To Awaken My Afflicted Brethren*, 12; William M. Reaves, *"Strength Through Struggle": The Chronological and Historical Record of the African-American Community in Wilmington, North Carolina, 1865–1950* (New Hanover County Public Library, 1998), 408.

13 **put his human possessions up for sale:** Hinks, *To Awaken My Afflicted Brethren*, 12.

13 **Howe bought Anthony:** Mary Greene, PhD, *Commissioned Research Report* (Legacy Finders, 2025).

13 **"palatial" three-story house:** *H. R. 17356, to Erect an Equestrian Statue at Wilmington, N.C., to the Memory of Maj. Gen. Robert Howe, of the American Revolution*, House of Representatives (Speech of Hon. John D. Bellamy of North Carolina), February 14, 1903, 3; William McKee Evans, *Ballots and Fence Rails: Reconstruction on the Lower Cape Fear* (University of Georgia Press, 2004), 7.

13 **educated in England:** Alan D. Watson et al., *Harnett, Hooper & Howe: Revolutionary Leaders of the Lower Cape Fear* (L. T. Moore Memorial Commission, Lower Cape Fear Historical Society, 1979), 94.

13 **"in affluence":** J. D. Bellamy, *H. R. 17356.*

13 **high-strung man; highest-ranking officer:** Charles E. Bennett and Donald R. Lennon, *A Quest for Glory: Major General Robert Howe and the American Revolution* (University of

North Carolina Press, 1991), 1, 71; Philip Ranlet, "Loyalty in the Revolutionary War: General Robert Howe of North Carolina," *Historian* 53, no. 4 (1991): 725–27.

13 **Continental Army:** Ranlet, "Loyalty in the Revolutionary War"; Bennett and Lennon, *A Quest for Glory*, 71.

13 **"the worst character":** Schaw, *Journal of a Lady*, 167.

13 **tar and feather:** Schaw, *Journal of a Lady*, 191.

14 **help from local accomplices:** Crow et al., *A History of African Americans*, 38.

14 **"repair the barns":** Cotton, "Anthony Walker."

14 **hired him out:** "Cotton, "Anthony Walker"; Reaves, *Strength Through Struggle*, 408; Watson et al., *Harnett, Hooper & Howe*, 71.

14 **not marry freely:** James A. Padgett, "The Status of Slaves in Colonial North Carolina," *Journal of Negro History* 14, no. 3 (1929): 325.

14 **Tuscarora Nation:** Thomas C. Parramore et al., "Tuscarora People," *Encyclopedia of North Carolina* (University of North Carolina Press, 2006).

14 **separated from her family:** Reaves, *Strength Through Struggle*, 408.

14 **"buy her as his wife":** Reaves, *Strength Through Struggle*, 409.

15 **technically in bondage:** James Howard Brewer, "Legislation Designed to Control Slavery in Wilmington and Fayetteville," *North Carolina Historical Review* 30, no. 2 (1953): 162.

15 **in the legal sense:** Greene, *Commissioned Research Report.*

15 **rice, indigo, tobacco:** Alfred Moore Waddell, *A History of New Hanover County and the Lower Cape Fear Region: 1723–1800* (self-published, 1909), 1:205–6; "NC.NEW.166.17880618.2.1646," Digital Library on American Slavery.

15 **ruining a silk shoe:** Schaw, *Journal of a Lady*, 145.

15 **small but prolific free Black community:** Richard C. Rohrs, "The Free Black Experience in Antebellum Wilmington, North Carolina: Refining Generalizations About Race Relations," *Journal of Southern History* 78, no. 3 (2012): 615–38.

15 **They worked alongside:** See Catherine Bishir's discussion of free Black builders in North Carolina, "Black Builders in Antebellum North Carolina," *North Carolina Historical Review* 61, no. 4 (1984): 447.

16 **fraught position:** John Hope Franklin, *The Free Negro in North Carolina 1790–1860* (University of North Carolina Press, 1943), 130.

16 **"status of these people":** Charles W. Chesnutt, "The Free Colored People of North Carolina," *Southern Workman* 31, no. 3 (1902).

16 **fearing the liberating influence:** Franklin, *The Free Negro*, 130; The Federal Writers' Project, *Slave Narratives: A Folk History of Slavery in the United States from Interviews with Former Slaves* (Library of Congress, 1941), 4.

16 **state's most prosperous:** Rohrs, "The Free Black Experience," 616.

16 **fellow carpenters:** Rohrs, "The Free Black Experience," 623; David S. Cecelski, *The Fire of Freedom: Abraham Galloway & the Slaves' Civil War* (University of North Carolina Press, 2015), 7–8.

16 **"same privilege":** New Hanover Co. NC, Superior Court, New Hanover County, NC General Index to Deeds, 1729–1954 & Deeds, 1734–1939; Deed from E. C. Bettencourt to A. Howe, image 456; database and images, FamilySearch, Deeds v. TT-UU, 1864–1867.

16 **only Southern state:** Irving Joyner, "Challenging Voting Rights and Political Participation in State Courts," *The Scholar: St. Mary's Law Review on Race and Social Justice* 21, no. 2 (2019): 237.

16 **"regulated by condition":** Chesnutt, "The Free Colored People."

16 **Black political consciousness:** Cecelski, *Fire of Freedom*, 7.

16 **abolitionist David Walker:** Hinks, *To Awaken My Afflicted Brethren*, 9–10.

16 **mother was free:** Hinks, *To Awaken My Afflicted Brethen*, 10; David Walker, *Walker's Appeal, in Four Articles; Together with a Preamble, to the Colored Citizens of the World but in Particular, and Very Expressly, to Those of the United States of America* (self-published, 1830).
17 **"more profitable":** Thomas Jefferson to John Wayles Eppes, June 30, 1820, Jefferson Quotes & Family Letters, The Thomas Jefferson Foundation.
17 **forced a son to beat his mother:** Imani Perry, *South to America: A Journey Below the Mason-Dixon Line to Understand the Soul of a Nation* (HarperCollins, 2022), 121.
17 **vowed to escape:** Walker, *Walker's Appeal*; Clement Eaton, "A Dangerous Pamphlet in the Old South," *Journal of Southern History* 2, no. 3 (1936): 327.
17 **"first sustained written assault upon slavery":** Herbert Aptheker, *One Continual Cry: David Walker's Appeal to the Colored Citizens of the World* (Humanities Press, 1965), 54.
17 **to be heard in Wilmington:** Marshall Rachleff, "David Walker's Southern Agent," *Journal of Negro History* 62, no. 1 (1977): 100–103; Cecelski, *Fire of Freedom*, 10.
17 **sixty copies:** Eaton, "A Dangerous Pamphlet," 469.
17 **"startling the land":** Philip S. Foner and Yuval Taylor, eds., *Frederick Douglass: Selected Speeches and Writings* (Chicago Review Press, 1999), 662.
17 **galvanized Black people:** Lori Leavell, "'NOT INTENDED EXCLUSIVELY FOR THE SLAVE STATES': Antebellum Recirculation of David Walker's 'Appeal,'" *Callaloo* 38, no. 3 (2015): 684; Eaton, "A Dangerous Pamphlet," 323.
18 **became a Union spy:** Cecelski, *Fire of Freedom*, 7, 43, 211.
18 **David Walker's father:** Hinks, *To Awaken My Afflicted Brethren*, 12–13.
18 **"*beasts of burden*":** Walker, *Walker's Appeal.*
18 **prospering patriarch:** Reaves, *Strength Through Struggle*, 409.

CHAPTER 2: THOSE PESTIFEROUS MOORES

19 **arrived in South Carolina:** L. H. Roper, "Moore, James, Sr.," *South Carolina Encyclopedia*, June 8, 2016; James M. Clifton, "Moore, Alfred," William S. Powell, ed., *Dictionary of North Carolina Biography* (University of North Carolina Press, 1991).
19 **thrived in his new environs:** John Kenneth Davis, *Patriarch of the Lower Cape Fear: Governor James Moore & Descendants* (New Hanover County Public Library, 2006), 2.
19 **Indian trade:** "Chapter I: Colonial Dames of America," in *Ancestorial Records and Portraits* (Grafton Press, 1910), 396–97; Bradley Joseph Dixon, "Surveys of Ambition: Indians, Carolina, and Empire, 1700–1715" (MA thesis, North Carolina State University, 2013).
19 **"most unjust warrs upon ye Indians":** Dixon, "Surveys of Ambition," 37.
19 **"plundering, raping, and murdering":** John Jay TePaske, *The Governorship of Spanish Florida, 1700–1763* (Duke University Press, 1964), 196–97.
20 **"largely illegal rush":** Robert Olwell and Alan Tully, eds., *Cultures and Identities in Colonial British America* (Johns Hopkins University Press, 2006), 56.
20 **eighty thousand acres:** Hinks, *To Awaken My Afflicted Brethren*, 2.
20 **leading enslavers were their kin:** Olwell and Tully, *Cultures and Identities*, 61.
20 **Stamp Act:** Maurice Moore, *The Justice and Policy of Taxing the American Colonies in Great-Britain* (self-published, 1765).
20 **reigned from Orton:** James Laurence Sprunt, *The Story of Orton Plantation* (self-published, 1958), 2–3.
20 **"loop-holed for fire arms":** Louis Toomer Moore, *Stories Old and New of the Cape Fear Region* (Louis T. Moore Memorial Fund, 1968), 14.

20 **"Orton rapidly became":** L. T. Moore, *Stories Old and New*, 14.
20 **scrappy Patriot force:** Dr. Chris E. Fonvielle Jr., "The 1776 Battle of Moores Creek Bridge," *Salt Magazine*, n.d.
21 **first American Moore—to the Supreme Court:** Clifton, "Moore, Alfred."
21 **returned home to Moorefields:** H. G. Jones, "Moorefields: National Register of Historic Places Inventory—Nomination Form," State of North Carolina Department of Archives and History, January 25, 1972; Alfred Moore Waddell, *Some Memories of My Life* (Edwards & Broughton Printing Company, 1908), 7.
21 **His own great-grandson:** "National Register of Historic Places Inventory—Nomination Form 10-300: Moorefields," United States Department of the Interior National Park Service, State Department of Archives and History, Raleigh, NC.
21 **born at Moorefields:** Waddell, *Some Memories*, 7.
21 **across Moorefields's expanses:** Waddell, *Some Memories*, 7–8.
21 **exaggeration upon overstatement:** Waddell, *Some Memories*, 11, 20–21.
22 **studied law privately:** Kent McCoury, "Alfred Moore Waddell (1834–1912)," *North Carolina History Project*.
22 **"Boston to New Orleans":** Waddell, *Some Memories*, 18–19.
22 **something of a sophisticate:** Waddell, *Some Memories*, 25, 35, 61.
22 **giver of jocular nicknames:** Waddell, *Some Memories*, 25, 61, 95.
22 **"old 'stamping ground'":** Waddell, *Some Memories*, 39.

CHAPTER 3: THE BELLAMYS BUILD

24 **a ridiculous house:** Catherine W. Bishir, "Urban Slavery at Work: The Bellamy Mansion Compound, Wilmington, North Carolina," *Buildings & Landscapes: Journal of the Vernacular Architecture Forum* 17, no. 2 (2010): 15–16.
24 **"a blue umbrella":** Diane Cobb Cashman, *The History of the Bellamy Mansion* (self-published, 1989), 25.
24 **first American John Bellamy:** Cashman, *History of the Bellamy Mansion*, 11–12; John D. Bellamy, *Memoirs of an Octogenarian* (Observer Printing House, 1942), 1–2.
25 **"culture and wealth":** J. D. Bellamy, *Memoirs of an Octogenarian*, 2.
25 **"from Murrell's Inlet":** Cashman, *History of the Bellamy Mansion*, 14.
25 **The will named:** Cashman, *History of the Bellamy Mansion*, 13–15; John Bellemee, will dated September 23, 1824, South Carolina Court of Ordinary (Horry District), "South Carolina, U.S., Wills and Probate Records, 1670–1980," Ancestry.com.
25 **"splendid heritage":** J. D. Bellamy, *Memoirs of an Octogenarian*, 2.
25 **set broken bones:** Cashman, *History of the Bellamy Mansion*, 15.
26 **"practice of physick":** Cashman, *History of the Bellamy Mansion*, 15–16.
26 **"in the springtime":** Cashman, *History of the Bellamy Mansion*, 15.
26 **returned to Wilmington:** J. D. Bellamy, *Memoirs of an Octogenarian*, 2.
26 **became responsible for:** Cashman, *History of the Bellamy Mansion*, 17.
26 **Bellamy household:** Population Schedule for New Hanover County, North Carolina, Sixth Census of the United States, 1840, NARA microfilm publication M704, Records of the Bureau of the Census, RG 29, National Archives, Washington, D.C.; Cashman, *History of the Bellamy Mansion*, 18.
26 **business interests multiplied:** Bishir, "Urban Slavery at Work," 16.
27 **"The copious rains":** Cashman, *History of the Bellamy Mansion*, 20.
27 **"prime Virgin Turpentine":** Cashman, *History of the Bellamy Mansion*, 20; Bishir, "Urban Slavery at Work," 16.

27 **John Dillard to invest:** Bishir, "Urban Slavery at Work," 16; Cashman, *History of the Bellamy Mansion*, 25–26.
27 **Only 0.5 percent of North Carolinians:** Cashman, *History of the Bellamy Mansion*, 26.
27 **"around these parts":** Quoted in Cashman, *History of the Bellamy Mansion*, 25.
27 **Belle had recently graduated:** Cashman, *History of the Bellamy Mansion*, 20.
27 **"independent gentlemen":** Catherine W. Bishir, *The Bellamy Mansion, Wilmington, NC: An Antebellum Architectural Treasure and Its People* (Historic Preservation Foundation of North Carolina, 2004), 12.
28 **political fray:** Margaret M. Mulrooney, *Race, Place, and Memory: Deep Currents in Wilmington, North Carolina* (University of Florida Press, 2018), 76; Evans, *Ballots and Fence Rails*, 9.
28 **"a certain cloud":** Cashman, *History of the Bellamy Mansion*, 19.
28 **had fine estates:** Tony P. Wrenn, *Wilmington, North Carolina: An Architectural and Historical Portrait* (Junior League of Wilmington, NC, 1984), 95.
28 **"spikes, knives, saws":** Katharine M. Jones, *Heroines of Dixie: Confederate Women Tell Their Story of the War* (Bobbs-Merrill Company, 1955), 70.
28 **"architecture of Southern nationalism":** James Patrick, *Architecture in Tennessee 1768–1897* (University of Tennessee Press, 1981), 181.
29 **THE UNION DISSOLVED!:** "The Union Dissolved!," *Daily Journal*, December 21, 1860.
29 **still unclear:** Horace W. Raper, "William W. Holden and the Peace Movement in North Carolina," *North Carolina Historical Review* 31, no. 4 (1954): 493–94; Cashman, "Time Line in the Life of the Bellamy Mansion," in *History of the Bellamy Mansion*.
29 **"were deeply stirred":** Cashman, *History of the Bellamy Mansion*, 31.
29 **"bonfire and procession":** J. D. Bellamy, *Memories of an Octogenarian*, 5–7.
29 **Leading the parade:** Evans, *Ballots and Fence Rails*, 9.
29 **lavish holiday dinner:** Ellen Bellamy, "Christmas Dinner at Uncle Taylors," unpublished manuscript, Lower Cape Fear Historical Society Archives; R. P. Paddison to Roger Moore, undated, Alice B. Moore Sisson Collection (Sp. Coll. #1266), box 6, folder 7, New Hanover County Public Library, Wilmington, NC.
29 **"see the Johnkannaus":** Harriet Ann Jacobs, *Incidents in the Life of a Slave Girl*, ed. Lydia Maria Francis Child (self-published, 1861), 179–80.
30 **"Cows' tails":** Jacobs, *Incidents in the Life*, 179–80.
30 **"kuner faces":** Douglas MacMillian, "John Kuners," *Journal of American Folklore* 39, no. 151 (1926): 53–54; Rebecca Cameron, "Christmas on the Buchoi Plantation," *North Carolinian*, December 26, 1895, 7.
30 **similar performance:** Cameron, "Christmas on the Buchoi Plantation."
30 **"copper pennies":** MacMillian, "John Kuners," 54; L. T. Moore, *Stories Old and New*, 76; Bellamy, "Christmas Dinner."
30 **leading the troupe:** Mulrooney, *Race, Place, and Memory*, 28–29.
30 **"exotic grotesquerie":** MacMillian, "John Kuners," 54.
30 **memories of the Kuners:** Bellamy, "Christmas Dinner."
30 **down to dinner:** Bellamy, "Christmas Dinner."
30 **"would play awhile":** Bellamy, "Christmas Dinner."
31 **main elements of the estate:** Catherine W. Bishir, *North Carolina Architecture* (University of North Carolina Press, 2005), 279–82; Ellen Douglas Bellamy, *Back with the Tide: Memoirs* (Bellamy Mansion Museum of History and Design Arts, 2002), 33.
31 **by a third:** Cashman, *History of the Bellamy Mansion*, 24.
31 **"one year's profit":** J. D. Bellamy, *Memoirs of an Octogenarian*, 8.

CHAPTER 4: THE HALSEYS ENTER THE RECORD

32 **husband and wife:** Joshua Halsey and Sallie Franklin Jones, marriage license, December 22, 1870, New Hanover County, North Carolina Marriage Records: 1741–2011, Ancestry.com; Hesketh (Nate) Brown Jr., "Let Me Tell You Something About Us Halsey's" (New Hanover County Community Remembrance Project, 2019).

32 **"little blind girl":** H. Brown, "Let Me Tell You Something."

CHAPTER 5: BREAKAWAY

34 **"great truth":** "Speech of A. H. Stephens," in Frank Moore, ed., *Rebellion Record: A Diary of American Events, with Documents, Narratives, Illustrative Incidents, Poetry, etc.* (G. P. Putnam, 1861), 1:45–46.

34 **responsible for every aspect:** Cashman, *History of the Bellamy Mansion*, 28.

34 **"they could foller":** Catherine W. Bishir et al., *Architects and Builders in North Carolina: A History of the Practice of Building* (University of North Carolina Press, 1990), 186–87.

34 **"*nothing but slaves*":** Cashman, *History of the Bellamy Mansion*, 28.

35 **strained to minimize:** J. D. Bellamy, *Memoirs of an Octogenarian*, 8.

35 **"credit to them":** Bishir, "Urban Slavery at Work," 17.

35 **"about all the work":** Bishir, "Urban Slavery at Work," 19; Reaves, *Strength Through Struggle*, 409; Cashman, *History of the Bellamy Mansion*, 29.

35 **"war on slavery":** "South Carolina Declaration of Secession (1860)," National Constitution Center.

35 **boycott Northern goods:** E. D. Bellamy, *Back with the Tide*, 25.

36 **"nor Weathersfield onions":** James C. Bonner, "Plantation Architecture of the Lower South on the Eve of the Civil War," *Journal of Southern History* 11, no. 3 (1945): 375.

36 **"the slavery question":** E. D. Bellamy, *Back with the Tide*, 25.

36 **"'dyed in the wool'":** Cashman, *History of the Bellamy Mansion*, 27–28.

36 **And so went the commission:** Cashman, *History of the Bellamy Mansion*, 27–28.

36 **lamplighters appeared:** Lawrence Lee, *New Hanover County . . . A Brief History* (North Carolina Division of Archives and History, Department of Cultural Resources, 1977), 52.

36 **chucking clamshells:** Sprunt, *Chronicles of the Cape Fear River*, 241; Rohrs, "The Free Black Experience," 634–35.

37 **two-hundred-foot spire:** Ben Steelman, "A Picture of Wilmington in 1861," *StarNews*, May 20, 2011.

37 **expense of William Seward:** "IMPORTANT PROCEEDINGS OF CONGRESS; MR. SEWARD'S SPEECH. Harmony, Conciliation and Compromise for the Sake of the Union," *New York Times*, January 14, 1861.

37 **unload cargoes:** Sprunt, *Chronicles of the Cape Fear River*, 133, 140, 142.

37 **"Gentlemen, your old customers are yet in market":** Advertisement, *Daily Journal*, January 24, 1861.

37 **Howe settlement:** "Almost a Fire—Incendiaries Still About," *Daily Journal*, March 24, 1870.

37 **two young relatives:** Population Schedule for New Hanover County, NC, Eighth Census of the United States, 1860, NARA microfilm publication M653, Records of the Bureau of the Census, RG 29, National Archives, Washington, D.C.

37 **his good character:** "Character Reference—Alfred Howe, 1861 January 24," box 1,

folder 2, McDonald–Howe Family Papers (SC-MS-034), Center for Southeast North Carolina Archives and History, UNCW Library.

38 **saffron-colored wax:** Sprunt, *Chronicles of the Cape Fear River*, 167.

39 **"two classes in the slaveholding States":** "Slaves and Free Persons of Color," *Weekly Standard*, December 7, 1859.

39 **"they might select masters and become slaves":** *Journal of the Senate of the General Assembly of the State of North Carolina at Its First Session: 1861–1862* (W. W. Holden, 1862), 95, quoted in Bernard H. Nelson, "Legislative Control of the Southern Free Negro, 1861–1865," *Catholic Historical Review* 32, no. 1 (1946): 37–39, 41–42.

39 **passenger log of the *Empire*:** *Empire* ship manifest, April 1, 1861, District of New York—Port of New York, *New York Passenger Lists, 1820–1891*, FamilySearch.org.

39 **certainly Elvin Artis:** Bishir, "Urban Slavery at Work," 16.

40 **"unparalleled reputation":** Claire Bourhis-Mariotti, "'Go to Our Brethren, the Haytians': Haiti as the African Americans' Promised Land in the Antebellum Era," *Miscellanées: Revue française d'études américaines*, no. 142 (2015): 9.

40 **"main topic" of conversation:** William Seraille, "Afro-American Emigration to Haiti During the American Civil War," *The Americas* 35, no. 2 (1978): 186.

40 **state funeral:** Leon D. Pamphile, "The Haitian Response to the John Brown Tragedy," *Journal of Haitian Studies* 12, no. 2 (2006): 138–39.

40 **package of enticements:** "Haytian Advertisements: Invitation," *Douglass' Monthly* 4, no. 3 (1861): 512.

40 **persuading Black Americans to immigrate:** Seraille, "Afro-American Emigration," 187, 193; Bourhis-Mariotti, "'Go to Our Brethren,'" 9, 18.

40 **heeded the call:** Seraille, "Afro-American Emigration," 194–95.

41 **"for English books can seldom be had":** Seraille, "Afro-American Emigration," 194–95.

41 **returned to the United States:** Claire Bourhis-Mariotti, *Wanted! A Nation! Black Americans and Haiti, 1804–1893* (University of Georgia Press, 2023), 19.

41 **Galloway also traveled to Haiti:** Cecelski, *Fire of Freedom*, 28–37.

CHAPTER 6: DELIVER US FROM EVIL

42 **"not-so-subtle reminder":** Cashman, *History of the Bellamy Mansion*, 34.

42 **"the grandest party":** E. D. Bellamy, *Back with the Tide*, 39.

42 **new Confederate capital:** Bishir, "Urban Slavery at Work," 28; J. D. Bellamy, *Memoirs of an Octogenarian*, 28.

42 **"said to me, 'Young man'":** J. D. Bellamy, *Memoirs of an Octogenarian*, 28.

43 **tenth and final child:** Cashman, *History of the Bellamy Mansion*, 36.

43 **survived being shot:** Cashman, *History of the Bellamy Mansion*, 38.

43 **rapidly changing city:** Sprunt, *Chronicles of the Cape Fear River*, 252, 288, 385, 413, 418.

43 **"rogues and desperadoes":** Sprunt, *Chronicles of the Cape Fear River*, 413.

43 **ordered a blockade:** Sprunt, *Chronicles of the Cape Fear River*, 372.

43 **quicksilver steamships:** Dr. Chris E. Fonvielle Jr., "A Plague Most Deadly," *Salt Magazine*, n.d.; Philip Gerard, "The South's Gibraltar: Fort Fisher," *Our State* 4 (2014).

43 **"cats watching a big rat hole":** Fonvielle, "A Plague Most Deadly."

43 **beating Union patrols:** Fonvielle, "A Plague Most Deadly"; Evans, *Ballots and Fence Rails*, 7; E. D. Bellamy, *Back with the Tide*, x.

44 **two million pounds of saltpeter:** Gerard, "The South's Gibraltar"; J. D. Bellamy, *Memoirs of an Octogenarian*, 27.

44 **"These were flush days":** J. D. Bellamy, *Memoirs of an Octogenarian*, 27.

44 **Nassau and Wilmington:** Evans, *Ballots and Fence Rails*, 11.

44 **blockade runner *Kate*:** Fonvielle, "A Plague Most Deadly"; David Silkenat, "How a Yellow Fever Outbreak Exacerbated the Civil War Refugee Crisis," National Museum of Civil War Medicine, June 19, 2017.

44 **"fellow named Swarzman":** Waddell, *Some Memories*, 55.

44 **Serving in no official capacity:** Armond W. Scott, "Negro Lawyer Expelled from Wilmington," *Wilmington Morning Star*, November 15, 1898.

44 **more than six hundred Wilmingtonians died:** Silkenat, "How a Yellow Fever Outbreak"; Philip Gerard, "A House Divided," *Our State* 1 (2011).

44 **"wagon-loads of corpses":** J. D. Bellamy, *Memoirs of an Octogenarian*, 27.

45 **enslaved cook named Sarah:** Cashman, "Time Line."

45 **"Pray in my bee half":** Silkenat, "How a Yellow Fever Outbreak."

45 **"fuliginous clouds":** Sprunt, *Chronicles of the Cape Fear*, 244–45.

45 **"safe a retreat":** E. D. Bellamy, *Back with the Tide*, x.

46 **"so sweet and different":** E. D. Bellamy, *Back with the Tide*, 8–9.

46 **its last conduit:** Evans, *Ballots and Fence Rails*, 7.

47 **"capture of Richmond":** Gerard, "The South's Gibraltar."

47 **scheme would likely have succeeded:** Evans, *Ballots and Fence Rails*, 16.

47 **hustled their children:** E. D. Bellamy, *Back with the Tide*, 5.

47 **exploding like rockets:** J. D. Bellamy, *Memoirs of an Octogenarian*, 28.

47 **binoculars trained south:** Cashman, *History of the Bellamy Mansion*, 40.

48 **abruptly switched camps:** Waddell, *Some Memories*, 52–54; David Zucchino, *Wilmington's Lie: The Murderous Coup of 1898 and the Rise of White Supremacy* (Grove Press, 2020), 12.

48 **"I was a Confederate soldier":** Waddell, *Some Memories*, 54.

48 **bloodshed in 1864:** "Alfred Moore Waddell," U.S. Civil War Soldier Records and Profiles: 1861–1865, *American Civil War Research Database*, Ancestry.com; Zucchino, *Wilmington's Lie*, 11.

48 **cousin Roger Moore:** Zucchino, *Wilmington's Lie*, 33.

48 **used the title Colonel:** Zucchino, *Wilmington's Lie*, 11; Waddell, *Some Memories*, 54–55.

48 **his Christmas sermon:** Evans, *Ballots and Fence Rails*, 19; Waddell, *Some Memories*, 57–58.

49 **prayer went up:** Waddell, *Some Memories*, 58; Leora Hiatt McEachern, *History of St. James Parish, 1729–1979* (self-published, 1982), 9.

49 **"splendidly equipped men":** Evans, *Ballots and Fence Rails*, 23.

49 **surrendered the city:** Thanayi Michelle Jackson, "'Devoted to the Interests of His Race:' Black Officeholders and the Political Culture of Freedom in Wilmington, North Carolina, 1865–1877," (PhD diss., University of Maryland at College Park, 2016), 22.

49 **"heathen have entered our land":** Cashman, *History of the Bellamy Mansion*, 42.

49 **"'Blow, Gabriel, blow'":** Waddell, *Some Memories*, 57.

49 **still living in slavery:** Reaves, *Strength Through Struggle*, 3; Ben Steelman, "Civil War Anniversary—Traces of Slavery Still Found in Wilmington," *StarNews*, August 31, 2011.

49 **sixteen hundred Black soldiers:** Jackson, "'Devoted to the Interests of His Race,'" 22–24; Walter Gilman Curtis, *Reminiscences of Wilmington and Smithville—Southport*, ed. Wolfgang Furstenau (first published in 1905; Southport Historical Society, 1999), 35–36.

50 **"How powerful it must have been":** Jackson, "'Devoted to the Interests of His Race,'" 24–25.

50 **Psalm 9:** Rev. L. S. Burkhead, "History of the Difficulties of the Pastorate of the Front Street Methodist Church, Wilmington, N.C., for the Year 1865," in *An Annual Publication of Historical Papers: Series VIII* (Historical Society of Trinity College, 1908–1909), 41–42; Cynthia J. Brown, *Strength from Our Past, Faith for Our Future: A History of St. Stephen African Methodist Episcopal Church* (St. Stephen African Methodist Episcopal Church Sesquicentennial Anniversary History Book Committee, 2015), 19.
50 **"Now you are all free!":** Evans, *Ballots and Fence Rails*, 25.
50 **"contrary to the laws of God":** C. J. Brown, *Strength from Our Past*, 13.
50 **Front Street congregation:** C. J. Brown, *Strength from Our Past*, 19.
50 **its own schism:** Reaves, *Strength Through Struggle*, 74.
50 **newly appointed pastor:** Reaves, *Strength Through Struggle*, 102; Burkhead, "History of the Difficulties," 38.
51 **"destroyed *as a race*":** Burkhead, "History of the Difficulties," 39; C. J. Brown, *Strength from Our Past*, 23.
51 **church property was rightfully theirs:** Burkhead, "History of the Difficulties," 50; Jackson, "'Devoted to the Interests of His Race,'" 44; C. J. Brown, *Strength from Our Past*, 26.
51 **"never-to-be-forgotten":** Burkhead, "History of the Difficulties," 41–43, 75; C. J. Brown, *Strength from Our Past*, 24.
52 **state's largest congregation:** C. J. Brown, *Strength from Our Past*, 36; Reaves, *Strength Through Struggle*, 102.

CHAPTER 7: CLOSER TO FREEDOM

53 **army surgeon:** J. D. Bellamy, *Memoirs of an Octogenarian*, 24.
53 **she'd poisoned it:** E. D. Bellamy, *Back with the Tide*, 10.
54 **"anxious to get home":** E. D. Bellamy, *Back with the Tide*, 12–13.
54 **"relieved our terrible plight":** J. D. Bellamy, *Memoirs of an Octogenarian*, 25.
54 **wrong or weak:** J. D. Bellamy, *Memoirs of an Octogenarian*, 24.
54 **"the silver intact":** E. D. Bellamy, *Back with the Tide*, 10–11.
54 **Union Army seized:** J. D. Bellamy, *Memoirs of an Octogenarian*, 29.
55 **"white and colored refugees":** Evans, *Ballots and Fence Rails*, 56, 58.
55 **"I have answered":** Cashman, *History of the Bellamy Mansion*, 45.
56 **"own old cook":** E. D. Bellamy, *Back with the Tide*, 6.
56 **"showy but uncomfortable":** Whitelaw Reid, *After the War: A Southern Tour, May 1, 1865 to May 1, 1866* (Moore, Wilstach, & Baldwin, 1866), 47; Cashman, *History of the Bellamy Mansion*, 46.
56 **"the drunken ass":** Emma LeConte, diary entry, April 21, 1865, Emma LeConte Diary: 1864–1865, folder 1, Southern Historical Collection, Wilson Library, University of North Carolina at Chapel Hill.
57 **ripped the pews out:** McEachern, *History of St. James Parish*, 9.
57 **kind of "prudent grief":** Evans, *Ballots and Fence Rails*, 50.
57 **draped the Bellamy Mansion in black:** Bishir, *The Bellamy Mansion*, 46.
57 **"a course of magnanimity":** "Citizens' Meeting," *Wilmington Daily Herald*, April 21, 1865.
57 **slave mortgages:** Sharon Ann Murphy, *Banking on Slavery: Financing Southern Expansion in the Antebellum United States* (University of Chicago Press, 2023).
57 **"Lincoln's death might change":** J. D. Bellamy, *Memoirs of an Octogenarian*, 10.
57 **"their best friend":** "Special Notices: Mass Meeting," *Herald of the Union*, April 26, 1865.

58 **crowd of mourners:** "Local Intelligence: The Celebration Yesterday," *Herald of the Union*, April 28, 1865.
58 **an enslaved artisan:** Bishir, *The Bellamy Mansion*, 46.
58 **"Negro political movement":** Evans, *Ballots and Fence Rails*, 51.
58 **"headquarters of General Hawley":** J. D. Bellamy, *Memoirs of an Octogenarian*, 30.
58 **members were women:** Cecelski, *Fire of Freedom*, 176.
58 **supporting Black enfranchisement:** Beverly Tetterton and Dan Camacho, *A Brief History of Wilmington, North Carolina* (Java Dog Press, 2018), 13–14.
58 **"could go take it":** John H. Jackson, "Memories of Uncle Jackson," in *Slave Narratives: A Folk History of Slavery in the United States from Interviews with Former Slaves* 11, no. 2 (1936): 4–5.
59 **"Year 1 of American Independence":** Edward Atkinson to John Murray Forbes, February 1, 1865, quoted in Eric Foner, *Reconstruction: America's Unfinished Revolution, 1863–1877, Updated Edition* (HarperPerennial, 2014), 66.
59 **"on the move":** Foner, *Reconstruction*, 80; Felix Haywood, interview, June 6, 1938, in *The American Slave: A Composite Autobiography, Texas Narratives, Vol. 5, Part 4*, ed. George P. Rawick (Greenwood Press, 1979), 1690.
59 **"common-sense protection":** "Wendell Phillips at Cooper Institute," *New York Times*, December 23, 1863.
59 **reinstating racial subjugation:** Foner, *Reconstruction*, 66.
59 **serfs of Russia:** William A. Darity Jr. and A. Kirsten Mullen, *From Here to Equality: Reparations for Black Americans in the Twenty-First Century* (University of North Carolina Press, 2022), 10.
59 **Georgia coastline:** Foner, *Reconstruction*, 71.
59 **purchase seized plantation land:** Akiko Ochiai, "The Port Royal Experiment Revisited: Northern Visions of Reconstruction and the Land Question," *New England Quarterly* 74, no. 1 (2001): 100.
60 **"toiled and suffered":** Jackson, "'Devoted to the Interests of His Race,'" 94, 101; "Address of the North Carolina Freedmen," *Daily Whig and Republican*, October 23, 1865, 2.
60 **published an appeal:** H. M. Turner, "Colored Men of Enterprise. Read This," *Christian Recorder*, April 29, 1865.
60 **to contact Fred:** Turner, "Colored Men of Enterprise"; Evans, *Ballots and Fence Rails*, 38.
60 **"most favorable opportunity for colored men":** Turner, "Colored Men of Enterprise."
60 **teemed with displaced people:** Zucchino, *Wilmington's Lie*, 4–6; Evans, *Ballots and Fence Rails*, 59.
60 **"cake and wine":** Evans, *Ballots and Fence Rails*, 65, quoted in Zucchino, *Wilmington's Lie*, 6.
61 **de facto spokesperson:** Zucchino, *Wilmington's Lie*, 11.
61 **"indeed daily outrages":** Alfred Moore Waddell to William Woods Holden, June 18, 1865, North Carolina Digital Collections, North Carolina Department of Natural and Cultural Resources.
62 **"truly, your friend":** "Local Intelligence: Public Meeting," *Wilmington Daily Herald*, July 25, 1865.
62 **red velvet curtain:** Mary Bason Broadfoot, "Thalian Hall," *Lower Cape Fear Historical Society, Inc., Bulletin* 13, no. 2 (1970): 1–3.
62 **"roar or laughter":** Waddell, *Some Memories*, 47.
62 **greeted the crowd:** "Africa in America: The State of the Freed Negroes," *Wilmington Daily Herald*, July 27, 1865.
63 **property or educational requirements:** "Africa in America"; Foner, *Reconstruction*, 192.

63 **industry and obedience:** "Africa in America," 4.
64 **seek absolution directly:** J. D. Bellamy, *Memoirs of an Octogenarian*, 33.
64 **got him a personal interview:** Cashman, *History of the Bellamy Mansion*, 47.
64 **"of executive clemency":** Bishir, *The Bellamy Mansion*, 49.
64 **firm cursive hand:** Bishir, *The Bellamy Mansion*, 49.
65 **lost an arm:** Cashman, *History of the Bellamy Mansion*, 50.
65 **settle his account:** Cashman, *History of the Bellamy Mansion*, 50; Bishir, *The Bellamy Mansion*, 51.
65 **"began life again":** E. D. Bellamy, *Back with the Tide*, 8.
66 **"Tell Ellen":** Cashman, *History of the Bellamy Mansion*, 50; Wrenn, *Wilmington, North Carolina*, 218.

CHAPTER 8: ALDERMAN HOWE

67 **"seven mystic years":** W. E. B. Du Bois, *Black Reconstruction in America, 1860–1880* (Free Press, 1996), 726.
67 **new political power:** Darity and Mullen, *From Here to Equality*, 173.
67 **Fred Howe seized:** Reaves, *Strength Through Struggle*, 409.
67 **stood bail:** "Local Intelligence: For Voting Twice—Examination in the Case of George L. Mason," *Daily Journal*, August 10, 1869.
67 **self-ventilating refrigerators:** "Notice: Winship's Patent Self-Ventilating Refrigerator," *Daily Journal*, May 29, 1869.
67 **state penitentiary board:** "The Legislature: Senate, Thursday, April 1, 1869," *Daily Standard*, April 2, 1869.
68 **institution's superintendent:** "Good Breeding," *Raleigh Sentinel*, May 26, 1869.
68 **"party of Lincoln":** Reaves, *Strength Through Struggle*, 239–40.
68 **Black volunteer firefighting brigades:** Reaves, *Strength Through Struggle*, 414–15; Cecelski, *Fire of Freedom*, 197; "Howe Family (fl. 1850s–1900s)," North Carolina Architects & Builders.
68 **one of his own sons:** Reaves, *Strength Through Struggle*, 411; for Alfred vs. Anthony, see Jackson, "'Devoted to the Interests of His Race,'" 213–22.
68 **Anthony prevailed:** "Municipal Election," *Wilmington Journal*, January 8, 1869; Jackson, "'Devoted to the Interests of His Race,'" 217–18, 222.
68 **"breathe substantive meaning":** Foner, *Reconstruction*, xxix.
68 **putting out fires:** "Local Intelligence," *Daily Journal*, September 29, 1870.
68 **mixed the brothers up:** On January 5, 1870, Wilmington's *Morning Star* printed a retraction at the top of page one that simply read: "The name of Alfred Howe occurred in our report of the vote in the First Ward, when it should have been Anthony Howe."
68 **"velocipede ring":** "Local Intelligence: Pugilistic Encounter Interrupted by 'Alderman' Howe," *Daily Journal*, May 18, 1869; "Local Intelligence: Wilson T. Morton," *Daily Journal*, August 31, 1869.
69 **in demographic terms:** LeRae Umfleet, *A Day of Blood: The 1898 Wilmington Race Riot* (North Carolina Office of Archives and History, 2009), 18.
69 **"vie with Oakdale":** *Wilmington Morning Star*, September 6, 1860, quoted in Reaves, *Strength Through Struggle*, 178–79; Jackson, "'Devoted to the Interests of His Race,'" 259.
69 **Black Masonic:** "Giblem Lodge: Saving Wilmington's First Black Masonic Lodge," Historic Wilmington Foundation.
69 **among its depositors:** Reginald Washington, "The Freedman's Savings and Trust Company and African American Genealogical Research," *Federal Records and African American History* 29, no. 2 (1977); "Washington Howe," "Valentine Howe," "Anthony

Howe" and "W. H. Howe," Freedman's Savings and Trust Company, *U.S. Freedman's Bank Records, 1865–1874*, Ancestry.com.

69 **1870 census:** Jackson, "'Devoted to the Interests of His Race,'" 40.

69 **"Knight of the White Plume":** Evans, *Ballots and Fence Rails*, 212.

69 **their own contest:** "The Tournament," *Wilmington Morning Star*, May 2, 1871; "Local Intelligence: Tournament," *Daily Journal*, May 2, 1871.

69 **Charles Posner:** "Local Intelligence: Beauties of Our Special Court—How Members of the Bar Are Treated and Civilities Regulated," *Daily Journal*, April 23, 1870.

70 **"I can never forget":** Waddell, *Some Memories*, 101–2.

71 **"allowed to vote unchallenged":** Zucchino, *Wilmington's Lie*, 37–38.

71 **enthusiastic turnout:** Zucchino, *Wilmington's Lie*, 38–39; Umfleet, *A Day of Blood*, 10; Foner, *Reconstruction*, 30.

71 **"The N—— Convention":** *Daily Journal*, February 26, 1868; Zucchino, *Wilmington's Lie*, 39.

71 **"under a deluge":** Evans, *Ballots and Fence Rails*, 101.

71 **"VAMPIRE-BOGUS-MONGREL":** "Glad Tidings," *Wilmington Morning Star*, April 21, 1868.

72 **supremacy through terror:** Zucchino, *Wilmington's Lie*, 33.

72 **transmission of the name:** "An Honorable Name Perpetuated," *Wilmington Semi-Weekly Messenger*, December 18, 1900.

72 **building materials:** Scott Nunn, "Back Then (June 1909): Fire Destroys Roger Moore's & Sons Brick Company," *StarNews*, June 6, 2009; "Bricks! Bricks! Bricks!," *Wilmington Messenger*, May 31, 1900; Wilmington Chamber of Commerce, *Wilmington Up-to-Date: The Metropolis of North Carolina Graphically Portrayed* (W. L. DeRosset Jr., 1902), 93.

72 **exemplary citizen:** Zucchino, *Wilmington's Lie*, 33; Evans, *Ballots and Fence Rails*, 99.

72 **He was also a recruiting asset:** William Lord DeRosset, *Pictorial and Historical New Hanover County and Wilmington, North Carolina, 1723–1928* (self-published, 1938), 30; Evans, *Ballots and Fence Rails*, 99.

73 **oath to the Klan:** "Roger Moore," in Samuel A. Ashe et al., eds., *Biographical History of North Carolina: From Colonial Times to the Present* (Charles L. Van Noppen, 1917), 8:383–84; Zucchino, *Wilmington's Lie*, 33; Evans, *Ballots and Fence Rails*, 99.

73 **"risen from Hell":** R. P. Paddison to Roger Moore, undated.

73 **"*Avenger Cometh*":** "Ku Klux—The Avenger Abroad," *Daily Journal*, April 18, 1868, quoted in Zucchino, *Wilmington's Lie*, 42.

73 **murdered Black people:** Du Bois, *Black Reconstruction*, 674.

73 **"they would capture":** R. P. Paddison to Roger Moore, undated.

73 **behind Confederate lines:** Cecelski, *Fire of Freedom*, 43.

74 **"hooting and yelling":** *Wilmington Morning Star*, April 21, 1868, quoted in Zucchino, *Wilmington's Lie*, 43; Evans, *Ballots and Fence Rails*, 101.

74 **"riotous parading":** Evans, *Ballots and Fence Rails*, 102.

74 **effectively disappeared:** Cecelski, *Fire of Freedom*, 203; Umfleet, *A Day of Blood*, 12.

74 **Galloway was elected:** Cecelski, *Fire of Freedom*, 203.

74 **"If white people":** Cecelski, *Fire of Freedom*, 206.

CHAPTER 9: A COMMUNITY OF INTEREST

75 **"We have turned":** *Reconstruction: Speech of Hon. Thaddeus Stevens, of Pennsylvania* (H. Polkinhorn & Son, 1865).

75 **Impoverished Southern Black people:** Foner, *Reconstruction*, 96–98.

75 **"show the world":** Joseph C. Hill et al., quoted in Reaves, *Strength Through Struggle*, 57.

75 **"a sea monster":** "Industrial Fair Exposition," *Wilmington Morning Star*, December 28, 1875.
75 **fair's second day:** "Industrial Fair Exposition."
76 **was already legendary:** Reaves, *Strength Through Struggle*, 186–88.
77 **"of much credit":** "Industrial Fair Exposition: Third Day—The Firemen," *Wilmington Morning Star*, December 30, 1875.
77 **"blowing a gale":** "The Great Fire," *Wilmington Morning Star*, February 23, 1886; "A Terrible Fire," *Wilmington Morning Star*, February 23, 1886.
77 **relief committee:** "The Fire Relief Committee," *Wilmington Morning Star*, March 6, 1886.
77 **ancestral corner:** Reaves, *Strength Through Struggle*, 410.
78 **city's board of education:** Jackson, "'Devoted to the Interests of His Race,'" 329–30.
78 **Williston Graded School:** Jackson, "'Devoted to the Interests of His Race,'" 329–30; Reaves, *Strength Through Struggle*, 152–53; "History of the Williston Industrial School," History of the Williston Industrial School: 1865–1937, SC-MS-034, box 1, folder 21, McDonald–Howe Family Papers, Special Collections Repository, Center for Southeast North Carolina Archives and History, UNCW Library.
78 **Williston had come a long way:** "History of the Williston Industrial School."
78 **Black faculty:** Reaves, *Strength Through Struggle*, 153.
78 **early teachers:** Jackson, "'Devoted to the Interests of His Race,'" 330.
78 **Mary Jane Langdon:** "Howe Family (fl. 1850s–1900s)," North Carolina Architects & Builders.
78 **credited as the architect:** "Howe Family (fl. 1850s–1900s)," North Carolina Architects & Builders.
79 **"a similar course":** Bishir, "Black Builders in Antebellum North Carolina," 456.
79 **William B. McKoy:** "Howe Family (fl. 1850s–1900s), North Carolina Architects & Builders; "Henry Bacon: American Architect," *Encyclopedia Britannica*, February 25, 2025.
79 **all the construction work:** Janet K. Seapker, "James F. Post, Builder-Architect," *Bulletin of the Lower Cape Fear Historical Society* 30, no. 3 (1987): 1.

CHAPTER 10: I.O.U. WADDELL

81 **Julia's family home:** "Local Intelligence: Real Estate Sale," *Daily Journal*, November 12, 1868.
81 **Alfred lived there:** Population Schedule for New Hanover County, NC, Ninth Census of the United States, 1870, NARA microfilm publication M593, Records of the Bureau of the Census, RG 29, National Archives, Washington, D.C.
81 **civil suit:** "Important Civil Suit—Five Thousand Dollars Damages," *Wilmington Morning Star*, December 24, 1869.
81 **"My nomination":** Waddell, *Some Memories*, 10.
82 **"his peculiar gifts":** Waddell, *Some Memories*, 100.
82 **special joint committee:** "Portraits in Oversight: Congress Investigates KKK Violence During Reconstruction," Levin Center Home, Wayne State Law School.
82 **Henry Louis Gates Jr.:** *Reconstruction: America After the Civil War*, directed by Stacey L. Holman (2019; PBS); *Congressional Globe and Appendix*: *First Session Forty-Second Congress* (Blair & Rives, 1871), 1:116.
82 **"shared my bed":** Waddell, *Some Memories*, 110.
82 **"encountered A MAN":** Waddell, *Some Memories*, 110.
83 **"waste of paper":** Waddell, *Some Memories*, 112.

83 **escape from jail:** Waddell, *Some Memories*, 91–92; Zucchino, *Wilmington's Lie*, 20–21; Evans, *Ballots and Fence Rails*, 31.

83 **series of articles:** "A. M. Waddell MC," *Wilmington Post*, April 7, 1876; "Judge McRoy," *Wilmington Post*, May 5, 1876; "Waddell Gambling," *Wilmington Post*, May 5, 1876; "Alfred Moore Waddell: Clerk and Master in Equity Sued on His Official Bond," *Wilmington Post*, May 5, 1876; "A. M. Waddell," *Wilmington Post*, June 2, 1876.

83 **serious accusations:** Evans, *Ballots and Fence Rails*, 223; Zucchino, *Wilmington's Lie*, 141.

83 **"true blue Southern":** "Alfred Moore Waddell," *Wilmington Post*.

83 **"without notice or warning":** J. J. Cassidey, "A Card," *Wilmington Post*, May 19, 1876.

84 **rickety character:** "A Campaign Incident," *Wilmington Post*, October 20, 1876.

84 **"a corrupt centralism":** "1876 Democratic Party Platform—June 22, 1876," American Presidency Project.

84 **kilt-wearing Celtic speaker:** Sprunt, *Chronicles of the Cape Fear River*, 675; Rev. Alexander MacRae, *History of the Clan MacRae, with Genealogies* (A. M. Ross & Company, 1899), 248; Susan Taylor Block, *Images of America: Cape Fear Lost* (Arcadia Publishing, 1999), 31.

85 **"go-a-headity":** Mulrooney, *Race, Place, and Memory*, 60; Bishir, *North Carolina Architecture*, 269.

85 **He married twice:** MacRae, *History of the Clan MacRae*, 250–55.

85 **enslaved eighteen people:** Slave Schedules for New Hanover County, North Carolina, Seventh Census of the United States, 1850, NARA microfilm publication M432, Records of the Bureau of the Census, RG 29, National Archives, Washington, D.C.; Mulrooney, *Race, Place, and Memory*, 61.

85 **"no political importance":** "Amnesty Petition of William MacRae, July 28, 1865," Civil War Era NC.

85 **five blockade runners:** "Clan MacRae," *Wrightsville Beach Magazine*, March 29, 2007.

85 **Navassa Guano Company:** MacRae Family Papers, David M. Rubenstein Rare Book & Manuscript Library, Duke University; "The Death of Mr. MacRae," *Wilmington Messenger*, September 22, 1892.

86 **Scottish keep:** Block, *Images of America*, 30–31.

86 **diversified portfolio:** Samantha Leonard et al., "Driving Through Time: Logging, Tourism, and the Blue Ridge Parkway in Linville, North Carolina," University of North Carolina, 2009–2012.

86 **enslaver-planters:** Mulrooney, *Race, Place, and Memory*, 59.

86 **matching rear gardens:** Block, *Images of America*, 31.

CHAPTER 11: YOU WON'T PUT ME OFF

87 **"This reporter has stabbed":** "Local Dots," *Wilmington Morning Star*, July 31, 1892.

87 **helped to build St. Marks:** "Howe Family (fl. 1850s–1900s)," North Carolina Architects & Builders.

88 **"Hurry up!":** "A Cruel Blow," *Wilmington Messenger*, August 2, 1892; "A Street-Car Fracas," *Wilmington Morning Star*; "The Kelly-Howe Affray Case," *Wilmington Messenger*, August 9, 1892.

88 **"You're a liar":** M. F. Heiskill, "The Difficulty on Sunday," *Wilmington Messenger*, August 3, 1892.

88 **"blow over the head":** "A Cruel Blow."

88 **"Howe's wounds":** "A Street-Car Fracas."

88 **"considerable prominence":** "A Cruel Blow."
88 **adjective *insolent*:** Foner, *Reconstruction*, 149.
89 **"invariably quarreled":** "The Kelly-Howe Affray Case."
89 **"Death of Alfred Howe":** "Death of Alfred Howe," *Wilmington Messenger*, October 7, 1892. This obituary states that Howe's altercation with Motorman Kelly took place on July 21, but it was surely a typo, as it was well documented at the time that it happened on July 31.
90 ***"post mortem"*:** Travis Souther, "Index of Names, Professions, Addresses and Other Details from the 1897–1905 Wilmington City Directories," New Hanover County Public Library, North Carolina Digital Heritage Center, 2020.
90 **Fred died with:** $25,000 in 1892 was worth $890,043.96 in 2025, according to the CPI Inflation Calculator.
91 **shot three Black owners:** "Three Black Grocers Lynched in Memphis, Tennessee," A History of Racial Injustice: March 9, 1892, Equal Justice Initiative.
91 **161 Black people:** Philip Dray, "A Lynching in New York 130 Years Ago Shows That the North Isn't Immune to Racial Hatred," *Time*, June 2, 2022.
91 **atmosphere soon soured:** "Serious Affray in a Bar-Room on South Front Street," *Wilmington Morning Star*, November 7, 1893.
91 **"cut his head off":** "Terrible Cutting Affray," *Wilmington Messenger*, November 7, 1893.
92 **"an iron crank":** "Terrible Cutting Affray."
93 **Kelly was still at large:** "Pithy Locals," *Wilmington Messenger*, November 8, 1893.

CHAPTER 12: RETRIBUTION IN HISTORY

94 **"twelve handsome residences":** "For the Exposition," *Wilmington Messenger*, November 12, 1895; *Wilmington Up-to-Date: The Metropolis of North Carolina Graphically Portrayed* (Wilmington Chamber of Commerce, 1902).
94 **electric fountain:** Sharon Foster Jones, *The Atlanta Exposition* (Arcadia Publishing, 2010), 7.
94 **exposition's official catalog:** *The Official Catalogue of the Cotton States and International Exposition: Atlanta, Georgia, U.S.A., September 18 to December 31, 1895* (Claflin & Mellichamp, 1895).
95 **Black representatives at the fair:** "The Colored People and the Atlanta Exposition," *Wilmington Messenger*, September 1, 1895.
95 **exposition's designated showcase:** *Official Catalogue*, 134–35.
95 **Dahomey African Village:** Jones, *Atlanta Exposition*, 98, 103; Mabel O. Wilson, *Negro Building: Black Americans in the World of Fairs and Museums* (University of California Press, 2012), 79–80.
95 **"racist representations":** Wilson, *Negro Building*, 79–80.
95 **scorching pamphlet:** Ida B. Wells, *The Reason Why the Colored American Is Not in the World's Columbian Exposition* (self-published, 1893), 4.
95 **allow Black participation:** Wilson, *Negro Building*, 52.
95 **segregated accommodations:** Wilson, *Negro Building*, 34; Jones, *Atlanta Exposition*, 7–8.
95 **venue was a triumph:** Wilson, *Negro Building*, 62.
96 **"its negro building":** J. Garland Penn, "To Open October 21, the Negro Building Will Open on That Date with Imposing Ceremonie," *Atlanta Constitution*, October 13, 1895; "What the Negro Is Doing," *Atlanta Constitution*, October 13, 1895.
96 **Atlanta Compromise address:** Mulrooney, *Race, Place, and Memory*, 21.

96 **Tuskegee Institute:** Ellen Weiss, *Robert R. Taylor and Tuskegee: An African American Architect Designs for Booker T. Washington* (NewSouth Books, 2012).
96 **"moral revolution":** "Negro Progress," *Atlanta Constitution*, October 22, 1895.
96 **"social equality carries with it civil equality":** Edwin S. Redkey, comp. and ed., *Respect Black: The Writings and Speeches of Henry McNeal Turner* (Arno Press, 1971), 165–66.
96 **"a new epoch":** Wilson, *Negro Building*, 72.
97 **Democrats finished "redeeming":** "1898 Wilmington Race Riot," 1898 Wilmington: Debunking the Myths [website], 1898 Wilmington Institute for Education and Research, 2005.
97 **"'judicious' cheating":** William Alexander Mabry, "Negro Suffrage and Fusion Rule in North Carolina," *North Carolina Historical Review* 12, no. 2 (1935): 80–81.
97 **"The interests of":** Edmonds, *The Negro and Fusion Politics*, 35.
97 **made it difficult for Black men to vote:** Edmonds, *The Negro and Fusion Politics*, 70, 74, 153.
98 **most consequential reform:** Edmonds, *The Negro and Fusion Politics*, 118; Mabry, "Negro Suffrage and Fusion," 88–89.
98 **"resurgence of the Negro in politics":** Edmonds, *The Negro and Fusion Politics*, 218.
98 **"fusion, confusion, and negroism":** Thomas W. Clawson, quoted by Jeffrey J. Crow, "'Fusion, Confusion, and Negroism': Schisms Among Negro Republicans in the North Carolina Election of 1896," *North Carolina Historical Review* 53, no. 4 (1976): 364.
98 **election of Daniel Russell:** J. D. Bellamy, *Memoirs of an Octogenarian*, 25.
98 **"hotly denounced as a scallawag":** J. D. Bellamy, *Memoirs of an Octogenarian*, 38–40.
98 **"retribution in history":** Josephus Daniels, *Editor in Politics* (University of North Carolina Press, 1941), 206.
98 **"Do this, do that":** "The Source of the Governor's Inspiration," *News & Observer*, September 30, 1898; Rachel Marie-Crane Williams, "A War in Black and White: The Cartoons of Norman Ethre Jennett & the North Carolina Election of 1898," *Southern Cultures* 19, no. 2 (2013): 12.
99 **"are largely savages":** "Judge Russell's Letter of Declination," in *Democracy Vs. Radicalism: Hand-book of N.C. Politics* (E. M. Uzzell, 1888), 21.
99 **a merely racist candidate:** Reaves, *Strength Through Struggle*, 244.
99 **colonial oppression:** Hossfeld, *Narrative, Political Unconscious, and Racial Violence*, 34.
99 **board of aldermen now comprised:** Umfleet, *A Day of Blood*, 29.
99 **"avoid being run down":** Harry Hayden, *The Story of the Wilmington Rebellion* (self-published, 1936).
100 **"If something is not done":** Hayden, *Story of the Wilmington Rebellion*.

CHAPTER 13: AN UNSAFE CONDITION

102 **"work they did":** John C. Dancy, *Sand Against the Wind: The Memoirs of John C. Dancy* (Wayne State University Press, 1966), 66.
102 **"lose their beauty":** "Advertisement: Women Lose Their Beauty," *Daily Review*, July 19, 1889.
102 **"sundry other articles":** "Systematic Robbery by a Domestic," *Wilmington Messenger*, August 28, 1891; "Sent to Jail for Larceny," *Wilmington Morning Star*, September 2, 1891.
102 **Sallie and Josh were arrested:** "Sent to Jail for Larceny," *Weekly Star*, September 24, 1891.
103 **prosecutors' failure:** "The Criminal Court," *Wilmington Messenger*, September 24, 1891.
103 **"an unsafe condition":** "City Affairs," *Wilmington Messenger*, February 6, 1897.
104 **"poured out their family stories":** Dylan C. Penningroth, *Before the Movement: The Hidden History of Black Civil Rights* (Liveright, 2023), 31.

104 **overturned the Civil Rights Act:** "Supreme Court Strikes Down Civil Rights Act, Legitimating Segregation," A History of Racial Injustice: October 15, 1883, Equal Justice Initiative.

104 **"consolidation of racism":** Kidada E. Williams, *They Left Great Marks on Me: African American Testimonies of Racial Violence from Emancipation to World War I* (New York University Press, 2012), 86.

CHAPTER 14: WHITE VIOLETS FOR EVENING TOQUES

106 **city of "promising distinction":** Turner, "Colored Men of Enterprise."

106 **working as dyers:** *African American Business Leaders, 1897: Compiled from a Database Supplied by Tod Hamilton Using the 1897 Wilmington City Directory* (New Hanover County Public Library), 385–92; Prather, "We Have Taken a City," in *Democracy Betrayed*, 17; *Wilmington, N.C.: City Directory, 1897* (J. L. Hill Printing Co., 1897).

106 **most integrated city:** Prather, "We Have Taken a City," in *Democracy Betrayed*, 16; Hayden, *Story of the Wilmington Rebellion*.

106 **outward-looking congregation:** Reaves, *Strength Through Struggle*, 105.

107 **never to arrest a white man:** Caleb Crain, "What a White-Supremacist Coup Looks Like," *The New Yorker*, April 20, 2020.

107 **"Dirty, Filthy Town":** "Wilmington's Fusion Rule: She Has Eighty-Six Negro Office-Holders," *Wilmington Messenger*, September 8, 1898.

107 **Black daily newspaper:** Prather, "We Have Taken a City," in *Democracy Betrayed*, 18.

107 **unacknowledged son:** Umfleet, *A Day of Blood*, 183.

107 **prestigious Hampton Institute:** Umfleet, *A Day of Blood*, 70.

107 **"goodly to look upon":** Caroline Sadgwar Manly to her sons, undated fourth letter, Alex L. Manly Papers, 0065-b1-fb, East Carolina Manuscript Collection.

108 **"every little petticoat":** Caroline Sadgwar Manly to her sons, undated fourth letter.

108 **"a very creditable colored paper":** Umfleet, *A Day of Blood*, 61.

108 **double-cylinder press:** "1898 Wilmington: A Secondhand Jonah Hoe Printing Press," *Object Project*, podcast, January 21, 2022; Zucchino, *Wilmington's Lie*, 99.

109 **"language of jewelry":** "The Language of Jewelry: Symbolism Is Carried into Articles for Female Adornment," *Daily Record*, August 28, 1898; "Agricultural Topics: Caring for Tulips," *Daily Record*, August 28, 1898; "Helps for Housewives: Croutons," *Daily Record*, March 26, 1898; "Helps for Housewives: Household Hints," *Daily Record*, March 26, 1898.

109 **paper covered fashion:** "For Women's Benefit: Fashion Fancies," *Daily Record*, March 26, 1898; "Local Briefs," *Daily Record*, August 30, 1898.

109 **poetry and stories:** "The Children's Pages," *Daily Record*, March 26, 1898.

109 **merchants alike advertised:** "Genuine Wine, Made by Henri Pateau, French Wine Maker," *Daily Record*, August 30, 1898.

109 **"Pine apple, Banana, Strawberry":** "Ice Cream Parlor," *Daily Record*, August 30, 1898.

109 **"of the Negro for the Negro":** "To Our Subscribers," *Daily Record*, September 28, 1895.

109 **"clever traps":** "The Air Is Full of Politics," *Daily Record*, September 28, 1895.

CHAPTER 15: WHITE MEN AND WHITE METAL

113 **"Negro domination" was responsible:** Daniels, *Editor in Politics*, 283.

113 **"and white metal":** Daniels, *Editor in Politics*, 283.

114 **"*The Nuisance Disturber*":** Daniels, *Editor in Politics*, 91, 88.

114 **most influential white men:** Daniels, *Editor in Politics*, 91.

114 **His primary backer:** Julian Shakespeare Carr Papers: 1892–1923, folder 26: addresses, 1912–1914: Scan 104, Southern Historical Collection, Chapel Hill, North Carolina.

114 **"a country paper":** Daniels, *Editor in Politics*, 92.

114 **"sometimes too lurid":** Daniels, *Editor in Politics*, 253.

114 **"few in number":** Daniels, *Editor in Politics*, 253.

114 **had never subscribed:** Daniels, *Editor in Politics*, 254; Umfleet, *A Day of Blood*, 40.

114 **"sovereign Negro state":** Frank Weldon, "Blacks Propose to Colonize and Control North Carolina," *Atlanta Constitution*, October 12, 1898.

115 **Lieutenants compiled daily:** Zucchino, *Wilmington's Lie*, 99; H. Leon Prather Sr., *We Have Taken a City: Wilmington Racial Massacre and Coup of 1898* (Associated University Press, 1984), 49–50.

115 **"Vigilance committees" whipped:** Umfleet, *A Day of Blood*, 55–56; Zucchino, *Wilmington's Lie*, 98–99.

116 **"an armed camp":** Umfleet, *A Day of Blood*, 57.

116 **antebellum-style insouciance:** Henry Bacon McKoy, *Wilmington, N.C.—Do You Remember When?* (Keys Printing Company, 1957), 75.

116 **"silently flirt":** Emma Woodward MacMillan, *A Goodly Heritage* (Wilmington Printing Company, 1961), 14; Umfleet, *A Day of Blood*, 57.

116 **Five black balls:** McKoy, *Wilmington, N.C.*, 75.

116 **"To become a member":** McKoy, *Wilmington, N.C.*, 75.

116 **new Confederate museum:** "Confederate Museum: List of Many Relics Received Yesterday," *Wilmington Messenger*, May 7, 1898; "The Confederate Museum Established by the Cape Fear Chapter, Daughters of the Confederacy," *Wilmington Messenger*, November 5, 1899.

116 **"a minnie ball":** "Confederate Museum Established"; "New Hanover County Museum," *Lower Cape Fear Historical Society Bulletin* 5, no. 1 (1961): 3; "A Valuable Souvenir for the Confederate Museum," *Wilmington Messenger*, November 7, 1899.

117 **"white tribe's castles":** David W. Blight, *Race and Reunion: The Civil War in American Memory* (Havard University Press, 2001), 278.

117 **"racial, political and industrial disorder":** Blight, *Race and Reunion*, 266, 294.

117 **"those stirring times":** "Confederate Museum Established."

117 **"'living monuments'":** Karen L. Cox, "The Confederacy's 'Living Monuments,'" *New York Times*, October 6, 2017.

CHAPTER 16: SOWING THE SEED

119 **"A Mrs. Felton":** Alexander Manly, "Editorial," *Daily Record*, August 18, 1898, reprinted in Umfleet, *A Day of Blood*, 63.

120 **reprinted Felton's speech:** Umfleet, *A Day of Blood*, 64.

120 **"sow the seed":** Manly, "Editorial."

121 **"kicking, disorganizing concern":** "Mischief Making Simpleton," *Wilmington Messenger*, August 25, 1898.

121 **Facing pressure to denounce:** "The Wilmington Race Riots," *New York Times*, November 21, 1898.

121 **Love and Charity:** Reaves, *Strength Through Struggle*, 17.

121 **"avoid these places":** "Local Briefs," *Daily Record*, September 5, 1898.

121 **formed Company K:** Umfleet, *A Day of Blood*, 35.

122 **pin-back buttons:** Umfleet, *A Day of Blood*, 41; Zucchino, *Wilmington's Lie*, 107–9.

122 **howitzer salute:** "Back from the War: The W.L.I. Returned Home Yesterday," *Wilmington Messenger*, September 23, 1898.
122 **his Republican neighbor:** Zucchino, *Wilmington's Lie*, 142.
122 **seigneurial monologues:** Waddell, *Some Memories*, 157, 178.
122 **"And thrice welcome!":** "Back from the War."
122 **roast beef banquet:** "Back from the War."
122 **immortalized the festivities:** "Villainous Conduct of Negroes in Brunswick County," *Semi-Weekly Messenger*, September 23, 1898.
123 **"blood of history":** Albert J. Beveridge, "March of the Flag," Address to an Indiana Republican Meeting, Indianapolis, Indiana, National Humanities Center, September 16, 1898.
123 **"rushing forward":** Charles W. Chesnutt, *The Marrow of Tradition* (Houghton, Mifflin and Company, 1901), 155.
123 **Black companies from Wilmington:** Umfleet, *A Day of Blood*, 35; Zucchino, *Wilmington's Lie*, 111.
123 **But unlike their white brethren:** *McKinley's Guns*, directed by Kent Chatfield (2021; Wind Tree Research Productions); Zucchino, *Wilmington's Lie*, 113.
123 **"white heat":** Daniels, *Editor in Politics*, 289.
124 **"lustful black brutes":** "More Negro Scoundrelism: Black Beasts Attempt to Outrage the Young Daughter of a Respectable Farmer," *Wilmington Morning Star*, September 22, 1898; "A Horrid Slander: The Most Infamous That Ever Appeared in Print in This State," *Wilmington Morning Star*, September 23, 1898.
124 **"an easy victory":** Minutes of the Organizational Meeting of the Association of Members of the Wilmington Light Infantry, December 14, 1905, North Carolina Collection, Wilson Library, University of North Carolina at Chapel Hill, Chapel Hill (hereafter cited as Minutes of the Organizational Meeting of the WLI), quoted in Umfleet, *A Day of Blood*, 64.
124 **fifty-four times:** "A Horrid Slander," *Wilmington Morning Star*, August 30, 1898; "A Horrid Slander," *Wilmington Morning Star*, November 6, 1898.
124 **"servants to register":** "A Few Hints," *Daily Record*, October 20, 1898; "What Is There to Fear?" *Daily Record*, October 20, 1898.
125 **"unholy war":** Umfleet, *A Day of Blood*, 30, 44.
125 **"farce that is about to be":** *Evening Star*, November 2, 1898, quoted in Zucchino, *Wilmington's Lie*, 159–60.
125 **"the retort which":** Jack Thorne [David Bryant Fulton], *Hanover, or The Persecution of the Lowly: A Story of the Wilmington Massacre* (M.C.L. Hill, 1901), 13–14.
125 **paid advertisement:** Umfleet, *A Day of Blood*, 68.

CHAPTER 17: CHOKE THE CAPE FEAR RIVER

127 **"a neighborhood fight":** Colonel F. D. Winston, quoted in Reaves, *Strength Through Struggle*, 245–46.
127 **"to suit ourselves":** Umfleet, *A Day of Blood*, 45.
127 **"by sending literature":** "1898 Constitution and By-Laws of the White Government Union," Block 185: 1865–1919, William B. McKoy Legal Papers, Lower Cape Fear Historical Society Archives.
128 **"gross libel":** "A Deceptive Letter Writer: The Willful, Malicious Attempt of W. H. Chadbourn to Libel the Whites of This Community," *Wilmington Messenger*, October 12, 1898; Umfleet, *A Day of Blood*, 45–46, 210; Prather, *We Have Taken a City*, 64–66.

128 **retracted his statement:** Umfleet, *A Day of Blood*, 46; Prather, *We Have Taken a City*, 64–66.
128 **"for his health":** James S. Worth to Josephine, November 4, 1898, James Spencer Worth Papers, Southern Historical Collection, quoted in Umfleet, *A Day of Blood*, 210n43.
128 **"all did it":** "A Letter of Eliza Yonge Wootten & the Rev. Edward Wootten," November 8, 1898, reprinted in the *Lower Cape Fear Historical Bulletin* 46, no. 3 (2002): 1, 3.
128 **"vigilance committee" tracked:** Iredell Meares, "The Wilmington Revolution," *Greensboro Patriot*, July 25, 1900.
128 **"doing practically nothing":** George Rountree, "Memorandum of My Personal Recollection of the Election of 1898," box 3, folder 41, Henry G. Connor Papers: 1744–1924, Southern Historical Collection, Wilson Library, University of North Carolina at Chapel Hill, 4–5.
128 **ride on a tugboat:** Zucchino, *Wilmington's Lie*, 103–5.
129 **"handsome naptha launch":** "A Commodious Naptha Launch," *Wilmington Semi-Weekly Messenger*, April 19, 1898, cited in the Family Files of the Bill Reaves Collection, New Hanover County Public Library.
129 **"wrecked in health":** B. F. Keith to William H. Hayes, February 19, 1919, Private Collection of Thomas Keith.
129 **bringing private utilities:** "1898 Wilmington Race Riot," 1898 Wilmington Institute for Education and Research.
129 **"Government by the People":** "Our Mission Is to Push: Wilmington Must Go Forward—It Has Advantages," *New Era*, May 6, 1896.
129 **headlines as "poke-juice":** B. F. Keith, *Memories* (Bynum Printing Co., 1922), 76.
130 **"the ultimate solution":** "B. F. Keith," *Wilmington Messenger*, September 4, 1898; "No Blood Spilt: Mr. B. F. Keith Assaults Mr. J. A. Fore in Consequence of an Article in the Messenger Last Sunday," *Wilmington Semi-Weekly Messenger*, September 9, 1898.
130 **"uncalled for abuse":** "B. F. Keith Replies," *Wilmington Semi-Weekly Messenger*, September 9, 1898; "B. F. Keith," *Wilmington Semi-Weekly Messenger*, September 4, 1898.
130 **"'civilization vs. barbarism'?":** "B. F. Keith Replies."
130 **"Murder!" Fore screamed:** Keith, *Memories*, 105–7.
130 **charged with assault and battery:** "Resented the Charge," *Wilmington Morning Star*, September 8, 1898.
130 **"mischievous animal":** "B. F. Keith."
131 **"God's creatures":** Keith, *Memories*, 102.
131 **"deep consideration":** Anonymous to B. F. Keith, October 21, 1898, Private Collection of Thomas Keith.
131 **"a lot of innocent people killed here":** Timothy B. Tyson, "The Ghosts of 1898: Wilmington's Race Riot and the Rise of White Supremacy," *News & Observer*, November 17, 2006.
131 **"too clean and brave to run":** B. F. Keith to Warren G. Harding, July 5, 1921, Private Collection of Thomas Keith.
131 **"drunken red shirts":** B. F. Keith to Warren G. Harding, July 5, 1921.
131 **"baluster supports":** Keith, *Memories*, 103–4.
133 **"engross her all the time":** Eliza DeRosset to Lossie Myers, November 13, 1863, quoted in Anna Koivusalo "'Nothing to Lose & *Everything* to Gain': Louis and Marie deRosset's Intimate Friendship with Edward Bulwer Lytton," *Australasian Journal of Victorian Studies* 26, no. 1 (2022): 26.
133 **Marie wrapped Gabrielle:** L. T. Moore, *Stories Old and New*, 166.
133 **"dark and stormy night"; "silver fork":** Edward Bulwer-Lytton, *Paul Clifford* (Henry Colburn and Richard Bentley, 1830), 1; Koivusalo, "'Nothing to Lose,'" 25.

133 **Orphaned at twelve:** Gilmore, *Gender and Jim Crow*, 109.
134 **she married Waddell:** Gilmore, *Gender and Jim Crow*, 109.
134 **"deafening cheers":** "Sizzling Talk"; Zucchino, *Wilmington's Lie*, 144–48.
135 **"choke the current":** "Sizzling Talk."
135 **"aflame with anger":** Catherine W. Bishir, "Landmarks of Power: Building a Southern Past, 1885–1915," in *Southern Cultures: The Fifteenth Anniversary Reader*, ed. Harry L. Watson and Larry J. Griffin (University of North Carolina Press, 2008), 64–65.

CHAPTER 18: RULE OR DIE

136 **blazing fall sunset:** Daniels, *Editor in Politics*, 293.
136 **enforcer caste:** Gilmore, *Gender and Jim Crow*, 65.
136 **"the dirty work of politics":** Chesnutt, *Marrow of Tradition*, 22.
136 **"especially invited and expected":** "Senator Ben. Tillman to Speak," *Fayetteville Observer*, October 13, 1898; "A White Man's Day: Eight to Ten Thousand People Out," *Fayetteville Observer*, October 22, 1898.
136 **"the jewel of her womanhood":** Zucchino, *Wilmington's Lie*, 123.
136 **make an example of Alexander Manly:** Tyson, "The Ghosts of 1898," 8H.
137 **prudently stayed inside:** Umfleet, *A Day of Blood*, 53.
137 **eleventh-hour deal:** Umfleet, *A Day of Blood*, 61.
137 **would run unopposed:** Umfleet, *A Day of Blood*, 67; "Local Ticket Withdrawn," *Evening Star*, November 4, 1898.
137 **"shoot him down":** Alfred Moore Waddell, quoted in "The North Carolina Race Conflict," *Outlook* 60 (1898), quoted in Umfleet, *A Day of Blood*, 59.
137 **"as Willie James":** Umfleet, *A Day of Blood*, 70.
138 **Black registrar:** Umfleet, *A Day of Blood*, 71–73.
138 **"thoroughly peaceable":** "White Supremacy: New Hanover County and the Sixth Senatorial District Redeemed," *Wilmington Morning Star*, November 9, 1898; Prather, *We Have Taken a City*, 96.
138 **"imperishable glory":** "Bellamy Is Elected Just as We Expected: The Great Victory," *Wilmington Morning Star*, November 9, 1898.
138 **"rule or die":** "Mother" to Sallie, November 9, 1898, Eliza Hall Parsley Papers, Southern Historical Collection, quoted in Umfleet, *A Day of Blood*, 73.
138 **"ATTENTION WHITE MEN":** "Attention White Men," *Wilmington Messenger*, November 9, 1898.
138 **"from the minister to the merchant":** Hayden, *Story of the Wilmington Rebellion*; "A Remarkable Meeting: The Negro Editor Banished from the City," *Wilmington Messenger*, November 10, 1898; Zucchino, *Wilmington's Lie*, 175–79; Prather, *We Have Taken a City*, 108.
141 **vacate their positions:** Prather, *We Have Taken a City*, 50.
142 **Brothers Hugh and Donald MacRae:** "A Remarkable Meeting."
142 **"vigorously carry out the action of the meeting":** Prather, *We Have Taken a City*, 110.
142 **stability and prominence:** Prather, *We Have Taken a City*, 110, 188.
143 **T. C. Miller, who had:** Zucchino, *Wilmington's Lie*, 180; Umfleet, *A Day of Blood*, 186.
143 **Dr. Thomas Mask:** Umfleet, *A Day of Blood*, 185.
143 **no such dialogue:** Umfleet, *A Day of Blood*, 75–78; Prather, *We Have Taken a City*, 111.
143 **"graphic and determined way":** "The Wilmington Riots: W. E. Henderson, an Exiled Negro, Vividly Describes Them," *Indianapolis Journal*, November 25, 1898; "Citizens Aroused: The Committee at Work," *Wilmington Morning Star*, November 10, 1898; "A Remarkable Meeting."

144 **John Harriss Howe had built:** Reaves, *Strength Through Struggle*, 412.

145 **"Please Deliver at House":** Prather, *We Have Taken a City*, 111; Zucchino, *Wilmington's Lie*, 184.

145 **Waddell had still not received:** Waddell, "The Story of the Wilmington, North Carolina, Race Riots"; Umfleet, *A Day of Blood*, 82–83.

145 **vacuum of leadership:** Umfleet, *A Day of Blood*, 82–83.

145 **"as if by magic":** Chesnutt, *Marrow of Tradition*, 178; Umfleet, *A Day of Blood*, 84.

145 **took an hour:** Umfleet, *A Day of Blood*, 84.

145 **"their return to power":** Henry Litchfield West, "The Race War in North Carolina," *The Forum* 26 (1899), in "Wilmington Riot of November 10, 1898" Source Documents Collection SC-MS-069, box 1, folder 38, Center for Southeast North Carolina Archives and History, UNCW Library.

146 **No one answered:** Waddell, "Story of the Wilmington, North Carolina, Race Riots."

146 **them to pieces:** Umfleet, *A Day of Blood*, 84; Prather, *We Have Taken a City*, 113.

146 **"set it afire":** Waddell, "Story of the Wilmington, North Carolina, Race Riots."

146 **Manly was long gone:** The exact timing of this story is disputed, as Manly didn't speak publicly about the event in the years following; however, the most reliable information comes from a letter written from his wife to his children after his death; Prather, *We Have Taken a City*, 96–98.

146 **"a pre-arranged 'lynching'":** Thomas W. Clawson, "The Wilmington Race Riot in 1898: Recollections and Memories," Thomas W. Clawson Papers #2792-z–1898, Southern Historical Collection, Wilson Special Collections Library, University of North Carolina at Chapel Hill.

146 **differently than Clawson:** Caroline Sadgwar Manly to her sons, January 14, 1954; Prather, *We Have Taken a City*, 96–98.

147 **triggered the alert:** Prather, *We Have Taken a City*, 113–14; "Awful Calamity: Wilmington's Dred Fear Realized," *Wilmington Messenger*, November 11, 1898.

148 **remaining walls teetering:** Prather, *We Have Taken a City*, 114.

148 **"We wrecked the house":** Waddell, "The Story of the Wilmington, North Carolina, Race Riots."

148 **dead snake:** Umfleet, *A Day of Blood*, 85.

148 **job well done:** Prather, *We Have Taken a City*, 114–15.

148 **"what might eventuate":** James H. Cowan, "The Wilmington Race Riot" (unpublished memoir, n.d.), Louis T. Moore Collection, New Hanover County Public Library, quoted in Umfleet, *A Day of Blood*, 87.

148 **Something very strange:** Prather, *We Have Taken a City*, 116; Rountree, "Memorandum of My Personal Recollection of the Election of 1898."

149 **"fighting at Sprunt's":** Prather, *We Have Taken a City*, 117.

149 **to the compress:** Umfleet, *A Day of Blood*, 87.

149 **"whole gang of Negroes":** Minutes of the Organizational Meeting of the WLI, quoted in Umfleet, *A Day of Blood*, 87–88.

149 **"bowie knife or two":** Umfleet, *A Day of Blood*, 97.

149 **"they had done nothing":** Rountree, "Memorandum of My Personal Recollection of the Election of 1898," 12.

149 **elsewhere in small groups:** Prather, *We Have Taken a City*, 118; Umfleet, *A Day of Blood*, 95.

149 **"guards, with their guns":** "A Pure-Bred Negro Relates It," *Wilmington Messenger*, May 24, 1905, "Wilmington Riot of November 10, 1898" Source Documents (SC-MS-069), box 1, folder 39, Center for Southeast North Carolina Archives and History, UNCW Library; Zucchino, *Wilmington's Lie*, 212.

150 **believed they were in control:** Umfleet, *A Day of Blood*, 88–92, 95.
150 **"go home and stay there!":** Umfleet, *A Day of Blood*, 88.
150 **Aaron Lockamy:** Umfleet, *A Day of Blood*, 93.
150 **firing back:** Umfleet, *A Day of Blood*, 91.
150 **"like striking a match":** Keith, *Memories*, 111.
150 **"riot alarm":** Umfleet, *A Day of Blood*, 93; Prather, *We Have Taken a City*, 120–21.
151 **"Negroes Shooting and Killing Whites":** Prather, *We Have Taken a City*, 121.

CHAPTER 19: MOTHER'S TATTERED SHAWL

152 **"boss stevedore":** "The Stevedore Trouble," *Wilmington Morning Star*, December 11, 1886.
152 **no secret in the family:** Cynthia Brown, interview with author, November 8, 2018.
153 **Athalia called to her mother:** Judge, "If It Ever Happens, Run."
153 **"shoot to kill":** Minutes of the Organizational Meeting of the WLI.
153 **"shrieking and crying":** J. Allen Kirk, "A Statement of Facts Concerning the Bloody Riot in Wilmington, N.C." (self–published, 1898); Zucchino, *Wilmington's Lie*, 229.
153 **"blaze away":** Minutes of the Organizational Meeting of the WLI.
153 **"stacked with men and guns":** Minutes of the Organizational Meeting of the WLI.
153 **their own hands:** Judge, "If It Ever Happens, Run."
154 **"mother's tattered shawl":** Charles Francis Bourke, "The Committee of Twenty-Five Men," *Collier's*, November 26, 1898; Prather, *We Have Taken a City*, 135.
155 **"The Red Shirts paraded":** Cotton, "A Historical Incident."
156 **"'do you think they were complicit'":** Barbara Bell Coleman, interview with author, October 5, 2020.
156 **interpreted these vigils:** June Nash, "The Cost of Violence," *Journal of Black Studies* 4, no. 2 (1973): 163–66, 76.
157 **"really the Wilmington massacre":** Cotton, "A Historical Incident."
157 **"wore that flag":** Nash, "The Cost of Violence," 164.

CHAPTER 20: IN TERROREM

158 **"fiery big horses":** Prather, *We Have Taken a City*, 124.
158 **"expression of manhood":** Kirk, "A Statement of Facts."
158 **fired at a white man:** Zucchino, *Wilmington's Lie*, 215; Prather, *We Have Taken a City*, 124.
158 **several Black businesses:** Zucchino, *Wilmington's Lie*, 215; Umfleet, *A Day of Blood*, 99.
158 **"Halt!" the white gunmen called:** Prather, *We Have Taken a City*, 130; Umfleet, *A Day of Blood*, 99.
159 **"look of s'prise":** Waddell, "The Story of the Wilmington, North Carolina, Race Riots."
159 **Inside they found:** Zucchino, *Wilmington's Lie*, 216; Prather, 124–25.
159 **"Hill Terry's house":** Minutes of the Organizational Meeting of the WLI.
160 **"The poor creature":** Jane Cronly, "An Account of a Race Riot in Wilmington, N.C., in 1898," Cronly Family Papers, David M. Rubenstein Rare Book & Manuscript Library, Duke University; Prather, *We Have Taken a City*, 125.
160 **self-appointed Democratic guardians:** Zucchino, *Wilmington's Lie*, 221–23.
160 **"made each officer resign *seriatim*":** J. D. Bellamy, *Memoirs of an Octogenarian*, 72.
160 **room as aldermen:** Prather, *We Have Taken a City*, 136.
160 **emerged powerless:** Zucchino, *Wilmington's Lie*, 222–24.

CHAPTER 21: OMELETS

161 **"old slave days":** "The Fisk Jubilee Singers, Birmingham," *Daily Mail*, February 1, 1898.
161 **prominent placement:** "White Versus Negro in America: Bloodshed at Wilmington," *Daily Telegraph*, November 11, 1898, 7; "Rioting at Wilmington," *London Standard*, November 11, 1898, 3; "Racial Troubles in the States," *Manchester Guardian*, November 11, 1898, 6.
162 **"tears will blot this":** Caroline Sadgwar Manly to her sons, January 14, 1954, Alex L. Manly Papers, 0065-b1-fb, East Carolina Manuscript Collection.
162 **targeted for banishment:** Zucchino, *Wilmington's Lie*, 249; Umfleet, *A Day of Blood*, 108.
162 **"heralding their miscegenation":** Hayden, *Story of the Wilmington Rebellion*.
162 **"wagon like cordwood":** Umfleet, *A Day of Blood*, 107.
162 **flipping real estate:** Zucchino, *Wilmington's Lie*, 238.
163 **"he talked and talked":** Minutes of the Organizational Meeting of the WLI.
163 **"followed the wagon":** Hayden, *Story of the Wilmington Rebellion*.
163 **"for safe keeping":** Hayden, *Story of the Wilmington Rebellion*.
163 **keeping the prisoners alive:** Prather, *We Have Taken a City*, 141.
163 **"a hollow square":** Umfleet, *A Day of Blood*, 108.
163 **"special police badge":** Umfleet, *A Day of Blood*, 110.
163 **"least of the insulting names":** "Arrived in Washington: Melton, Bunting, and Gilbert—Three of the Scoundrels Expelled from Wilmington at Department of Justice," *Wilmington Morning Star*, November 15, 1898.
163 **"war of purification":** Umfleet, *A Day of Blood*, 113.
163 **conscious of appearances:** Umfleet, *A Day of Blood*, 113.
164 **"appointed and recognized":** Mrs. Roger Moore to *The Messenger*, A Communication by Mrs. Roger Moore Collection (SC-MS-130), box 3, folder 1, Center for Southeast North Carolina Archives and History, UNCW Library.
165 **"Mrs. So-and-So":** Hossfeld, *Narrative, Political Unconscious, and Racial Violence*, 127.
165 **checkpoints and searches:** Umfleet, *A Day of Blood*, 123.
165 **"victims of exposure":** "Register Lyon's Ringing Letter," *Richmond Planet*, December 10, 1898.
165 **wrote to his wife:** James S. Worth to "Josephine," November 16, 1898, Worth Family Papers: 1844–1955, David M. Rubenstein Rare Book & Manuscript Library, Duke University; Umfleet, *A Day of Blood*, 124.
165 **"a low voice":** "The Wilmington Riots: W. E. Henderson, an Exiled Negro, Vividly Describes Them," *Indianapolis Journal*, November 25, 1898.
166 **via his father:** Andrea Smythe, "Scott, Armond Wendell," *NCpedia*, State Library of North Carolina, June 2023; Zucchino, *Wilmington's Lie*, 233–34.
166 **"cause to be thankful":** "Lawyer Scott Banished," *Wilmington Messenger*, November 11, 1898.
166 **"never to return":** "Local Dots: Lawyer Scott Banished," *Wilmington Morning Star*, November 11, 1898.
166 **swarming with Red Shirts:** Zucchino, *Wilmington's Lie*, 240–41; Kirk, "A Statement of Facts."
167 **"an inoffensive deportment":** Umfleet, *A Day of Blood*, 123; Reaves, *Strength Through Struggle*, 254.
167 **short of crucial labor:** Zucchino, *Wilmington's Lie*, 253.
167 **new white policemen:** Umfleet, *A Day of Blood*, 121.

167 **"decency and respectability":** Rev. Peyton Hoge in 1898, quoted by Amanda Greene, "1898 Riots Still Resonate with Wilmington's Black Churches," *StarNews*, November 6, 2008.

167 **"make an omelet":** "Interview of Rev. C. T. Blackwell White minister of First Baptist Church," *Messenger*, November 14, 1998, 1898 Foundation Papers (SC-MS-217), box 4, Center for Southeast North Carolina Archives and History, UNCW Library.

168 **"to congratulate you":** Wade H. Harris to A. M. Waddell, November 10, 1898, "Wilmington Riot of November 10, 1898" Source Documents (SC-MS-069), box 1, folder 11, Center for Southeast North Carolina Archives and History, UNCW Library.

168 **"mud and degradation":** J. M. Cameron to Waddell, November 11, 1898, "Wilmington Riot of November 10, 1898" Source Documents (SC-MS-069), box 1, folder 12, Center for Southeast North Carolina Archives and History, UNCW Library.

168 **"Sunday all the time":** Waddell, "The Story of the Wilmington, North Carolina, Race Riots."

168 **"will prove conclusively":** "Good Order Rules: Business Has Been Resumed and the City Has Regained Its Normal Tranquility," *Wilmington Morning Star*, November 13, 1898.

168 **"Negro aggressor":** "Riot Refugees: Negroes Who Fled to the Woods Suffering," *Wilmington Semi-Weekly Messenger*, November 15, 1898.

169 **had been shot in the back:** *Transactions of the Medical Society of the State of North Carolina, Forty-Sixth Annual Meeting Held at Asheville NC, May 30, 31, and June 1, 1899* (Observer Printing and Publishing House, 1899), 134, 166.

169 **"Please send releif [*sic*]"; "Why do you forsake the Negro?":** Anonymous to President William McKinley, November 13, 1898, Documents on the 1898 Wilmington Massacre, Local History Room, New Hanover County Public Library; Anonymous to Mr. Mc Kinly [*sic*], November 15, 1898, Documents on the 1898 Wilmington Massacre, Local History Room, New Hanover County Public Library.

169 **"this one-horse town":** *New York Journal* article, reprinted in the *Indianapolis Freeman*, December 3, 1898, quoted in Zucchino, *Wilmington's Lie*, 268.

169 **"fatal race riots":** "Nine Negroes Shot to Death," *New York Times*, November 11, 1898.

169 **The paper's headline:** "Horrible Butcheries at Wilmington," *Richmond Planet*, November 19, 1898.

169 **demanding federal action:** "Wilmington Refugees," *Fayetteville Weekly Observer*, November 17, 1898; Zucchino, *Wilmington's Lie*, 286.

170 **"ringing letter":** "Register Lyons' Ringing Letter," *Richmond Planet*, December 10, 1898, first published in the *New York Herald* on December 4, 1898.

170 **"If we can't get protection now":** "The Wilmington Riots: W. E. Henderson, an Exiled Negro, Vividly Describes Them."

170 **"irreversible judgment of battle":** John Ascher, "Remembering President William McKinley 100 Years After His Assassination," *New Federalist*, September 2001.

170 **"disgrace to the state":** Zucchino, *Wilmington's Lie*, 287; Prather, *We Have Taken a City*, 151.

170 **"greatly burdened":** Booker T. Washington, *Up from Slavery: An Autobiography* (Doubleday & Co., 1900), 304.

170 **"an inveterate conciliator":** Blight, *Race and Reunion*, 351.

170 **"exacerbated racial antagonism":** Blight, *Race and Reunion*, 352.

170 **"Don't do it"; "men of white skins":** National Archives materials relating to the 1898 Wilmington Race Riot, RG 60, General Records of the Department of Justice, box 117A (1887–1904), file 17743–1898, transcribed August 2002, and Julian Shakespeare

Carr in the *Wilmington Messenger*, November 12, 1898, both quoted in Zucchino, *Wilmington's Lie*, 291.

171 **"incomprehensible silence":** "Open Letter to President McKinley by Colored People of Massachusetts," October 3, 1899, Library of Congress Archives.

171 **"echoes of the wreck reverberating":** "The Political Horoscope," *Colored American*, September 20, 1902.

CHAPTER 22: FLAMING MUTILATIONS

172 **"BELLAMY IS ELECTED":** "Bellamy Is Elected Just as We Expected," *Weekly Star*, November 11, 1898.

172 **with free liquor:** Zucchino, *Wilmington's Lie*, 164.

172 **delivered him:** "Negroism Defunct: She Is Again Placed in Line with Her Sister States of the South," *Wilmington Semi-Weekly Messenger*, November 11, 1898; "Glorious Victory: New Hanover Goes for White Supremacy," *Wilmington Semi-Weekly Messenger*, November 11, 1898.

172 **"the vilest slanderer":** Hayden, *Story of the Wilmington Rebellion*.

172 **"his hospitable home":** "Congressman Bellamy: The Second Regiment Band Serenaded Him Last Night—Delightfully Entertained," *Wilmington Morning Star*, November 16, 1898.

173 **factotums, not guests:** Umfleet, *A Day of Blood*, 127.

173 **"farce, a mockery":** *Contested Election Case: Oliver H. Dockery vs. John D. Bellamy, From the Sixth Congressional District of the State of North Carolina* (Government Printing Office, 1899), 5.

173 **denied Dockery's charges:** J. D. Bellamy, *Memoirs of an Octogenarian*, 140.

173 **"simply a uniform":** *Contested Election Case*, 6.

174 **"plantation literature":** J. D. Bellamy, *Memoirs of an Octogenarian*, 140.

174 **inside job:** J. D. Bellamy, *Memoirs of an Octogenarian*, 140.

174 **"not one word of condemnation":** William E. Henderson, Lisa Adams Address, University of North Carolina Wilmington, November 1998, quoted in Zucchino, *Wilmington's Lie*, 321.

175 **tacit agreement that once:** "Cape Fear S. F. E. Company," *Wilmington Morning Star*, November 11, 1897; Umfleet, *A Day of Blood*, 126.

175 **Waddell fired:** Zucchino, *Wilmington's Lie*, 276.

175 **gold-headed cane:** "'Mike' Dowling Honored," *Wilmington Morning Star*, December 6, 1898; "Funeral of Mrs. Dowling," *Wilmington Morning Star*, January 25, 1911; Janet F. Davidson, "The 1898 White Supremacist Campaign and Massacre: A Brief Narrative," Cape Fear Museum of History and Science, n.d., 11n34.

175 **he was arrested:** "Funeral of Mrs. Dowling."

175 **"beautiful and substantial":** Reaves, *Strength Through Struggle*, 412.

176 **His only heir:** Reaves, *Strength Through Struggle*, 412; Population Schedule for New Hanover County, North Carolina, ED 109, Fourteenth Census of the United States, 1920, NARA microfilm publication T625, Records of the Bureau of the Census, RG 29, National Archives, Washington, D.C.

176 **severely beat:** "Believed to Be Manly," *Wilmington Morning Star*, November 13, 1898.

176 **resurfaced in Asbury Park:** Zucchino, *Wilmington's Lie*, 279.

176 **uncharacteristic caution:** "Manly Defends the Negro," *Baltimore Sun*, November 17, 1898.

177 **"he had lost everything":** "Manly Is at Asbury Park," *Baltimore Sun*, November 14, 1898.

CHAPTER 23: A PERMANENT MEMORIAL

182 **"spirit of revenge":** Edmonds, *The Negro and Fusion Politics*, 193.
183 **"to protect fish":** Edmonds, *The Negro and Fusion Politics*, 193.
183 **"getting in position":** Hon. H. G. Connor, "Presentation of the Portrait of Hon. George Howard to the Supreme Court of North Carolina," February 13, 1917, in *North Carolina Reports Vol. 173: Cases Argued and Determined in the Supreme Court of North Carolina, Spring Term, 1917* (Bynum Printing Company, 1955), 877–96.
183 **mandating Jim Crow:** Edmonds, *The Negro and Fusion Politics*, 189.
183 **"SEPARATE CARS":** Nash, "The Cost of Violence," 171.
183 **oppressive measures followed:** Edmonds, *The Negro and Fusion Politics*, 191–92.
183 **"buy a ticket":** Philip Gerard, interview with author, February 13, 2019.
183 **so-called grandfather clause:** Paul D. Escott and David R. Goldfield, eds., *Major Problems in the History of the American South, Volume II: The New South* (D.C. Heath and Co., 1990), 179.
184 **"must show his faith":** "The General Assembly," *Union Republican*, February 23, 1899, quoted in Edmonds, *The Negro and Fusion Politics*, 182.
184 **"how can you explain away the actions":** "That North Carolina Constitution," *Richmond Planet*, December 3, 1898.
184 **"great sledge hammer":** "The General Assembly," *Union Republican*, February 23, 1899, quoted in Edmonds, *The Negro and Fusion Politics*, 182.
184 **"a permanent memorial":** John Haley, "Race, Rhetoric, and Revolution," in *Democracy Betrayed*, 219.
184 **silencing Black voters:** Zucchino, *Wilmington's Lie*, 315.
184 **thirty thousand:** Gilmore, *Gender and Jim Crow*, 124.
184 ***two votes*:** Edmonds, *The Negro and Fusion Politics*, 233; Tom Keith, email to author, July 20, 2021.
184 **"lily white":** Quoted in Edmonds, *The Negro and Fusion Politics*, 213; Gilmore, *Gender and Jim Crow*, 115.
185 **wastewater situation:** Meares, "Wilmington Revolution."
185 **strategy the North Carolina Way:** Haley, "Race, Rhetoric, and Revolution," in *Democracy Betrayed*, 220.
185 **"hollow pretext":** Edward Ball, *Life of a Klansman: A Family History in White Supremacy* (Farrar, Straus and Giroux, 2020), 277.
185 **"flame of passion":** Meares, "Wilmington Revolution."
185 **"in terms of savagery":** Chestnutt, *Marrow of Tradition*, 327.
186 **"recent experiences in":** Waddell, *Some Memories*, 244; Alfred Moore Waddell, "The Franchise in the South," in *Race Problems of the South: Report of the Proceedings of the First Annual Conference Held Under the Auspices of the Southern Society for the Promotion of the Study of Race Conditions and Problems in the South at Montgomery, Alabama, May 8, 9, 10, 1900* (B. F. Johnson Publishing Co., 1900), 39–48.
186 **"greatest political crime":** Waddell, "The Franchise in the South," 44.
186 **"the bob-tailed dog":** Waddell, "The Franchise in the South," 42.
186 **"much fairer-colored man":** Waddell, *Some Memories*, 245.

CHAPTER 24: CUFFS

187 **employed in domestic service:** "Black Domestic Workers," *Women & the American Story (Free Curriculum Website)*, The New York Historical.

188 **"impossible to convict":** Meares, "Wilmington Revolution."
188 **"articles of raiment":** "Kitchen Robbery: Two Colored Women Tried for the Crime and Bound Over," *Wilmington Messenger*, September 7, 1899.
189 **containing napkins and a butter jar:** "Woman Sneak Thief Caught," *Wilmington Messenger*, August 28, 1900.
189 **jury convicted Sallie:** "The Criminal Court: Several Convictions Yesterday at the Third Day's Session," *Wilmington Semi-Weekly Messenger*, November 27, 1900.
189 **care of their toddlers:** Population Schedule for New Hanover County, North Carolina, Twelfth Census of the United States, 1900, NARA microfilm publication T623, Records of the Bureau of the Census, RG 29, National Archives, Washington, D.C.
189 **"black man's Waterloo":** "The Political Horoscope."
190 **"most fair-skinned Negroes":** Prather, *We Stole a City*, 162.
190 **"elevator man":** Twelfth Census of the United States.
190 **as a bellhop:** "Armond W. Scott Dies; Municipal Court Judge," *Evening Star*, September 19, 1960.
190 **"Hell, this isn't Scott?":** "I Sent Thousands of Men to Jail," *Ebony*, September 1958, 84–90.
190 **"colorful, often fiery":** "Judge Armond Scott's Estate Valued at $140,000," *Jet* 19, no. 3: (1960): 7.
190 **"to one drink":** "Armond W. Scott Dies."
191 **"Up from Hell":** "I Sent Thousands of Men to Jail," 84.
192 **a white majority:** Umfleet, *A Day of Blood*, 18, 152.
192 **thousand fewer Black:** Umfleet, *A Day of Blood*, 151–52.
192 **donning red bandannas:** McKoy, *Wilmington, N.C.*, 141–43.
192 **Black businesses withdrew:** Umfleet, *A Day of Blood*, 151, 155.
192 **steamboat captain:** Prather, *We Have Taken a City*, 162.
192 **John Singer Sargent:** Holland Cotter, "John Singer Sargent's Drawings Bring His Model Out of the Shadows," *New York Times*, May 7, 2020.
192 **principals in Philadelphia:** Isabel Wilkerson, *The Warmth of Other Suns: The Epic Story of America's Great Migration* (Vintage Books, 2011), 533.
192 **"colonies of refugees":** "Wants Refugees to Return: Recent Wilmington Race War Responsible for John Green's Mission to Brooklyn," *Brooklyn Eagle*, August 25, 1899.
192 **"a permanent basis":** "Influx of Colored People," *Brooklyn Daily Eagle*, January 30, 1899.
193 **"live on scraps":** "Wants Refugees to Return."
193 **"a man in Wilmington":** Quoted in Hossfeld, *Narrative, Political Unconscious, and Racial Violence*, 131.
193 **desperate to return home:** Umfleet, *A Day of Blood*, 186.
193 **"worse than a dog":** Umfleet, *A Day of Blood*, 230–31.
194 **The next year, he died:** Umfleet, *A Day of Blood*, 230–31.
194 **"insolent negro":** Alston Watts in the *News & Observer*, March 5, 1901, quoted in Zucchino, *Wilmington's Lie*, 323.
194 **a Red Shirt organizer:** A. Christopher Meekins, "Kitchin, Claude," *NCpedia*, 2020.
194 **"civil death sentence":** Gilmore, *Gender and Jim Crow*, 119.
194 **"I cannot live in North Carolina":** "Southern Negro's Plaint; Congressman G. H. White Forced to Leave North Carolina," *New York Times*, August 26, 1900; Zucchino, *Wilmington's Lie*, 323.
194 **hosted Alexander Manly's wedding:** "The Political Horoscope."
194 **resurrected the newspaper:** John Jeremiah Sullivan, "Daily Record Remnants Issue Vol. 1," *Third Person Project*, August 2, 2019.

194 **land was fertile:** "History Whitesboro," Concerned Citizens of Whitesboro, Inc.
195 **"a black city":** George W. Reid, "The Post-Congressional Career of George H. White, 1901–1918," *Journal of Negro History* 61, no. 4 (1976): 369.
195 **"Progressive Whitesboro":** "History Whitesboro"; "Whitesboro, N.J.," August 17, 2007, Beinecke Rare Book & Manuscript Library, Yale University.
195 **mothers and fathers:** Population Schedule for Cape May County, New Jersey, Middle Township, ED 92, Thirteenth Census of the United States, 1910, NARA microfilm publication T624, Records of the Bureau of the Census, RG 29, National Archives, Washington, D.C.
196 **Labor Day reunion:** Kam Williams, "Best Known for His High-Profile Relationship with Oprah, Stedman Graham Has Quietly Built a Reputation for Community Service," *Bay State Banner*, August 10, 2010.
196 **Whitesboro scholarship fund:** Bill Duhart, "N.J. Town's Oprah Connection Is Just the Beginning. It Was Also a Haven from Racist South," NJ.com, November 26, 2021.

CHAPTER 25: A CHILD'S BOX OF LETTERS

197 **"elaborate scale":** *Dispatch*, September 14, 1899, quoted in Block, *Images of America*, 27.
197 **known as the German Helmet:** Block, *Images of America*, 27.
198 **"serve us at the cottage":** J. D. Bellamy, *Memoirs of an Octogenarian*, 154–55.
198 **152 turtle eggs:** "Turtles and Turtle-Eggs," *Wilmington Morning Star*, June 22, 1893.
198 **"Henry Brewington will serve them":** "Oyster Roast," *Wilmington Messenger*, February 13, 1894.
198 **Republican politics in Wilmington:** "The Political Experiment," *Wilmington Morning Star*, July 14, 1869.
198 **traumatic experience:** Ben Steelman, "MyReporter Talks About Famous Local Hurricanes," *StarNews*, September 1, 2020.
198 **his guest's lace-ups:** J. D. Bellamy, *Memoirs of an Octogenarian*, 155.
199 **"ignorant negro":** J. D. Bellamy, *Memoirs of an Octogenarian*, 155.
199 **Lost Cause remade:** Blight, *Race and Reunion*, 278.
199 **"record the truth":** "Alfred Moore Waddell, Enlightened Wilmingtonian," Cape Fear Historical Institute Papers, Cape Fear Historical Institute.
200 **"like a child's box":** Alfred Moore Waddell quoting James Anthony Froude, quoted in Bishir, "Landmarks of Power," 59–60.
200 **"suppression of black supremacy":** Hossfeld, *Narrative, Political Unconscious, and Racial Violence*, 54.
200 **"in their place":** Thomas E. Watson, quoted in Clifford Kuhn and Gregory Mixon, "Atlanta Race Massacre of 1906," *New Georgia Encyclopedia*, September 23, 2005.
200 ***Use violence*:** Tyson, "The Ghosts of 1898."
200 **"with hanging carcasses":** "Fleming Makes Answer to Smith and Hardwick," *Atlanta Constitution*, November 9, 1906.
200 **"black devils"; "extreme insolence":** Various articles, *Atlanta Journal*, September 22, 1906.
200 **kissed her hand:** "Negro Kissed Young Girl on Hand," *Atlanta Journal*, September 22, 1906.
200 **streamed into Atlanta's Black neighborhoods:** "The Atlanta Race Massacre of 1906: A Brief History," *National Center for Civil & Human Rights*, August 2022.
201 **lucrative real estate:** Hossfeld, *Narrative, Political Unconscious, and Racial Violence*, 53–54.
201 **Lumina was lit:** "Lumina Part 1," *Wrightsville Beach Magazine*, June 24, 2008.

201 **Society had been founded:** "History," The North Carolina Society of New York.
201 **Sons and Daughters:** David Cecelski, "The Sons and Daughters of North Carolina," September 19, 2021.
201 **"Southern Progress":** "*Speeches Delivered at the Dinner of the North Carolina Society of New York, at the Hotel Astor, December 7, 1908* (n.p., 1908).
202 **"What are we going to do with":** Edwin Bjorkman, "Hugh MacRae: Builder of Human Happiness: A Study in Agricultural Engineering," Federal Writers' Project Papers #3709, Southern Historical Collection, quoted in J. Vincent Lowery, "The Transatlantic Dreams of the Port City Prophet: The Rural Reform Campaign of Hugh MacRae," *North Carolina Historical Review* 90, no. 3 (2013): 290.
202 **"Diversify, diversify":** Ida M. Tarbell, "Will Your Home Be Happy as Theirs?," *Collier's*, July 15, 1922, 5–6.
202 **regressive to the core:** Lowery, "Transatlantic Dreams," 290.
202 **allowed them to exploit:** Alexis Clark, "How Southern Landowners Tried to Restrict the Great Migration," History.com, January 4, 2022.
203 **"constant withdrawal of brains":** Tycho de Boer, *Nature, Business, and Community in North Carolina's Green Swamp* (University Press of Florida, 2008), 134, quoted in Lowery, "Transatlantic Dreams," 290.
203 **"race improvement":** Ellen H. Richards, *Euthenics: The Science of Controllable Environment* (Whitcomb and Barrows, 1910,), viii, quoted in Lowery, "Transatlantic Dreams," 294–96.
203 **end reliance on Black workers:** Marcia G. Synnott, "Replacing 'Sambo': Could White Immigrants Solve the Labor Problems in the Carolinas?," *Proceedings of the South Carolina Historical Association* (1982), 77, cited in Lowery, "Transatlantic Dreams," 296.
203 **recruit settlers from Europe:** Lowery, "Transatlantic Dreams," 296.
203 **"direct from Italy":** "Immigrants Arrive: Came to Wilmington from Italy and Will Take Up Farms on Wilmington and Weldon Road," *Wilmington Messenger*, December 13, 1905.
203 **"Florence and Milan":** Hugh MacRae, *Bringing Immigrants to the South: Address Delivered Before the North Carolina Society of New York*, December 7, 1908, quoted in Lowery, "Transatlantic Dreams," 300.
203 **ten-acre plot:** "About the Village of St. Helena," Village of St. Helena, NC, March 4, 2019.
204 **Dutch, German, Polish, and Hungarian:** Lowery, "Transatlantic Dreams," 298, 301.
204 **Nazi persecution:** "Van Eeden (D-117)," NC Department of Natural and Cultural Resources, December 12, 2023.
204 **"carload of strawberries":** Hugh MacRae, quoted in Tarbell, "Will Your Home," 22.
204 **"and ice cream cones":** Anonymous visitor, quoted in Lowery, "Transatlantic Dreams," 303.
205 **"'do not blame the negro'":** Quoted in Lowery, "Transatlantic Dreams," 320.
206 **pineapple finial:** Mark Darrough, "Masonboro Sound Historic District: An 'Oasis of Extraordinary Beauty' Threatened by Clear-Cutting Development," *Port City Daily*, April 25, 2021.
206 **moved in on Thanksgiving Day:** "Masonboro Sound Historic District: Architectural Description," National Register of Historic Places, North Carolina Department of Natural and Cultural Resources, 1992, 17.
206 **"On moonlight nights":** Crockette W. Hewlett and Mona Smalley, *Between the Creeks, Revised: Masonboro Sound, 1735–1985* (New Hanover Printing & Publishing Co., 1985), quoted in Samantha Smith, "Cazau–Williams-Crow House (Halcyon Hall)," Application for City of Wilmington Local Landmark Designation, November 2019, 18.

206 **"comfortable this winter":** Agnes Parsley to Anna Parsley Love, October 26, 1910, Anna Parsley Love Letter (SC-MS-086), Special Collections, Center for Southeast North Carolina Archives and History, UNCW Library.
206 **working as a cooper:** Population Schedule for New Hanover County, North Carolina, ED 67, Twelfth Census of the United States, 1900, NARA microfilm publication T623, Records of the Bureau of the Census, RG 29, National Archives, Washington, D.C.
207 **"a color scheme":** "Society: Gives Birthday Party," *Wilmington Morning Star*, December 10, 1922.
207 **"thirty of the younger set":** "Oyster Roast at 'Live Oaks,'" *Wilmington Morning Star*, January 2, 1920.
207 **fifty-two weeks:** Population Schedule for New Hanover County, North Carolina, ED 65–23, Sixteenth Census of the United States, 1940, NAID 131449027, Records of the Bureau of the Census, RG 29, National Archives, Washington, D.C.
207 **total of $468:** Athalia Howe [Whitfield], Population Schedule for New Hanover County, North Carolina, Sixteenth Census of the United States, 1940, Records of the Bureau of the Census, RG 29, National Archives, Washington, D.C.
208 **right to a minimum wage:** Jennifer Guglielmo and Diana Sierra Becerra, "Finally, Minimum Wage," A History of Domestic Work and Worker Organizing, 2021.
208 **send a chauffeur:** Cynthia Brown, interview with author, December 28, 2021.
208 **president of the state chapter:** United Daughters of the Confederacy, *Fourteenth Annual Minutes of the United Daughters of the Confederacy, Rocky Mount, N.C.: October 12–14, 1910*, North Carolina Division, 1910.
208 **George Davis Committee:** "All Wilmington Honors Mr. Davis," *Wilmington Morning Star*, April 21, 1911.
208 **raised the $5,010:** "George Davis Monument, Wilmington," Documenting the American South (DocSouth): Commemorative Landscapes of North Carolina, University of North Carolina.
208 **"land without memories":** February 1895 clipping, Branch Papers, North Carolina Division of Archives and History, quoted in Bishir, "Landmarks of Power," 59.

CHAPTER 26: THE HERB THAT FLOURISHETH

210 **found Wilmington boring:** Arthur S. Link, "Woodrow Wilson: The American as Southerner," *Journal of Southern History* 36, no. 1 (1971): 7–8.
210 **barques, brigs, brigantines:** J. D. Bellamy, *Memoirs of an Octogenarian*, 112; L. T. Moore, *Stories Old and New*, 229.
210 **Sir Walter Scott:** William Allen White, *Woodrow Wilson: The Man, His Times, and His Task* (Riverside Press, 1924), 57; Cashman, *History of Bellamy Mansion*, 107–8; J. D. Bellamy, *Memoirs of an Octogenarian*, 112.
210 **"haunted each other's":** White, *Woodrow Wilson*, 58.
210 **"find Mr. Tommy":** White, *Woodrow Wilson*, 58–59.
211 **"talking about a book":** Cashman, *History of the Bellamy Mansion*, 109.
211 **"somber and implacable":** White, *Woodrow Wilson*, 62.
211 **"always in pairs":** White, *Woodrow Wilson*, 58.
212 **"humiliations and misery":** Haitian Memorial Presented to President Harding, quoted in "Haitian Delegates Want U.S. to Get Out—Memorial to Handing Charges," *New York Times*, May 9, 1921.
212 **introduced Jim Crow:** Brenda Gayle Plummer, "The Afro-American Response to the Occupation of Haiti, 1915–1934," *Phylon* 43, no. 2 (1982): 129.

212 **Before Wilson's election:** "Wilson and Race: Segregation of the Federal Government," The President Woodrow Wilson House, National Trust for Historic Preservation.

212 **"cage built":** W. E. B. DuBois, "Another Open Letter to Woodrow Wilson," September 1913, quoted in Dylan Matthews, "Woodrow Wilson Was Extremely Racist—Even by the Standards of His Time," *Vox*, November 20, 2015.

212 **"state-sanctioned":** Abhay Aneja and Guo Xu, "The Costs of Employment Segregation: Evidence from the Federal Government Under Woodrow Wilson," *Quarterly Journal of Economics* 137, no. 2 (2022): 911–58.

212 **"old-fashioned poke bonnets":** "Call President 'Tommy,'" *Argus Leader*, September 26, 1913.

212 ***Birth of a Nation*:** *Washington Post*, February 19, 1915, cited in Mark E. Benbow, "Birth of a Quotation: Woodrow Wilson and 'Like Writing History with Lightning,'" *Journal of the Gilded Age and Progressive Era* 9, no. 4 (2010): 513.

213 **"Adventurers swarmed out of the North":** Woodrow Wilson, *A History of the American People* (Harper & Brothers, 1902), quoted in a title card for *The Birth of a Nation*, directed by D. W. Griffith (1915).

214 **"veritable empire":** Wilson, *A History of the American People*, in a different title card for *The Birth of a Nation*.

214 **violent intervention:** Sprunt, *Chronicles of the Cape Fear River*, 554.

214 **"Anglo-Saxon race has been reunited":** Thomas Dixon Jr., *The Leopard's Spots: A Romance of the White Man's Burden, 1865–1900* (Doubleday & Co., 1902), 414.

214 **practical insights:** Henry Louis Gates Jr., *Stony the Road: Reconstruction, White Supremacy, and the Rise of Jim Crow* (Penguin Press, 2019), 105.

214 **summer of 1919:** For a fuller accounting of the horrors and impact of the summer of 1919, see Cameron McWhirter, *Red Summer: The Summer of 1919 and the Awakening of Black America* (St. Martin's Press, 2011).

214 **fought for abroad:** "Targeting Black Veterans: Lynching in America," Equal Justice Initiative Report, 2017.

214 **"blood now raging":** Letters to Hon. Key Pittman, May 31, 1917 [Image 150] and June 2, 1917 [Image 152], Woodrow Wilson Papers, Series 4: Executive Office File, 1912–1921, 5A (244-336), Manuscript/Mixed Material Division, Library of Congress; "'We Need Scarcely to Say That You Have Grievously Disappointed Us': The Broken Promises of Wilson in Letters from Black Americans," Library of Congress.

214 **"over his boyhood":** Woodrow Wilson, *Robert E. Lee: An Interpretation* (University of North Carolina Press, 1924), v, quoted in Link, "Woodrow Wilson," 13.

215 **local problem:** "Red Summer of '19," The Woodrow Wilsom Presidential Library & Museum, February 27, 2020.

CHAPTER 27: MRS. HALSEY

216 **pulmonary tuberculosis:** Death Certificate of Bessie Cato, April 29, 1916, Wilmington, New Hanover County, North Carolina, North Carolina State Board of Health, Bureau of Vital Statistics, North Carolina State Archives, Raleigh.

217 **Sallie is sixty-five:** Population Schedule for Union County, New Jersey, Summit, ED 160, Fourteenth Census of the United States, 1920, Records of the Bureau of the Census, RG 29, National Archives, Washington, D.C.

217 **Juanita stays home:** Population Schedule for Union County, New Jersey, Summit, ED 20–154, Sixteenth Census of the United States, 1940, NAID 131967989, Records of the Bureau of the Census, RG 29, National Archives, Washington, D.C.

CHAPTER 28: VISIBLE WORK

219 **"educational governor":** Rupert B. Vance, "Aycock of North Carolina," *Southwest Review* 18, no. 3 (1933), 288.

219 **"your setter pups":** Charles B. Aycock Speech, quoted in Vance, "Aycock of North Carolina," 296.

219 **"actual hard labor":** Second Charles B. Aycock Speech, quoted in Vance, "Aycock of North Carolina," 298.

220 **"dirty treatment":** B. F. Keith to Warren G. Harding, July 5, 1921, Private Collection of Thomas Keith.

220 **"we ought to be ashamed":** J. O. Carr (Chairman Board of Education), "New Hanover County: Board of Education Report," August 10, 1916, 20.

221 **"better equip themselves":** "Growth and Development of Wilmington Schools During Past Six Years," *Wilmington Morning Star*, June 4, 1916.

221 **Female students:** "Superintendent J. J. Blair Reviews Past School Year," *Wilmington Morning Star*, June 14, 1915.

221 **Their Black teachers:** Carr, "New Hanover County: Board of Education Report," 7, 85–86.

221 **lowered to half-mast:** "Death of Col. A. M. Waddell: Passed Away Last Night After Brief Illness," *Wilmington Dispatch*, March 18, 1912.

222 **smothered by a pet cat:** "Col. Roger Moore's Little Grandson Smothered on Christmas Eve," *Wilmington Messenger*, December 26, 1896.

222 **"Good Roads":** "Meeting Tomorrow Morning," *Wilmington Dispatch*, September 9, 1911.

222 **Black men enlisted in droves:** J. A. Jamieson et al., "Why Black Men Fought in World War I, 1919," The Gilder Lehrman Institute of American History, 2019.

222 **"extraordinary heroism":** "Hargrove Bellamy," World War I: Army Recipients of the Distinguished Service Cross, Home of Heroes: Medal of Honor & Military History, 2018.

222 **"prominently connected":** "Hargrove Bellamy Freed by Germans; Sails for U.S. Soon," December 6, 1918, Clippings File, Lower Cape Fear Historical Society.

222 **Carolina Shipbuilding:** "Lay First Ship's Keel During July," *Wilmington Morning Star*, June 14, 1919.

222 **MacRae's Tidewater Power:** Hossfeld, *Narrative, Political Unconscious, and Racial Violence*, 58.

222 **Quince served as mayor:** "Arrest Former Mayor upon Blackmail Charge," *News & Observer*, June 22, 1932.

223 **chairs called "Afromobiles":** Henry Knight Lozano, "Race, Mobility, and Fantasy: Afromobiling in Tropical Florida," *Journal of American Studies* 51, no. 3 (2017): 805–13.

223 **countryside filling station:** "Arrest Former Mayor upon Blackmail Charge."

223 **"died without a word":** "Death of Col. Roger Moore: He Died Suddenly of Apoplexy at 11 O'Clock Last Night," *Wilmington Messenger*, April 22, 1900.

223 **his co-conspirator:** Laurie Gunst, *Off-White: A Memoir* (Soho Press, 2006), 261.

223 **shot himself:** Death Certificate of Alfred Moore Waddell Jr., July 31, 1930, Wilmington, New Hanover County, North Carolina, North Carolina State Board of Health, Bureau of Vital Statistics, North Carolina State Archives, Raleigh.

223 **"made for me":** Photograph of Roger Moore with inscription, Alice Borden Moore Sisson papers (Sp. Coll. #1266), box 1, folder 2, North Carolina Collection, New Hanover Public Library.

225 **"to the wall":** *State's Defense*, August 17, 1920, quoted in Elna C. Green, "Those Opposed: The Antisuffragists in North Carolina, 1900–1920," *North Carolina Historical Review* 67, no. 3 (1990): 327; Gilmore, *Gender and Jim Crow*, 209.
225 **so-called mammy monument:** Tony Horwitz, "The Mammy Washington Almost Had," *The Atlantic*, May 31, 2013.
225 **chamber acted quickly:** Blight, *Race and Reunion*, 288.
225 **"lived more free":** *Congressional Record*, 67th Cong., 4th sess., January 9, 1923, vol. 4, pt. 2, 1509, quoted in Micki McElya, *Clinging to Mammy: The Faithful Slave in Twentieth-Century America* (Havard University Press, 2007), 148.
225 **proposed designs:** "Award of 'Mammy' Statue Causes War Between Artists," *Baltimore Sun*, July 8, 1923.
225 **"publicity and acclaim":** McElya, *Clinging to Mammy*, 118–19.
226 **"symbol of servitude":** Quoted in McElya, *Clinging to Mammy*, 153.
226 **"bomb under it":** *Washington Eagle*, reprinted in "Senate Okeyed Statue over Protests," *Baltimore Afro-American*, March 9, 1923, quoted in McElya, *Clinging to Mammy*, 159.

CHAPTER 29: I WANT IT ALL EXACTLY

227 **confined to a few rooms:** Cashman, *History of the Bellamy Mansion*, 63.
227 **passing out ginger biscuits:** Bishir, *The Bellamy Mansion*, 63.
227 **"an unreconstructed rebel":** Quoted in Bishir, *The Bellamy Mansion*, 63.
227 **historian John Haley:** E. D. Bellamy, *Back with the Tide*, viii.
227 **"so vividly impressed":** E. D. Bellamy, *Back with the Tide*, 3.
227 **"lusty shoots":** Phil Wright, "Flamboyant Bellamy Mansion May Become Shrine," *Sunday Star-News*, November 9, 1947.
228 **show of disdain:** Bishir, *The Bellamy Mansion*, 63.
228 **two most powerful families:** "Miss Bellamy to Wed," *Charlotte Observer*, February 10, 1924.
228 **"Count at Genoa":** J. D. Bellamy, *Memoirs of an Octogenarian*, 191.
228 **"best linseed oil":** J. D. Bellamy, *Memoirs of an Octogenarian*,193.
228 **supported another candidate:** J. D. Bellamy, *Memoirs of an Octogenarian*, 111–13.
229 **In other words, he was lobbying:** J. D. Bellamy, *Memoirs of an Octogenarian*, 113.
229 **"curt and offensive":** J. D. Bellamy, *Memoirs of an Octogenarian*, 113–14.
229 **"competent white men":** W. C. Allen, *A Child's History of North Carolina* (Authors Co-operative Pub. Co, 1916), 414, quoted in Tyson, "The Ghosts of 1898," 16.
229 **"the dark cloud":** Andrew J. Howell, *The Book of Wilmington* (self-published, late-1920s), 182.
230 **no horror surpassed:** E. D. Bellamy, *Back with the Tide*, 8.
230 **"Not an easy matter":** E. D. Bellamy, *Back with the Tide*, 8.
230 **"four-hundred-year-old social order":** Isabel Wilkerson, *Caste: The Origins of Our Discontents* (Random House, 2020), 17.
231 **"great, gray apparition":** Bishir, *The Bellamy Mansion*, 63.
231 **"'lavender and old lace'":** Maude Waddell, "Writers Visit Historic Old Bellamy Home in Wilmington," *Wilmington News*, September 4, 1934, Bill Reaves Collection, New Hanover County Public Library.
231 **"first boarding school":** Susan Taylor Block, "Oral History, 2007 November 2," Susan Taylor Block Collection (SC-MS-122), box 1, folder 16, Center for Southeast North Carolina Archives and History, UNCW Library, 19:00.
231 **fell in easily:** "1943 Hugh MacRae II," in *In Memoriam*, St. Paul's School Alumni Horae, January 10, 2019.

231 **Boston to Wilmington:** Bambi MacRae, interview with author, March 31, 2022.
232 **had shot himself:** "Obituaries: Nelson MacRae," *Wilmington Morning Star*, February 13, 1942; "Nelson MacRae Found Dead of Bullet Wound," *Asheville Citizen-Times*, February 12, 1942.
232 **attribute it to depression:** Hugh MacRae III, interview with author, July 14, 2021.
232 **without a will:** Nelson MacRae, estate record, February 23, 1942, Administrators' Bonds: 1844–1946, New Hanover County, North Carolina Superior Court.
232 **Aviation Cadet Program:** "Hugh MacRae: November 24, 1924–October 8, 2018," Andrews Mortuary & Crematory.
233 **"friend for five decades":** Talbot Hamlin and Jessica Hamlin, *We Took to Cruising: From Maine to Florida Afloat* (Sheriden House, 1951), 100.
233 **thick with dust:** Hamlin and Hamlin, *We Took to Cruising*, 100–101.
233 **dime-store plates:** Cashman, *History of the Bellamy Mansion*, 64.
233 **still working at seventy-three:** Population Schedule for New Hanover County, North Carolina, ED 65–19, Sixteenth Census of the United States, 1940, NAID 131448897, Records of the Bureau of the Census, RG 29, National Archives, Washington, D.C.
233 **Ellen forbade anyone:** A. G. Dickson, "Bellamy Home May Be Painted," *Sunday Star-News*, April 26, 1959.
233 **"I want it all exactly as it was":** Dickson, "Bellamy Home May Be Painted."
233 **Ellen died:** Cashman, *History of the Bellamy Mansion*, 64–65; Wright, "Flamboyant Bellamy Mansion."
233 **upon her father's death:** Cashman, *History of the Bellamy Mansion*, 64.
233 **More than fifty heirs:** Wright, "Flamboyant Bellamy Mansion."
233 **neglected to pay property taxes:** Wright, "Flamboyant Bellamy Mansion."
233 **Lina Stallings refused to vacate:** Wright, "Flamboyant Bellamy Mansion."
233 **beyond the grave:** "Deaths & Funerals: Final Rites for Beloved Aged Wilmington Woman [Ellen Bellamy]," *Robesonian*, February 4, 1946.

CHAPTER 30: FLEAS IN A JAR

235 **"Brooklyn to Brooklyn!":** H. Brown, "Let Me Tell You Something."
235 **magazine report:** Ernest Dunbar et al., "When the Negro Faces North," *Look*, December 17, 1963, 30–35.
235 **"definitely adverse influence":** 1930s appraiser, quoted in Emily Badger, "How Redlining's Racist Effects Lasted for Decades," *New York Times*, August 24, 2017.
236 **"pain or bitterness":** Hesketh Brown Jr., "Lima Bean Soup," unpublished essay, n.d.
237 **"clam right up":** Hossfeld, *Narrative, Political Unconscious, and Racial Violence*, 132.
237 **"fleas in a jar":** Anonymous, quoted in Hossfeld, *Narrative, Political Unconscious, and Racial Violence*, 139.
237 **fact-gathering mission:** Hubert A. Eaton, *Every Man Should Try* (Bonaparte Press, 1984), 42; John L. Godwin, *Black Wilmington and the North Carolina Way: Portrait of a Community in the Era of Civil Rights Protest* (University Press of America, 2000), 64.
238 **"dummy intermediary owner":** Eaton, *Every Man Should Try*, 25.
238 **Black players were barred:** Matthew Prensky et al., "A Return to Segregation: Neighborhood Schools Policy Fuels Inequities, Erases New Hanover's Progress," *StarNews*, April 19, 2022.
238 **house rules were simple:** Eaton, *Every Man Should Try*, 25.
238 **arranged for Althea:** "What Connection Did Althea Gibson Have with Wilmington?," *StarNews*, October 12, 2021.

238 **"two cardboard suitcases":** Eaton, *Every Man Should Try*, 28.
238 **Wimbledon trophy:** Althea Gibson, *I Always Wanted to Be Somebody* (Harper & Brothers, 1958), 117.
238 **"place a towel over my face":** Eaton, *Every Man Should Try*, 22.
238 **"exceedingly strong":** Eaton, *Every Man Should Try*, 75.
239 **Eaton was impatient:** Eaton, *Every Man Should Try*, 43.
239 **"pervasive fears":** Eaton, *Every Man Should Try*, 43.
239 **"good race relations":** Godwin, *Black Wilmington*, 64–65.
239 **Hugh MacRae Morton:** Eaton, *Every Man Should Try*, 46.
240 **Black facilities' value:** Eaton, *Every Man Should Try*, 47.
240 **"tenor of politics had changed":** Eaton, *Every Man Should Try*, 124.
240 **"gloomy pronouncements":** Godwin, *Black Wilmington*, 72.
240 **losing each time:** Eaton, *Every Man Should Try*, 124.
240 **registered to vote doubled:** Eaton, *Every Man Should Try*, 126.
241 **"courage to join the cause":** Eaton, *Every Man Should Try*, 47.
241 **got a job in Brooklyn:** Eaton, *Every Man Should Try*, 50.
241 **"ultramodernistic" brick:** "Williston High School Dedication Sunday," *Wilmington Morning Star*, May 14, 1954.
241 **"intercommunication system":** Eaton, *Every Man Should Try*, 48.
242 **first Black police officers:** Godwin, *Black Wilmington*, 75.
242 **"I was determined":** Eaton, *Every Man Should Try*, 132.
242 **fruit of a form:** Karl E. Campbell, "Pupil Assignment Act," in *Encyclopedia of North Carolina* (University of North Carolina Press, 2006).
243 **"built to comply":** Eaton, *Every Man Should Try*, 51.

CHAPTER 31: VERY PERTINENT FACTS

244 **"a sweeping challenge":** James L. Hunt, "Creating North Carolina Populism, 1900–1960: Part 2: The Progressive Era Legacy, 1930–1960," *North Carolina Historical Review* 97, no. 3 (2020): 320.
244 **takeover a "coup d'état":** Edmonds, *The Negro and Fusion Politics*, 171.
245 **"distinctly a REVOLUTION":** Hossfeld, *Narrative, Political Unconscious, and Racial Violence*, 75–79.
245 **secured a weekly spot:** Susan Taylor Block, *Wilmington Through the Lens of Louis T. Moore* (Lower Cape Fear Historical Society, 2001), 9.
246 **"friendly interest":** L. T. Moore, *Stories Old and New*, 75, 184.
246 **"long-range protector":** Louis Moore Bacon, "Foreword," in Block, *Wilmington Through the Lens*, 5–6.
246 **vouching personally:** Louis T. Moore to librarian at the University of North Carolina, May 22, 1944, Thomas W. Clawson Papers, Southern Historical Collection, University of North Carolina Wilson Library.
247 **"ignorance, prejudice, carelessness":** Lambert Davis to Gordon Gray, June 7, 1951, UNC Press Papers, quoted in Hunt, "Creating North Carolina Populism," 324.
247 **"culminated in a racial conflict":** Quoted in L. T. Moore, *Stories Old and New*, 220.
248 **"What kind of historian":** John Hope Franklin to Mrs. Isaac B. Grainger, May 4, 1964, New Hanover County Public Library, Wilmington, NC.
248 **better to fail:** L. T. Moore, *Stories Old and New*, 236.

CHAPTER 32: THE GREATEST SCHOOL UNDER THE SUN

251 **install a darkroom:** John Staton, "What to Know About a Wilmington Icon Whose Legacy of School Desegregation Is in Peril," *StarNews*, May 10, 2023.

251 **Kansas City Monarchs:** Cynthia Brown, interview with author, December 28, 2021.

251 **421 to Seabreeze:** Cynthia Brown, interview with author, November 1, 2020.

251 **Their granddaughter, JoAnne:** Assata Shakur, *Assata: An Autobiography* (Lawrence Hill Books, 1987), 22.

252 **"We don't put our family in a nursing home":** Cynthia Brown, interview with author, December 28, 2021.

252 **wore pearls:** *The Willistonian: 1954* (Williston Senior High School), 16.

252 **"a ray emitted":** *The Willistonian: 1964* (Williston Senior High School), 20–40.

253 **class of 1954:** *The Willistonian: 1954*, 20–40.

253 **the prologue:** "Alumni Recall Williston, 'Greatest School Under the Sun,'" *StarNews*, June 28, 2015.

253 **the Picture Man:** Peter Applebome, *Dixie Rising: How the South Is Shaping American Values, Politics, and Culture* (Harcourt Brace & Co., 1996), 223.

253 **concerts, symposia, lectures:** Applebome, *Dixie Rising*, 223.

253 **"huge black dandelions":** Wayne Moore, *Triumphant Warrior: A Soul Survivor of the Wilmington Ten* (Warrior Press, 2014), 23.

253 ***"I would not be a Gold Bull"*:** W. Moore, *Triumphant Warrior*, 21.

254 **implemented the Pearsall Plan:** Adrienne Dunn, "Pearsall Plan: North Carolina's Response to Brown v. Board of Education," North Carolina History Project.

254 **single Black student:** Eaton, *Every Man Should Try*, 84.

254 **sued the school board for violating:** Godwin, *Black Wilmington*, 178.

255 **"over the Board's failure":** Robert R. Bond to E. A. Laney, January 6, 1964, Dr. Heyward C. Bellamy Collection (SC-MS-167), box 4, folder 14, Center for Southeast North Carolina Archives and History, UNCW Library.

255 **underreporting his income:** Eaton, *Every Man Should Try*, 159.

255 **pay additional taxes:** Eaton, *Every Man Should Try*, 160.

255 **Ann Landers:** "Soviets Hint Gal Next Space Pilot," *Wilmington Morning Star*, August 11, 1964; "Ann Landers Says: He'd Charge for His Dates," *Wilmington Morning Star*, August 11, 1964.

255 **formerly white restaurants:** Eaton, *Every Man Should Try*, 160.

256 **"I did everything in my power":** Sam Ervin to Cyrus Hogue, June 23, 1964, Dr. Heyward C. Bellamy Collection (SC-MS-167), box 4, folder 14, Center for Southeast North Carolina Archives and History, UNCW Library.

256 **patient in question:** "Physician Faces Charge of Murder," *Wilmington Morning Star*, August 12, 1964.

256 **"more emotional trauma":** Eaton, *Every Man Should Try*, 161.

258 **soaked in local history:** John J. Burney interview with Adina Lack, March 6, 2003, Voices of UNCW, Randall Library Oral History Collection, University of North Carolina Wilmington Archives and Special Collections.

258 **"This man's employer is white":** Gary E. Trawick, *Just Throw a Rock . . . and Run: A Son of the South Talks Race* (SlapDash, 2022), 262.

258 **killed the patient:** T. C. Jervay, "Wilmington Dentist Cleared of Murder," *Pittsburgh Courier*, November 28, 1964.

258 **"I'd never sleep again":** Eaton, *Every Man Should Try*, 163; John J. Burney interview with Adina Lack.

258 **star witness for the prosecution:** Jervay, "Wilmington Dentist Cleared of Murder."

CHAPTER 33: WHY IT WAS THE WORST

260 **investigation into the Klan:** Walter Goodman, "H.U.A.C. Meets the K.K.K.," *New York Times*, December 5, 1965.

260 **resurgence of the Klan:** *The Present-Day Ku Klux Klan Movement: Report by the Committee on Un-American Activities, House of Representatives, 90th Cong., 1st Sess.* (Government Printing Office, 1967), 19.

260 **"the most active state":** Russell Clay, "Tar Heels Reject State's Label of No. 1 for Klan," *News & Observer*, October 24, 1965.

260 **North Carolina klaverns:** David Cecelski, "The Klan Last Time—Part 3: Hot Dogs and Cake Raffles," September 13, 2017, DavidCecelski.com; *Present-Day Ku Klux Klan Movement*, 27.

260 **"Looking for a Handout":** Oliver Williams, "Rebirth of Klan Counters Moderate Action in State," *News & Observer*, August 23, 1964, quoted in "North Carolina Resurgence of the Ku Klux Klan," Greensboro Truth and Reconciliation Commission Final Report, 2006, 100.

260 **Grand Dragon Bob Jones:** "Klansville U.S.A.: Bob Jones and the North Carolina Klan," *American Experience* (PBS, January 2015).

261 **"nearly all walks":** Arnold Kirk, "New Hanover Klan One of the Strongest: SBI," *Wilmington Morning Star*, August 1, 1964; *Activities of the Ku Klux Klan Organization in the United States: Part 1 Hearings Before the Committee on Un-American Activities, House of Representatives, 89th Cong., 1st Sess.* (U.S. Government Printing Office, 1966), 1964.

261 **took the Fifth Amendment:** "Ku Klux Klan Probe Completed," in *CQ Almanac 1966* (CQ Press, 1967).

261 **any written reports:** John Herbers, "Sheriff Says He and 6 Deputies Joined Klan to Keep an Eye on It," *New York Times*, October 27, 1965.

261 **publicly denied:** Kirk, "New Hanover Klan"; *Activities of the Ku Klux Klan Organization*, 1989.

261 **they didn't have any suspects:** *Activities of the Ku Klux Klan Organization*, 1981.

262 **"wait-and-see":** "Local Officials to 'Wait, See,'" *Wilmington Morning Star*, October 27, 1965.

262 **It bears noting:** "Sheriffs to Issue Local Press Cards," *Wilmington Morning Star*, January 29, 1963.

262 **"man does a good job":** Scott Nunn, "Back Then—New Hanover Sheriff in 1960s Joined Klan," *StarNews*, December 1, 2015.

262 **only about a third:** Carolyn Zimmerman, "Dr. Martin Luther King to Speak in Wilmington," *Wilmington Morning Star*, February 14, 1968, 2.

262 **Dr. King planned to swing through:** Michael B. Richardson, "'Not Gradually . . . but Now': Reginald Hawkins, Black Leadership, and Desegregation in Charlotte, North Carolina," *North Carolina Historical Review* 82, no. 3 (2005): 347–79.

262 **choosing Wilmington:** Williston H. Lofton, "The Elimination of the Negro from Politics," *Journal of Negro Education* 23, no. 1 (1954): 66–67.

263 **local voters chose:** Godwin, *Black Wilmington*, 185.

263 **Wilmington was growing whiter:** Godwin, *Black Wilmington*, 187–88.

263 **propaganda arm:** "City Briefs: Mrs. Julia Brown," *Wilmington Morning Star*, February 25, 1968; "Julia Brown Talk Scheduled in Wilmington," *Wilmington Morning Star*, February 23, 1968.

263 **"DO NOT BE FOOLED":** "Vote White" handbill, Wilmington Citizens Council, 1960s, Bellamy Papers, folder: African American History, Wilmington 10, Lower Cape Fear Historical Society Archives.

263 **King postponed:** "King Cancels Stop in Wilmington Thursday," *Wilmington Morning Star*, April 2, 1968; for more on the John Birch Society, see Don Terry, "Bringing Back Birch," *Intelligence Report*, no. 149 (2013): 25–30.

263 **approximately the same time:** "Findings on MLK Assassination," National Archives.

263 **"We Shall Overcome":** Bertha Todd, quoted in Jennifer Whitmer Taylor, "Protest in the Port City: The Story of the Wilmington Ten" (MA, University of North Carolina at Wilmington, 2006), 18.

263 **Sheriff Marion Millis, still in:** Godwin, *Black Wilmington*, 217.

264 **call in the National Guard:** "Rioting Hits City; Curfew Is Ordered," *Sunday Star-News*, April 7, 1968; "Wilmington Has Siege on Sunday," *Durham Herald-Sun*, April 8, 1968.

264 **police presence:** Wiley McKellar, "Curfew Is Ended in Wilmington," *Wilmington Morning Star*, April 11, 1968.

264 **Allsbrook moved the curfew:** "Essentials: Along the Cape Fear," *Wilmington Morning Star*, April 8, 1968; "Firm Guard and Curfews Dampen Tar Heel Violence," *Durham Herald-Sun*, April 8, 1986.

265 **"double disaster":** Larry Reni Thomas, *The True Story Behind the Wilmington Ten* (U.B. & U.S. Communication Systems, 1982), 31.

265 **Wilmington's violence as the state's worst:** "Firm Guard Grip, Curfews Dampen Tar Heel Violence."

265 **"not afraid to retaliate":** Thomas, *True Story*, 46–47.

CHAPTER 34: A NEST OF COILED SNAKES

266 **"I remember former slaves":** Heyward C. Bellamy, *With All Deliberate Speed: The Reminiscences of Heyward C. Bellamy* (self-published, 2009), 3.

267 **"to welcome them":** H. C. Bellamy, *With All Deliberate Speed*, 51.

267 **"freedom-of-choice":** Green v. County School Board of New Kent County, 391 U.S. 430 (1968); Vivian Hopp Gordon, "Green v. County School Board of New Kent County," *Britannica Encyclopedia*, May 20, 2025.

268 **"jig was up":** William Hill to Howard Manning, July 30, 1968, Dr. Heyward C. Bellamy Collection (SC-MS-167), box 4, folder 5, Center for Southeast North Carolina Archives and History, UNCW Library.

268 **three high schools:** Heyward Bellamy to Eloise Severinson, August 14, 1968, Dr. Heyward C. Bellamy Collection (SC-MS-167), box 1, folder 9, Center for Southeast North Carolina Archives and History, UNCW Library; Godwin, *Black Wilmington*, 207.

268 **entirely segregated schools:** Carolyn Zimmerman, "Judge Orders Single School System," *Wilmington Morning Star*, July 24, 1968.

268 **Not a single white:** Godwin, *Black Wilmington*, 206.

268 **To achieve the racial balance:** "School Board Votes to Close Williston," *StarNews*, June 27, 1968.

268 **"We invite anybody":** "'Outlook Is Bleak' for Retaining 'Free Choice,'" *Charlotte Observer*, July 17, 1968.

269 **Gainsborough painting:** "Routine Stop Yields $60, in N.C. Art," *News & Observer*, September 5, 1968.

269 **"It is inhuman":** H. M. Roland, "An Introduction to 'Handicaps to the New School Program,'" in Dr. Heyward C. Bellamy Collection (SC-MS-167), box 9, folder 6, Center for the Southeast North Carolina Archives and History, UNCW Library.

269 **"startling increase":** "Statement of Charles J. Hause, President, Save Our Country, Inc., Wilmington, NC, Accompanied by the Former School Superintendent," in *Hearing Before Subcommittee No. 2 of the Committee on the Judiciary House of Representatives*,

Ninety-Second Congress, Second Session on H.R. 13694 and H.R. 13828 to Amend the Joint Resolution Establishing the American Revolution Bicentennial Commission as Amended: Serial No. 30 (U.S. Government Printing Office, 1972), 558.

269 **"property more important than our lives":** Assata Shakur, "To My People," July 4, 1973, Freedom Archives.

269 **"no greater delight":** Zora Neale Hurston, "August 11, 1955 Letter to the Orlando *Sentinel*," BlackPast.org, 2016.

270 **"our track record":** W. Moore, *Triumphant Warrior*, 36.

271 **"waved a rebel flag":** Carolyn Zimmerman, "School Board Votes to Close Williston High," *Wilmington Morning Star*, June 27, 1968; Frances Weller, "First Black Student to Integrate New Hanover County Public Schools Dies at 65," WECT News, October 6, 2015.

271 **voting unanimously:** State Board of Education to Heyward Bellamy, July 1, 1968, Dr. Heyward C. Bellamy Collection (SC-MS-167), box 5, folder 7, Center for the Southeast North Carolina Archives and History, UNCW Library.

271 **organizations dissolved:** Hossfeld, *Narrative, Political Unconscious, and Racial Violence*, 86.

271 **in the trash:** *Pardons of Innocence: The Wilmington Ten*, directed by Cash Michaels (2014).

271 **"desegregation punctured it":** Eaton, *Every Man Should Try*, 214.

271 **"nest of coiled snakes":** W. Moore, *Triumphant Warrior*, 59.

271 **last-ditch lawsuit:** Eaton, *Every Man Should Try*, 116.

271 **boarded buses:** W. Moore, *Triumphant Warrior*, 57.

272 **early retirement:** W. Moore, *Triumphant Warrior*, 51.

272 **only eight remained:** Leslie T. Fenwick, *Jim Crow's Pink Slip: The Untold Story of Black Principal and Teacher Leadership* (Harvard Education Press, 2022), 10.

272 **couldn't stop sweating:** Michaels, *Pardons of Innocence*, 21:00.

272 **examination about the Constitution:** James E. Lanning to William L. Hill, May 26, 1970, Dr. Heyward C. Bellamy Collection (SC-MS-167), box 5, folder 12, Center for Southeast North Carolina Archives and History, UNCW Library.

272 **"hitting blacks":** Wiley McKellar, "Violence Flames at High Schools," *Wilmington Morning Star*, May 8, 1970.

273 **"of metal prongs":** "Committee for Legal, Constitutional Education for Everyone," Dr. Heyward C. Bellamy Collection (SC-MS-167), box 9, folder 6, Center for Southeast North Carolina Archives and History, UNCW Library.

273 **"'I'll kill you'":** W. Moore, *Triumphant Warrior*, 51.

273 **"the constant agitation":** Anonymous to Concerned Citizens, May 25, 1970, Dr. Heyward C. Bellamy Collection (SC-MS-167), box 5, folder 12, Center for Southeast North Carolina Archives and History, UNCW Library.

274 **Most of the group's members:** Michael Praats, "Crimes of the Cape Fear: 'The Rights of White People' a Homegrown Hate Group," WECT News, March 24, 2021.

274 **"What are we supposed":** Jon Nordheimer, "Anti-Negro Group Vexing Police in Wilmington, NC," *New York Times*, October 7, 1971.

274 **more dangerous than the Klan:** Praats, "Crimes of the Cape Fear."

274 **"stay white":** Praats, "Crimes of the Cape Fear"; Nordheimer, "Anti-Negro Group."

275 **"terror of the populace":** Chief H. E. Williamson, "Arrests Occurring February 6–10, 1971, Relative Civil Disorders: Case #221083—Hilton Murdie Jones," Dr. Heyward C. Bellamy Collection (SC-MS-167), box 9, folder 7, Center for Southeast North Carolina Archives and History, UNCW Library.

275 **"Communist-inspired":** Leroy Gibson, quoted in Nordheimer, "Anti-Negro Group."

275 **secede from the Union:** Account of ROWP Meeting, Dr. Heyward C. Bellamy Col-

lection (SC-MS-167), box 9, folder 7, Center for Southeast North Carolina Archives and History, UNCW Library.

275 **"ready to settle":** Leroy Gibson, quoted in Nordheimer, "Anti-Negro Group."

275 **"integration and rioting":** Leroy Gibson, quoted in Timothy B. Tyson, *Blood Done Sign My Name: A True Story* (Three Rivers Press, 2004), 275.

CHAPTER 35: DO NOT CALL OUR BLUFF

277 **"traffic's for us":** H. C. Bellamy, *With All Deliberate Speed*, 61.

277 **congregated there:** John Staton, "50 Years Later, Fire That Destroyed Hemenway Hall in Wilmington Remains a Mystery," *StarNews*, May 19, 2021.

277 **"Stop Bussing":** Staton, "50 Years Later."

278 **"Bellamy has to go":** *Hanover Sun* article, quoted in H. C. Bellamy, *With All Deliberate Speed*, 63.

278 **start sawing boards:** Mary Louise Bellamy, interview with author, April 8, 2021.

278 **Mary won a Fulbright:** Mary Louise Bellamy, interview with author.

278 **"what is possible":** Heyward Bellamy, quoted in Mary Louise Bellamy interview with author.

279 **"like a second mother":** H. C. Bellamy, *With All Deliberate Speed*, 55.

279 **"betterment of this community":** H. C. Bellamy, *With All Deliberate Speed*, 55; Marjorie Smith, "School Contracts Ready for Signatures," *Wilmington Morning Star*, July 18, 1974.

279 **in shaving cream:** Mary Louise Bellamy, interview with author.

279 **vandal had broken into the school:** H. C. Bellamy, *With All Deliberate Speed*, 58.

279 **"gets his head blown off":** Heyward Bellamy, quoted in Mary Louise Bellamy interview with the author.

280 **"need to study the history":** H. C. Bellamy, *With All Deliberate Speed*, 55.

281 **Black history syllabus:** Ethan J. Kytle and Blain Roberts, *Denmark Vesey's Garden: Slavery and Memory in the Cradle of the Confederacy, A 150-Year Reckoning with America's Original Sin* (New Press, 2018), 277.

281 **impromptu sit-in:** W. Moore, *Triumphant Warrior*, 65.

281 **expelling fifteen students:** Philip Gerard, "The 1970s: The Wilmington 10," *Our State*, March 2, 2021.

281 **fight spilled onto campus:** John C. Beane Statement, April 6, 1971, Dr. Heyward C. Bellamy Collection (SC-MS-167), box 9, folder 7, Center for Southeast North Carolina Archives and History, UNCW Library.

281 **reported her injury:** Kenneth Robert Janken, *The Wilmington Ten: Violence, Injustice, and the Rise of Black Politics in the 1970s* (University of North Carolina Press, 2021), 11.

281 **"made a flying tackle":** McKellar, "Violence Flames."

281 **"not a call boy":** Heyward Bellamy, "What We Want: What We Believe," Dr. Heyward C. Bellamy Collection, (SC-MS-167), box 7, folder 13, Center for Southeast North Carolina Archives and History, UNCW Library.

281 **"We believe that we":** H. Bellamy, "What We Want."

282 **boycotting their classes:** Janken, *Wilmington Ten*, 19.

282 **"dirty underwear":** Willie Earl Vereen, *Wilmington Ten Willie: Guilt by Association* (self-published, 2019), 39.

282 **"we were standing up":** W. Moore, *Triumphant Warrior*, 53.

283 **stagnated economically:** Godwin, *Black Wilmington*, 189.

283 **In 1966, 42:** Godwin, *Black Wilmington*, 187–88.

283 **"not getting an education anyway":** Janken, *The Wilmington Ten*, 24–25.

283 **strong tradition of social justice:** "UCC Firsts," United Church of Christ [Timeline].

283 **North Carolina mountains:** Alfred W. Stuart, "General Demographics," *NCpedia* (reprinted from *The North Carolina Atlas Revisited)*, 2010.
284 **"I was totally isolated":** Eugene Templeton, interview with author, April 6, 2021.
284 **"very little about community organizing":** Templeton, interview with author.
284 **"the most learned Black man":** Tyson, *Blood Done Sign My Name*, 130.
285 **"bashed in his skull":** Tyson, *Blood Done Sign My Name*, 133.
285 **"full-length fur coat":** W. Moore, *Triumphant Warrior*, 70–71.
285 **"more like a pimp":** Janken, *The Wilmington Ten*, 25.
285 **has recently resurfaced:** Jacey Fortin, "The Long History of the 'Outside Agitator,'" *New York Times*, June 8, 2020; Patrik Jonsson and Story Hinckley, "Outside 'Agitators' in Protests Have a Long History—in Myth and Fact," *Christian Science Monitor*, June 12, 2025.
285 **"having more violence":** "Statement by H. E. Williamson Chief of Police," Dr. Heyward C. Bellamy Collection, (SC-MS-167), box 7, folder 2, Center for Southeast North Carolina Archives and History, UNCW Library.
285 **"wipe out the Black community":** Hossfeld, *Narrative, Political Unconscious, and Racial Violence*, 91.
285 **boys on the bottom:** Janken, *The Wilmington Ten*, 21.
286 **"not liar, but lie":** Dr. Heyward C. Bellamy Collection, (SC-MS-167), box 7, folder 13, Center for Southeast North Carolina Archives and History, UNCW Library.
286 **"Do not call our bluff!":** W. Moore, *Triumphant Warrior*, 91.
286 **their school principals:** Janken, *The Wilmington Ten*, 27–28.
286 **would be suspended:** Janken, *The Wilmington Ten*, 28.
286 **"less and less occasion for trouble":** Hugh T. Lefler and Patricia Stanford, *Harcourt Social Studies: North Carolina* (Harcourt Brace Jovanovich, 1972), 406.
287 **"utter illogic":** "Editorials: The Reasoned Approach," *Wilmington Morning Star*, February 4, 1971.
287 **"bunch of youngsters":** Quoted in Jon Nordheimer, "Guard Is Ordered to Wilmington, NC," *New York Times*, February 8, 1971,
287 **"were not afraid to say":** Larry Thomas, quoted in Janken, *The Wilmington Ten*, 31.
288 **dinner at Lum's:** Mary Louise Bellamy, "House Evacuation," diary entry, February 3, 1971, emailed to author.
288 **Black arsonists:** Janken, *The Wilmington Ten*, 29–30.
288 **conflagrations across the city:** "Fire Guts NHHS Fieldhouse as Violence Resumes," *Wilmington Morning Star*, February 6, 1971.
288 **daughter to a private school:** "Our History," Highlander Academy on the Historic Flora MacDonald Campus.

CHAPTER 36: JR. BABYLON

289 **"slave master's classrooms":** Janken, *The Wilmington Ten*, 28; Anonymous Flyer signed "Power Peace and Liberation to All Black People," Dr. Heyward C. Bellamy Collection (SC-MS-167), box 9, folder 4, Center for Southeast North Carolina Archives and History, UNCW Library.
289 **unfurled a black flag:** Janken, *The Wilmington Ten*, 31.
290 **blasted party tunes:** W. Moore, *Triumphant Warrior*, 99.
290 **Black minister was shot:** W. Moore, *Triumphant Warrior*, 102–3.
290 **"promising to destroy everything":** W. Moore, *Triumphant Warrior*, 104.
290 **killing him with three:** Janken, *The Wilmington Ten*, 37; John Hendrix, "Curfew Proclaimed in City and County," *Wilmington Morning Star*, February 8, 1971.

291 **taking sniper fire:** Kenneth R. Janken, "Remembering the Wilmington Ten: African American Politics and Judicial Misconduct in the 1970s," *North Carolina Historical Review* 92, no. 1 (2015): 15.
291 **police claimed that Black:** W. Moore, *Triumphant Warrior*, 106.
292 **"struck in the temple":** Hendrix, "Curfew Proclaimed in City and County."
292 **blown through the police barricade:** Janken, *The Wilmington Ten*, 37.
293 **"Mrs. Cumber Faints":** Rip Collins, "The Cumber Family Unites in Mourning," *Wilmington Morning Star*, February 13, 1971.
293 **"I think Daddy would have wanted it":** Collins, "Cumber Family Unites."
294 **"to regain control":** Hendrix, "Curfew Proclaimed in City and County."
294 **illicit weapons:** Trawick, *Just Throw a Rock*, 208.
294 **reasons to be upset:** Nordheimer, "Guard Is Ordered to Wilmington, NC."
294 **"million candlepower" infrared:** Rick Nichols, "Wilmington Strife Marked by Communications Gap," *News & Observer*, February 9, 1971.
294 **"weapons of mass death":** John Hendrix, "Situation Reported Improving: Fires Mar Second Night of Curfew," *Wilmington Morning Star*, February 9, 1971.
294 **No one was inside:** Nichols, "Wilmington Strife."
294 **"sniper nests":** Nichols, "Wilmington Strife"; Janken, *Wilmington Ten*, 38; Hendrix, "Situation Reported Improving"; Wiley McKellar, "Gregory Church Taken Over by Guard, Police," *Wilmington Morning Star*, February 9, 1971.
294 **"struggle has just begun":** Nichols, "Wilmington Strife."
294 **"*Has it come to this?*":** W. Moore, *Triumphant Warrior*, 111.
295 **"I don't know whether I hit anyone":** McKellar, "Gregory Church Taken Over."
295 **had been incinerated:** W. Moore, *Triumphant Warrior*, 116.
295 **nonviolent boycott into a "small war":** Wayne King, "The Case Against the Wilmington Ten," *New York Times Magazine*, December 3, 1978, 30–31.
295 **"largely bloodless":** W. Moore, *Triumphant Warrior*, 117.

CHAPTER 37: THE HAPPIEST DAMN POLICE CHIEF

296 **"burning like Roman candles":** "Flames Ravage Hemenway Hall," *Wilmington Morning Star*, May 28, 1971.
296 **"rusting typewriters":** H. C. Bellamy, *With All Deliberate Speed*, 61.
297 **simply be too much:** H. C. Bellamy, *With All Deliberate Speed*, 62.
297 **"a fire trap":** H. C. Bellamy, *With All Deliberate Speed*, 62.
297 **"remain a mystery forever":** Wiley McKellar, "Hemenway Hall Fire Will Probably Remain a Mystery, Says Williamson," *Wilmington Morning Star*, May 26, 1971.
298 **"clean the place up":** Janken, *The Wilmington Ten*, 40.
298 **ROWP set up a headquarters:** Janken, *The Wilmington Ten*, 46.
298 **"They can't arrest the chickens":** Janken, *The Wilmington Ten*, 52.
298 **"Key Extremist":** Janken, *The Wilmington Ten*, 43, 69–72.
298 **"caught up in the dragnet":** Janken, *The Wilmington Ten*, 77.
299 **racially motivated "assassination":** Janken, *The Wilmington Ten*, 72.
299 **"happiest damn police chief":** "Ben Chavis Charged in Conspiracy," *News & Observer*, March 17, 1971.
299 **sat in jail for months:** W. Moore, *Triumphant Warrior*, 144.
299 **arrests were politically motivated:** Janken, *The Wilmington Ten*, 79.
300 **"we are now held prisoners":** "Letter from Wilmington 11," *African World*, April 15, 1972.

CHAPTER 38: ISN'T THIS BEAUTIFUL?

301 **petitioned for a venue change:** "Racial Disorders Trial Launched," *Wilmington Morning Star*, June 6, 1972.
301 **"LET FUTURE GENERATIONS REMEMBER":** "Pender County Confederate Monument, Burgaw," Documenting the American South (DocSouth): Commemorative Landscapes, University of North Carolina.
301 **"gateway to hell":** W. Moore, *Triumphant Warrior*, 163.
301 **Judge Joshua James:** Janken, *The Wilmington Ten*, 87; Irving Joyner, email to author, November 17, 2022.
302 **calling people by the wrong names:** Janken, *The Wilmington Ten*, 90–91.
302 **eliminate potential Black jurors:** W. Moore, *Triumphant Warrior*, 170.
302 **evidence of guilt:** Janken, *The Wilmington Ten*, 95–96.
302 **"come up here and cause trouble":** Gary Trawick, interview with author, August 22, 2025.
303 **"something connected":** Eugene Templeton, interview with author, April 6, 2021.
303 **reform school:** Janken, "Remembering the Wilmington Ten," 37.
303 **awaiting sentencing:** W. Moore, *Triumphant Warrior*, 185.
303 **significant mental disabilities:** W. Moore, *Triumphant Warrior*, 172; Janken, *The Wilmington Ten*, 75.
303 **lunging at them:** Janken, *The Wilmington Ten*, 99.
304 **received the longest:** Trial Transcript, North Carolina v. Benjamin Franklin Chavis, Marvin Patrick, Connie Tyndall, et al. (also known as "The Wilmington Ten Case"), Volume 4: Part 4, Civil Rights Division, U.S. Department of Justice.
304 **"taking our boys away":** Janken, *The Wilmington Ten*, 103.
304 **"black oppression would go on":** W. Moore, *Triumphant Warrior*, 184.

CHAPTER 39: THEY BLASTED MY SHOP

305 **seven miles in each direction:** John Randt, "Blast Site Probed," *Wilmington Morning Star*, May 30, 1973.
305 **mistaking the booming:** John Randt, "Explosion Destroys Wilmington Journal," *Wilmington Morning Star*, May 29, 1973.
305 **"part of the game":** Randt, "Blast Site Probed"; John Randt, "Publisher: It Is Part of the Game," *Wilmington Morning Star*, May 30, 1973.
306 **had lived next door:** Rhonda Bellamy, *Moving Forward Together: A Community Remembers 1898* (SlapDash, 2008), 110.
306 **"without fear or favor":** Quoted in Reaves, *Strength Through Struggle*, 317.
306 **"devastating to historians":** Reaves, *Strength Through Struggle*, 317.
306 **"never missed an issue":** Jervay, quoted in R. Bellamy, *Moving Forward Together*, 110.
306 **"My daddy was very, very plain":** Michaels, *Pardons of Innocence*, 1:11:42.
307 **"abhor this kind of thing":** "Wilmington: Racial Hotbed," *Daily Times-News*, October 9, 1973.
307 **explosion went off:** "Wilmington: Racial Hotbed"; "Blast Rips Synagogue," *Wilmington Morning Star*, June 20, 1973.
307 **Ku Klux Klan klavern:** William J. Coughlin, "Klan Going Public to Test Political Waters," *StarNews*, April 4, 1982; John Randt, "Arrest Made in Bombings," *Wilmington Morning Star*, July 10, 1973.
307 **"the Wilmington One":** "Wilmington: Racial Hotbed."
307 **With Ellen's debts:** Cashman, *History of Bellamy Mansion*, 65.

307 **Eventually, the heirs:** Dickson, "Bellamy Home May Be Painted."
308 **commercial tenants:** Cashman, *History of Bellamy Mansion*, 66.
308 **"let us say hello to you":** A. L. Bulluck, "You Are Cordially Invited to Visit and Shop at Deedie's Fabric Shop," *Wilmington Morning Star*, April 19, 1953.
308 **damage was extensive:** "The Museum: Our Story," Bellamy Mansion Museum.
308 **set by Black activists:** Gareth Evans, interview with author, October 9, 2018.

CHAPTER 40: PRISONERS OF CONSCIENCE

310 **"As a concerned citizen":** "Action Line: Sounding Off," *Wilmington Morning Star*, June 17, 1973.
311 **"We are all fighting for our lives":** Angela Davis, quoted in Jim Hefner, "'Watergate' Justice Seen Here," *Wilmington Morning Star*, June 18, 1973.
311 **"*Qui connaît Ben Chavis?*":** Dominique Pouchin, "Qui connaît Ben Chavis?," *Le Monde*, March 19, 1977.
311 **"prisoners of conscience":** Janken, *The Wilmington Ten*, 126.
311 **"human rights of the Wilmington Ten":** Letter to President Jimmy Carter, quoted in King, "The Case Against the Wilmington Ten."
311 **"just won't go away":** Morley Safer, quoted in W. Moore, *Triumphant Warrior*, 258.
311 **"gambled, drank, and smoked":** W. Moore, *Triumphant Warrior*, 264; King, "The Case Against the Wilmington Ten."
311 **head of the local Ku Klux Klan:** W. Moore, *Triumphant Warrior*, 264.
311 **"I need a woman":** Allen Hall, quoted in Cash Michaels, "Letters from Wilmington Ten Prosecution Witness Confirms Frame-Up," *Milwaukee Courier*, December 14, 2012.
312 **claimed he'd burned:** Janken, *The Wilmington Ten*, 131.
312 **declined to grant a new trial:** Janken, *The Wilmington Ten*, 136.
312 **Soviet news agencies:** Janken, *The Wilmington Ten*, 145.
312 **"World opinion is demanding the release":** "An Interview with Fidel Castro," in *The Black Scholar: Africa in Struggle* 10, no. 1 (1978): 33–43.
313 **"you racist dunce!":** Janken, *The Wilmington Ten*, 151; W. Moore, *Triumphant Warrior*, 270.
313 **only accept a pardon:** "Last Defendant in a Firebombing Is Released from Carolina Prison 'Long Struggle' for Freedom," *New York Times*, December 15, 1979.
313 **still had two years to serve:** W. Moore, *Triumphant Warrior*, 270.
313 **"satisfy your racist constituency":** Robert J. Lipshutz (Counsel to the President) to Imani Kazana, February 22, 1978, quoted in Janken, *The Wilmington Ten*, 153.
313 **urged the attorney general:** W. Moore, *Triumphant Warrior*, 262.
313 **Carter evaded the issue:** Janken, *The Wilmington Ten*, 146.
313 **"fundamental unfairness":** W. Moore, *Triumphant Warrior*, 260.
313 **served eight years:** "Last Defendant in a Firebombing Is Released."

CHAPTER 41: LEGACIES OF PERSEVERANCE

317 **certain problems:** John Coggins, "Progress of Race Relations Positive, Negative," *Sunday StarNews*, December 23, 1979; John Coggins, "Schools Relatively Calm Now," *Wilmington Morning Star*, December 24, 1979; John Coggins, "Individual Must Figure Race Relations Balance Sheet," *Wilmington Morning Star*, December 25, 1979.
318 **"racial disturbances":** "Race Poll Called 'Disturbing,'" *Wilmington Morning Star*, December 30, 1993.
318 **community gutted and Black residents displaced:** Matthew Prensky, "Wilmington's

Northside Is Changing. Meet the People with Deep Roots There," *StarNews*, July 25, 2022.

319 **through the car window:** PJ Brown, interview with Sameen Gauhar, November 13, 2025.

319 **"paint was flaking off":** Cynthia Brown, interview with author, August 19, 2020.

320 **"us against the world":** Nicole Ganglani, "'I Was Very Racist'—Michael Jordan Opens Up About the Racist Encounter That Formed His View of Race Growing Up," Basketball Network, August 27, 2022.

320 **murdered James Jordan:** Andrew Lawrence, "James Jordan's Murder Was About More Than the Death of a Superstar's Father," *The Guardian*, April 2, 2021.

320 **"it's complicated":** John Staton, "What Does Michael Jordan Mean to Wilmington? It's Complicated," *StarNews*, April 12, 2022.

320 **"This is home":** Emma Dollenmayer, "'This Is Home': Michael and Deloris Jordan Speak at Clinic Grand Opening in Wilmington," WECT News, May 7, 2024.

320 **Dawson Jordan:** Ben Steelman, "Review—A Portrait of Michael Jordan," *StarNews*, June 1, 2014.

320 **famous habit:** Wright Thompson, "Michael Jordan: A History of Flight," ESPN, May 19, 2020.

320 **"might have been a strategic effort":** Perry, *South to America*, 223.

320 **happened to her at the library:** Aaron Hoover, "Remembering 1898: 100 Years Later, Wilmington Looks Back; City Looks Back at Painful History," *StarNews*, November 10, 1996.

320 **"legacy of deceit":** Cynthia Brown, "Opinion: One Family's Memories," in *1898 Centennial Foundation Program*, Bertha Boykin Todd Papers Collection (SC-MS-390), box 1, folder 6, Center for Southeast North Carolina Archives and History, UNCW Library.

321 **election and subsequent reelections:** "Sizzling Talk."

322 **"lively gayety":** Jane R. Jenkins, "Social Dance in North Carolina Before the Twentieth Century—An Overview" (PhD diss., University of North Carolina, 1978), 28.

322 **silk pouch:** Jenkins, "Social Dance in North Carolina," 45.

323 **"it'll be all over town":** Bambi MacRae, interview with author, March 31, 2022.

324 **amateur musician; passionate sailor:** Jill Gerard, "In Memoriam: Revered Author, UNCW Professor Philip Gerard to Be Celebrated This Month," *Port City Daily*, December 3, 2022; Philip Gerard, "What They Don't Tell You About Hurricanes," *Creative Nonfiction, Special Double Issue: A View from the Divide: Creative Nonfiction on Health and Science*, no. 11 (1998): 100–109.

324 **"believe in writing":** J. Gerard, "In Memoriam: Revered Author."

325 **"only white faces":** Philip Gerard, "Afterword," in *Cape Fear Rising: 25th Anniversary Edition* (Blair, 2019).

325 **"every cocktail party":** Philip Gerard, interview with author, February 13, 2019.

325 **"passions and agendas":** P. Gerard, "Afterword."

325 **samizdat style:** Wayne Lofton, interview with author, April 17, 2024.

325 **had given a lecture:** Ben Steelman, "Writer Exposes Wilmington 'Coup D'état,'" *Wilmington Morning Star*, July 15, 1985.

326 **"extensive remodeling":** Cashman, *History of the Bellamy Mansion*, 57.

326 **"the protagonists' motivations":** P. Gerard, interview with author.

326 **would use their real names:** Philip Gerard, "Riot of 1898 Isn't Behind Us Yet," *StarNews*, February 13, 1994.

326 **historical novelist:** P. Gerard, "Afterword."

327 **some urgent concerns:** P. Gerard, interview with author.

327 **"highly exaggerated":** Hoover, "Remembering 1898."

327 **"not a very nice thing":** Beejay Grob, "Letter to the Editor," *Wilmington Morning Star*, February 19, 1994; Hossfeld, *Narrative, Political Unconscious, and Racial Violence*, 97.
328 **"'He's making that stuff up'":** P. Gerard, interview with author.
328 **"awful phone calls":** J. Gerard, "In Memoriam: Revered Author."
328 **his book launch:** P. Gerard, "Afterword."
328 **rescinded an invitation:** P. Gerard, interview with author.
328 **penalizing Gerard:** "Philip Gerard's 'Cape Fear Rising' Reveals the Truth About the 1898 White Supremacist Coup in Wilmington, N.C," episode 54, *Charlotte Readers Podcast*, October 1, 2019.
328 **ten-thousand-dollar gift:** P. Gerard, "Afterword."
329 **perfect metaphor:** P. Gerard, interview with author.

CHAPTER 42: DANGEROUS MEMORIES

330 **"appropriate remembrance":** Quoted in Hossfeld, *Narrative, Political Unconscious, and Racial Violence*, 103.
331 **"Old Wilmington friend":** Quoted in Hossfeld, *Narrative, Political Unconscious, and Racial Violence*, 116.
331 **mounted machine gun:** Kent Chatfield, interview with author, January 22, 2020.
331 **stockpiling guns:** Hossfeld, *Narrative, Political Unconscious, and Racial Violence*, 109.
331 **"stir up animosities":** Hossfeld, *Narrative, Political Unconscious, and Racial Violence*, 104, 106.
331 **sober memorial:** Bolton Anthony, "Confronting Dangerous Memories: Wilmington's Centennial Commemoration of the Coup of 1898," 1898 Foundation Papers (SC-MS-217), box 1, folder 1, Center for Southeast North Carolina Archives and History, UNCW Library.
331 **gave the foundation ballast:** Hossfeld, *Narrative, Political Unconscious, and Racial Violence*, 107.
331 **"most potentially divisive issue":** Melton A. McLaurin, "Commemorating Wilmington's Racial Violence of 1898: From Individual to Collective Memory," *Southern Cultures* 6, no. 4 (2000): 52.
331 **"far from the truth":** Inez Campbell-Eason, interview with author, February 16, 2019.
332 **glowing 1985 newspaper profile:** Debbie Norton, "MacRae Finds Long Family Tradition to Be No Burden," *Wilmington Morning Star*, November 3, 1985.
332 **"with all the vigor":** George Rountree III, quoted in Hoover, "Remembering 1898."
332 **"official history":** Hossfeld, *Narrative, Political Unconscious, and Racial Violence*, 115.
332 **mayor of Tulsa:** McLaurin, "Commemorating Wilmington's Racial Violence," 47.
332 **"dialogue sessions":** McLaurin, "Commemorating Wilmington's Racial Violence," 49.
332 **"interracial community garden":** "Friendship Garden Grows from Talk," *1898 Centennial Foundation Program*, Bertha Boykin Todd Papers Collection (SC-MS-390), box 1, folder 6, Center for Southeast North Carolina Archives and History, UNCW Library.
332 **"first step of atonement":** "Commemorate 1898????," *Wilmington Journal*, November 19, 1998, quoted in Hossfeld, *Narrative, Political Unconscious, and Racial Violence*, 106.
333 **"Show me the money!":** Lethia Hankins, "Our Voice: Show Me the Money," *Wilmington Journal*, March 12, 1998.
333 **observances of the Tulsa massacre:** Sam Howe Verhovek, "75 Years Later, Tulsa Confronts Its Race Riot," *New York Times*, May 31, 1996.
333 **"must be handled with care":** Bertha Todd Solicitation, 1998, Bertha Boykin Todd Papers Collection (SC-MS-390), Center for Southeast North Carolina Archives and History, UNCW Library.

333 **"settle the matter":** Bambi MacRae, interview with author, March 31, 2022; Hossfeld, *Narrative, Political Unconscious, and Racial Violence*, 105.

333 **"*dangerous memories*":** Isaiah Madison, "Confronting Dangerous Memories: Wilmington's Centennial Commemoration of the Coup of 1898," 1898 Foundation Papers (SC-MS-217), Center for Southeast North Carolina Archives and History, UNCW Library.

334 **"hushed, tension-filled":** McLaurin, "Commemorating Wilmington's Racial Violence," 50.

334 **Haley opened the program:** McLaurin, "Commemorating Wilmington's Racial Violence," 50.

334 **"childhood mammy":** McLaurin, "Commemorating Wilmington's Racial Violence," 50.

334 **"the high point":** R. Bellamy, *Moving Forward Together*, 55.

334 **"cannot foist":** "Another View: A Conversation with George Rountree III," *News & Observer*, November 1, 1998.

335 **"Wilmington has been kind to me":** George Rountree III to Bertha B. Todd, November 17, 2006, Private Collection of Bertha B. Todd.

335 **famously bragged:** McLaurin, "Commemorating Wilmington's Racial Violence," 53; Umfleet, *A Day of Blood*, 85.

335 **"God's restoration plan":** "The Riots of 1898: A Prophetic Perspective from the Mind of God," flyer, December 1998, New Hanover County Public Library.

336 **"hear something like hail":** Buck Colbert "B. C." Franklin, "The Tulsa Race Riot and Three of Its Victims," August 22, 1931, Smithsonian Institution Transcription Center, National Museum of African American History and Culture.

336 **"great holocaust":** Cory Reiss and Mark Schreiner, "'Breakdown of Social Order' Bred Violence, Scholar Says," *StarNews*, October 24, 1998.

336 **standing ovation:** Mark Schreiner, "Racial Unrest Revisited; Historians Optimistic That Lessons Were Learned from 1898," *StarNews*, October 25, 1998.

336 **"no longer turn a blind eye":** James Leutze, interview with author, December 17, 2025.

CHAPTER 43: GROUNDBREAKING

337 **"honor the memory" of 1898:** R. Bellamy, *Moving Forward Together*, 26.

337 **"tolerance and understanding":** R. Bellamy, *Moving Forward Together*, 14.

337 **tear down any structure:** McLaurin, "Commemorating Wilmington's Racial Violence," 54.

337 **cochairs of the 1898 Memorial:** R. Bellamy, *Moving Forward Together*, 118.

338 **"gracefully and without rancor":** R. Bellamy, *Moving Forward Together*, 14.

338 **"forgive ourselves and each other":** Brian Feagans, "Vigil Emphasizes Healing Wounds," *StarNews*, November 10, 1997.

338 **state agreed to donate the land:** R. Bellamy, *Moving Forward Together*, 26.

338 **Fundraising began in 2000:** R. Bellamy, *Moving Forward Together*, 26.

338 **gave ten thousand dollars:** R. Bellamy, *Moving Forward Together*, 113.

338 **"wanted a memorial that did not blame anyone":** Quoted in Trista Talton, "Remembering 1898; City Picks Atlanta Group's Model," *StarNews*, January 16, 2001.

339 **"It won't provide":** Amy E. Turnbull, "Wright Suggests 1898 Park Move," *StarNews*, February 12, 2002.

339 **Odeleye's payment deadlines:** Melton McLaurin, "1898 and Odeleye" email to Bertha B. Todd, June 11, 2005, Private Collection of Bertha B. Todd.

339 **Democratic Party to issue a formal apology:** Chris Fitzsimon, "Reparations Advised

for 1898 Riot in Wilmington," NC Newsline, June 2, 2006; Veronica Gonzalez, "N.C. Dems Apologize for 1898 Riot," *StarNews*, January 21, 2007.

339 **sue for damages:** Angela Mack, "Bill Allowing Civil Action by 1898 Riot Victims Advances," *StarNews*, March 15, 2007.

339 **fraud and obstruction of justice:** Allyson Lorick, "Former State Representative Thomas Wright Released from Prison," WWAYTV3, May 26, 2014.

339 **prison sentence:** Lorick, "Former State Representative."

339 **"I'm not going to sit here":** Wayne Moore, interview with author, August 25, 2020.

340 **"Nobody really understands":** Wayne Lofton, private video of Nate Brown, October 10, 2023, shared with author.

CHAPTER 44: RETURN TO LIVE OAKS

341 **"believe it's impossible":** Aaron Hoover, "'People Fall All the Time in Life, but the Real Test Is How Well You Get Up'; 'Hues' Won't Be Stopped by the Blues," *StarNews*, September 1, 1997.

342 **lasted fifteen years:** Pressley Baird, "Community Action, Nonprofit Agency That Ran Head Start, Closes," *StarNews*, August 13, 2013.

342 **"Kellogg's person":** Angela Mack, "Local Woman's Work Against Heart Disease Celebrated," *StarNews*, July 5, 2007.

CHAPTER 45: PARDONS OF INNOCENCE

345 **"We were kids":** Gina White, "The Wilmington 10 Case: Trial and Prison," *Wilmington Morning Star*, February 10, 1986.

345 **"rumor and innuendo":** "N.C. Governor Resisted Pressure Not to Pardon Wilmington Ten," *Washington Informer*, January 14, 2013.

346 **"ugly stain":** Bev Perdue Statement, quoted in "Gov. Perdue Issues Pardon of Innocence for Wilmington 10," WECT News, December 31, 2012.

346 **dead victims' families compensation:** Fran T. Norton, "Wilmington Ten—Families of Deceased Won't Get Compensation," *StarNews*, August 4, 2015.

346 **"I just want to go forward":** Jason Gonzales, "Gov. Perdue Pardons Wilmington 10," *StarNews*, December 31, 2012.

346 **trove of papers:** Cash Michaels, "N.C. Governor Grants Pardon to 'Wilmington Ten,'" *Bay State Banner*, January 16, 2013.

346 **"Fresh start with new jury":** Janken, *The Wilmington Ten*, 93.

347 **Stroud's jury selection:** Janken, *The Wilmington Ten*, 97; "NC NAACP Reaffirms Plea for Governor to Pardon Wilmington Ten," WHQR Public Media, November 28, 2012.

347 **"injustice and political repression":** Janken, *The Wilmington Ten*, 1.

347 **"I want my forty acres and a mule":** Vereen, *Wilmington Ten Willie*, 97.

CHAPTER 46: A MATTER WHICH HAS BEEN SETTLED

348 **Among other amenities:** "Long Leaf Park," Wilmington N.C. River District & Island Beaches.

348 **donated the land:** Frances Weller, "Hugh MacRae Park Name Change to Take Place Immediately, Signs Removed," WECT News, July 14, 2020.

349 **"white citizens" alone:** John Staton, "Hugh MacRae Descendant Says Wilmington Park Should Be Renamed," *StarNews*, July 7, 2020.

349 **"unstated and secret":** Philip Gerard, interview with author, February 13, 2019.
349 **"bad guys win":** Philip Gerard, "Opinion: Why We Should Rename Hugh MacRae Park," *StarNews*, September 27, 2015.
349 **"Being in the Secret Nine":** Hugh MacRae II, quoted in Hossfeld, *Narrative, Political Unconscious, and Racial Violence*, 162.
350 **"helpful, appropriate, or constructive":** Hugh MacRae II, "Letter to the Editor," *StarNews*, October 1, 2015.

CHAPTER 47: MOM-OSAS

353 **population increased:** Tim Buckland, "150 Years of Change," *StarNews*, July 13, 2017.
353 **Lara returned home often:** "Lara Trump, President's Daughter-in-Law, Returns Home for Baby Shower," WECT News, July 10, 2017.
353 **"'this is my home'":** Hannah Leyva, "Wrightsville Beach Native Lara Trump Loves Coming Home to Campaign for Father-in-Law Donald Trump," *Port City Daily*, September 2, 2016.
354 **"Southern blood in the Trump family":** Hunter Ingram, "Trump's Daughter-in-Law Likely to Speak at NC Rally," *Blue Ridge Now*, August 8, 2016.
354 **"But people will":** "Donald Trump Campaign Event in Wilmington, North Carolina," C-SPAN, August 9, 2016.
354 **"most restrictive voting law":** N.C. State Conference v. McCrory, No. 16-1468 (4th Cir. 2016).
354 **aided by gerrymandering:** Dahlia Lithwick, "What's the Matter with North Carolina?," *Slate*, July 24, 2013.
354 **Sweeping into power:** "99 Reasons to FLIP NC," Flip NC, 2018; Lucille Sherman, "'We Are in Control': How a Decade of Republican Majorities Reshaped North Carolina," *News & Observer*, October 31, 2020.
355 **"Second Amendment People":** "Trump Suggests 'Second Amendment People' Could Stop Clinton," *The Guardian*, August 9, 2016.
355 **required curriculum:** "Boseman's Bill Would Add 1898 Riots to Education Curriculum," *StarNews*, February 2, 2009.

CHAPTER 48: UNRAVELING

356 **glee club carried:** "Williston Alumni Community Choir Celebrates Their Centennial," WHQR Public Media, June 5, 2015.
356 **"buy-in" and "kinship":** Sam Scott, "Board Takes Next Step on Redistricting," *StarNews*, April 1, 2006.
356 **all Black or all white:** Kris Nordstrom, *Stymied by Segregation: How Integration Can Transform North Carolina Schools and the Lives of Its Students* (North Carolina Justice Center, 2018), 3.
357 **"unraveling before our eyes":** Marian Wright Edelman, "EDITORIAL: Marian Wright Edleman [*sic*] on NHC Middle School Redistricting," WWAYTV3, April 7, 2010.
357 **"back to the same place":** Mayor Bill Saffo, quoted in Cammie Bellamy, "Wilmington Mayor: Schools 'Re-Segregated,'" *StarNews*, May 19, 2017.
357 **"equity and achievement gaps":** Scott, "Board Takes Next Step on Redistricting."
357 **ranking plunged:** Jonathan Haynes, "'Businesses Won't Come Here': Wilmington Warned About School Segregation," *StarNews*, November 24, 2020.
358 **one of the most segregated schools:** Matthew Prensky et al., "A Return to Segregation:

Neighborhood Schools Policy Fuels Inequities, Erases New Hanover's Progress," *StarNews*, April 19, 2022.

358 **public-school curriculum:** LeRae Umfleet, *1898 Wilmington Race Riot Report* (North Carolina Department of Cultural Resources—Office of Archives and History, 2006), 2; "Boseman's Bill Would Add 1898 Riots."

358 **without ever hearing mention:** T. Keung Hui, "Schools Have 'Failed Us.' Some NC Students Say More Black History Needs to Be Taught," *News & Observer*, April 21, 2021.

358 **downtown walking tour:** "Tar Heels Go Walking," Historic Wilmington Foundation.

358 **"act like historians":** "Social Studies 6–8," New Hanover County Schools, www.nhcs.net.

359 **"a formal apology for the events":** Brenna Flanagan, "NHCS Board Member Expresses Discomfort with 1898 Curricula, Questions If It's Being Taught Factually," *Port City Daily*, August 4, 2022.

359 **social studies standards:** "North Carolina Unpacking Document for Grade 4," North Carolina Department of Public Instruction, November 18, 2025.

359 **"I'm so glad":** Cara Ward, interview with author, January 8, 2026.

359 ***Britannica Kids*:** Flanagan, "NHCS Board Member Expresses Discomfort with 1898 Curricula."

359 **"rough draft version":** Whitney Coonradt, quoted in Hunter Ingram, "Is the Wilmington 1898 Coup Getting Lost in the Classroom?," *StarNews*, August 19, 2020.

359 **is not mandatory:** Ingram, "Is the Wilmington 1898 Coup Getting Lost."

359 **"we just don't have that time":** Whitney Coonradt, quoted in Ingram, "Is the Wilmington 1898 Coup Getting Lost."

CHAPTER 49: ALEXANDER MANLY PARK

360 **"Third Reconstruction":** Rev. Dr. William J. Barber II and Jonathan Wilson-Hartgrove, *The Third Reconstruction: How a Moral Movement Is Overcoming the Politics of Division and Fear* (Beacon Press, 2016), 62.

360 **With the publication of David Zucchino's:** Ben Steelman, "Author of 1898 Best Seller 'Wilmington's Lie' to Speak with Port City Readers," *StarNews* Online, November 5, 2020.

360 **nearly unseated:** Benjamin Schachtman, "Devon Scott Reflects on His Wilmington Mayoral Campaign and Looks Ahead to What's Next," *Port City Daily*, November 9, 2019.

360 **Donny Williams, a Black Wilmington:** "A Look Back: Defining Images of Wilmington Protests," *StarNews*, August 14, 2020.

361 **"Today is a challenging day":** Michael Praats, "Fired Wilmington Cop: 'We Are Just Going to Go Out and Start Slaughtering Them F—— N——. I Can't Wait. God, I Can't Wait,'" *Port City Daily*, June 24, 2020.

361 **two years after Jerry Spivey:** "D.A. Removed for Racial Slur," *Charlotte Observer*, August 30, 1995.

361 **described a Black official:** Praats, "Fired Wilmington Cop."

362 **spray-painted "BLM":** Frances Weller, "Vandalized Signs at Hugh MacRae Park Taken Down for Repairs," WECT News, June 22, 2020.

362 **staged a sit-in:** "Kenan Memorial Fountain, Wilmington," Documenting the American South (DocSouth): Commemorative Landscapes DocSouth, University of North Carolina.

362 **"someone who conspired to murder":** Lettie Gore, quoted in "Hundreds Take Part in Sit-In at Hugh MacRae Park," WECT News, July 1, 2020.

363 **America's ten best:** Daniel Seamans, "Hugh MacRae Park Tops 'The Best Playgrounds of 2017' List," WWAYTV3, May 24, 2017.

363 **couldn't change history:** Si Cantwell, "Opinions Mixed, but Most Say Keep Hugh MacRae Park Name," *StarNews*, July 26, 2015.

363 **white supremacy began to fall:** Rachel Treisman, "Nearly 100 Confederate Monuments Removed in 2020, Report Says; More Than 700 Remain," NPR, February 23, 2021.

363 **undisclosed location:** John Staton, "Emails Point to Origins of Wilmington's Plan for the Removal of Confederate Monuments," *StarNews*, August 16, 2021.

363 **"time is right":** "Statue of White Supremacist Josephus Daniels Removed from Raleigh's Nash Square," ABC11, June 16, 2020.

364 **covered the sign:** Hunter Ingram, "Hugh MacRae Park Sign Covered with One Honoring Wilmington 1898 Figure," *StarNews*, June 29, 2020.

364 **"grandeur of the Old South":** John Brannon Albright, "A Walk Through Wilmington's Past," *New York Times*, January 13, 1985.

366 **"not going to help":** Bambi MacRae, interview with author, March 31, 2022.

366 **"not allowed to fade":** Edward Ball, *Slaves in the Family* (Farrar, Straus and Giroux, 1998), ix.

367 **"I'm not against":** Meg MacRae, quoted in Staton, "Hugh MacRae Descendant."

367 **Meg's half brother:** Frances Weller, "Hugh MacRae III Meets with Organizers of Petition Pushing to Rename Namesake Park," WECT News, July 3, 2020.

367 **"pendulum has swung":** Nelson MacRae, interview with author, December 28, 2025.

368 **"kind of like a release":** Sonya Patrick, quoted in Staton, "Hugh MacRae Descendant."

368 **"get a petition":** Nelson MacRae, interview with author.

368 **informal rule:** Scott Jaschik, "UNC Changes Name of Stadium, Which Has Honored Racist," *Inside Higher Ed*, October 3, 2018.

369 **billboard erected:** Hunter Ingram, "'1898. 2020. Vote.' Billboard, Downtown Signs Evoke Wilmington Massacre Memory in Call to Vote," *StarNews*, November 2, 2020.

CHAPTER 50: WOOOOOOO!

370 **must act now:** Brian Naylor, "Read Trump's Jan. 6 Speech, a Key Part of Impeachment Trial," NPR, February 10, 2021.

371 **Cuban American leader:** Christopher Rhodes, "Why 'White' Supremacists Are Not Always White," *Al Jazeera*, June 2, 2023.

371 **White nationalist paramilitaries:** Tom Dreisbach and Tim Mak, "Yes, Capitol Rioters Were Armed. Here Are the Weapons Prosecutors Say They Used," NPR, March 19, 2021.

371 **connoting white power:** "Identifying Far-Right Symbols That Appeared at the U.S. Capitol Riot," *Washington Post*, January 15, 2025.

371 **they wore red hats:** Matthew Rosenberg and Ainara Tiefenthäler, "Decoding the Far-Right Symbols at the Capitol Riot," *New York Times*, January 13, 2021.

371 **The nation watched:** "Rioters Break Windows and Breach US Capitol," CNN, January 6, 2021.

372 **"Boo, fucking n——!":** Quoted in Nick Niedzwiadek, "Capitol Police Officer Says Jan. 6 Rioters Used N-Word Against Him, Others," *Politico*, July 27, 2021.

372 **died after suffering strokes:** Chris Cameron, "These Are the People Who Died in Connection With the Capitol Riot," *New York Times*, January 5, 2022.

372 **Confederate flag was paraded:** Eliott C. McLaughlin, "Before January 6, Insurgents Waving Confederate Flags Hadn't Been Within 6 Miles of the U.S. Capitol," CNN, January 7, 2021.

372 **Trump showered the insurrectionists with praise:** "'We Love You, You're Very Special': President Trump Tweets Message, Later Removed, to Rioters Storming the U.S. Capitol," CBS News, January 6, 2021.
372 **The prosecution of:** Jake Grumbach, "How Did We Get Here: Protecting Democracy from State Level Threats in the Age of National Parties," in *More than Red and Blue: Political Parties and American Democracy*, October 13, 2023.
372 **went to jail:** "Here's Where Jan. 6 Trials Stand on the Fourth Anniversary of the Capitol Riot" (PBS, January 6, 2025).
373 **both the FBI:** Adam Gabbatt, "US Is Failing to Address 'Persistent and Lethal Threat' of Domestic Terrorism, Report Finds," *The Guardian*, November 29, 2022; United States Senate Committee on Homeland Security & Government Affairs, *The Rising Threat of Domestic Terrorism: A Review of the Federal Response to Domestic Terrorism and the Spread of Extremist Content on Social Media* (U.S. Senate, 2022).
373 **"American greatness":** "Presidential Actions: Restoring Names That Honor American Greatness," The White House, January 20, 2025.
373 **immediately pardoned:** Dan Barry and Alan Feuer, "Reframing Jan. 6: After the Pardons, the Purge," *New York Times*, August 24, 2025.
373 **purge of the Justice Department:** Barry and Feuer, "Reframing Jan. 6."
373 **Confederate partisans:** Mike Wendling, "Trump Pardons Give Jan. 6 Defendants Nearly Everything They Wanted," BBC, January 21, 2025; Ibram X. Kendi (@ibramxk), "As Trump pardoned almost all of the Jan. 6th insurrectionists, lest we forget that President Andrew Johnson pardoned almost all Confederates . . . ," Instagram post, January 21, 2025.

CHAPTER 51: THE GUN

375 **acquired the gun:** "History of the 3rd North Carolina Cavalry Regiment," The Civil War in the East.
376 **Moore Capital Management:** Thomas Franck, "A Legendary Trader Who Made Billions Betting on Wars, Other Macro Events Is Hanging It Up," CNBC, November 21, 2019.
376 **"a childhood dream":** Louis Moore Bacon, interview with author, January 13, 2026.
376 **"original landscape":** Richard Stradling, "Closed to Public, Orton Plantation Is Transforming on a 'Grand Scale,'" *Charlotte Observer*, July 30, 2012.
376 **supported efforts to preserve:** "North Carolina," Moore Charitable Foundation.
376 **"opportunity to commemorate":** Richard Stradling, "A Billionaire Is Trying to Restore Rice Fields Worked by Slaves. It Hasn't Been Easy," *News & Observer*, July 8, 2017.
377 **His Klan activity:** Bill Sisson, interview with author, February 19, 2022.
379 **Sisson worked with chi:** "The Past Is Present," *StarNews*, August 22, 2007.
379 **"focus on being American":** Bettie Fennell, "Museum's Focus on Education Is Rejected," *StarNews*, December 20, 1994.
380 **Shore Acres House:** "Ready for a Plaque?," Historic Wilmington Foundation Inc.
381 **"only through the lens of current values":** Bill Sisson, interview with author, March 12, 2021.

CHAPTER 52: NEVER FORGOTTEN

383 **"making minimum wage":** Nate Brown, interview with author, March 9, 2022.
384 **he found his grandparents:** Juanita Starks, Population Schedule for New Hanover

County, North Carolina, Sixteenth Census of the United States, 1940, NAID 131449027, Records of the Bureau of the Census, RG 29, National Archives, Washington, D.C.

387 **"that horse-drawn carriage":** Kendall McGee, "Great Grandchildren of 1898 Victim React to Discovery of Joshua Halsey's Gravesite," WECT News, October 13, 2021.

388 **"a chance to grow something hopeful":** "Community Remembrance Project," Equal Justice Initiative.

CHAPTER 53: THE INVOICE

393 **tax incentives:** Umfleet, *1898 Wilmington Race Riot Report*, 1.

394 **close its school system for five years:** Darity and Mullen, *From Here to Equality*, 17–21.

394 **"bill of particulars":** Darity and Mullen, *From Here to Equality*, 2.

394 **"complex web of harms":** Darity and Mullen, *From Here to Equality*, 6, 31.

394 ***lower* median net worth:** Darity and Mullen, *From Here to Equality*, 33.

394 **"The invoice for reparations":** Darity and Mullen, *From Here to Equality*, 257.

394 **"price we must pay":** Ta-Nehisi Coates, "The Case for Reparations," *The Atlantic*, June 2014.

394 **One of them, Viola Fletcher:** Alex Traub, "Viola Fletcher, Oldest Survivor of the Tulsa Race Massacre, Dies at 111," *New York Times*, November 24, 2025.

394 **"I live through the massacre":** "Written Testimony of Viola 'Mother' Fletcher Before the Subcommittee on the Constitution, Civil Rights, and Civil Liberties," 117th Cong., 1st sess., May 19, 2021.

395 **Support for reparations:** Carrie Blazina and Kiana Cox, "Black and White Americans Are Far Apart in Their Views of Reparations for Slavery," Pew Research Center, November 28, 2022.

395 **"appropriate remedies":** *H.R. 40, Commission to Study and Develop Reparation Proposals for African Americans Act*, House Judiciary Subcommittee on Constitution, Civil Rights, and Civil Liberties, 117th Cong., 1st sess., January 4, 2021.

395 **"a nonstarter":** Barack Obama, quoted in Bailey Aldridge, "Obama Says 'White Resistance and Resentment' Stopped Him from Pushing for Reparations," McClatchy DC, February 25, 2021.

395 **finally voted to advance:** Juana Summers, "A Bill to Study Reparations for Slavery Had Momentum in Congress, But Still No Vote," NPR, November 12, 2021; Beatrice Peterson, "Rep. Cori Bush Says $14 Trillion Reparations Bill Will 'Eliminate the Racial Wealth Gap,'" ABC News, May 19, 2023.

395 **pursued local redress:** Wesley Lowery, "Viola Fletcher Waited 102 Years for Reparations. She's Still Waiting," *Washington Post*, October 4, 2023.

395 **Restorative Housing Program:** Robin Rue Simmons, "How the City of Evanston Is Paying Reparations," *Next City*, September 14, 2022.

395 **filed a class-action lawsuit:** Alex Harrison, "Class Action Suit Claims City's Reparations Program Is Unconstitutional," Evanston Roundtable, May 24, 2024.

396 **"bears responsibility":** Brentin Mock, "As Asheville Pursues Reparations, North Carolina Seeks Silence," Bloomberg, November 1, 2023.

396 **planned to bring:** "Reparations for Slavery," CBS News, November 4, 2000.

396 **this one languished:** Kimberly Cook, "Reparations for Historical Violence Against African American People in New Hanover County," Change.org, August 26, 2020.

397 **New Hanover Community Endowment:** "History," New Hanover Community Endowment.

397 **draw attention away:** John Staton, "Wilmington Community Reflects on Hugh MacRae Park Renaming," *StarNews*, July 16, 2020.
397 **honors Alfred "Fred" Howe:** "Background," The Howe Scholarship Endowment.
397 **"the lying stops":** Lucy McCauley, "Toward the Truth of the 1898 Wilmington, N.C. Massacre and Coup d'Etat," Bittersweet: Linked Through Slavery, April 16, 2023.
398 **existential dilemma:** Lowery, "Viola Fletcher Waited 102 Years for Reparations."

CHAPTER 54: YOU KNOW THE WAY

399 **Chief Watcoosa:** William G. DiNome, "Cape Fear Indians," in William S. Powell, ed., *Encyclopedia of North Carolina* (University of North Carolina Press, 2006).
399 **enslaved on area plantations:** Si Cantwell, "Church Caretaker Searches for Missing Bell," *StarNews*, January 19, 2010.
400 **church bell:** "Glory, Glory," March 25, 1998, Scripts and Production Documents, Fincannon and Associates Script Collection (SC-MS-175), Center for Southeast North Carolina Archives and History, UNCW Library.
400 **"that's a war crime":** Marvin Graham, interview with author, March 16, 2021.
401 **"Movie and a Mixer":** "125th Anniversary of 1898 Wilmington Massacre: Commemoration Activities: October 20th," New Hanover County.
401 **"Part of me was afraid":** Rachel Lewis Hilburn, "CoastLine: 'It Broke My Hip.' Kieran Haile, Alex Manly's Great-Great-Grandson, on the 'Dark and Terrible' Intergenerational Trauma of Slavery," WHQR, November 2, 2021.
401 **"return to those families":** Kieran Haile, quoted in Mara McJilton, "'We Still Have These Gaps in Our Stories': Descendants of Alex Manly Speak on Impacts of 1898 Massacre," WECT News, November 10, 2023.
402 **"We couldn't even say the word":** John Staton, "Wilmington's 1898 Coup and Massacre at 125: 'Healing Forward' with More Work to Be Done," *StarNews*, November 1, 2023.
402 **who had been abruptly transferred:** Xavier Board, "Just a Regular School Closing? Williston Legacy Graduation to Take Place for Classes '69, '70," *Port City Daily*, June 19, 2023.
402 **"legacy graduation":** "Williston Graduation Video and Pictures," New Hanover County Schools, July 1, 2023.
402 **"more of a listener":** Hugh MacRae III, interview with author, November 28, 2023.
405 **"changed and repackaged":** Flanagan, "NHCS Board Member Expresses Discomfort with 1898 Curricula."
406 **"opt our kids out":** Katie Gates, quoted in "County School Board Temporarily Limits Controversial Book," *Carolina Journal*, September 11, 2023.
406 **had abruptly resigned:** Johanna F. Still and Ben Schachtman, "The Dive: Out with the New," *The Assembly NC*, February 8, 2024.
406 **"what is the reaction supposed to be":** Derrick Anderson, quoted in Brenna Flanagan, "'Margin of Error Is a Lot Smaller': Black Community Members Speak Out on Foust Firing," *Port City Daily*, July 20, 2024.
406 **twenty projects chosen:** "Professional Development Programs," National Endowment for the Humanities.
407 **"We want this history":** Leigh Carter, interview with author, October 24, 2024.

Selected Bibliography

Ball, Edward. *Slaves in the Family*. Farrar, Straus and Giroux, 1998.

Bellamy, Ellen Douglas. *Back with the Tide: Memoirs*. Bellamy Mansion Museum of History and Design Arts, 2002.

Bellamy, Heyward C. *With All Deliberate Speed: The Reminiscences of Heyward C. Bellamy*. Self-published, 2009.

Bellamy, John D. *Memoirs of an Octogenarian*. Observer Printing House, 1942.

Bellamy, Rhonda. *Moving Forward Together: A Community Remembers 1898*. SlapDash, 2008.

Bishir, Catherine W. *The Bellamy Mansion, Wilmington, NC: An Antebellum Architectural Treasure and Its People*. Historic Preservation Foundation of North Carolina, 2004.

———. *North Carolina Architecture*. University of North Carolina Press, 2005.

———. "Urban Slavery at Work: The Bellamy Mansion Compound, Wilmington, North Carolina." *Buildings & Landscapes: Journal of the Vernacular Architecture Forum* 17, no. 2 (2010): 13–32.

Blight, David W. *Race and Reunion: The Civil War in American Memory*. Havard University Press, 2001.

Block, Susan Taylor. *Images of America: Cape Fear Lost*. Arcadia Publishing, 1999.

Brown, C. J. *A Metamorphosis of the Soul: Lessons from My Journey on Faith, Hope, Love and Perseverance*. Westbow Press, 2014.

Brown, Cynthia J. *Strength from Our Past, Faith for Our Future: A History of St. Stephen African Methodist Episcopal Church*. St. Stephen African Methodist Episcopal Church Sesquicentennial Anniversary History Book Committee, 2015.

Brown, Hesketh (Nate), Jr. "Let Me Tell You Something About Us Halsey's." New Hanover County Community Remembrance Project, 2019.

Cashman, Diane Cobb. *The History of the Bellamy Mansion*. Self-published, 1989.

Cecelski, David S. *The Fire of Freedom: Abraham Galloway & the Slaves' Civil War*. University of North Carolina Press, 2015.

Cecelski, David S., and Timothy B. Tyson, eds. *Democracy Betrayed: The Wilmington Race Riot of 1898 and Its Legacy*. University of North Carolina Press, 1998.

Chesnutt, Charles W. *The Marrow of Tradition*. Houghton, Mifflin and Company, 1901.

Daniels, Josephus. *Editor in Politics*. University of North Carolina Press, 1941.

Darity, William A., Jr., and A. Kirsten Mullen. *From Here to Equality: Reparations for Black Americans in the Twenty-First Century*. University of North Carolina Press, 2022.

Dixon, Thomas. *Leopard's Spots: A Romance of the White Man's Burden, 1865–1900*. Doubleday & Co., 1902.

Eaton, Hubert A. *Every Man Should Try*. Bonaparte Press, 1984.

Edmonds, Helen G. *The Negro and Fusion Politics in North Carolina, 1894–1901*. University of North Carolina Press, 1951.

Evans, William McKee. *Ballots and Fence Rails: Reconstruction on the Lower Cape Fear*. University of Georgia Press, 2004.

Everett, Christopher, dir. *Wilmington on Fire*. Speller Street Films, 2015.

Foner, Eric. *Reconstruction: America's Unfinished Revolution, 1863–1877, Updated Edition*. HarperPerennial, 2014.

Gates, Henry Louis, Jr. *Stony the Road : Reconstruction, White Supremacy, and the Rise of Jim Crow*. Penguin Press, 2019.

Gerard, Philip. *Cape Fear Rising*. Blair, 1994.

Gilmore, Glenda Elizabeth. *Gender and Jim Crow: Women and the Politics of White Supremacy in North Carolina 1896–1920*. University of North Carolina Press, 1996.

Godwin, John L. *Black Wilmington and the North Carolina Way: Portrait of a Community in the Era of Civil Rights Protest*. University Press of America, 2000.

Hayden, Harry. *The Story of the Wilmington Rebellion*. Self-published, 1936.

Hinks, Peter P. *To Awaken My Afflicted Brethren: David Walker and the Problem of Antebellum Slave Resistance*. Pennsylvania State University Press, 1996.

Hossfeld, Leslie H. *Narrative, Political Unconscious, and Racial Violence in Wilmington, North Carolina*. Routledge, 2005.

Jackson, Thanayi Michelle. "'Devoted to the Interests of His Race': Black Officeholders and the Political Culture of Freedom in Wilmington, North Carolina, 1865–1877." PhD diss., University of Maryland at College Park, 2016.

Jacobs, Harriet Ann. *Incidents in the Life of a Slave Girl*. Edited by Lydia Maria Francis Child. Self-published, 1861.

Janken, Kenneth Robert. *The Wilmington Ten: Violence, Injustice, and the Rise of Black Politics in the 1970s*. University of North Carolina Press, 2021.

Judge, Phoebe, host. *Criminal*, podcast, episode 158, "If It Ever Happens, Run." *Vox*, February 12, 2021.

Keith, B. F. *Memories*. Bynum Printing Co., 1922.

Kirk, J. Allen. "A Statement of Facts Concerning the Bloody Riot in Wilmington, N.C." Self–published, 1898.

McKoy, Henry Bacon. *Wilmington, N.C.—Do You Remember When?* Keys Printing Company, 1957.

Michaels, Cash, dir. *Pardons of Innocence: The Wilmington Ten*. 2014.

Moore, Louis Toomer. *Stories Old and New of the Cape Fear Region*. Louis T. Moore Memorial Fund, 1968.

Moore, Wayne. *Triumphant Warrior: A Soul Survivor of the Wilmington Ten*. Warrior Press, 2014.

Mulrooney, Margaret M. *Race, Place, and Memory: Deep Currents in Wilmington, North Carolina*. University of Florida Press, 2018.

Prather, H. Leon, Sr. *We Have Taken a City: Wilmington Racial Massacre and Coup of 1898*. Associated University Press, 1984.

Reaves, William M. *"Strength Through Struggle": The Chronological and Historical Record of the African-American Community in Wilmington, North Carolina, 1865–1950*. New Hanover County Public Library, 1998.

Rohrs, Richard C. "The Free Black Experience in Antebellum Wilmington, North Carolina: Refining Generalizations About Race Relations." *Journal of Southern History* 78, no. 3 (2012): 615–38.

Schaw, Janet. *Journal of a Lady of Quality; Being the Narrative of a Journey from Scotland to the West Indies, North Carolina, and Portugal, in the Years 1774 to 1776.* Edited by Evangeline Walker Andrews and Charles McLean Andrews. Yale University Press, 1923.

Sprunt, James. *Chronicles of the Cape Fear River, 1660–1916.* Edwards & Broughton Printing Co., 1916.

Umfleet, LeRae. *A Day of Blood: The 1898 Wilmington Race Riot.* North Carolina Office of Archives and History, 2009.

Waddell, Alfred Moore. *Some Memories of My Life.* Edwards & Broughton Printing Company, 1908.

White, William Allen. *Woodrow Wilson: The Man, His Times, and His Task.* Riverside Press, 1924.

Wilson, Mabel O. *Negro Building: Black Americans in the World of Fairs and Museums.* University of California Press, 2012.

Zucchino, David. *Wilmington's Lie: The Murderous Coup of 1898 and the Rise of White Supremacy.* Grove Press, 2020.

Image Credits

Page xxiii: Wilmington, N.C., race riot, 1898. Library of Congress, Prints & Photographs Division.

Page xxvi: Courtesy the author

Page 3: Courtesy the Brown Family

Page 22: Waddell, Hon. Alfred Moore of N.C. Delegate to Constitutional Union National Convention at Baltimore, 1860. Library of Congress, Prints & Photographs Division, LC-BH832-416 [P&P].

Page 38: Courtesy Center for Southeast North Carolina Archives and History/ UNCW Library/University of North Carolina Wilmington

Page 46: Courtesy Bellamy Mansion

Page 65: Courtesy Bellamy Mansion

Page 104: Courtesy the author

Page 132: Courtesy Collection of Lori Keith Robinson

Page 164: Courtesy Cape Fear Museum of History and Science, Wilmington, North Carolina

Page 191: Courtesy Johnson Publishing Company Archive/J. Paul Getty Trust and Smithsonian National Museum of African American History and Culture

Page 195: Courtesy Cape Fear Museum of History and Science, Wilmington, North Carolina

Page 202: Courtesy New Hanover County Public Library, Local History Room

Page 204: Hugh Morton Photographs and Films/Wilson Special Collections Library/ UNC-Chapel Hill Library

Page 207: Courtesy the Brown Family

Page 224: Courtesy New Hanover County Public Library, Local History Room

Page 234: Courtesy Nate Brown

Page 236: Copyright © Bob Adelman

Page 247: Courtesy New Hanover County Public Library, Local History Room

Page 254: Courtesy Cape Fear Museum of History and Science, Wilmington, North Carolina

Page 257: SECO/USA TODAY NETWORK/Imagn Images

Page 278: Herman Benton/USA TODAY NETWORK/Imagn Images

Page 289: Courtesy Center for Southeast North Carolina Archives and History/ UNCW Library/University of North Carolina Wilmington

Page 291: Andy Howell/USA TODAY NETWORK/Imagn Images

Page 312: Harold Valentine/Associated Press

Page 340: Ayokunle Odeleye/Odeleye Sculpture Studios LLC

Page 351: Courtesy Bellamy Mansion

Page 367: John Staton/USA TODAY NETWORK/Imagn Images

Page 369: Courtesy *Port City Daily*

Page 375: Courtesy the author

Page 389: Melissa Sue Gerrits/Getty Images

Page 403: Jahi Chiwendiu/*Washington Post*

Index

Page numbers in *italics* indicate photographs.